AF540631

A Text Book of Psychology

A TEXT BOOK OF PSYCHOLOGY

By

William McDougall

DISCOVERY PUBLISHING HOUSE
NEW DELHI-1100 02

Published by:

DISCOVERY PUBLISHING HOUSE
4383/4B, Ansari Road, Darya Ganj
New Delhi-110 002 (India)
Phone : +91-11-23279245; 23253475; 43596065
E-mail : discoverybooksindia@gmail.com
discoverypublishinghouse@gmail.com
namitwasan9@gmail.com
web : www.discoverypublishinggroup.com

Reprinted: 2026

ISBN: 978-81-7141-505-2

A Textbook of Psychology

Printed at:
Infinity Imaging Systems
Delhi

TO
THE HONOURED MEMORY OF
WILLIAM JAMES, GREAT PHILOSOPHER, GREAT
PSYCHOLOGIST, AND GREAT MAN

PREFACE

The time has gone by when any one man could hope to write an adequate text-book of psychology. The science has now so many branches, so many methods, so many fields of application, and such an immense mass of data of observation is now on record, that no one man can hope to have the necessary familiarity with the whole. But, even when a galaxy of learning and talent shall have written the text-book of the future, there will still be need for the book which will introduce the student to his science, which will aim at giving him at the outset of his studies a profitable line of approach, a fruitful way of thinking of psychological problems, and a terminology as little misleading as possible. The present volume is designed to render these services.

The need of such a book is greater in psychology than in any other science. In the physical sciences the student needs only to refine upon the methods of observation and reasoning which he has learned to apply in dealing with the physical world about him, regarding all events as links in a mechanical chain of cause and effect. Most students have begun, by the time they approach psychology, to regard this as the true and only way of science. And many of the books on psychology encourage them in this belief. Having begun in this way myself, and having slowly and painfully extricated myself and found what seems to me a much more profitable attitude toward psychological problems, I hold that the path of the student may be made smoother by setting clearly before him at the outset the alternative routes; so that, whichever he may choose to follow, he may at least make his choice with his eyes open, and may constantly be aware of the alternatives. The two principal alternative routes are (1) that of mechanistic science, which interprets all its processes as mechanical sequences of cause and effect, and (2) that of the sciences of mind, for which purposive striving is a fundamental category, which regard the process of purposive striving as radically different from mechanical sequence. The aim of this book is, then, to introduce the student to psychology by this second route; and throughout I have kept in the foreground the question of the relative merits of the two routes; for this is the most important issue before psychologists at the present time, the one which divides them most fundamentally.

The mechanical psychology, naturally and almost inevitably, adopts the atomistic or "mosaic" theory of mental process, the theory that what in these pages is called thinking is a "stream of consciousness" consisting of discrete elements, units, particles, or atoms of conscious stuff, commonly called "sensations" or "units of feeling," cohering somehow in clusters. When it seeks to explain the clusterings and sequences of these "elements," it does so by imagining each one to be attached in some manner to an elementary process in the brain; and it seeks to explain the conjunctions and sequences of the elementary brain-processes in a purely mechanical fashion, by aid of the laws of the physical and chemical sciences.

This mechanical psychology is decidedly preponderant at the present time; and my book therefore is largely a polemic against all psychology of this type and on behalf of purposive psychology. For I am sure that nothing is to be gained by disguising or slurring over this issue, and that it must be frankly faced and resolved before psychology can go forward with the harmony and general agreement upon fundamentals which prevail in the physical sciences.

The fact and the importance of the issue were most interestingly illustrated by the work of the two eminent men to whom I have the honor to be in some sense the successor in Harvard College. Hugo Münsterberg began as a forceful, brilliant, and dogmatic exponent of the mechanical mosaic psychology. But more and more, as he became increasingly interested in the practical applications of psychology, he recognized the claims of the purposive psychology. And, in his later works, he may almost be said to appear as a self-made convert to this way of thinking.

In William James a similar evolution is traceable; less clearly, because all of his strictly psychological work was published at one period of his development, when he was still trying to balance himself upon and to reconcile the two incompatible foundations. His great work, "The Principles of Psychology," shows this divided allegiance in almost every chapter. Where I have criticised the mechanistic mosaic psychology, I have usually chosen James's exposition of it, because it is incisive and brilliant. This may give the impression that I disagree with James more widely than is actually the case. For there were two Jameses—James the physiologist and sensationist psychologist, and James the author of the purposive psychology which was the root of his pragmatic philosophy. It is only the former James with whom I am in wide disagreement, and whom I have criticised.

In spite of this disagreement, I regard the "Principles" as perhaps the best book upon which serious students of psychology can begin to whet their appetite. To such students I am inclined to say: "Begin, as I did, by reading James's 'Principles' carefully and thoroughly, and then take up this book and see if it can help to clarify your thinking and to clear up some of the major tangles left by James."

As compared with James's great work, this book is simplified by consistent adhesion to a single point of view, that of the purposive psychology. But it makes no attempt to conceal the difficulties and complexities of psychological study. In the past, both descriptions and explanations of mental life have suffered much from the natural endeavor of psychologists to simplify their expositions. This tendency to simplification is, in fact, the root of the mechanistic mosaic psychology, that which describes mental process as made up of static elements, "units of feeling," "atoms of sensation," "particles of mind-dust," "neutral entities," or what not. And this type of psychology is still with us, and still predominant. Its latest exponent, Mr. Bertrand Russell, has performed the service of reducing it to the lowest level of banality (in his "Analysis of Mind"). Recently it has begotten upon physiology a most misshapen and beggarly dwarf, namely, "behaviorism," which just now is rampant in this country. But fortunately there are signs of a better future.

The work of Henry Head in England, and of Pierre Marie and of Bergson in France, has thrown doubt upon the interpretations of mental disturbances following on brain-lesions in terms of the mosaic theory, interpretations which, not long ago, were very confidently advanced as justifying that theory. The psychoanalytic movement, however great its errors may prove to be, must always be memorable as a breaking loose from the tradition of mental life as a mechanical mosaic, and a demonstration that we must interpret it as a play of purposive forces rather than as an aggregation or mechanical streaming of mental atoms. In Germany, whence the mosaic psychology was imported into this country, there seem to be clear indications that its course is well-nigh run. Among the academic psychologists, those of the group represented by *Psychologische Forschung* have set their feet upon a better way. And, in a report upon the Congress held at Marburg in 1922, Doctor Henning writes: "Until the turn of the century it was believed that one could grasp the mind with number and measure. This was the direction of the Wundtian School; but few papers of this kind were presented to the Congress; for since 1900 there has developed a qualitative psychology which concerns itself less with numbers and more with kinds of experience and qualitative analysis. We know to-day that the complications and structure of experience cannot be analyzed into simple qualitative elements or built up by joining one such element to another." In America also this return to sanity is not without its pioneers. Professor R. M. Ogden, for example, in a recent article ("Are There Any Sensations?" *Am. Journ. of Psych.*, 1922) raises a "doubt as to the genuineness of the hypothetical elements of sensation," and proposes that we should no longer strive "to reconstruct mental life as a certain number of conscious entities merely joined one to another in a mosaic of sensory particles." And some leading psychologists, notably Doctor Morton Prince and Professor M. W. Calkins, have never wholly deserted the purposive route, even when they have compromised with the other by admitting "mental elements" as units of composition of "consciousness."

I venture to regard my book as an endeavor to carry to its logical conclusion that critical rejection of the "mosaic psychology" which has been a main theme of the psychological writings of Messrs. James Ward, F. H. Bradley, Dawes Hicks, and G. F. Stout. My exposition is most nearly allied to and owes most to the works of the last named. Although I always feel humble in face of the clarity and penetrating quality of Professor Stout's writing, I venture to hope that in certain respects I may have attained greater consistency and a more complete emancipation from the evil influence of the "mosaic" tradition.

Any introduction to psychology written from the mechanistic and mosaic standpoint naturally begins with a description of the structure and functions of the nervous system, and goes on to discuss at some length the "sensations" of the various senses. I have touched on these topics very lightly only; because any attempt to treat of them adequately would have made the book unduly large, and because they seem to me of very secondary importance for the beginner.

Our knowledge of the functions of the nervous system is very rudimentary, and as regards many of those of greatest interest to psychology we are still entirely in the dark. The schematic oversimplified view which can be presented in one or two chapters seems to me of little value, and apt to be seriously misleading.

The psychophysiology of the senses is a field rich in accumulated observations, the fascination of which as a field of research is not unknown to me. But I cannot see that a brief and bald statement of the principal facts and theories is of primary importance to the young student of psychology. And the student who approaches psychology by this route is almost inevitably led into the mechanical atomistic way of thinking which I would have him avoid.

To begin with the study of the senses is seductive; for this is one way of simplifying psychology and of enabling the student to feel that he is acquiring a solid basis of facts. But it is a simplification achieved at the cost of an abstraction from actual experience, the degree of which the young student does not easily understand. I have preferred to lead the student up to the complexities of the human mind by way of the simpler processes of the animal mind. For there, although we are confined to the observation of behavior for evidence of mental life, we do at least deal with concrete realities rather than with abstract and artificial entities, such as "the sensations" are.

I have not attempted to make direct use of the large and rapidly increasing body of knowledge derived from the study of abnormalities of mental life. For this also is not of primary importance for the beginner; and it seems to me that little is to be gained by inserting snippets of psychopathology into an introductory book. I hope to publish shortly a volume on the abnormal processes, in which I shall endeavor to show how these may be satisfactorily conceived in terms of the general principles laid down in this volume. Although it is intended that the two volumes shall be independent, they will naturally supplement one another; and, for brevity's sake, I have on several pages referred to this projected volume as Part II.

I have printed in smaller type a number of passages in which I have discussed problems of peculiar difficulty or of secondary importance. The main part of the text in larger type may be read continuously; and the beginner may safely omit, on first reading, both the sections in smaller type and the foot-notes. In adopting this plan I have aimed to make the book useful both to junior and to more advanced students. I would also warn the beginner that the introductory chapter is a very difficult one. He should not be discouraged, if he should find that he cannot understand all of it at the first reading. He should return to it after reading the rest of the book.

Readers of my "Social Psychology" will notice that I have modified in certain respects my account of instinct. The present account is, I hope, not only fuller, but also clearer and nearer to the truth. The statement of the theory of laughter, included in Chapter V, has appeared in *Scribner's Magazine*, and I thank the publishers for permission to make use of it here.

I have to thank Professor Arthur Thomson and the publishers of "An Outline of Science," and Sir F. W. Mott and the publishers of his "Human Voice in Speech and Song," for permission to reproduce the two plates (Figs. 1 and 2), and to thank also Mr. L. H. Horton, who has read part of my manuscript and made valuable suggestions for its improvement.

W. McD.

HARVARD COLLEGE,

PREFACE TO THE FOURTH EDITION

This edition has merely been corrected and improved in some small points. I would take the opportunity to draw the reader's attention to some more recent discussions of character; for I regard my account of character as my best and most original contribution to psychology; and in this book limitations of space have confined me to a very condensed treatment of this supremely important topic. A chapter on "The Structure of Character" has been added to my "Social Psychology" (21st edition); in that chapter character is concisely defined and described as an organized and integrated system of sentiments. In a new book, "Character and the Conduct of Life," I have dealt in a popular way with the practical problems of influencing the formation of character; and in my "Outline of Abnormal Psychology" (referred to in this volume as Part II) I have shown how the theory of character first sketched in my "Social Psychology" is borne out by its application to the interpretation of various forms of failure of integration, especially the hysterical dissociations of permality, schizophrenia, and the manic-depressive psychoses.

I desire also to point out that the now so influential German school of *Gestalt*, or configurational psychology, is bringing about reforms which I have long advocated and which are represented in this volume, especially in the chapters on perception and on the growth of mental structure. In all their criticisms of the atomizing tendency that has for so long a time been widely prevalent I am entirely at one with the members of that school. I find myself at variance with them chiefly in respect to three features of their teaching, which I venture to regard as defects. First, they seem to me too much dominated by the hypothesis of psycho-neural parallelism, a dominance which seems somewhat old-fashioned in these days of the triumph of "emergent and creative evolution." Secondly, they do not sufficiently regard that distinction which I have made a prominent feature of this book, namely, the distinction between mental structure and mental functioning or activity; this finds expression in their neglect to undertake that supreme effort of constructive imagination by means of which alone we can hope to penetrate into the depths of our mental constitution and, aided by the study of mental growth of the individual and the comparative study of mental life in its simpler expressions, to build up, with constant correction and refinement, some adequate picture of our mental structure, its roots, its stem, its many branches, and some conception of their functional relations. Thirdly, I find most of the writers of that school somewhat neglectful of the conative aspect of mental process. The experimental study of perception is that field of psychology in which we can go furthest without taking due account of the conative basis of all our mental life. The fact that the work of this school has been chiefly concerned with that field accounts for their inadequate and hesitant recognition of the purposive or goal-seeking nature of all human and animal activities. This criticism, however, is not applicable to one member of the school, Dr. Kurt Lenin; he, by means of most interesting experimental studies, is achieving an insight into the conative processes which in very many respects I find to be in close agreement with the teachings of this book. It may be hoped that his work will strongly influence the other members of this the most promising movement of contemporary German psychology and by so doing bring German and British psychology more nearly into accord. But there are other interesting movements of German psychology in the same convergent direction. There are a number of influential contemporary workers in Germany who may be roughly classified as exponents of the *Geisteswissenschaftliche Psychologie*; the common and distinctive feature of this school (led by Prof. Ed. Spranger) is the repudiation of the mechanical atomistic psychology which has been until recently dominant in the universities, and their frank recognition of the fact that any psychology that is to be of value to the social sciences or to aid us in the tasks of understanding and influencing human nature must at every point take account of the purposive nature of all mental process. The same is true also of two other schools of contemporary German psychology, namely, the *personalistische* and the *verstehende* (represented by Dr. William Stern and Dr. Fr. Erismann, respectively). Add that

Prof. Hans Driesch has recently thrown his weighty influence on the side of purposive psychology and that the influence of the psycho-analytic schools continues to spread, without perhaps securing many whole-hearted adherents, and it appears that the atomistic mechanical psychology of the nineteenth century is rapidly losing ground in its own home and head-quarters.

It is pleasant also to note that in Austria Professor and Frau Dr. Bühler are leading a similar convergent reform of academic psychology. In America, on the other hand, the signs are less auspicious; for, in spite of the attention excited by the work of the *Gestalt* school, the universities continue in the main either to follow the way of mechanical sensationism which they learnt from Germany in the last century or to cherish the home-bred dogmas of mechanical behaviourism.

W. McD.

DUKE UNIVERSITY

CONTENTS

CHAPTER I

CHAPTER II

CHAPTER III

CHAPTER IV

CHAPTER V

CHAPTER VI

CHAPTER VII

CHAPTER VIII

PAGE

CHAPTER XIII

CHAPTER XIV

CHAPTER XV

CHAPTER XVI

CHAPTER XVII

CHAPTER I

INTRODUCTORY

Psychology is, or aspires to become, a science, a systematically organized and growing body of knowledge. Entering upon the study of this science, we shall naturally expect to be told what is the class of things or processes with which the science is concerned; what kind of knowledge, what sort of increase of understanding, we may hope to gain from the study of it.

The most satisfying answer is that it should help us to a better understanding of human nature. The aim of psychology is to render our knowledge of human nature more exact and more systematic, in order that we may control ourselves more wisely and influence our fellow-men more effectively. There is probably no psychologist who would find serious fault with this statement. As a definition of the province of the science it falls short in two respects. Such a definition should indicate all that falls within the province and should exclude everything that does not. And in both these respects the statement falls short of perfection. For one well-established branch of psychology studies animals, and is properly called the study of animal behavior. And, on the other hand, we have anthropology, a study which by its very title claims to be, and in practice is, the science of mankind; but which, as generally understood, includes much that falls outside the province of psychology. We should not attach great importance to these imperfections; for similar difficulties arise when we attempt to define concisely any science or branch of science. The fields of the various sciences overlap. It is inevitable that they should do so; for, if there are sharp divisions in nature, we do not know exactly where to find them, and therefore cannot draw any precise boundaries between the sciences. And such overlapping of the sciences is really advantageous; for it brings the workers in the several sciences into touch and co-operation one with another.

The psychologist may and should study animal behavior; in doing so, he enters the field of the zoologist, needs his help and may hope to render some help in return. But he studies animals for the sake of the light which such study may throw upon his own problems, the problems of human nature. The relation of psychology to zoology is not unlike that of zoology to geology. The zoologist or biologist needs some knowledge of geology, and is able to make returns to the geologist for the help he gets from him; and there is a large field of overlap, the science of fossil remains or palæontology, which is dependent upon and supplementary to both these more fundamental sciences. In a very similar way, the science of animal behavior stands between zoology and psychology, as a field of overlap which is dependent upon both and in which they may come into helpful relations.

The other weakness of our definition of psychology, namely, that it may seem to claim too much and so encroach upon the field of anthropology, is no more serious. Anthropology, broadly conceived, concerns itself with man as an animal species. Within this wide science are several more special anthropological sciences, none of which can be sharply marked off from the more inclusive science or from one another; such are ethnology and human morphology and physiology. Psychology is a member of this group of anthropological sciences; it may be distinguished from the wider science of anthropology by saying that it is concerned, not with man as one animal species among others, but with man in his distinctively human aspect. Now every one knows that man is chiefly distinguished from the animals by his mental powers. Why not then be content (as some of the earlier writers were) to define psychology as the science of mind, or of the human mind, or of mind as manifested in the human species? There are several objections to such a definition. First, "mind" is a vague word, itself in need of definition. The meaning of the word can not be defined by pointing to one mind after another and saying: "This and this and this is what I mean by 'a mind.'" Although the words "mind" and "mental" are in common usage, we can only gradually by prolonged study build up and clarify our conception of "mind" or of "a mind." Secondly, there are other sciences of mind than psychology: such are logic, and metaphysic, and epistemology, and theology, all of which claim to tell us about mind or minds.

Those who have been content to define psychology as the science of mind have for the most part conceived of human nature as a combination of two very unlike things or principles, mind and body. But this is an assumption the validity of which is highly disputable; it has been not only disputed, but also confidently rejected, by a great number of philosophers, as well as by many of the leaders of modern science. And, even if we regard the assumption as well founded, we have to confess that it is impossible to distinguish clearly and confidently between body and mind, between the working of the body and the manifestations of mind in or through the body.

Psychology is Based on Observations of Three Kinds. Introspection

The difficulty is that each of us has no direct or immediate acquaintance with minds other than his own. Each one of us experiences pain and pleasure and various emotions, thinks and strives, remembers and expects and resolves. And it is generally agreed that all such experiences are manifestations of his mind or mental capacities. By reflection upon such experiences a man may form some notion of what his mind does and can do. And, by comparing notes with other men, he learns that they have similar experiences upon similar occasions, and infers that they have minds not unlike his own. Such observation of the varieties of one's own experience is called *introspection.* Every intelligent person can and does to some extent notice and remember his experiences; and there are very few who do not sometimes describe their experiences in words, reflect upon them and discuss them with their fellows. When such introspection, reflection, and interchange of descriptions of experiences and reflections upon them are conducted systematically, the process constitutes one of the great methods of psychology. It has for a long time been a well-recognized method; it has in fact often been declared to be the sole practical method of psychological study, the only legitimate and effective method of obtaining knowledge of the mind. During the last half century, this method of study has been greatly refined by the use of systematic experiment; that is to say, the person who wishes to notice and describe his experiences of any particular kind, instead of waiting until in the natural course of events such an experience occurs, deliberately seeks or arranges conditions under which some such experience is likely to occur, expects it and notices it, and describes it as carefully as possible. By the aid of a laboratory, all sorts of ingenious apparatus, and skilled assistants, much may be done to refine introspection and to record its results more accurately; and such work is a large part, though by no means the whole, of what is called "experimental psychology." Experimental introspection has obvious limitations. Many of the most vital and interesting experiences, such as grief or joy or fear or moral struggle, cannot be induced at will, except, perhaps, in very slight degrees. And, under the most favorable conditions, introspection of our more vivid and vital experiences is difficult, because we are apt to be primarily interested in the events of the outer world in which we are taking part, if only as observers. Then again the very act of introspection does to some extent modify the experience we wish to observe and describe; so that in introspecting we partially defeat our own purpose.

Another great difficulty meets us when we come to exchange notes with others upon our introspections; namely, the language in which we describe our experiences to one another is always sadly inadequate and imperfect. It is not true, as has sometimes been said, that language was evolved purely for the description of material things and events; it seems more nearly true to say that language was in the first place essentially a means for communicating and describing our experiences, and that, throughout its development, this has been a very important function of language. Nevertheless, in respect of this function, language, in spite of all the efforts of literary men and of psychologists to render it more precise and effective, remains a very inadequate instrument. For the description and discussion of things and events of the material world language has become very efficient; because we all have, or may have, the same kind of acquaintance with those things and events; and the efficiency of language for this purpose affords a strong guarantee of the essential similarity of such knowledge and acquaintance obtained by men in general.

But, in respect of the description of our experiences, language can never attain the same efficiency; just because each man has one kind of acquaintance with his own experience, namely, a direct acquaintance, and another, a very indirect kind of acquaintance only, with the experiences of other men.[1] Yet here again the fact that we do succeed by the aid of language in making one another understand in some degree our descriptions of our experiences shows that one man's experiences are not wholly unlike another's, but rather have much in common. In many cases of the description of experience, language is but little less efficient than for the description of objective fact. If I say "I saw the moon rise over the hill just now," you understand what I mean almost as fully and as surely as when I say "The moon rose over the hill just now." Yet in the former case my words describe a fact of my experience of which you can have only indirect acquaintance through my description; while in the second case the words describe an objective event which you may be acquainted with in the same way as myself and may objectively verify in other ways. Again, I say "I am truly sorry"; and (if I am speaking truly) I describe a fact with which you can have no direct acquaintance, such as I have; yet you know very well what I mean, and you adjust your conduct accordingly. And if, instead of "sorry," I had used any one of some hundreds of words, and had said "I am, or I feel, weary or angry, or anxious, or afraid, etc.," you might have felt the same confidence that you took my meaning. This confidence is justified by the success with which we use such language to influence one another.

[1] This statement is sometimes disputed. There is some striking evidence in support of the view that one man, A, may sometimes become aware of the thoughts or feelings of another, B, or otherwise be influenced by them, in some more direct fashion than the usual roundabout processes of bodily or verbal expression by B and the perception of those expressions by A by aid of his senses. Such communication by unknown means is generally called "telepathic"; but its reality is not regarded as fully established.

Observation and Description of the Conditions of Experience

The introspective method has, then, peculiar difficulties and limitations; yet, in spite of these, it is possible for it to achieve a generalized description of types of experience. It could and did achieve in this way a certain stage of psychological science, namely, the descriptive classificatory stage, which is but the first stage of the development of a science. But even this could be achieved only by taking note of the conditions under which we enjoy the experiences that we more or less successfully describe in words. For it is largely by noting and pointing out to one another such conditions that we attain to a common use and understanding of the words by aid of which we describe our experiences. We note, for example, that "hot" is the right word for the description of our experience when we closely approach the fire, "pain" when any part of the body is injured, "weary" when we have worked long and hard, "pleased" when we attain what we seek, and so on. Some of these conditions are facts of the outer world, some are facts of experience; and by noting systematically such occasions or conditions of various types of experience, it is possible to establish a certain number of empirical rules which raise to the explanatory stage the purely descriptive psychology attainable by introspection alone. This has been done with good effect.

Observation and Description of Behavior

A third great type of observation enables us to carry yet further our understanding of our experience, and at the same time raises another group of problems. This is the observation of conduct or behavior, both our own and that of other persons. By the term "conduct or behavior of any person" we denote every movement and every other observable change of bodily condition which seems to express his experience. We know from observation of our own behavior that movements of the limbs, the face, the throat and chest, and other bodily changes, such as sweating and shedding of tears, are apt to accompany or follow upon experiences of certain types, in a more or less regular and orderly fashion. And observation of other persons, combined with their statements about their accompanying experiences, enables us to formulate a number of general rules, stating the correlation or conjunction of types of experience with types of bodily expression or behavior. Common observation has embodied in common speech a number of such empirical rules of correlation between modes of experience and modes of behavior; and, aided by these and by his own observations, every man, without special study, acquires some skill in interpreting modes of behavior as expressions of experiences.

Popular and Literary Psychology

These three kinds of observation—namely, (1) introspection, or the noticing of one's own experiences, (2) observation of the conditions or occasions of experiences, (3) observation of the expressions of experiences—are practised by all men with some degree of success; and common speech embodies many general propositions based upon them. Such propositions constitute the popular psychology which we inevitably acquire in learning the use of language. Until we begin to study psychology scientifically, we inevitably make use of these forms of speech and accept more or less uncritically the propositions expressed or implied by them. Most of these implications of common speech are more or less true; for they embody the wisdom of the ages. But most of the words used in popular psychology are so vague and ill-defined that it is very difficult to formulate in such terms any unambiguous propositions or to convey any clear meaning. The literary art largely consists in so combining the words and phrases of popular psychology as to convey such meaning more effectively than the common speech of the common man can do. The cultivation of literature or the art of letters has thus greatly refined the psychology of common speech; and, when we speak of a cultivated man, we generally mean one who has learnt to appreciate and to make use of this more subtle and effective literary psychology. Persons whose education has been mainly literary, and who have learnt to appreciate highly and to use with some skill this more subtle literary psychology, are very apt to take the view that it is the only form of psychology of any value and that the attempt to deal scientifically with the facts of experience, or to make a scientific psychology, is mistaken and fruitless. But this anti-scientific view is ill-founded; there need be and should be no antagonism between literary and scientific psychology. From this point onward I shall use the terms "psychology" and "psychologist" to denote the scientific varieties; but in doing so, I shall imply no disrespect for the achievements in this sphere of poets and biographers and writers of romance. The wise psychologist will regard literature as a vast store-house of information about human experience, and will not neglect to draw from it what he can.

Divergence of Scientific Psychology

For long ages the literary and the scientific treatments of human nature and human experience were but little differentiated; but as, under the stimulus and example of the other natural sciences, psychology began to be studied more systematically for its own sake, it drew further away from the popular and literary traditions, and a spirit of antagonism showed itself. This tendency was perhaps inevitable; for the psychologists, in attempting to specialize the words of common speech and to give them precise meaning, and in endeavoring to formulate exact generalizations and explanations of experience, formed hypotheses or theories, as is done in all the other natural sciences; their statements about experience and even their observations were then apt to be distorted or perverted by their theories; for such theories could at the best only approximate to the truth, and at the worst were very misleading. This tendency of psychology to diverge from the common and the literary traditions culminated about the end of the nineteenth century, when the artificial character of psychology was carried so far by some of its exponents that their writings seemed to have no relation to human nature or experience and no bearing upon practical life. To some psychologists this was evidence that their science was still in a very crude and unsatisfactory condition; for they saw that the true purpose of psychology, in the progressive realization of which its justification must be found, is the improvement of our understanding, and therefore of our control, of human experience and behavior. But others took a high line and reacted against the charge that psychology was a useless and purely academic pursuit, by retorting that it made no claim to be anything else; that it could have, and should not aspire to have, any bearing whatever on real life; that it was a game like any other, to be played according to accepted rules or conventions; that the enjoyment to be had from the game and the sharpening of wits that it might bring were its sole justification and *raison d'être.*

Applications of Psychology Restore It to Sanity

This stage, however, did not long endure. One of the most prominent of the "strictly scientific" psychologists who dogmatically expounded this remarkable doctrine, in accordance with his principles and in defense of the strictly useless psychology which he had produced, shortly afterward published a long series of books on the applications of psychology to life; and, as these books were not without value, they provided a convincing demonstration of the falsity of the doctrine. In thus turning from false theory to practical endeavor, this inconsistent psychologist exemplified the condition and the development of psychology at the time. For by the impartial inquirer the so-called science might well have been described as a mass of observations of the three kinds we have noticed, mixed with and distorted by a chaotic jumble of theories.

Nevertheless, it began to be apparent, even to some practical men, that this jumble of facts, expressed by various writers in terms of the most diverse and inconsistent theories, though it might hardly deserve the name of a science, had yet something to offer of value for practical life. And the psychologists kept plugging away, accumulating observations, refining their methods, and discussing their theories, vastly encouraged by these indications of a coming recognition and practical application of their hard-won knowledge. Nothing succeeds like success. And so these first successful applications of psychology have brought many more students into the field, have turned many into the paths of direct attack upon practical problems (*i. e.*, of applied psychology) and have excited a wide-spread popular interest in this now flourishing science. Even literary men are beginning to pay some attention to it and to find in it some help toward understanding and describing human experience and behavior. Thus psychology is coming into its own; and the psychologist, instead of ploughing his lonely furrow in the vague hope of contributing to a science that may some day be recognized as of value to mankind, finds himself embarrassed by the fact that men of the most varied occupations are calling on him for help, expecting from him definite pronouncements and safe guidance in a multitude of practical problems.

This revolution of the popular attitude toward psychology, from one of complete indifference to that of excessive trust and expectation of practical guidance from it, brings serious drawbacks and dangers to the orderly development of the science. But in the long run it must tend to its advancement. And we may now confidently say that psychology is destined to go forward, answering more fully the practical demands made on it, and gradually building itself up into the master science of human nature; a science which will provide for all the social sciences the foundation for lack of which they have long remained relatively sterile.

The Use of Hypotheses Is Necessary

I have said that the theories of psychologists have colored their descriptions, and often have distorted their observations. What, then, is to be our attitude toward theories or hypotheses in psychology? Are we to banish them and to build up a science without hypotheses? That would be quite impossible, even if we were content to remain on the plane of purely descriptive psychology. For, in order to describe, we must use general and abstract terms; and every such word implies a theory or hypothesis. Description requires classification of like with like; and the use of any word which denotes a class of like objects of thought implies the hypothesis that these objects are so far of common nature as to justify us in thinking of them as alike—for the particular purpose we have in view. Classificatory hypotheses of this kind are necessarily made by every science; and they have to justify themselves by their successful working. Without them, not only science but all intelligent discourse is impossible, whether about human nature or any other topic. The discussion of experience, of its conditions and its expressions, necessarily makes use of such classificatory hypotheses. But the question remains—Should we restrict the use of hypothesis as much as possible? Or is it advantageous deliberately to devise and use hypotheses that go beyond the bare minimum necessary for description, hypotheses of a more gratuitous nature, designed to explain the facts we describe? Here opinions differ very widely. Some authors profess a horror of hypotheses, and pretend to proscribe them from all science. This is mere ignorance and pedantry. We have seen that the hypotheses invoked in the use of general terms are inevitable; and the more far-reaching, more deliberately designed hypotheses, which are commonly distinguished as explanatory, are not really of a different nature; for description and explanation are not really distinct processes; explanation is only description in terms more general and more abstract than those of simple description. In making and using such hypotheses, it is all-important to be aware of what we are doing and to be ready to modify or abandon them at need. If we maintain this attitude, hypotheses are great aids to discovery, and, in so far as they are well designed, they greatly simplify description and facilitate explanation.

Some Historical Hypotheses

When psychology began to separate itself as a science from the popular and literary traditions, it did not start with a clean sheet in respect of hypotheses. Not only was it obliged to use and to revise, as best it could, the classificatory hypotheses of common speech; but also it found in these traditions certain hypotheses of the more far-reaching or explanatory kind, which, though vague and ill-designed for scientific purposes, were so firmly established that it was difficult to escape their influence. The very name of the science embodies such a hypothesis; for it implies that the science is concerned to study the soul or *psyche*, which for long ages had been regarded as a vital principle inhabiting and animating each human body and somehow the ground of each individual's experience. Many of these hypotheses were launched on their careers by great writers, or were developed by philosophers and by their authority established more securely in the common and literary traditions. Almost all psychologists make use of hypotheses having some such history. And the mischief is that there is no agreement as to which are the better of them; and, worse still, some hold them dogmatically, shape all their psychology upon them, and look with scorn upon all other types of psychology determined by the acceptance of other hypotheses. Wide divergences due to acceptance of widely different hypotheses are not peculiar to psychology. In physical science there are those who accept the ether, and those who do not; those who believe in absolute space and time, and those who do not; those who make use of the hypotheses of causation, energy, and force, and those who profess to have thrown them overboard as useless impedimenta. Similar differences in psychology are, then, no reproach to it and no ground for regarding it as in a peculiarly bad or hopeless position.

We may glance at some of the chief of these divergent types of psychology, resulting from different views as to the use of hypotheses.

Psychology of Pure Experience

Those who would restrict the use of hypothesis most severely aim at describing and explaining experience in terms of experience alone. They are allied with the pure idealists among the philosophers, for whom experience alone is real and all that exists, or is real, is experience. They are apt to define psychology as the science of individual experience or of pure experience. Apart from the insuperable difficulties of the metaphysical doctrine implied, psychology of this type may confidently be said to condemn itself to sterility by its self-denying ordinance.

Psychology of the Soul and Faculty Psychology

Ancient psychology accepted the soul, and was chiefly concerned to distinguish the various functions of the soul and to assign them seats in the various parts of the body. In the modern period this type developed into what is generally called "faculty psychology." Experience was regarded as a function or activity of the soul, or of a part of the soul distinguished as the mind; or "the mind" was used as synonymous with "soul"; and experiences of each of the principal types, such as remembering, desiring, judging, comparing, were said to be due to the exercise of a corresponding faculty, a faculty of the mind or soul; each such faculty being a subsidiary hypothesis. Faculty psychology had a considerable career; and early in the nineteenth century it received a new lease of life in the modified form of phrenology, which taught that each faculty had its seat in some particular part of the brain. Both the older and the later form of faculty psychology have long been discredited. Even though it be admitted that the conception of a soul or mind endowed with certain most fundamental faculties is one that we cannot wholly dispense with; yet we must recognize that in itself this assumption can carry us but a little way, and that to multiply the faculties and merely ascribe each type of experience to the exercise of such a faculty is a fruitless procedure.

The Psychology of Ideas

The great rival of the faculty theory was the *theory of ideas.* This theory has had a most varied and influential career in both philosophy and psychology; and, though no one has ever been able to make of it a consistent and intelligible theory, its influence still lives on. It is so firmly entrenched in the popular, the literary, and the psychological traditions, that the word "idea" is perhaps the most frequently used of all psychological terms, and few psychologists succeed in avoiding the use of it, even when they reject the theory it implies. In Plato's theory of ideas each "idea" was a supernatural archetype of a class of things; and the "ideas" existed in some remote and inaccessible region.[1] But at a later period "ideas" were brought into the mind and changed their character. John Locke was chiefly

[1] This is the traditional interpretation of Plato's language, but in recent years it has been seriously questioned.

responsible for establishing "the new way of ideas" in modern psychology. He began by defining "an idea" as anything whatsoever of which a man thinks[1] And, since Locke accepted the common-sense view of the physical world, the view namely that material things exist independently of our minds, this definition seemed to identify material things with "ideas." But Locke's further discussion made it seem that "the ideas" were somehow within, and a part of, the mind. The quick-witted Irishman, Bishop Berkeley, seized upon this inconsistency of the ponderous Englishman, and pointed out that, if all things of which we can think are "ideas," and "ideas" are in, or of, the mind, then all things of which we can think are in and of the mind; and, therefore, all things of which we can have any thought or knowledge are mental things. In this way he started a stream which swelled into that vast sea of troubled speculation called modern idealism. David Hume also took the "ideas" into the mind; but, in doing so, made them a substitute for the mind itself. Locke's use of the theory of "ideas" was a compromise between this extreme position and the faculty psychology; between "the new way of ideas" and the old way of faculties. For he continued to use the hypothesis of the mind endowed with faculties, and described the mind as exercising its faculties upon or about its "ideas." But, said Hume, all we know directly is the stream of "ideas" (and "impressions" which for him did not differ essentially from "ideas") and what we call the mind or soul is a mere empty stage which we unnecessarily assume to exist as the scene upon which the "ideas" play their parts. From that time onward "ideas" have played a very prominent part in psychology.[2] Experience became a mere stream of "ideas," and the course of experience was to be explained by the action of "ideas" upon one another. Thinking of any object was described as "having an idea of it"; and to think of it a second time, or a third, was described as "having the same idea again." Then arose the question—Where was the "idea" in the interval between my first and second thinking

[1] "Whatsoever is the object of the understanding when a man thinks."

[2] The more modern term "presentation" is almost synonymous with "idea" and has the advantage of denoting also "sense-perceptions."

of the object? Two answers, often confused together, became current. One described "ideas" as capable of existing in two conditions, the conscious and the unconscious conditions; when I am thinking of an object, my "idea" of it is said to be in the conscious condition; when I cease to think of it, the "idea" subsides into the unconscious condition. Some authors, seeing that the "idea" was, if it was anything at all, essentially a section or piece of experience, sought to avoid the inconsistency of the expression "unconscious idea," by supposing that, in the interval between its successive appearances, the "idea" became, not unconscious, but only subconscious or very slightly conscious The mind for this school was then no longer a stage or scene for the "ideas"; but consisted in and of the mass of "ideas," unconscious or subconscious for the most part, but passing in turn into the conscious condition.

The other answer was that the mind, the stage on which "ideas" play their parts, is also a store-house; that beneath the stage, which is illuminated, is a dark chamber in which "ideas" are stored. From this dark chamber they issue in turn, to appear upon the illuminated stage; afterward sinking down again into the dark store-house. Thus, for this theory, the mind consists of two chambers, one illuminated, one dark; the illumination is "consciousness," a sort of light which plays upon the "ideas" as they emerge from below; the plane of emergence, that of the trap-doors in the stage, came to be spoken of as "the threshold of consciousness"; and the "ideas" were said to rise above or fall below this threshold, the transition from light to darkness being usually more or less gradual. This way of describing experience is full of inconsistencies and obscurities. And, though it may have played a useful part in the past, as, for example, in the psychology of Herbart, there is no justification for continuing to use it. My own opinion is that any service performed by these confused and confusing fictions (namely, the "ideas," the dark and the illuminated chambers of the mind, "the threshold of consciousness," and "consciousness" as a light which illuminates "ideas") is far outweighed by the vast mass of confused and loose thinking which they have engendered. They should be sternly banished to the psychological museums.

Yet they still thrive; as we see in the Freudian psychology, which has flourished so greatly of late years, and in the usage of many writers of other schools.

Psychology as Science of Consciousness

Others define psychology as the science of consciousness; which is not far from the definition of it as the science of individual experience. For "consciousness" is generally taken to be almost, if not quite, synonymous with "experience"; although, as we have just seen, there are other usages of the word. "Consciousness" is a thoroughly bad word; and it has been a great misfortune for psychology that the word has come into general use. If it be used as synonymous with "experience," it must be admitted that "experience" is much the better term; because, even when it is used in the substantival sense, it retains the form of the verb from which it is derived, so that we can hardly forget that experience implies some one who experiences and something which is experienced by the experiencer. Whereas "consciousness," having the form of a substantive which cannot be used as a verb, allows us to forget that it stands for the fact of being conscious of something, and that it implies some one who is conscious of that something. And many of the writers who use the word allow themselves to fall into this error; though the etymology of the word should help them to avoid it. For it is derived from *conscire*, which is the Latin for "to know things together"; and "consciousness," if it is used at all, should be used to mean "the act of knowing or thinking of things." The word "conscience" would have been a better word than "consciousness" for psychological purposes, if it had not been appropriated by the moralists and given a special popular meaning. The French language is more fortunate than ours in that it retains the word "conscience" in its original sense.

The Atomistic or Mosaic Psychology

The havoc wrought in psychology by the word "consciousness" is chiefly due to our deep-seated tendency to reïfy (to make a thing or a stuff of) every object that we think and speak of, especially when we think or speak of it by aid of a word of substantival form. Yielding to this tendency, very many psychologists have fallen into the way of speaking of consciousness (*i. e.*, of the act of thinking of things) as though it were a stuff. Then, on contemplating this stuff, it appears obvious that it is not a simple stuff of uniform texture, but rather highly complex and variegated; more like a mosaic or a piece of tapestry than a uniform white sheet. Moreover, it appears like a stuff that perpetually changes, as though an endless strip of tapestry were drawn along before our eyes. Therefore, proceeding to analyze this stuff, they seem to themselves to discover that it is a mosaic, made up of small pieces of stuff; and they then set themselves to find the smallest particles, the irreducible elements or atoms, of this stuff.

The question then arises whether all these particles, of which "consciousness" is supposed to be made up, are of one kind; and, while some maintain that they are of several or of many kinds, the majority assert that they are fundamentally of one kind only, which they call "sensations," or "sensory elements." And some speculators of a metaphysical turn go further and say that these particles are not really the ultimate elements; but that, just as the atoms of the older chemistry are now commonly said to consist of electrons, or of particles of electricity or of some other stuff, so the sensory elements or atoms really consist of still finer particles of "consciousness" which they like to call "mind-stuff" or "mind-dust." Some of them go so far as to assert that, not only ourselves or our minds, but all things in the universe are made up of such mind-dust, arranged and compounded in many different conjunctions. And then, in order to make plausible this fantastic view, the view that the seas and mountains, stars and planets and all things else are made up of this stuff, they fall back on the expressions "subconsciousness," and "threshold of consciousness," and "consciousness as a light which illuminates one chamber of the mind and all that enters into it"; striving in this way to make intelligible their doctrine that the stuff they call "consciousness" exists in two forms, namely, "conscious consciousness" and "unconscious consciousness."

Fusion of Atomistic with Idea Psychology

This way of treating of experience readily combines with "the way of ideas." For "ideas," regarded as things, are a product of the same tendency to reïfy whatever we think of. The "consciousness psychologist," accepting "ideas" as things, as innocently as he accepts "consciousness" as a stuff, asks himself—Of what stuff are these things called "ideas" composed? The answer is not far to seek. Obviously "ideas" are composed of "sensory elements"; and so arises a full-blown "sensationism" or sensationist psychology. It is generally held by the exponents of this doctrine that it has the great merit of solving or abolishing the perplexing problem of the relations between mind and matter; and, since matter is said by them to be composed of the same stuff as "consciousness" or "ideas," they proudly claim for it the title of "idealism." [1] Any one who is capable of contemplating the history of psychology in a detached spirit will be inclined to agree that this "consciousness" is not only stuff but also non-sense. And some of the exponents of "sensationism," having carried the doctrine as far as they can, have themselves arrived at this conclusion. For, turning round upon their own doctrine in a moment of illumination, they have asked—Does this stuff that we call "consciousness" really exist? Does consciousness exist? And they have been constrained to reply—No, obviously it does not exist; it is an illusion, a fiction.

Having thus displayed the purely fictitious and fallacious character of "consciousness psychology," some of the more thoroughgoing thinkers have deduced from its failure a new philosophy which they call "neo-realism." Thus has been evolved the very latest form of materialism which, instead of saying, with the old-fashioned materialists, that the brain secretes consciousness, says rather that the distinction between

[1] The word "idealism" has two entirely different meanings which are often confused implicitly and sometimes deliberately. In the one meaning it denotes any doctrine which asserts that the whole world consists of mind or minds or mental operations. In the other meaning it stands for any moral attitude of striving to realize an "ideal"—to make real or actual a state of affairs that seems to us better than the existing state.

consciousness or experience and things known or experienced is fictitious and illusory, that "ideas," and "perceptions," and all the other things said to be composed of bits of "consciousness," are really identical with the objects of the physical world. Thus the wheel comes full circle, and we are brought to the position from which Locke started out—"ideas" are once more the things of which a man thinks; that is to say, they are identified with all "the furniture of earth," while "the choir of heaven," including all such things as minds, souls, selves, or spirits, with all their modes of activity and experience, is left out from the picture of the universe.

Most of the exponents of "consciousness" and "sensationism" do not achieve this last turn of the wheel. In order to understand their position, which is perhaps the one most widely held at the present day, we must consider a very important influence in modern psychology of which up to this point I have made no mention, the influence, namely, of physiology.

Influence of Physiology on Psychology

The ancient philosophers knew nothing of the functions of the brain. But, early in the modern period, it was made clear that the functions of the human brain are very important and that they are somehow bound up with or concerned in our knowing and feeling and striving, with our experience in short. Therefore, many ardent spirits set to work to solve the secrets of experience by investigating the brain. An immense and ever-increasing amount of human energy has been devoted to this very difficult research, and a multitude of facts have been established. And the school which seeks to explain all human experience and activity in terms of the structure and functions of the brain, or of the nervous system, has constantly gained in numbers and influence. The program of this school was crudely formulated in the eighteenth century by the notorious dictum that the brain secretes thought as the liver secretes bile. But various more-detailed formulations were made by the physiologists, according to the type of psychological doctrine which they chose to adopt for assimilation with the facts of their own science.

Early in the nineteenth century, the phrenologists, of whom Francis Gall was the leader, combined a crude brain-physiology with the "faculty psychology." Even before this date the "idea psychology" had been given (by David Hartley, 1749) a physiological turn which greatly added to its plausibility, and which went far to make the fortune of that type of "idea psychology" known as "the psychology of association." The "association psychology," which was long dominant in England, of which Locke and Hume were the founders, and of which Hartley, the two Mills and Bain, were the leading exponents, claimed to explain all experience as a succession of "ideas"; these were said to be linked or associated together and to draw one another along into consciousness by means of their links or automatic couplings. Now, though "ideas" seemed to be facts or real things, it was difficult to give any adequate picture of the links or couplings; and therefore Hartley, one of the first of the associationists, devised, no doubt with a sense of great relief, the plan of attributing to the brain the couplings and all the pulling and pushing, in short, the whole business of shunting and shifting "ideas" into and out of "consciousness." And the more the brain was studied, the better it seemed to lend itself to this purpose.

The doctrine of localization of cerebral functions, which, in the crude form of Gall's phrenology, had proved untenable, seemed to become more definitely established as knowledge grew rapidly in the later part of the nineteenth century. The brain became revealed as a vast jungle of cells connected by a tangle of nerve fibres, each of which cells seemed to be in some sense a vital unit. The "idea psychology" was then translated into physiological terms by supposing that each "idea" had its home in some one cell, where it dwelt at peace and in darkness during the greater part of its time; and that occasionally, when a nervous current reached the cell, the "idea" within it glowed and became "conscious" or was projected into "consciousness."[1] And it was conceived that, whenever the excitement of one cell followed upon that of another, the two cells became linked to-

[1] T. H. Ziehen ("Outlines of Physiological Psychology") is the best contemporary exponent of this view.

gether by a path of low resistance; so that thereafter the excitement of one would easily spread over to the other, leaving the path between them still more open. In this way all experience was physiologically explained as the successive emergence of "ideas" out of their holes or cells, according to the law of neural habit. Then, when "sensationism" analyzed "ideas" and displayed them as made up of "sensory elements" or "sensations," these elements or atoms were assigned each to its own nerve cell; and the "idea" or "cluster of sensations" had then for its neural counterpart a cluster of cells which worked together as a functional unit. And this unit could grow by the inclusion of more cells, as the "idea" could become more complex by the inclusion of more "sensory elements"; and the group of cells could become linked with others to form a group of groups, which might come into action simultaneously or successively.

To those who accepted this scheme it naturally seemed that there was no longer any need to postulate a "mind," a "soul," a "subject of experience," a "self"; an experiencer or a thinker of any kind who thinks, desires, remembers, expects, or in any way experiences, was deemed unnecessary; or, if it seemed convenient at times to use language of this kind, it was sufficient to say that "the idea" of the moment does the thinking, or that the passing thought thinks and is the only thinker.[1] But in the main the active mode passed out of fashion in the description of experience; and the laws of thought became the mechanics of the brain. "Consciousness," it was said, was reduced to the role of a passive spectator. But even this was an overstatement of the position assigned to it; even a spectator is active to the extent of observing. It would be more true to say that "consciousness" was given the role of a "super."

The Mechanical Reflex Theory

The full persuasiveness of this translation of psychology into terms of brain-mechanism is only to be understood when it is realized that, in addition to providing what seemed an equiva-

[1] This last was the subterfuge preferred by James, who, in his great work, "The Principles of Psychology," made an heroic effort to work out a consistent "Sensationism."

lent in the brain for every "sensation" or other discoverable element of "consciousness," and a plausible scheme of the way in which these brain-elements might be supposed to play upon one another, physiology was working out at the same time a scheme which claims to be able to explain, in principle, all human action in terms of the mechanics of the nervous system. This scheme is a development of the principle of *reflex action*, which was first clearly formulated by the great philosopher Descartes at the opening of the modern period. Descartes suggested that the principle would suffice to account for all the bodily activities of animals; but he himself and most other psychologists continued to regard the bodily actions of men as expressions of their experience, as somehow determined by their thinking, by their feeling, their desiring, their remembering, their recognizing, and so forth.

Descartes' account of reflex action was merely a brilliant guess; but the subsequent course of physiological discovery has justified it abundantly. It has been shown that, in both men and animals, some elementary but seemingly purposive movements may be evoked, even when the brain is wholly out of action or destroyed and the individual remains unaware of the whole process. Thus, if the sole of the foot is pricked, most men and most animals will quickly draw away the foot. Common sense says: "He feels the prick and draws away the foot in order to avoid the painful impression." Well, physiologists have shown that this withdrawal of the foot may occur in a very similar way, when the spinal cord has been separated from the brain. And a man in this condition, though he may see his foot move when pricked, does not feel the prick or the movement; and he knows nothing of them, if his eyes are closed. They have shown that the prick excites a nerve in the foot, that this excitement spreads up the nerve to the spinal cord as a wave of physical change (not unlike a current of electrical change in a telephone-wire) leaps across from the sensory nerve to a motor nerve (much as the electric spark leaps from one terminal to another) and so issues along the motor nerve and, reaching the muscles of the leg, causes in them an explosion which in turn causes them to contract and so withdraw the foot. That is the type of reflex action as conceived by Descartes and studied by modern physiologists. The latter have shown that many simple movements and secretions may be produced in animals and in the human organism in this relatively simple way; the whole action or reaction being a sequence of processes which seem in principle capable of being adequately described and explained in terms of physics and chemistry; although as a matter of fact we are still far from having achieved any such description.

Physiologists have shown also that the spinal cord (the part of the central nervous system which lies in the spine and to which all the sensory nerves pass in and from which all the motor and gland-exciting nerves issue) consists essentially of a large number of such mechanisms for effecting reflex actions; each mechanism being a more or less complicated conjunction of sensory with motor nerves, by means of which the nervous current excited in any sensory nerve is led over into some group of motor or gland nerves. Further, they have found reason to believe that the whole nervous system, including the brain, is built up on the pattern of these reflex mechanisms or sensori-motor nervous arcs, which lead on from sense-organs to the executive organs, namely, muscles and glands. The brain seems, in fact, to consist merely of a multitude of such nervous paths or arcs, differing only from those of the spinal cord in being longer and more complicated, and in having more abundant connections with one another. The mysterious "nerve-cells," which had been supposed to be the abodes of "ideas," are shown to be merely swellings upon the fine protoplasmic threads which are the nerve fibres. Those of the surface or cortex of the brain (the famous gray matter) seem to be in no way essentially different from those which occur in the spinal cord on the simplest reflex arcs; and their essential function seems to be to regulate the nutrition and growth of the nerve fibres which are parts of the same cells.

Thus all human action is made to appear to be of the type of reflex action, to be the issue merely of the play of nervous currents, started in the sense-organs by stimulations from the physical world and propagating themselves through the jungle of the nervous system, finding always the paths of least resistance according to purely physical principles All human action is reflex action, or, as the principle is more commonly formulated, every human action is a mechanical response to a stimulus.

Memory and the Reflex Theory

If you, my reader, are new to this sort of thinking, you may say: That is all very well, but how about memory? Surely many of my actions are prompted and guided not by sense-impressions, but by memory, by memories of past experiences! The physiologist has his answer to this question also. The nervous system contains many reflex paths innately organized; that is to say, they develop and become ready to lead off sensory excitation to the appropriate muscles spontaneously; just as the blood-vessels develop spontaneously in such a way as to lead the currents of blood wherever they are needed. But, unlike the network of the blood-vessels, the nervous network is plastic. Every reflex arc is connected with a multitude of others; so that, under the most favorable conditions (as when, for example, all nervous pathways are rendered very open by a large dose of strychnine) excitement started in any sensory nerve may spread like an avalanche throughout a multitude of channels and throw practically every muscle in the body into violent action. Any nervous current is normally restricted to a comparatively few pathways, leading it over to the muscles, by the fact that every sensory nerve-path is more intimately connected with certain motor nerves than with any others; but these connections, junctions or synapses between nerves or neurones (as the complete units, consisting of nerve-cell and fibre together, are now called) are very delicate structures. Each synapse presents a certain resistance to the passage of the current of nervous energy. But this resistance is not a fixed quantity; it varies from moment to moment, according to the conjunctions of many influences that play upon it. Hence the unpredictable and variable character of all reactions, save the simplest reflexes. Of all influences that affect the resistance of the synapse, the most important is conceived to be the actual passage of the nervous current across it from neurone to neurone; for, it is held, this renders the resistance of that synapse permanently lower than it previously was, or leaves it with a diminished power of resisting the passage of the current. Granting this, imagine that an entirely novel odorous object is presented to your nose; this "stimulus" excites, by way of well-organized reflex paths, the reaction of biting. The object then stimulates your mouth or tongue in such a way as to excite another reflex action, that of spitting it out (in common parlance, we say: The object has a pleasing odor, but a bad taste). Now suppose further that a similar object is presented to your nose on a second occasion. It is probable that you will not bite, but rather will make (incipiently at least) the motion of spewing it out. Common sense would say that you remember the bad taste and that this leads you to refrain from repeating your bite; or it might say that, owing to your prior experience of the bad taste, the odor is now unpleasant to you; or that it now, instead of exciting your appetite, excites disgust. But the physiologist says that the close succession of the two reactions on the first occasion has established a more intimate connection between the two reflex paths through which the two reactions were evoked, by lowering the resistance of certain synapses; so that now the nervous current excited by the odor, instead of flowing on to the muscles which do the biting, flows over directly to the second set of muscles which effect the movement of spewing out. Thus an alteration of resistances at certain synapses has produced a new reflex path. A reaction established or acquired in this way is called a "conditioned reflex." All that used to be called profiting by experience, or intelligent adaptation of behavior, or the acquirement of habits, in short, all facts that used to be classed under the terms "memory" and "habit" we are now to regard as essentially a matter of the establishment of "conditioned reflexes." No wonder that in these days the young student of psychology swears by "conditioned reflexes" and is apt to regard the term as the key to most of the riddles of the universe, or at least as the master key of human fate! Having grasped this master principle, he feels, and in some quarters he is encouraged to feel, that he need no longer rack his brains over the traditional puzzles of psychology. For it has become clear to him that love, honor and duty, faith, hope and charity, reason, will and moral effort, are merely so many names by which we denote as many varieties of "conditioned reflex," of somewhat complicated pattern no doubt, but not essentially different from the scratch-reflex of the dog's hind-leg. He sees clearly that the good dog is the one whose "conditioned reflexes" lead him to the softest spot and the best bone. Equally clearly he sees that the good man is he whose conditioned reflexes have been established by a judicious system of rewards and punishments; and that the wise man is he whose conditioned reflexes lead him to avoid pain and to pursue pleasure. *Sic itur ad astra.*

Consequences of the Mechanical Reflex Theory

Having arrived at this point of his career in the pursuit of understanding, two courses lie open to the aspiring student of human nature; he may attach himself to either of two schools. If he is of a severely practical turn of mind, he will give ear to the "Behaviorists." The official representatives of this flourishing school will tell him that he need trouble himself no further over the problems of experience or of "consciousness"; need not ask the troublesome questions: Does consciousness exist? Can consciousness do this or that? How is it related to the reflex processes of the brain? He will be told that the conduct or behavior of any man is merely the sum of his conditioned reflexes; that this is all we know and all we need to know. But, accepting this position, he has one more choice still to make. He may elect to fall in with the crowd marching behind Dr. J. B. Watson[1] and to say with him: What has been called experience or consciousness may occur or exist for all I know or care. But I am not interested in it. I am concerned only to understand human behavior. I know that all behavior is mechanically determined by reflex processes; let me get on with the study of "conditioned reflexes."

Or, if he feels the need of a metaphysical justification of his position, he may follow the forlorn banner of Dr. E. B. Holt,[2] the most thoroughgoing of the neo-realists, who with a sublime consistency will tell him that what he has been accustomed to call his experiences or his consciousness of pleasure or of pain,

[1] "Psychology from the Standpoint of the Behaviorist."
[2] "The Concept of Consciousness."

of desire, of effort, of knowing, of remembering, and the rest, that all these are really movements of particles or of currents of energy in the world about him; and who will explain to him how and why, from the dawn of reflection to the end of the nineteenth century, the whole human race has been the victim of the illusion that thinking of a material object is not identical with the existence of that object, but rather a fact of a different order.

But the student who has accepted the principle of the conditioned reflex as all-sufficient may nevertheless find it impossible to appreciate Dr. Holt's extreme position; and he may also refuse to copy Dr. Watson in his devil-may-care attitude toward experience. For he may feel that his experience is too real to be explained away as an illusion; and he may argue that, even though behavior be merely a sequence of reflex actions mechanically determined, yet we cannot afford to repudiate introspective observation entirely. For, he may reflect, our knowledge of these reflex processes is still rudimentary and schematic only; and, if "sensations" or "sensory elements" faithfully attend the workings of the brain, each drawn along by some "conditioned reflex" like a slave at the chariot-wheel of his master, we may hope, by continuing the study of them, to throw more light upon these theoretically so clear, but practically so obscure, master-factors of human nature, the "conditioned reflexes." If he takes this line, he will fall in with a large and excellent company of psychologists who are following just this road. Not all of these pin their faith to the conditioned reflex conceived in the strictest and narrowest sense; but for all of them (and probably this group comprises a majority of the academic psychologists of the present day) human conduct is determined wholly and strictly by the mechanical action of the bodily organs, and chiefly by that of the nervous system; that is to say, by physical and chemical changes in the nervous and other tissues, processes which are in principle strictly predictable and describable as movements in space, obeying laws or conforming to equations no other than those which are found to hold good for inorganic processes. For them the nervous system has taken the place of the soul, or mind, or self, or the subject of experience; the brain, or at most "the passing thought that thinks," is the sole thinker, and thinking is mechanical brain action or its "epi-phenomenon." A large number of psychologists who agree in this respect (though they differ widely in other matters) do not, like the late Hugo Münsterberg, loftily assert that, because "sensations" or other elements which compose their "consciousness" are artificial abstractions, their psychology has no bearing upon human life and no practical value; nor do they, like Dr. Watson, cease to take an intelligent interest in their own introspective findings and those of other observers. They rightly recognize that, even if their physiological assumptions be true, it is nevertheless a fact that research into the functions of the brain has been greatly aided in the past by introspective observations; and, though they anticipate that the mechanistic physiology of the brain will more and more supersede and ultimately wholly absorb psychology, they hold that its advance may be greatly aided by the continued and more refined study of experience. Professor Titchener may perhaps be named as standing unambiguously for this type and program of psychology.[1]

The Mechanical Reflex Not the Foundation Stone of Psychology

Now let us go back to consider the student confronted by the consequences drawn from the study of the nervous system. He is told that his experiences are merely mosaics of sensory elements, each of which is called into being, or into "consciousness," by a physico-chemical process of the brain; that his belief in his power of choosing, resolving, striving, "of seeking the good and ensuing it," in purposive action in a word, is a delusion; that his hardest choice is not, as the older determinists used to say, determined by his strongest desire, is not in fact at all influenced by desire or by anything of that nature; and that even pleasure and pain, which for so long were widely held to be the springs of all human action, have no influence upon it.

We have seen how, confronted with these conclusions, which are supported by an imposing array of authority, and feeling

[1] "A Text-book of Psychology."

themselves unable to criticise the observations and reasonings upon which they are based (for indeed the full appreciation of these would demand several years of special physiological study, which few psychologists find time to undertake) the majority capitulate, and follow one or other of the lines I have briefly sketched.

But some (and I hope that this book may add to their number) will hesitate, remembering vividly perhaps some devastating conflict of desires, some moral struggle hardly won, some intense pain, some base temptation, some impulse of profound pity or of tender devotion, of fierce anger or horrible fear. They may ask themselves: Is there not something radically wrong with a system of thought which tells us that these experiences are of no account in the world? Must there not be some flaw, some ill-founded premise or assumption, in the argument which leads to this incredible conclusion; a conclusion which runs counter to the teachings of the moral leaders of all ages; which represents man as no more capable of creative activity or of self-determination than the humblest animal or the crystal in the test tube; which regards the Bible, or the works of Shakespeare, of Beethoven, of Newton, as fortuitous concourses of atoms, whose arrangement in space is due to mechanical processes of natural selection no other than that which sorts the pebbles from the sand upon the beach?

It is said that he who hesitates is lost. But sometimes it happens that he who hesitates is saved, especially when it is a question of dashing down a steep slope. Let the beginner in psychology who hesitates at the brink of the slope that leads to materialism and a rigid determinism look round again and critically survey the ground. Let him also look down the slope; and there in imagination he may see the sturdy figure of T. H. Huxley, struggling in vain in his old age to lay the spectre he had so confidently helped to create;[1] there also he may descry the forlorn figure of Herbert Spencer, once acclaimed the king of mechanists, but now remembered as the author of a "chromo-philosophy" of scandalous vagueness. Let him turn and look upward, and he will see the serene figures of Charles Darwin

[1] "Evolution and Ethics."

and Newton and Faraday, of Herman Lotze, of Leibnitz and Plato and Wordsworth, and of all the great poets, an august company of great men who refused to "lay the intellect to rest upon a pillow of obscure ideas," whose voices still ring down the ages, insisting that Man is more than mechanism and may yet be master of his fate.

The Assumptions of the Reflex Theory

Thus warned and encouraged, the student may be prepared to give due weight to the following reflections. All the varieties of psychology which propose to abdicate in favor of a mechanistic physiology, which propose to replace the hypothesis of a mind, a soul, a self, a subject, an experiencer, by that of a brain or a bodily organism working on strictly mechanical or physical principles (that is to say, behaviorism, sensationism, associationism, presentationism), may be conveniently classed together as mechanistic psychologies.[1] All of these are based upon certain assumptions which, though they have a certain plausibility, have not been justified by the best efforts of those who make use of them so confidently. The chief of these assumptions are: (1) that mechanistic physiology will at some remote date prove adequate to the task that lies before it, namely, the working out of a complete description and explanation of the bodily processes of organisms (including the human organism) in terms of the mechanistic principles of physics and chemistry; (2) that it is, or may become, possible to give an intelligible account of the relation between the facts of experience and the facts of behavior, in terms compatible with such mechanistic physiology.

Let us examine briefly these two assumptions. The assumption which underlies mechanistic physiology is part of a wider twofold assumption which underlies the whole of mechanistic biology; namely, that the mechanistic description of the inorganic world is in principle correct, and that organisms have

[1] These psychologies are not necessarily mechanistic. Any one of them might be combined with a belief in the reality of purposive action. But they all lend themselves readily to alliance with the mechanistic view of organisms which denies the reality of purposive action; and as a matter of fact they are usually so allied. Behaviorism especially seems to be deduced implicitly from the mechanistic dogma and to lie, somewhat uneasily, in this metaphysical bed.

been evolved from inorganic matter by the operation of natural selection, without the intervention of any influences, forces, or modes of action other than those operative in the inorganic world. Although this assumption has been very often and very confidently made, its validity appears more doubtful now than it did a generation ago. It is beginning to be generally admitted by leading biologists that Darwin's great principle of natural selection will not suffice to account for organic evolution and for that appearance of purposive adaptation of organisms to their environment which forces itself on our attention throughout the realm of life. As our knowledge of living things grows, the problem of life and its evolution appears more, rather than less, resistant to mechanical principles. The same is true within the narrower field of general physiology. The researches of the last one hundred years have brought us a vast mass of knowledge about the physical and chemical processes that go on within the body; but each new step reveals more problems of regulation and adaptation than it solves. We are told by some of the more philosophically minded leaders in physiological research[1] that we seem to be moving ever further from the goal of the mechanistic program, rather than approaching it. Again, within the still more special field of the physiology of the nervous system, our knowledge is astonishingly defective in view of the confidence with which it is put forward as a substitute for psychology. We do not know the nature of the change which propagates itself along the nerve fibres, as the so-called nervous impulse; and opinion is acutely divided as to whether this is of one kind only, or of two, or of many kinds. We know nothing about the nature of the inhibitory process which is involved in all co-ordination of nervous activity. We know next to nothing of the peculiar constitution and processes of the all-important synapses. The doctrine of "specific energies of sensory nerves," which, under several successive forms, has been as a ray of light in a great darkness, is now much blown upon and most by those who have no intelligible substitute for it. The doctrine of the localization of functions in the cerebral cortex, which, about the beginning of this century, seemed to be well established, at least

[1] E. g., Doctor J. S. Haldane, "Life, Mechanism, and Personality."

for the elementary sensory and motor functions, is also rocking insecurely and seems to need at the least a complete recasting in some form not yet suggested.[1] The facts of restitution of function, after destruction of tissue, remain as completely refractory to mechanistic interpretation in this as in all other fields of biology.[2]

As regards their second great assumption, the mechanistic psychologies are in no better case. The proposal of the behaviorists "to look this problem boldly in the face and pass on" cannot be acceptable to any man not entirely lacking in scientific curiosity; for, even though experience be notning but a kind of phosphorescence upon the brain, it is yet that without which life would have no value and no meaning for us. The proposals of the neo-realists would, if carried to their extreme, abolish the problem; but only one author has had the moral courage to attempt to carry them to this ridiculous extremity. The "sensationists" are divided between, or vacillate uncertainly between, the doctrine of *epiphenomenalism* (which would make "sensations" a kind of phosphorescence called into being by the nervous current traversing the cortex) and the mind-stuff theory, according to which "sensations" are things which exist in their own right as the primordial stuff of which the world is composed. Both doctrines utterly fail to give any intelligible account of the conditions under which these "sensations" come together to form "consciousness" as we know it introspectively, the conscious activities of perceiving, imagining, remembering, or otherwise thinking of an object.[3] And both fail to carry through the program whose simplicity is the main strength of the mechanistic position, namely, that of describing and explaining the whole of nature in one set of terms or categories, the categories of

[1] Cf. S. I. Franz, presidential address to the American Psychological Association, *Psychological Review*, 1921.

[2] *Ibid.* See also "The Science and Philosophy of the Organism," by Hans Driesch, for discussion of facts of this order.

[3] Professor C. A. Strong ("The Origin of Consciousness") has made the most thorough and sustained effort to carry out the "mind-stuff" program; but finds himself constrained to introduce into his sketch of the universe "given essences" which are "logical entities or subsistents . . . not either physical or psychological," and which seem to be so inconsistent with the general program as to constitute an admission of the impossibility of working it out consistently.

physical science. For, if the matter of the brain can generate "sensations," that matter is more than, and other than, the matter or physical processes described by physical science; and, if all matter is "sensations," or of the same nature as "sensations" which can combine to constitute the various forms of experience, then the account of it which physical science gives is most misleading, and the categories of that science, however useful they may have been, are only distant approximations to the truth.

Indeed, in the present state of physical science, it is absurd to pretend that its categories must prescribe the type of all legitimate description and explanation. For these are in perpetual flux. In the palmy days of materialism, it was common form to assert dogmatically that the universe consists of atoms of matter, that all energy was the momentum of such atoms, and all change the transmission of momentum by impact of one hard and resilient particle upon another. But those days of the "billiard-ball-universe" are gone forever, save perhaps in the imagination of a few belated biologists who have picked up their views of physical science from old-fashioned text-books. All the categories of physical science, matter, energy, motion, momentum, mass, and Space and Time themselves, are in question; and no man can say whether any one of them will emerge alive from the fermenting chaos of modern physical speculation.[1]

This being the state of affairs, it is surely premature, to say

[1] Let the student ponder the following words with which a leading physicist (A. S. Eddington, professor of astronomy at Cambridge) concludes a recent work on "Space, Time, and Gravitation": "The theory of relativity has passed in review the whole subject-matter of physics. It has unified the great laws, which by the precision of their formulation and the exactness of their application have won the proud place in human knowledge which physical science holds to-day. And yet, in regard to the nature of things, this knowledge is only an empty shell —a form of symbols. It is knowledge of structural form, and not knowledge of content. All through the physical world runs that unknown content, which must surely be the stuff of our consciousness. Here is a hint of aspects deep within the world of physics, and yet unattainable by the methods of physics. And, moreover, we have found that where science has progressed the farthest, the mind has but regained from nature that which the mind has put into nature. We have found a strange footprint on the shores of the unknown. We have devised profound theories, one after another, to account for its origin. At last, we have succeeded in reconstructing the creature that made the footprint. And lo! it is our own."

the least of it, to assume that human nature and human action are capable of being adequately explained or described in terms of the categories of physical science. The only wise course for the psychologist, as for the biologist in general, is the bold one of asserting the relative independence of his science and his right to choose and use the categories that are most profitable for his purpose, the better understanding and control of human nature. Let him leave to the future the most difficult task of harmonizing the conclusions of the biological and the physical sciences, while keeping an open mind and a critical attitude toward all attempts in that direction.

Acceptable Hypotheses

In this book, then, I shall attempt to show my readers how we may describe human nature and human experience, and in a proximate (*i. e.*, in a scientific rather than a metaphysical) sense explain the facts, by the aid of working hypotheses which make no claim to be ultimately true, but claim merely to be useful at the present time. The hypotheses to be adopted must determine the method of description; and the language of description will imply these hypotheses.

I shall try to avoid the language implying the hypotheses which I have adversely criticised in the foregoing pages, namely "ideas," "consciousness" as a stuff compounded of "sensations" or other elements or units of composition, and mechanical reflexes as the units of action. It is not easy to adhere strictly to this program; for the language of "ideas" and "sensations" is common, not only to most psychologies, but also to the literary and the common-sense traditions; and I must pray for indulgence if here and there I should lapse into these convenient and familiar but misleading modes of speech.

I will indicate here in briefest outline the hypotheses that seem to me most acceptable and the terms which we may most profitably use. First—What is to be our attitude toward physiological knowledge, especially our knowledge of the structure and functions of the nervous system? We have seen that many psychologists at the present day have given up altogether the use of the terms "mind," "soul," and "subject." Recognizing that the mind can be profitably described neither as merely a bundle of faculties, nor as a more or less organized mass of "ideas" regarded as enduring things that pass in and out of "consciousness," they have substituted for the mind the nervous system or the brain; with the results that we have glanced at. Now, if we refuse to follow this modern practice, we must go back to, or adhere to, the older practice and still speak of "the mind." For what the older psychology meant by "the mind" was that *something* which expresses its nature, powers, and functions in two ways: (1) the modes of individual experience; (2) the modes of bodily activity, the sum of which constitutes the behavior of the individual. The mechanistic psychology says—this *something* which expresses its nature in these two ways is essentially the brain, as described to us by the mechanistic physiology. There can be no question that we are bound to postulate this *something;* and that, if we are not content to regard it as merely the brain mechanically conceived, we must have some name for it, and must recognize that it has a very complex nature, or is a very complex organization; that it first manifests itself in the relatively simple behavior of the new-born infant; and that it grows in complexity and definiteness, partly in virtue of its innate or hereditary tendencies, partly in virtue of the influences that play upon it from within and without the body and of the modes of activity with which it responds to these influences.

The Hypothesis of the Mind

I do not think that we can find a better word to denote this *something* than the old-fashioned word "mind." The mind, then, of the individual organism is that which expresses itself in his experience and in his behavior; and we have to build up our description of the human mind by gathering all possible facts of human experience and behavior, and by inferring from these the nature and structure of the mind. I say nature *and* structure; for we may usefully distinguish between these. It seems probable that Mind has the same nature wherever and whenever it exists or manifests itself, whether in animals, men, or superhuman beings, whether in the new-born infant, the fool, or the wise man. On the other hand, the structure of the mind seems to be peculiar to each individual; not only is it very various in the various species of animals (if they have minds) and in man; but the structure of the mind of one man is different from that of every other man; and, in any one man at each stage of his career or life-history, it is not quite the same as at any other stage, because, as we said, it constantly develops or evolves into greater complexity and definiteness during the years of growth, and later perhaps, in extreme old age, undergoes a regressive change or involution.

The mechanistic psychologist will say: What you call "the mind" is just what I call "the brain." Why go out of your way to set up this vague, mysterious, purely hypothetical *something* which, as you admit, no one has ever seen or handled or can hope to see or handle, while all the time you have the brain, as solid and as real as a lump of cheese, which we positively know to be concerned in all experience and in all behavior, and about which the labor of thousands of expert workers has built up an immense mass of knowledge? To this I would reply: I do not underrate the value of this physiological knowledge and research; but I assert that, in the present state of science, it is not profitable to substitute the brain for the mind. To do so limits unduly our freedom of thought; it ties us down to one kind of explanation, leads us to absurd consequences (of the kind we have noticed), and, worst of all, is apt to blind us to facts of observation, and biases our interpretation of other facts.

On the other hand, I have no sympathy with certain psychological purists who would banish all physiological facts and theories from psychology, on the ground that psychology and physiology are two distinct sciences whose facts and categories can not be mingled without confusion. I would say: Let the psychologist make the fullest possible use of all the help that physiology can give; let him regard it as one of his tasks to harmonize or co-ordinate the facts and descriptions of his own science with those of physiology. But let him not capitulate to the unjustified demand that his science shall abdicate its functions in favor of a mechanistic physiology Ultimately we may learn how to harmonize the findings of the two sciences far more satisfactorily than it is possible to do at the present day. Let us push explanation in terms of nervous structure and function as far as ever we can; but in doing so, let us not suppose that such explanations are ultimately and completely true.[1]

The Definition and Divisions of Psychology

After thus defining what meaning we are to attach to the word "mind," we may return to the question of the proper or most useful definition of psychology. Provisionally we defined it as the study of human nature, admitting that this is unsatisfactory in that it seems to claim the whole of human physiology as within the province of psychology; whereas it is clear that at present it is to the best interests of both sciences that they shall be kept distinct, the nature of their relations being left for better and more exact determination as both sciences progress. Psychology clearly is concerned with human nature in its mental aspect, physiology with human nature in its bodily aspect. At present there are many facts of importance to the one science which the other can afford to neglect. If it is objected that this division of labor implies the old view of radical dualism of mind and matter, or soul and body, we reply that it need not and should not carry this implication; that this question of dualism is a metaphysical problem with which science is not immediately concerned, one which it may and should leave undecided; that, since no certain answer can be given to it, science should not hamper itself by accepting dogmatically, or even provisionally, one or other answer.

With this understanding, then, psychology may be defined as

[1] I have myself followed this plan and indulged in a good deal of physiological speculation. To the young student of psychology who intends to make psychology, either as pure science or in any of its applications, his business in life, I would say—Learn all you can of physiology and especially of the nervous system. It is worth while to devote several years to the study of physiology, while you are still young. It is noteworthy that some of the greatest psychologists have followed this plan, and have made themselves acquainted not only with physiology but with the whole range of medical studies of their day. I may cite the names of John Locke, R. H. Lotze, William James. It may be claimed also that some experience of the actual practice of medicine is of great value to the psychologist. In no other way can he come into the most intimate contact with other persons and study them from all points of view.

the science of the human mind; we may make the definition more exact by adding the words "positive" and "empirical"; "empirical" to mark the fact that psychology relies upon the great method common to all the natural sciences, namely, observation of concrete facts and the induction of general rules or laws from these concrete particulars, rather than upon deduction from any *a priori* principles; "positive" to mark it as the science of mind as it actually exists and operates, to distinguish it from the sciences primarily concerned with the ideals, norms, standards, or rules of right thinking and conduct.[1]

The psychologist has, then, to build up his description of the human mind by inference from the observed facts of behavior, the behavior of men and of animals, and from the observed facts of experience, facts of his own experience observed introspectively and facts of others' experience described and recorded by them.

[1] As long ago as 1905 I suggested that psychology might be defined as the positive science of conduct or behavior (in my "Primer of Physiological Psychology"), and in later works I have used and defended this definition. I preferred this definition to any of the others current, for two reasons: (1) it seems to mark off the field of psychology clearly from the fields of other sciences and to include everything that properly pertains to psychology; whereas ambiguities, and logical and other difficulties, are involved in all the other definitions; (2) it lays stress on the importance of the objectively observable facts, the facts of outward behavior or bodily action in which mental activity expresses itself; and these facts had usually been unduly neglected in favor of the other class of expressions of mind, the introspectively observable facts. I still regard this definition as a good one, logically perhaps the best. But since my suggestion was made, it has been adopted and carried to an extreme by the "behaviorists." In protesting against a too exclusive study of the introspective data, and rightly insisting on the importance of the study of behavior as a psychological method, they have overshot the mark and swung into the untenable position noticed above. Hence I am disposed to say: "If you are going to get on, it's time for me to get off." This question of the definition of psychology is after all one of minor importance. All our lines of separation between the sciences are provisional only and liable to readjustment as knowledge grows. We ought to aim not so much at perfectly logical definitions, which will only be possible when the sciences are completed, but at definitions stated in terms of the practical purposes with which we pursue the several sciences. Accepting this principle, we may define physiology, as it exists to-day, as the science which aims to give us better understanding and control of the chemical and physical processes of the various organs of the body; and psychology as the science which aims to give us better understanding and control of the behavior of the organism as a whole. This is the demarcation proposed in my "Psychology, the Study of Behavior," Home University Library, 1912.

This is the fundamental kind of psychology, the general psychology presupposed by all the more special kinds of psychological study, such as the study of individual or racial peculiarities of mental constitution, the study of group life or collective psychology, the study of abnormal or disordered minds. Sometimes the name of one or other of the principal methods of study is prefixed to the word psychology, as though to denote a specialized branch, such as experimental, or physiological, or comparative or genetic, or introspective; but, though these are convenient divisions, justified by practical exigencies of study, they are not logically distinct branches of the science; and the student should not let himself be misled into thinking of them in that way. Indeed the special branches themselves must also be regarded as capable of lending valuable aid in the attack on the problems of general psychology; and in so far they may be regarded as methods of study rather than as distinct special branches of the science.

The Subject is an Indispensable Hypothesis

In the main our minds have been evolved in the course of our efforts to comprehend and control our physical environment. We deal with this most successfully, for all practical purposes, by regarding it as made up of enduring things which undergo changes and act upon one another and upon us. In consequence, when we turn to describe experience, we tend to treat it in similar fashion, as though it were made up of things. Whatever phase of experience we think of we make an object of our thinking; and we tend to regard every object of our thinking as a thing. But experience is not made up of things; it is a process and perhaps in all cases a train of activity.[1]

[1] Professor Bergson has made much of this tendency to reïfy whatever we think of; he describes it as a natural and unavoidable weakness of the human intellect which unfits it to deal with the facts of life and experience. He recognizes a mode of mental activity which he calls "intuition" and regards as fundamentally distinct from intellect or intelligence; and he assures us that this faculty alone is capable of coping with the facts with which psychology is concerned. I have never been able to comprehend the nature of this alleged faculty, nor am I convinced by his arguments against the competence of intellect. But I do recognize the need of conducting our intellectual processes with the greatest circumspection in this sphere and the need of choosing our language in such a way as to give as little scope as possible to this falsifying tendency to reification.

The most general and fundamental facts about experience as we know it, or enjoy it, are two. First, experience or experiencing is always an experiencing of something, it is always a thinking about some object, even when, as in psychologizing, that object is itself an experiencing or thinking. Secondly, all experiencing or thinking is the experiencing or thinking of *some one*, some subject, some person, some organism. So far as we positively know, this *some one*, this subject, is always a material organism, or is embodied in, and manifests itself to us only in and through the medium of, a material organism. That is to say, experience, as we know it, is always the thinking of some subject of or about some object. Therefore I propose to use the verb "to think" as the most general word for the description of experience. This usage is wider than the usual one; but it has good precedent in Descartes' famous phrase, "*Cogito, ergo sum*"—*cogito*, or I think, is the most general form of experience. If we use this word, we shall be more likely to avoid the error of reïfying our mental processes; for it will constantly remind us that, whenever we refer to a fact of experience, we imply *some one* thinking of *some thing*.

Let the student ask himself whether he has ever chanced to find "a percept," or "a concept," or "an idea," or "a sensation" lying about loose in the world, as he may find a pebble, or a star, or a bone, or any other physical thing. He will realize that he has never done so, nor is likely to do so. He might as well expect to find "a falling" or "a movement" without something that falls or moves, as "a perceiving" or "a remembering," detached and isolated from the subject who perceives or remembers. And surely to say "I think of X," or "I perceive X," is a more direct and accurate statement than to say "I have an idea of X" or "I have a percept of X," or than to say "An idea or percept of X has come into my mind or risen into consciousness." The former is a plain and simple statement of fact; the other modes of expression are circumlocutions that imply strange and highly disputable theories, such as those we have glanced at in this chapter. Even if we use these perverse traditional expressions, we have to admit, when the question is raised, that these "ideas" or "percepts" or "concepts" and the "consciousness," into and out of which they are said to pass, always belong to some one, to some person or other organism,[1] which we naturally denote either by a proper name or by a pronoun, I, you, he, she, or it. All experience then is the experience of some subject. Whether all experience takes the form of thinking of an object is a debatable question. It has been pointed out that, while every experience that any one can introspectively observe and report upon is a thinking of an object, yet sometimes we seem to be almost purely passive, to approximate to mere suffering or enjoying without being aware of any object; and it has been argued that we may justifiably postulate a kind of experience that, going yet further in this direction, becomes a pure passivity. Such hypothetical purely passive experience would not be thinking of an object and might be called "anoëtic experience."

Mental Structure and Mental Functions

By adhering to the direct and natural form of speech, we may secure another great advantage, namely, we may distinguish clearly between facts of mental activity and facts of mental structure. Mental structure is that enduring growing framework of the mind which we infer from the observed manifestations of mind in experience and in behavior; and, since this develops, grows and, even when the mind is at rest, endures, we may properly describe it and its parts in substantival terms, which terms we shall have to select and define with care. The distinction between mental structure and mental process or functioning or activity is comparable to that between the structure and the functioning of a machine or of a bodily organ such as a muscle. It is of course impossible to find any true analogy or parallel to illustrate the task of the psychologist in building up his account of the structure of the mind; but the following crude illustration may help to make it clearer. Suppose a

[1] Some modern philosophers and logicians speak of our acts of thinking as "ideas," and "concepts," and "concrete universals," and "neutral entities," and so forth, and thus, misleading themselves into the belief that such entities exist, they are led to the monstrous conclusion that whatever we can imagine has or enjoys actual existence; all of which is a natural outcome of the "idea" theory, which in turn is merely the outcome of a loose usage of words.

mechanical toy or doll, actuated by a complicated clockwork, which reacts in a variety of ways under different conditions; and suppose that the investigator, who wishes to ascertain the nature of the machinery within it, can only watch its movements under various conditions and hear a variety of sounds emitted by its mechanisms when they are in motion. From data of these two kinds he could build up by inference some account of the structure of the hidden mechanisms. It is one of the allurements of the "idea theory" that "ideas" are treated at will as either functions or parts of the structure, a very convenient procedure, but one which leads to endless confusion. Many other words are frequently used in this ambiguous and confusing manner which we must try to avoid.

In speaking of mental structure and likening it, as I did just now, to the structure of a machine, we must not be misled into taking the word "structure" in the sense of a material structure or any spatial arrangement of parts. We commonly and properly speak of the structure of a poem or of a musical composition, meaning a whole consisting of parts in orderly functional relations with one another; and, though the structure of the mind is not of the same order as these structures, yet these, rather than the material structure of a machine, should be thought of as offering the closer analogy. Those students who find it useful to picture, or visualize, or represent in diagrammatic form whatever they think about may visualize the structure of the mind in spatial terms without danger, if they bear this warning in mind. And, in accordance with what was said above of the use in psychology of knowledge of the nervous system, we may, without serious danger, allow schematic diagrams of nervous structure to represent features of the mental structure, if we hold fast to the truth that the mind and its processes cannot be literally translated into, or adequately represented by, or supplanted by, any description of the structure and functions of the nervous system mechanically conceived. The structure of the mind is a conceptual system that we have to build up by inference from the data of the two orders, facts of behavior and facts of introspection.

CHAPTER II

THE BEHAVIOR OF THE LOWER ANIMALS

I have used the word "behavior" hitherto as though it stood in no need of definition; and practically we all understand and use the word in pretty much the same sense. We all learn early in life to distinguish two great classes of things in the world about us, living things and lifeless things, or the animate and the inanimate. Primitive men make the same distinction; but they do not draw the line as accurately as we do. They easily regard any unusual appearance or happening among lifeless things as evidence of their animation; this is the tendency known as primitive animism or anthropomorphism. But the spread of scientific knowledge has made it easy for us to draw this distinction without hesitation, and usually without error.

The Marks of Behavior

By "behavior" we commonly mean the action or actions of some living thing. It is true that we may say of a ship or of an automobile: "She is behaving badly to-day." But the fact that we are apt to use the personal pronoun on such occasions shows that we more or less playfully personify the ship or the machine. And, if the "behavior" of the ship or of the machine is extremely bad, we are apt to "lose our temper" and swear at it—a further degree of the same tendency to personification. Behavior, then, is peculiar to living things. When an animal is dead, its corpse does not "behave"; it has become inert, the sport of the forces that play upon it from without.[1] This indi-

[1] About plants we are in doubt. When a tree sways in the breeze, we do not speak of its motions as behavior; but when a flower turns its face toward the sun, or opens and closes its petals, or when a climbing plant seems to reach out and grasp a support, we are more inclined to speak of its behavior. And science cannot yet tell us whether such language is justified. In the opinion of some leading botanists it is.

cates one of the marks of behavior, namely, a *certain spontaneity of movement.* In behaving, an animal is not simply pushed or pulled by forces external to itself; but, if it actively resists the push or pull, it is behaving. It is true that the behavior of an animal often appears to be a response or reaction to some sense-impression, a sound, a touch, or a ray of light. And some of the mechanists dogmatically lay down the law that every movement is a response to some such impression, which they call the "stimulus to the reflex action"; and when, as is often the case, the movement cannot be traced to any impression on an external sense-organ, they postulate some internal stimulus, some impression upon a sensory nerve from within the body, and so bring the apparent exception under their "law." Whether this assumption is well founded we can not at present say. But, even if it be true that every instance of behavior is initiated by a "stimulus," it is evident that the movement or train of behavior, once initiated, often continues independently of the initiating stimulus. A momentary noise, such as the snapping of a twig, may send the rabbit scurrying to his burrow, put to flight a flock of birds, and throw the timid deer into the attitude and motions of alert watchfulness; or the taking of my hat from its peg, or a single word uttered, may provoke in my dog a violent and prolonged outburst of activity, a general excitement which may long persist and may break out afresh many times. This is a second mark of behavior; namely, the *persistence of activity independently of the continuance of the impression which may have initiated it.*

An inanimate object, when set in motion, continues to move in the same direction, if not acted upon by any forces which deflect or arrest it; it continues so to move until by friction, or by impact against some greater mass, it is brought to rest. Its movements and changes are in principle strictly predictable according to physical laws. And if the object contains, like a rocket, or a torpedo, or an automobile, some supply of energy which maintains the movement in spite of friction or other resistances, the exact prediction of the rate, extent, and direction of the movements is in principle equally possible, through more complicated calculations. But, when an animal persists in the movements initiated by a sense-impression, its movements are not predictable in detail. If we are familiar with the behavior of animals of the same species, we may predict with some confidence the general character and the final outcome of its movements under particular circumstances. When, for example, like a rabbit, it belongs to some timid species which normally shelters itself in holes in the earth, we may predict that, if it is set running by a sudden noise, it will continue to run until it finds such a shelter, and that, if the course it first takes leads to no such shelter, it will dodge hither and thither until shelter is found. Such *variation of direction of persistent movements* is a third mark of behavior.

The movements of an animal are commonly continued, with more or less variation of direction, until they bring about that kind of change in its situation which, as we have noted, is predictable in general terms from a knowledge of the species; and when that new situation is achieved, the train of activity commonly ceases, perhaps giving place to some activity of an altogether different kind. We naturally say in such a case that the activity has come to an end. This *coming to an end of the animal's movements as soon as they have brought about a particular kind of change in its situation* is a fourth mark of behavior.

Again, we may often observe that, while the animal's movements are maintained, they seem to show in some degree preparation for, or anticipation of, the new situation which will bring them to an end or will give rise to a new and very different train of movements. The dog which, when shut in a room, is aroused by the sound of his master's voice without may rush to the window and then to the door, and may keep looking at the door or scratching at it. Or the house-dog, when a strange dog or man approaches the house, may advance toward him with teeth bared, hair bristling, and every muscle stiffened in preparation for attack or combat. Or the cat, aroused by the squeak of the mouse behind the wainscot, stealthily approaches the hole and there lies in wait in the attitude of preparation for the spring upon the prey. Such *preparation for the new situation toward the production of which the action contributes* is a fifth mark of behavior.

It is almost impossible to describe actions which show these five marks of behavior, especially the third, fourth, and fifth, in purely objective terms, that is, without using words which attribute to the animal certain modes of experience. We naturally say that the animal is seeking and anticipating the new situation which is the natural end or goal of its behavior, and that it directs its actions toward this goal.

When we observe movements which exhibit all of these five peculiarities, we do not hesitate to regard them as manifestations of Mind or mental activity. No movements of lifeless things combine these five peculiarities; and it is just because the movements of plants do not unmistakably show them that we hesitate to ascribe Mind to plants.

A sixth mark of behavior, which is less easy to observe, has been very commonly accepted as the most trustworthy indication of mental life; namely, *some degree of improvement in the effectiveness of behavior, when it is repeated by the animal under similar circumstances.* When such improvement occurs, when, on the recurrence of a particular situation, the animal is excited on this second occasion to behavior which attains the same natural goal, but attains it more rapidly, more directly, more neatly, with fewer steps and less of seemingly random movement, we naturally say that it has profited by its experience on the former occasion. No doubt, when such improvement may be observed, it provides the surest criterion; but, without this sixth mark, we may infer mental activity from the other five. And it is to be noted that this sixth mark implies the others; if the train of movements did not present those characters, we should not be able to infer Mind from the sixth alone. For many machines, as every one who has driven a new automobile knows, improve in efficiency with repetition of their movements, owing to the nicer adjustment of parts to one another which results from friction and wearing of the surfaces.

Behavior is Purposive

Now, when the movements of a human being exhibit the first five marks of behavior, we do not hesitate to infer that they are purposive; by which we mean that they are made for the sake of attaining their natural end, and that this end is more or less clearly anticipated or foreseen. For any one of us, when he acts in this way and reflects upon his behavior, may observe introspectively that he himself foresees, however vaguely, the kind of end his actions will attain. In the typical case of purposive action, we foresee or imagine the end very clearly and definitely, and we desire or resolve to attain it; and we may also foresee and deliberately adopt the various steps of action which are the means to the attainment of the desired or resolved end. The natural end of a train of action foreseen and desired, or consciously chosen or intended, is properly called the goal of action or endeavor. We are said to strive toward the goal. The attainment of the goal is said to be the purpose of our action or our striving.[1]

We have to recognize that in many cases our foreseeing of the goal and of the steps toward it is very vague and sketchy; and that the steps and the goal itself become clearly defined in our minds, only in the course of action and attainment. Yet we do not feel it improper to describe such actions as purposive. Sometimes one may perform an action or train of actions rapidly and impulsively, as we say; perhaps there is no time for deliberation or introspection. And, if one looks back upon such action, it may be impossible to recover any clear description of one's experience during action. Perhaps one may be able to say: I suddenly noticed a child in the roadway before an oncoming car, and, without having time to think what I should do, I found that I had snatched it up. In such moments one is wholly absorbed in action. But the difficulty of making any clear retrospective survey of one's experience does not prevent us from properly regarding such an action as purposive.

[1] While the adjective "purposive" may be applied to action or bodily movement clearly and unambiguously in the sense defined in the foregoing pages, it remains very difficult to use the substantive "purpose" without ambiguity.

A Scale of Degrees of Purposiveness

By reflecting upon a variety of actions, we may realize that our actions may be arranged in a scale; at the upper end of the scale may be put such actions as are most deliberately purposive, the goal and means having been pondered, developed in imagination, and deliberately chosen among various alternative possibilities, before overt action began. Lower in the scale would be those actions the goal and the steps toward which we have thought of, clearly perhaps, but without pondering and choosing. Lower still are such actions as we perform with only a very vague and sketchy foresight of the goal and of the means, or perhaps of the goal only. And, at the lower end of the scale of purposiveness, would be such impulsive actions as the snatching the child from imminent danger. As regards action of this last class, although we cannot give any retrospective account of our experience which would include the foreseeing of the goal of the action, we see that the action is such that, if we had acted a little more slowly and deliberately, we should have foreseen the goal we sought or purposed, and perhaps also the steps of the action we actually took. We rightly feel that we did not act as a mere machine, but that the action was a purposive action in which our nature was truly expressed; and we may confidently infer that the goal was foreseen, however vaguely and incompletely, at the moment of action. There is no obvious lower limit to the scale of purposiveness; and we may fairly ascribe to other men in moments of impulsive action the same vague foreseeing that we infer on our own part at such times. And, though here the inference is more debatable, we may ascribe to an animal whose action exhibits the first five marks of behavior the same kind of vague anticipation of the goal.

Purpose Implies Foresight

Purposive action is, then, action that seems to be governed or directed in some degree by prevision of its effects, by prevision of that which still lies in the future, of events which have not yet happened, but which are likely to happen, and to the happening of which the action itself may contribute. *Purposiveness in this sense seems to be of the essence of mental activity;* and it is because all actions which have the marks of behavior seem to be purposive, in however lowly and vague a degree, that we regard them as expressions of Mind.

We cannot provide any final and conclusive proof of the truth of this ascription of purposive or mental quality to the action of any animal. Some of the mechanists would scornfully repudiate the claim that we may reasonably regard animal behavior as purposive; they would stigmatize such interpretation as anthropomorphic; and this word is one of their strongest terms of reproach for those who do not agree with them. Logically they should equally repudiate the attribution of purpose to their fellow-men, or to those men who give no introspective account of their purposive actions; and some of them do not hesitate to do this, and to deprecate as "anthropomorphic" such interpretation of human action. If they admit the word "purposive," they define it in a non-psychological manner, and describe as purposive all actions which seem to be serviceable to the life of the animal or the species. Applying this objective and non-psychological criterion, they point out that simple reflex actions, such as the withdrawal of the foot from a sharp contact, or the scratch-reflex of the dog's hind-leg, are serviceable, and therefore purposive. Yet we see that such reflex actions may be provoked by suitable stimulation in an animal whose brain has been destroyed; or in a man in whom the part of the spinal cord concerned in the action is severed from the brain, and who remains entirely unaware of the whole process. They argue from these facts as follows: such serviceable reflex actions appear to be purposive; yet they are accompanied by no experience and are purely mechanical processes of which the successive steps can be traced in the nerves and muscles as purely chemical and physical events; hence, when we observe the more complicated trains of action in which the processes of the brain play some essential part, we are justified in regarding them as merely more complex processes of the same mechanical type; and, if the actions are those of a man who tells us that he foresaw the end of his action and desired it, and directed his action in such a way as to attain this goal, that makes no essential difference; the brain mechanisms, the complicated arrangements of nervous paths laid down in his brain, would have brought about the serviceable train of action of his limbs just as securely and effectively, if he had not foreseen or desired the end.[1]

Now, if the mechanist could point to any processes or movements of inanimate things which presented all the foregoing marks of behavior, his argument would be a strong one. We might feel compelled to admit that he was right in assimilating all animal and all human behavior to the type of the mechanical reflex, and in explaining behavior from below upwards; leaving the relation of experience to such actions a blank mystery, as the "parallelists" do in their formula that experience runs parallel with brain-action in a relation of temporal concomitance merely, like two parallel rays of light projected into space, which continue to run parallel, but which never meet or influence one another.

But it is impossible to find any instance of such movements of lifeless objects; and for this reason we are justified in claiming, provisionally at least in the present state of science, that nature presents two classes of things, the non-living and the living, and two classes of movements, the mechanical and the purposive, characteristic of the two classes of things respectively.

There is a class of things which in a sense stands between these two classes, namely, machines. The machine achieves a purpose, and its movements may therefore be said, in a certain sense, to be purposive. But the purpose which they express and achieve is not that of the machine, but rather that of the man who designs and constructs the machine, and who sets it in movement, or sets it ready to move when some part of it is touched. It is the existence of complicated and delicate machines that gives plausibility to the mechanistic view of human and animal behavior. If such machines occurred in nature without the intervention of living beings, their existence would go far

[1] This is the position common to all the mechanistic psychologists (behaviorists, epiphenomenalists, and parallelists). The psychic monist would disclaim it, but for all practical purposes, that is to say, pragmatically, and therefore really, his position is not essentially different so long as he accords primacy or superior validity and reality to the laws or categories of physical science. For definition and discussion of these views and the further justification of the view here taken, the reader is referred to the final chapter of Part II.

to justify this view. And, in a much less degree, the view would find some justification, if any man could devise and construct a machine which would exhibit all the marks of behavior. But even this has not been accomplished. The complicated machine is not in principle different from the simple tool, the mechanical aid to our purposive action. If I throw a stone at my enemy's head and stun him, the stone effects my purpose or intention; it is directed by it and may be said to embody it. In the same way, if I construct an infernal machine of the greatest subtlety which will explode under my enemy's bed at a given hour, or whenever he may lie down upon it, the machine equally and in the same sense effects and embodies my purpose. But, even if it were made so perfect that it would explode only on the approach of my enemy and not on that of any other man, it would still be only a more complicated example of the principle of action illustrated by the stone thrown from the hand.

In the first chapter I argued that the psychologist should and must choose the fundamental categories appropriate to his science, if he is to make progress toward his proper goal, the better understanding and control of human nature and human behavior. *Purposive action is the most fundamental category of psychology;* just as the motion of a material particle according to the mechanical principles of Newton's laws of motion has long been the fundamental category of physical science. Behavior is always purposive action, or a train or sequence of purposive actions.

Purposive and Reflex Actions Contrasted

Let us look a little more closely at the distinction between *purposive action* and the *reflex action* which the mechanists attempt to put in its place, with the consequences that we have already glanced at; namely, "sensations" or "ideas" confusedly thought of as mysterious entities, dragged passively into and out of that other mysterious entity "consciousness" by the mechanical reflex processes of the brain. I do not mean to assert that reflex processes as conceived by physiology do not occur. Human organisms, as well as the higher animals, do exhibit reactions of the mechanical reflex type. If the reader, comfortably seated, will cross his right knee over the other and sharply tap the tendon below the right knee-cap, his right foot will jerk forward owing to the contraction of the large muscles of the front of the thigh. That is a very simple reflex action.

Many other such tendon-reflexes can be provoked in similar fashion; the observation of them is of great value to the neurologist as throwing light upon the condition of the nervous system. Others can be provoked by gently scratching the skin in various parts; *e. g.*, "the abdominal reflex," a sharp contraction of the muscles of the wall of the abdomen, by scratching the skin of the flank; or the closing of the eyelid at the slightest touch on the skin over the eyeball. Many other reflex processes, resulting in contractions of the muscles of the visceral organs, such as the heart, blood-vessels, respiratory and digestive organs, or in secretion of tears, saliva, gastric and other juices, may be provoked by stimulation of various sensory nerves. Such reflex actions have been elaborately studied in animals whose brains have been destroyed.[1] It has been shown that the simple reflexes are, in many instances, functionally linked in such a way that they naturally succeed one another, producing a more or less complicated train of movement of a serviceable type, the first movement producing a stimulus for the second, the second for the third, and so on. For example, the legs of a dog whose brain has been destroyed may be thrown by stimulation of the soles of the feet into a sequence of movements resembling the movements of walking.[2] Such a sequence of reflex actions is commonly called a chain-reflex; and it is by imagining the arrangements of nerve-paths which subserve such chain reflexes to be multiplied and complicated enormously, but on the same mechanical principles, that the mechanists seek to explain all human behavior. And recently it has been shown that the human spinal cord, when detached from the brain by a wound, is richer in such complicated reflex mechanisms than had previously been supposed.[3]

[1] By no one so thoroughly as by Professor Sir Charles Sherrington, the President of the Royal Society of London, whose great work embodying his studies of reflex action ("The Integrative Action of the Nervous System") should be mastered by every serious student of psychology.

[2] The animal in this condition cannot, however, walk; for walking is a very much more complex process than the mere sequence of leg movements; the balancing of the whole body is involved in it.

[3] Especially by the studies of Doctor Henry Head. Cf. "Studies in Neurology," London, 1920.

But, although such reflex movements are serviceable, in the sense that they are such as the organism makes use of in the course of its normal behavior (for example, the reflex walking movements of the legs of the brainless dog) when we examine them closely, we see that they do not exhibit the characteristic marks of behavior, the objective criteria of purpose.

The reflex lacks (1) the spontaneity of behavior: the legs of the brainless dog only execute the walking reflex when stimulated in a particular manner: the normal dog gets up from sleep in a dark quiet corner and walks, without being excited to this behavior by any assignable stimulus. The reflex lacks (2) the persistency of behavior: that is to say, the reflex movements continue only so long as the stimulus is applied to the appropriate sense-organ. The chain-reflex is no exception to the rule, though it may seem to be so to the casual observer; for each movement produces the stimulus to the next in the sequence; just as, when one shell in a "dump" is exploded, a sequence of explosions may result. (3) The reflex is stereotyped or fixed, the movements evoked by the same stimulus falling on the same sensory nerve are, approximately, the same on all occasions; whereas purposive movements are indefinitely variable. If we saw a dog walking steadily forward over a smooth road, we might be in doubt whether his movements were purely reflex; and, if the movements were long continued, we should be inclined to suspect this; just by reason of the absence of those perpetual variations of movement which are so characteristic of behavior. But, when we see a dog, aroused by his master's whistle, run from door to window and back again, varying his movements in a hundred ways as he does so, we confidently regard this as behavior.

(4) The reflex movements do not present that appearance of seeking a goal which is common to all behavior, and of which the essential feature is the persistence of movements with variation *until*, and *only until*, that goal is attained. It is true that the cessation of the stimulus which provokes the reflex might be claimed as the analogue of the goal of purposive behavior; as when the foot is withdrawn from a prick, or the dog's hind-foot scratches its irritated flank. But the natural goal of

behavior (*i. e.*, of a purposive movement) is more than the cessation of a stimulus; its attainment, which brings the movement to a close, involves some positive novelty in the total situation. Thus, if we saw a dog lying in the sunlight and then saw him get up and wander about, we might suppose that the heat of the sun's rays had stimulated him to reflex walking; but, if we saw him walk to a patch of shade and there lie down and resume his slumber, we should confidently infer that this was behavior, a purposive movement attaining its natural goal.

(5) Reflex action does not show that preparation for the coming situation (the situation which will result from the action) which in behavior suggests anticipation of that future situation. Conceiving the dog as a reflex machine, a bundle of reflexes, we might legitimately imagine such a mechanism to be stimulated by a sudden noise, such as the sound of his master's voice, to rouse up from sleep, get upon his feet, and wander about. But nothing that we know of reflex action would justify us in supposing that he could be led by similar reflex processes to make all those preparations for a joyous and riotous welcome with which the normal dog responds to such a sense-impression.

(6) Reflex processes are not improved by repetition, as the movements of behavior are. The same stimulus, applied again and again under the same conditions, repeatedly evokes the same movements or train of movements. It is possible that by repetition a reflex movement may be rendered more fixed or more easily evocable; but even that has not, I think, been shown to be true. Still less has it been shown that any reflex process becomes more nicely adjusted, or more effective on repetition. The scratch-reflex of the brainless dog's hind-foot, which superficially resembles so closely a purposive movement, always shows a lack of nicety of direction toward the spot irritated, as compared with the scratching movements of the normal dog. And there is no evidence to suggest that any amount of repetition of stimulation at any one point of the skin of the brainless dog would result in a nicer direction of the foot toward the spot.

The mechanist will point to the "conditioned reflex," and say—here is evidence of "learning" or "profiting by experience" among reflex processes. But just here the weakness of the mechanist's position appears very clearly.

The typical instance of "the conditioned reflex," on the study of which the doctrine is chiefly based, is the salivary reflex of the dog. Professor Pavloff showed that, when a savory morsel is presented to the nose of a dog, saliva is secreted; and that if, on repeated occasions, a bell is sounded at the same moment that the food is presented, the sound of the bell will (after a certain number of repetitions of this conjunction of impressions) suffice to evoke a flow of saliva. This appears to involve both a profiting by experience and a preparation for the coming situation. But in claiming this reaction as a reflex and the whole process as purely mechanical, the mechanist begs the very question in dispute.

If it could be shown that a "conditioned reflex" of this sort can be established in a brainless dog, or in a dog or other animal deeply anesthetized with chloroform or ether, the mechanist's interpretation of the particular facts would be strongly supported and his general position greatly strengthened. But this has not been shown to be possible. The attempt to demonstrate this possibility should be the all-absorbing task of the behaviorist. But I do not know of any attempt at such demonstration; and all we know of the functions of the nervous system tends to make it appear very improbable that any such attempt can succeed. For we know that dogs (and other animals) deprived, not of the whole brain, but of the cerebral cortex only, seem incapable of learning, of profiting by experience, or of acquiring "conditioned reflexes." Yet an animal in this condition, retaining intact the cerebellum and basal ganglia of the great brain, is very much more like a normal animal than is one in which the whole brain is out of action. An animal in the former condition will wander about restlessly, will eat and perform all the bodily movements essential to continued living; and he may be provoked to what seem to be emotional expressions (especially anger). Yet, in spite of the fact that his movements show some of the marks of behavior, he never seems to learn or to profit by experience. Though he may be fed by the same man for months, he seems to show no recognition of the man or of the approach of food, by anticipatory actions such as the mechanist would call "conditioned reflexes."

The mechanist may be disposed to challenge also my statement that the reflex process does not exhibit variation of character and direction. He may point to the much celebrated instance of the brainless frog which, if a bit of blotting-paper soaked in vinegar is placed on one flank, will wipe it away with the hind foot of the same side, and which, if that hind foot is forcibly restrained, will wipe it away with the hind foot of the other side. In face of this instance (and of similar instances) we must admit that we cannot interpret the facts confidently. But there are two alternative interpretations, either of which is consistent with the distinction between reflex and purposive action which I have drawn. First, it may be that this is a true reflex action, mechanically explicable; that is to say, it may be that the resisted contractions of the leg, first excited reflexly by the stimulus, give rise to additional stimuli which provoke reflexly the movements of the other leg, or determine the excitement from the irritated spot to flow over to the other leg. If this is the true interpretation of this movement, it remains an interesting example of complicated reflex action. Secondly, it may be that the action is purposive in a lowly sense. When we deal with animals so low in the scale of life as frogs, we cannot argue safely from their anatomy to their functions. The brain of the frog is but very little developed; and a little lower in the scale we find animals which exhibit behavior in spite of having no brains, as we shall presently see. It may be, then, that at the level of organization of the frog, the brain is not essential to purposive action—as it seems to be in animals higher in the scale of life.

A Seventh Mark of Behavior

In contrasting reflex action with purposive action or behavior, we must take notice of yet another distinction of great importance, which perhaps deserves to rank as a seventh objective mark of behavior; namely, a reflex action is always a partial reaction, but a *purposive action is a total reaction of the organism.* Let us examine this distinction more nearly. If your dog is lying idly by your side, perhaps occasionally snapping at a fly, you may, by pulling a hair or otherwise stimulating his flank, repeatedly provoke the scratch-reflex of his hind leg, without interfering with his repose; he may continue to snap, cocking his eye now and then at some interesting object, apparently quite unaware of your stimulus and of the machine-like movements of his leg—with a very comical effect. In a similar way, various reflex reactions may be simultaneously evoked by independent stimuli; and, so long as they do not affect the same organs, they do not interfere with one another; each is a strictly local reaction of a segment (or of some few segments) of the animal.[1] In a similar way in ourselves, many reflexes may be excited simultaneously and independently of one another; the pupil may contract to increase of light, the foot jerk to a tap on the tendon, the respiration or blood-vessels or heart respond to various stimulations.

In purposive action, on the other hand, the whole organism is commonly involved; the processes of all its parts are subordinated and adjusted in such a way as to promote the better pursuit of the natural goal of the action. If, while you amuse yourself by repeatedly exciting the scratch-reflex in your dog, some sound excites him to behavior, then, even though the behavior

[1] A few highly complex reflex movements involve many segments, *e. g.*, the walking movements of the dog's legs; and here, as in all opposed reflexes of the same limb, such as those of extension and flexion, the *law of reciprocal inhibition* holds good; that is to say, the more strongly excited reflex inhibits the less strongly excited and incompatible reflex.

consists in nothing more than assuming an alert attitude with eyes and ears directed toward the disturbing object, your stimulation of his flank becomes ineffective; at the same time the fly is ignored, and even your voice, raised in command, may fail to provoke any sign of obedience. If the sound is followed by the appearance of a stranger (dog or man) your dog springs to his feet with every muscle and organ at work in preparation for attack; and, while this condition continues, all his reflexes are subordinated to this major purposive activity; stimuli which, when he was at rest, would have evoked a wide range of reflexes produce no appreciable effect, and objects which might have provoked him to other trains of behavior are ignored. That is the type of the total reaction. The vital energies of the whole organism are concentrated upon the task in hand.[1]

The Relation of the Human to the Animal Mind

Having now studied the essential peculiarities of purposive action objectively observed, we may turn to review very briefly the actions of animals at various levels in the scale of life. The study of animal behavior teaches four lessons of high importance for psychology: (1) It makes clearer the nature of purposive action and reveals its prevalence throughout the whole of the animal world: (2) it elucidates the very foundations of human nature, by displaying in relative simplicity among the animals the modes of action (namely, instinctive actions) which are fundamental in human behavior, but which in human life are so complicated and obscured by the great development of our intellectual powers that their full importance is only now beginning to be recognized: (3) it shows us how we may conceive the structure of the relatively simple mind of an animal, and so gives us a valuable cue for building up our description of the structure of the human mind: (4) for it reveals some of the stages which the mind must have passed through in the long course of mental evolution from animalcule to man.

We have to regard the human mind, not as different in kind

[1] For a more detailed discussion of the distinction between reflex and instinctive action, I would refer the senior student to my article, "The Use and Abuse of Instinct in Social Psychology" (*Journal of Abnormal and Social Psychology*, 1922).

from the animal mind, but rather as built up on a foundation which is essentially similar to the animal mind, especially to that of the animals nearest to us in the tree of life. We must look for evidence of the persistence of the types of structure and function of the animal mind, remembering that these fundamental structures are overlaid by later evolved structures, and that their functioning is complicated and disguised by the activities of the more recently evolved structures.

This way of regarding the relation of the human to the animal mind finds strong support in the comparative study of the nervous system of the vertebrates. When we go outside the vertebrate group, the anatomy of the nervous system is found to be so differently planned that it is difficult to point with confidence to any of its parts as strictly homologous with parts of the vertebrate nervous system. But within the vertebrate group we can trace these homologous parts (parts of similar function) without difficulty; and we find that we can select and arrange in an evolutionary scale a number of types of nervous system which may be regarded as roughly representing stages on the line of evolution of the human nervous system from one like that of the simplest existing vertebrate.

When we construct such a scale and compare its various members, we find that the parts which constitute the simplest vertebrate nervous system are represented throughout the scale, and that evolution seems to have taken the form of the successive superposition of new structures upon the older. It seems that the essential functions of the older structures are not abrogated or altogether superseded by those of the more recently evolved parts, but, retaining their fundamental importance, become complicated, and variously controlled and modified by the functions of the later evolved superimposed structures.[1] Now, though we have refused to regard the nervous system as identical with the mind, and though we maintain that the mind has a nature, a

[1] Some general understanding of the parts and functions of the nervous system is necessary for every student of psychology. The student should study the diagrams in some such book as Herrick's "Introduction to Neurology"; and he who intends to study psychology intensively should at least make himself thoroughly master of this book, as well as of Sherrington's "Integrative Action of the Nervous System."

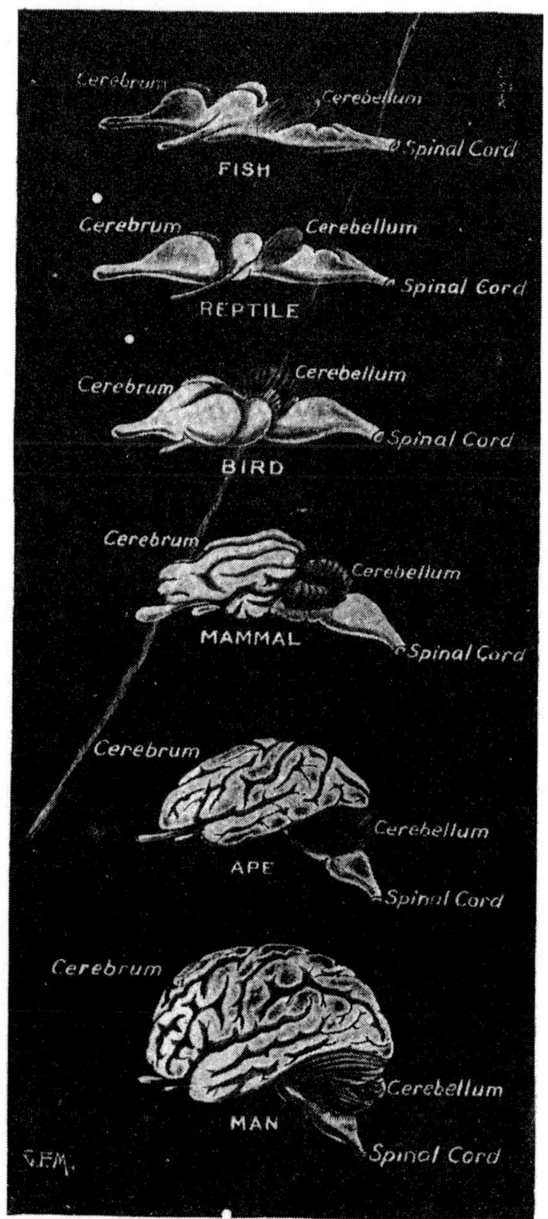

From "The Outline of Science." By permission of G. P. Putnam's Sons

FIG. I.—THIS DRAWING SHOWS THE EVOLUTION OF THE BRAIN FROM FISH TO MAN

structure, and functions which cannot be adequately described, represented, or explained in terms of nervous structure and functions, we have to recognize that the nervous system is at least the immediate instrument and servant of the mind, through which it maintains its relations with the rest of the bodily organism and with the physical world about it, as well as with

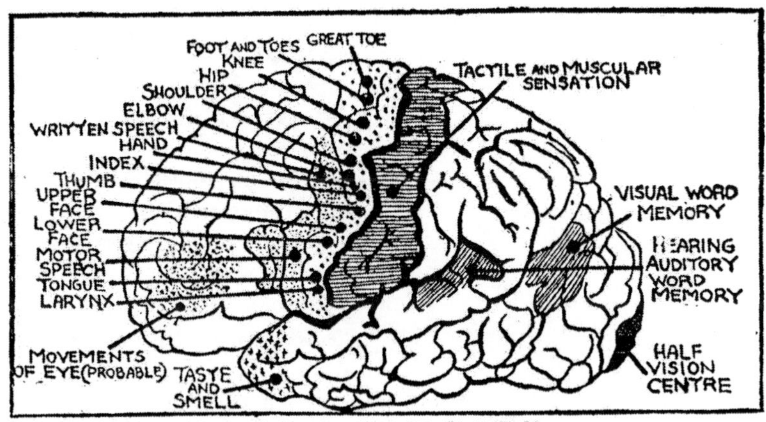

From "The Brain and the Voice in Speech and Song," by Sir F. W. Mott. Courtesy of Harper & Bros., London.

FIG. 2.

This picture of the human brain (seen from the left side) illustrates the large extent of the areas of the cortex which surround the areas immediately concerned in sensory and motor functions. These, the "association areas," the areas of highest function, are small in the ape's brain and are hardly distinguishable in the brain of the dog.

other minds embodied in other organisms. Hence the story of the evolution of the nervous system, which we can reconstruct from the comparative study of existing types, affords valuable, though always indirect and disputable evidence, of the course of mental evolution.

The Nature of Tropisms

One of the very obvious difficulties of the theory that behavior is merely a conjunction or series of mechanical reflexes, is the fact that the reflex is peculiar to those animals which have a well-developed nervous system. For the behavior of animals that have no such nervous system, the mechanists are therefore driven to devise some other explanation than the reflex. We may best bring out the purposive quality of the movements of the lower animals by examining the mechanistic explanation and pointing out its inadequacy.

The principle of the *tropism* has been confidently offered as adequate to explain all these lower sub-reflex forms of behavior.[1] The principle may be best illustrated by imagining a simple, free-swimming, bilaterally symmetrical organism whose movements are effected by two paddles, one on each side, as represented in Fig. 3. We may suppose the animal to have also a pair of rudimentary eyes, mere spots of pigment which absorb the light and are stimulated by light to a degree proportional to its intensity. And we may suppose each eye-spot to be connected with the muscles of the paddle of the same side by a thread of conducting protoplasm, a rudimentary nerve. Then we may suppose that each paddle will work strongly in proportion to the intensity of the light falling upon the eye-spot of the same side. If a ray of light passes through the water in the direction shown by the arrow, it will stimulate

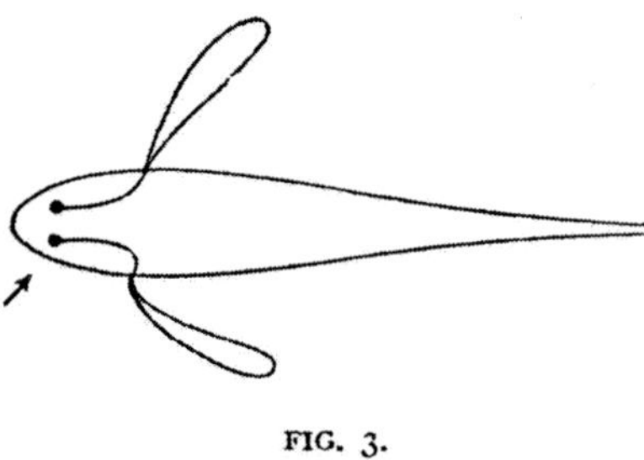

FIG. 3.

[1] By none more confidently than by Doctor Jacques Loeb, whose experimental observations have done much to secure acceptance for the principle, their brilliance blinding many students to the weakness of the reasoning applied to the facts of observation. Cf. "The Mechanistic Conception of Life," Chicago, 1912. Loeb seeks to identify instincts with "tropisms" rather than with reflexes. He writes: "That in the case of our inner life a physico-chemical explanation is not beyond the realm of possibility is proved by the fact that it is already possible for us to explain cases of simple manifestations of animal instinct and will on a physico-chemical basis; namely, the phenomena . . . of animal tropisms." Further: "Our wishes and hopes, disappointments and sufferings, have their source in instincts, which are comparable to the light instinct of the heliotropic animals. The need of and the struggle for food, the sexual instinct with its poetry and its chain of consequences, the maternal instincts with the felicity and the suffering caused by them, the instinct of workmanship, and some other instincts are the roots from which our inner life develops. For some of these instincts the chemical basis is at least sufficiently indicated to arouse the hope that their analysis, from the mechanistic point of view, is only a question of time."—Pp. 26 and 30.

the left eye more strongly than the right; and therefore the left paddle will work more strongly than the other. This will cause the creature to turn toward the right; and the turning movement will continue until the animal swims away from the source of light and parallel to the ray. That direction will be one of stable equilibrium; for the least deflection from this direction will produce inequality of stimulation of the two eyes, and so make the direction of movement parallel to the ray once more. Accordingly, if a number of such animals were swimming freely in a long glass tank in the dark, they might be found swimming in all directions and irregularly distributed throughout the water. But, if a ray of light were then thrown through the tank from end to end, all the animals would turn away from it; and presently all would be found butting their noses against the end of the tank remote from the light; or, if one part of the tank were shaded from the light, all or most of them would be found swimming in this shaded part. The ordinary man, contemplating this effect of the light on the animals, would be inclined to interpret it anthropomorphically, by saying that the animals dislike or fear the light, and therefore flee from it to seek the shade. But the mechanist would smile pityingly and say: "No, liking and disliking, fear, discomfort, satisfaction, pain and pleasure have no more part in this little drama than they have in the drama of human life. The whole process of redistribution of the animals in space is completely explicable in terms of physics and chemistry. The turning of the animals from the light is a tropism; they are negatively photo-tropic."

Now imagine an animal of similar structure, different only in that each eye-spot is connected with the paddle of the opposite side only. It is obvious that such an animal would turn toward the light rather than away from it; and that, if a ray of light were passed through the glass tank, all the animals would swim toward the source of light, and would presently be found butting against the end of the tank at which the light enters. And, if one part of the tank were shaded, they would seem to avoid this shaded part and to seek the light. Such animals would be positively photo-tropic.

All animals are constantly subjected to chemical and physical influences, many of which are directed upon them somewhat in the fashion of a ray of light; especially is this true of all forms of radiant energy, heat, electricity, and that mysterious energy we call gravity. And chemical substances are apt to diffuse themselves through air and water in a way which results in a graded density of the solution, and thus may give rise to chemotropisms. The mechanists are inclined to regard all the behavior of the lower forms of life as tropisms of these various kinds; and they do not hesitate to extend the principle to explain the behavior of animals that have well-developed nervous systems. For example, larvæ of a certain insect (*Porthesia chrysorrhœa*) climb upward on the tree on which they are hatched, and so find the young buds on the tips of the branches. This is said to be due to positive heliotropism; light directs their movements upward. When they have climbed to the top of the branch and eaten all the leaves, they turn downward and descend, as though in search of more food. This offers no difficulty to the mechanist interpretation. When they have eaten all the leaves, they lose their positive heliotropism. Hence their descent.[1] This is a mild sample of what can be accomplished

[1] Professor Loeb writes: "They *can* now creep downward, and the restlessness which is characteristic of so many animals forces them to creep downward until they reach a new leaf, the odor or tactile stimulus of which stops the progressive movement of the machine and sets their eating activity again in motion." (*Op. cit.*, p. 48.) He adds, in a foot-note: "The physico-chemical cause of this 'restlessness,' which is noticeable in many insects and crustaceans, is at present unknown." The implication is that if, and when, the chemical condition of this restlessness shall be discovered, this train of behavior will be wholly explained in physico-chemical terms. But that is far from true. Why downward? Why not down and up and to and fro in perfectly random fashion? If it be suggested that feeding renders the larvæ negatively heliotropic, the theory would encounter the difficulty that, on coming across more leaves, the larvæ cease to descend. This simple case illustrates the fact that the tropic theory, although it no doubt points to a real factor influencing behavior in many cases, cannot wholly explain any train of behavior. This inadequacy of the tropic theory and of the reasoning of the mechanists is well illustrated by Loeb on his next page, where he shows that ants and bees, at the time of the nuptial flight, seem to be positively heliotropic. He adds: "I gained the impression that this nuptial flight is merely the consequence of a very highly developed heliotropic sensitiveness." The significant word here is "merely." The author neglects a host of the facts of the nuptial flight which render it very different from a mere flying toward the sun, and concludes in characteristic fashion: "Thus, according to these observations the bees at the time of the nuptial flight are positively heliotropic machines."

by the principle of tropism. Its most enthusiastic exponents seem to believe that by the same principle all behavior, even human behavior, is explicable; and they even seem to resent the fact that the higher animals possess nervous systems and reflexes; for this fact narrows the field of application of their favorite principle, and restricts the scope of their ingenuity in applying it, or at least brings a serious rival into the field.

Tropism a Valid Principle but Not All-Sufficient

It is worth while to reflect that, if a monstrous visitor from another planet were to study the behavior of a colony of human beings through a powerful magnifying glass, he might well come to the conclusion that human behavior is largely, if not wholly, a matter of tropic reactions. For he would observe that, when they are fatigued by a day's activity, they become negatively phototropic, seeking dark places and lying quiet there; but after a period of rest the sign of their tropism is reversed, so that they become positively phototropic and seem to seek the light. He would observe that in cold weather these queer creatures become positively thermotropic and congregate about fires and stoves; and that, when they are hungry, they become positively chemotropic toward the chemical substances which diffuse themselves from the cook-house door. He might observe also that the males tend to congregate about young females; and, if he were a mechanist of the school of Loeb, he would confidently infer that the young female emits some unknown form of radiant energy towards which the males are positively tropic.[1]

The evidence on which this observer would base his interpretations would be not unlike that which we have for the application of the principle of tropism to the animalcules. I do not wish to suggest that the principle is not sound and valid in certain cases. When, for example, the moth flies into the flame, consumed by a desire for immortality, as the poets tell us, or fascinated by the pleasing glow, as perhaps the man-in-the-street would say, it is, I think, not improbable that a positive heliotropism is really the determining factor. And in many

[1] Cf. Bethe's interpretation of the "homing" of bees on p. 81.

other instances tropism may play a part in determining the behavior of animals. But there seems to be no possibility of explaining all the behavior of any animal in terms of this principle. Even some of the most plausible applications of the principle come upon nasty snags, as we have seen in the instance of the larval *Chrysorrhœa.* In other cases we can only work the tropic principle by piling supposition upon supposition. But more important is the consideration that the movements of an animal, guided by tropisms alone, would show none of the marks of behavior; yet the movements of even the simplest animals do show such marks. The tropic principle presupposes that spontaneity and that persistence of movements which we called the first two marks of behavior. For, if the animal makes no movements of locomotion, there is nothing for the tropic guidance to work upon.

Further, movements governed by tropism, when they do not at once attain their natural end, should show none of that variation of direction which is the third mark of behavior. Yet almost every instance of animal locomotion shows this mark. Even the moth does not usually fly directly into the flame; but more commonly hovers round it uncertainly, as though both attracted and repelled, before he blunders into it.

It is among the unicellular animals that the tropic principle might, if anywhere, be expected to celebrate its completest triumph. For surely, it may be said, it is absurd to postulate anything of the nature of mind in a tiny speck of jelly, which appears almost structureless under the highest powers of the microscope. Yet we must remember that each one of us, even the most magnificently endowed, begins life as just such a speck of jelly. The only difference known to us is that one speck remains a speck, or becomes many similar specks, while the other becomes a man and, perhaps, a philosopher.

Behavior of Protozoa

Of such animals (*Protozoa*) the humblest and simplest is the *Amœba.* Yet here is a condensed chapter from the lives of two such creatures.[1] These unicellular specks of protoplasm creep

[1] H. C. Jennings, "The Behavior of Lower Organisms," p. 17.

over solid surfaces submerged in fresh water. A larger specimen, C, comes in contact with a smaller one, B. C thereupon changes the direction of its locomotion and sends out two long protuberances which begin to enclose B, as B continues on its path. This process continues until C completely encloses B, together with a quantity of water. C then stops and changes its direction, carrying B within it in a quiescent condition. After a brief period, the quiescent B bestirs itself and begins to emerge from C, sending protuberances out through a small canal left open in the substance of the enclosing C. Thereupon C reverses its movement and again completely encloses B, and again moves off in the opposite direction, carrying B within. Again B, by a few rapid movements, escapes from the "posterior end" of its captor C, and becomes completely free and separated from C by a clear interval. Again C reverses, overtakes B, again engulfs it, and starts away in a new direction. B then seems resigned to its fate; it remains contracted to a spherical mass within C for some five minutes. But, after that time, B again bestirs itself, forces its way through the containing wall of C's substance, and finally escapes.

It is clear that this series of movements resembles behavior, a series of purposive actions, far more closely than a series of tropisms. At any rate, the tropic theory is very far from having an adequate explanation to offer.

Consider the movements of the slipper animalcule (*Paramœcium*). This is a tiny slipper-shaped animal. Although it consists of a single cell only, it has highly specialized parts or organs, including the cilia, whose whiplike movements propel it with blunt end foremost and sweep particles of food into its mouth. Its activity consists in little more than these almost constant movements of its cilia. And it is one of the most machinelike of the animalcules. Yet it exhibits unmistakably some of the marks of behavior. Especially it exhibits spontaneity in its almost perpetual activity and in the renewal of it after short periods of quiescence. Usually, upon coming into contact with a solid object, it reverses the motion of its cilia, backs away, turns through a small angle and again swims forward. But sometimes it remains quiescent, anchored to the surface, then shifts its position upon it, remains quiet again, and then swims away. "All this may happen without the slightest evident change in the outer conditions. So far as can be seen, the Paramœcium first responds to the solid by the avoiding reaction, later by the positive contact reaction, and still later suspends the contact reaction, all without any change in external conditions. The changes inducing the change in reaction must then be within the animal." (Jennings, *op. cit.*)

Even more suggestive of behavior or purposive action are the following reactions of Stentor, a slender vaselike creature. It consists of a single cell, but has a more differentiated structure than most other *Protozoa*. The apex of its conical body is commonly attached to some solid surface; the base of the cone is surrounded with cilia, whose movements drive a current of water into a soft-walled depression, which is the mouth. This creature was bombarded with a stream of innutritious particles by Jennings, who describes the following series of reactions: (1) Stentor sweeps the particles into its "mouth" for a short time; (2) it bends to one side, repeating this movement several times at short intervals; (3) it reverses the action of the cilia about its "mouth," so that the particles, instead of being ingested, are driven away; (4) after repeating this reversal two or three times, it contracts its whole body toward its base of attachment; (5) if, after several repetitions of this withdrawal, Stentor still encounters the stream of particles on extending itself, it makes a more violent contraction of its whole body, which results in its detachment from its fixed base; it then swims away and takes up a new position, again attaching itself to some solid surface. This sequence of reactions to the unvarying stimulus seems to exhibit in a rudimentary way all the marks of behavior. The mechanist may suggest that the continued bombardment reverses the sign of Stentor's tropism toward such stimulation; but this hardly meets the case. The significant fact is that, after repeating one movement several times, the animal, under the same external conditions of stimulation, makes a quite different movement which more effectually removes it from the harmful influence. It is at least a striking instance of *variation* of movement in face of constant stimulation; and each of the successive movements is an adaptive reaction. Perhaps it deserves to be classed as a very simple instance of learning or of profiting by experience.

Professors H. S. Jennings and S. J. Holmes, who seem to be strictly impartial and who have studied the behavior of these animalcules most intensively, agree in holding that we cannot explain all the movements of these simplest animals as tropisms and reflexes, and that we are justified (provisionally at least) in regarding them as constituting behavior, that is to say, as very simple and lowly examples of purposive action.[1]

Behavior of the Earthworm

We might with advantage dwell upon hundreds of examples of behavior among very simple animals. But I will cite only one more from the quite lowly region of the scale of life, a well-known bit of behavior of the common earthworm. It has long

[1] Professor Jennings writes of the Amœba as follows: "Can the behavior of Amœba be resolved throughout into direct unvarying reactions to simple stimuli—into elements comparable to simple reflexes? For most of the behavior . . . the stimuli can be recognized in simple chemical or physical changes in the environment. Yet there are certain trains of action for which such a resolution into unvarying reactions to simple stimuli seems unsatisfactory. This is notably true for some of the food reactions. In watching an Amœba following a rolling food-ball, one seems to see the animal, after failing to secure the food in one way, try another. Again, in the pursuit of one Amœba by another, it is difficult to conceive each phase of action of the pursuer to be completely determined by a simple present stimulus. For example [in the pursuit described above], after Amœba B has escaped completely and is quite separate from Amœba C, the latter reverses its course and recaptures B. What determines the behavior of C at this point? . . . One who sees the behavior as it occurs can hardly resist the conviction that the action at this point is partly determined by the changes in C due to the former possession of B, so that the behavior is not purely reflex." ("Behavior of the Lower Organisms," p. 24.) Again he writes: "We may classify the various changes in behavior due to stimulation into three main types, which may be called the positive reaction, the negative reaction, and the food reaction. . . . These types are not stereotyped; each varies much in details under different conditions. The movements in these reactions are clearly not the direct results of the simple physical action of the agents inducing them. As in the higher animals, so in Amœba the reactions are indirect. . . . It is therefore not possible to predict the movements of the organisms from a knowledge of the direct physical changes produced in its substance by the agent in question." (*Op. cit.*, p. 23.)

Jennings writes also: "Thus we find in the unicellular organisms very little in the behavior that can be interpreted in accordance with this local action theory of tropisms. The latter does not by any means express the fundamental nature

been common knowledge that an earthworm, when about to draw a leaf into its burrow, will seize it by the narrower end. Experiment on this cue with pieces of paper of various shapes has shown that an earthworm, whose sense-organs and nervous system are very simple, will explore the piece of paper which it is about to draw into its burrow, and will generally seize it by the most suitable corner for its purpose. Thus, if the paper be a triangle, having one angle distinctly more acute than the other two, it will seize the paper at the apex of this angle, which obviously is the one that any intelligent being would choose, if its purpose was to drag the paper into a narrow round burrow.[1]

of their behavior in directed reactions. These are based chiefly on the performance under stimulation of varied movements, with selection from the resulting conditions. . . . The prevalence of this local action theory of tropisms as a general explanation of behavior in lower organisms is based only on an incomplete knowledge and an insufficient analysis of the facts of behavior." Further, he writes: "Intelligence is commonly held to consist essentially in the modification of behavior in accordance with experience. . . . It appears clear that we find the beginnings of such adaptive changes of behavior even in the Protozoa. . . . This fundamental basis [of intelligent adaptation] then clearly exists even in the Protozoa; it is apparently coextensive with life. It is difficult if not impossible to draw a line separating the regulatory behavior of lower organisms from the so-called intelligent behavior of higher ones; the one grades insensibly into the other. . . . We have asked merely whether there exist in the lower organisms objective phenomena of a character similar to what we find in the behavior of man. To this question we have been compelled to give an affirmative answer. So far as objective evidence goes, there is no difference of kind, but a complete continuity between the behavior of lower and of higher organisms." He then discusses the question—Is the behavior of lower organisms such as to "suggest to the observer the existence of consciousness"? He is of the opinion "that Paramœcium . . . makes such an impression that one involuntarily recognizes it as a little subject acting in ways analogous to our own. Still stronger, perhaps, is this impression when observing an Amœba obtaining food. . . . The writer is thoroughly convinced, after long study of the behavior of this organism, that if Amœba were a large animal, so as to come within the every-day experience of human beings, its behavior would at once call forth the attribution to it of states of pleasure and pain, of hunger, desire, and the like, on precisely the same basis as we attribute these things to a dog. . . . We attribute consciousness to the dog, because this is useful; it enables us practically to appreciate, foresee, and control its actions much more readily than we could otherwise do. . . . I believe it beyond question that we should find similar attribution to it [Amœba] of certain states of consciousness a practical assistance in foreseeing and controlling its behavior. Amœba is a beast of prey, and gives the impression of being controlled by the same elemental impulses as higher beasts of prey."

[1] Charles Darwin seems to have been the first to put these facts on scientific record in his book on earthworms. His observations have been confirmed. Professor

I confess that this behavior is staggering. It certainly cannot be explained as either a tropism or a conditioned reflex. In some sense the animal appreciates by successive touches the shape of the paper, or at least the nature of its angles; and in some sense it compares these, and chooses the one most suitable to its purpose. The behavior seems to imply and express a comparative judgment, as clearly as when I choose a shoe to fit my foot. We shall see that other animals a little higher in the scale behave in a variety of ways which seem to imply such judgment.

Insects and Instinctive Behavior

Let us turn now to the insects, whose fascinating behavior has attracted the intensive study of many fine observers and which lend themselves so much better than most wild animals to minute observation. The difficulty is to choose amidst a wealth of material. The insects have a relatively simple nervous system, consisting of a chain of ganglia (small clusters of cells); each ganglion is connected with its neighbors by a longitudinal bundle of nerve fibres; and each receives sensory fibres from the sense organs, and sends out motor fibres to the muscles of its segment. Each ganglion seems to be a small group of typical reflex mechanisms.

Further, the insect is strictly bilaterally symmetrical, and thus lends itself well to explanation by the tropic principle. Here, if anywhere, we might expect a combination of reflexes, condi-

G. Kafka writes (in his very thorough and critical "Tierpsychologie," Leipzig, 1914) as follows: "Dass es tatsächlich Formreize sind, welche die Reaktionen der Tiere [earthworms] bestimmen, ergibt sich aus den Versuchen Hanels, in denen ihnen drei- oder viereckige Papierstückchen zum verstopfen ihrer Röhren dargeboten und diese Figuren wiederum weitaus am häufigsten in unmittelbarer Nähe des spitzesten Winkels ergriffen wurden, selbst wenn etwa in einem gleichschenkeligen Dreieck das Verhältnis des Schenkels zur Basis nur 9: 10 betrug." (Vol. 1, p. 494.) Without wishing to reflect upon the scientific impartiality of Herr Kafka, I would draw the student's attention to his use of the term "Formreiz," literally, "shape stimulus." This is a mild example of a practice common among mechanists. They fit all behavior to their "stimulus-response formula," by means of the simple device of classifying as "stimuli" everything in heaven and earth, from a flash of light or a simple touch to a religious or political system of beliefs, or an institution such as the Roman Church or the British Empire.

tioned reflexes, and tropisms to yield fairly adequate explanations of what to a superficial view looks like behavior.

Some of the mechanists have rightly seen that here is the proper field for the demonstration of the adequacy of their principles, and have boldly thrown out their challenge to the anthropomorphists.[1]

The behavior of insects is particularly interesting also, because insects are rightly held to illustrate in the richest and purest manner the operation of "Instinct." The problem of "Instinct" is of fundamental importance. Instinctive action, rather than reflex action, is in my view, and in that of many other psychologists, the key to the understanding of human behavior. It is the teaching of this book that human behavior is built up on a basis of innate tendencies which are in all essentials very similar to the instinctive tendencies of animals.

Others, notably Professor Bergson, take a different view. They assert that Instinct and Intelligence are two diverse developments of Mind that have little in common. They suggest that in the course of evolution Mind arrived at a parting of the ways, that the path of evolution was split into two divergent paths, Instinct and Intelligence; and that, while the insects followed the former and developed Instinct in a very high degree and Intelligence hardly at all, the vertebrates and mammals followed the other path and developed Intelligence till it culminated in the intellect of man; Instinct in this line remaining comparatively inactive, until it was rediscovered by Professor Bergson and recognized by him as the essential function involved in philosophic intuition.

The mechanists form a third party who see in Instinct nothing more than complex reflex action, often of the type of the chain-reflex, and sometimes modified or controlled by tropisms.

We have then to keep in mind these three rival views during our study of insect behavior; and we must attempt to find grounds of decision in favor of one or other of them.

The definition and demarcation of Instinct and Intelligence have been much debated of recent years; but no general agreement as to the precise use of the words has yet been reached,

[1] Cf. especially the attempt of A. Bethe discussed in the following chapter.

nor can be reached until agreement as to the nature of the facts denoted shall have been achieved. But the great majority of all parties would agree that we may properly call "instinctive" those actions of animals which seem to be purposive (*i. e.*, exhibit the marks of behavior) and which are performed by any animal independently of previous experience of similar situations. The surest evidence of such independence of prior experience is the performance of an action immediately after the animal emerges from its egg, or after some similar radical change of environment and mode of life; though in many other cases it is possible to be sure that, in spite of the lapse of time since such a change of life, the animal has not had contact with any object or situation similar to that which evokes the instinctive response. In defining instinctive action, some authorities would add that an instinctive action or tendency is one which is common to all members of the species. This is, no doubt, very generally true, but seems to be an unnecessary and extrinsic addition.

Intelligent action, on the other hand, is generally defined as one which seems to show that the creature has profited by prior experience of similar situations, that it somehow brings to bear its previous experience in the guidance of its present action. Instinct (abstractly conceived and with a capital letter) is native or inborn capacity for purposive action; Intelligence is the capacity to improve upon native tendency in the light of past experience.

The Hormic Theory

A word must be said here on the meaning of the word "teleological." I have insisted that all mental activity is purposive, that it is a striving toward a goal, however vaguely the goal may be thought of. The word "teleological," which means directed toward a goal, has often been applied to animal behavior, or to the realm of life in general, to imply that the processes of organisms are adjusted to bring about certain results which are the goal designed or willed by the Creator. If organic processes are described as teleological in this sense of the word, the view is compatible with the theory that all animals are merely machines or mechanisms. For the processes of a man made machine are teleological in this same sense: they bring about the results designed and willed by the maker of the machine. We may, however, use the word "teleological" as equivalent to "purposive" in the sense in which it is defined in this chapter. The difference between the two meanings is very important. Applied to the whole process of organic evolution, the term "teleological" may mean that the process is realizing a goal conceived and willed by the Creator in the minutest detail. On the other hand, if it is used as synonymous with "purposive" in the sense defined in this chapter, it means that in the process of organic evolution the goal of the process is progressively created and defined, as evolution advances and as Mind becomes increasingly capable of conceiving the future in terms of alternatives between which it chooses.

The view that all animal and human behavior is purposive in however vague and lowly a degree, and that purposive action is fundamentally different from mechanical process, may be conveniently called the *hormic theory.* The word "hormic" is from the Greek "horme" (ὅρμη), which means a vital impulse or urge to action. Schopenhauer's "will-to-live," Professor Bergson's "*élan vital,*" and Doctor C. G. Jung's "*libido,*" are alternative expressions for the purposive or hormic energy that is manifested in human and animal behavior. In adopting this word I am following the suggestion of Professor T. P. Nunn in his very excellent little book, "Education, Its Data and First Principles." He states the theory so admirably that I cannot forbear to cite a few sentences:

"Are we, since our bodies are 'matter,' to seek in physical laws an explanation for the whole of life; or are we, since our bodies are alive, to interpret their activity by what we know of life where its character appears in the highest and clearest form—namely, in the conscious life of the mind?" "The animal's life is, of course, permeated (as human physiology is) by chemical and physical factors; but just as a poem, though permeated by grammar, is more than a sum of grammatical expressions, so the behavior, even of a protozoan, escapes beyond the conception of a physico-chemical machine. In short, the humblest creature is autonomous." "Stupendous as the distance is between the lives of the protozoan and the creature who has been made a little lower than the angels, it consists—like the difference between a village church and a cathedral—not in any radical unlikeness of the essential features, but rather in the differing richness, variety, and subtlety of the details in which a single scheme has been worked out at different evolutionary levels."

"Starting from the position that there is more than physics and chemistry even in the humblest animal, it [the hormic theory] comes to view the history of life as a striving toward the individuality which is expressed most clearly and richly in man's conscious nature, and finds, therefore, in that goal toward which the whole creation moves the true interpretation of its earlier efforts."

"We need a name for the fundamental property expressed in the incessant adjustments and adventures that make up the tissue of life. We are directly aware of that property in our conscious activities as an element of 'drive,' 'urge,' or felt tendency toward an end. Psychologists call it *conation,* and give the name *conative process* to any train of conscious activity which is dominated by such a drive. . . . For instance, the reader's endeavor to understand the present sentence is a conative process in which a relatively complex system of mental acts moves toward a more or less clearly envisaged end. . . . While the reader's mind is pursuing the printed argument, his neuromuscular mechanisms are keeping his head aloft upon his shoulders, his digestive glands are dealing with his latest meal. None of these purposive processes may be called conative, for they lie below, and even far below, the conscious level; yet a suprahuman spectator, who could watch our mental behavior in the same direct way as we can observe physical events, would see them all as instances of the same class, variant in detail but alike in general plan. In other words, he would see that they all differ from purely mechanical processes by the presence of an internal 'drive.' . . . To this element of drive or urge, whether it occurs in the conscious life of men and the higher animals or in the unconscious activities of their bodies and the (presumably) unconscious behavior of lower animals, we propose to give a single name—*horme* (ὁρμη). In accordance with this proposal all the purposive processes of the organism are hormic processes, conative processes being the subclass whose members have the special mark of being conscious." Again he writes: "Horme, as we have defined the term, is the basis of the activities that differentiate the living animal from dead matter." Further, they, the hormic processes, undergo a "development in which they become organized into ever wider and more complex hormic systems. Beginning as a cell in his mother's body, a very part of her flesh, he [each man] becomes a 'parasite' nourished by her blood and feeding on her food, yet already a being with a life and destiny of his own. The hormic processes, both conservative and creative, in which that life consists, are still mainly unconscious, though, as his nervous system determines and his sense organs form, his 'will to live' may be enriched by some vague conational, that is, conscious elements, while he still lies in his mother's womb. As soon as he has left her body and has entered on the long task of picking his way through the labyrinth of the outer world, the conational elements acquire a new significance, and their development becomes the centre of the spectator's interest. Conation rises slowly from the level of blind, or purblind, impulse to that of clear-eyed desire, and eventually from the level of desire seeking an immediate good to that of will fixed upon a distant and perhaps ideal goal. Meanwhile, subserving this advance in the character of the horme, there is a parallel development in its organization—showing itself first in the emergence of his physiological organs and in the correlation of their functions, then after birth, in the co-ordination of the powers of sense and movement in systems of ever-increasing complexity and effectiveness, and lastly in the gradual building up of great conative hierarchies, which determine the form of the man's individuality and are the measure of his life's achievement."

CHAPTER III

BEHAVIOR OF INSECTS

Many great naturalists have devoted much of their lives to the study of the ants, bees, and wasps; and the behavior of these insects is of the utmost interest to the psychologist, because it presents so many clear instances of the blending of Intelligence with Instinct, of undeniable Intelligence with unmistakable Instinct. But, before turning to these, let us consider a single example of what may fairly be called purely instinctive behavior. I select for description a train of actions, each of which is normally performed once only by each insect, and which therefore can owe little or nothing of its nicety of adaptation to the previous experience of the individual performer. Instances of such actions abound among the insects; the following one differs from many others only in being exceptionally complex.

Purely Instinctive Behavior

The Yucca moths "emerge from their chrysalis cases just when the large, yellowish-white, bell-shaped flowers of the Yucca open, each for a single night. From the anthers of one of these flowers the female moth collects the golden pollen and kneads the adhesive material into a little pellet, which she holds beneath her head by means of the greatly enlarged bristly palps. Thus laden, she flies off and seeks another flower. Having found one, she pierces with the sharp lancets of her ovipositor the tissue of the pistil, lays her eggs among the ovules, and then, darting to the top of the stigma, stuffs the fertilizing pollen-pellet into its funnel-shaped opening."[1] In this way the moth places her eggs where they can develop, if the ovules develop; but the ovules can develop only if the moth pushes the pollen from another flower into the open stigma. Nature has so con-

[1] I cite from Professor Lloyd Morgan's account in "Habit and Instinct."

stituted the moth that she performs this cycle of nicely adjusted actions, essential to the continuance of the species, shortly after emerging from the chrysalis, when she cannot have acquired any knowledge of the flower or of her grub and its needs.

This is a fine example of the working of a *chain-instinct.* Why should we not be content to call it a chain-reflex? Each step in the train of action brings the moth into a new situation in which new stimuli affect its sense-organs. Why not be content to suppose, with the mechanists, that each step is simply a reflex reaction to some new stimulus? The available descriptions of this train of action do not enable us to say whether or no it presents all the marks of behavior. The first three marks of our list—spontaneity, persistence, variation—are not described; though it is probable that minute and repeated observation would discover them. Preparation for the coming situation is conspicuous. Direction toward an end might perhaps be claimed; but it does not clearly appear, because its clear appearance involves the first three marks, not reported in this instance. There is no evidence of improvement on repetition, because no repetition has been observed. But each step does seem to be a total reaction. And there is another feature of the process which, though not an essential mark of behavior (because not present in many of the lower instances of behavior, and not always present in instinctive action), yet, when it is present, very clearly marks off instinctive from merely reflex action and from tropism. *Reflex action is response to a stimulus; instinctive action is in many cases a response to an object.* Subjectively the distinction between response to a stimulus and response to an object is fairly clear, though the line may not be sharply drawn. For example, if particles of pepper enter my nostrils they may provoke a sneeze, even though I do not perceive the odor or the irritation; the sneeze is then a reflex action, a reflex response to a stimulus. But, if I perceive the odor and the irritation and then blow my nose, that is behavior initiated by perception, a purposive reaction upon an object.

In attempting to apply this distinction in the study of animal behavior, we have to rely upon objective criteria; therefore, when we observe reaction upon some simple sense-impression, such as an odor, a simple sound, a touch, or a ray of light, we remain in doubt. But, if a nicely adapted reaction is found to be evoked only by some complex conjunction or sequence of sense-impressions, then we may infer on the part of the animal a *synthetic activity* which makes from a complex of sense-stimuli a unitary object.[1]

Synthetic activity of this kind is of the essence of perception. Thus, when the humble earthworm slowly explores, by successive touches, the borders of a leaf or of a piece of paper, then seizes it by its acutest angle and drags it into his burrow, we may infer on his part an act of perception; we may infer it as confidently as when we see a blind man spell out a word or recognize a child by touch; or as when, with closed eyes, a man recognizes by touch alone a complex object placed in his hand. For the earthworm's behavior *is not merely a response to a stimulus;* it is action guided by an appreciation of the shape of the object, an appreciation gained through a series of sense-impressions. And it implies far more than a mere summation of stimuli. If a stimulus is weak, it may fail to evoke a reflex action; and yet may evoke such action, if it is repeated several times in quick succession. That is what is meant by "summation of stimuli." But the earthworm, in order to seize the acutest angle, must appreciate in some sense the shape of the leaf, must relate the successive stimuli or sense-impressions of contact in a complex and orderly whole; and *such relating synthetic activity is the essence of perception.* Such relating synthetic activity is most prominent in ourselves in relation to impressions of sight and hearing; that is why we call these the most intellectual of the senses. In the animals also sight and hearing seem to be prominent in the same way; but the behavior of some animals, of the ants, for example, implies that complex and successive impressions of both touch and smell are synthesized by them more elaborately and effectually than by the normal average man.

Let us return to the Yucca moth, whose train of behavior may seem to a superficial view so machinelike. Consider a single step of this behavior, the placing of the egg in the one

[1] More strictly—the subject responds to a complex conjunction or sequence of sense-impressions with awareness of a unitary object.

position in all the world where it can develop, that is, among the ovules of the flower. Even if we assume that an odor emanating from the ovules exerts some tropic influence on the moth, it is obvious that this will not suffice to determine the placing of the egg in the right spot. That can be effected only under the guidance of a multitude of simultaneous and successive sense-stimuli; and these must be not merely summated, but rather synthesized and related into an appreciation of the shape of the parts of the flower concerned. In other words, the response of the moth to the flower is a *perceptual response*, not a mere reaction to a stimulus.[1]

Instinct and Intelligence Co-operate in Homing

Among the hymenoptera the solitary wasps are the most interesting in the present connection. For the behavior of the social species is more difficult to analyze, and at present many of its features are far beyond our comprehension. M. Henri Fabre, the aged prince of entomologists, has devoted some of his many fascinating reports to the solitary wasps.[2] And Mr. and Mrs. Peckham have given us minute studies of them in a very charming volume.[3] There are many species of these solitary wasps, all of which lead much the same sort of life; but the behavior of each species is in some respects peculiar to itself.

In so far as all the members of one species behave in the same ways, and especially when such behavior is peculiar to that one species, we may confidently regard such behavior as instinctive. The solitary mode of life of these wasps presents great advantages to the student of their behavior. When we are observing the behavior of animals that are gregarious or that are brought up by parents in a family group, it is often difficult to distin-

[1] This is one of the respects in which an uncritical adhesion to the mechanist theory of behavior is apt to blind the theorist to facts. Starting out with the formula that all behavior is a reaction to a "stimulus," such a theorist is apt to ignore altogether this highly important distinction between "stimuli" and "objects." This abuse of the word "stimulus" reaches its extreme when the mechanist seeks to bring, say, the political or religious activities of a man under the stimulus-response formula by describing his system of political or religious beliefs as an internal institutional stimulus.

[2] "Souvenirs Entomologiques."

[3] "Wasps, Social and Solitary."

guish instinctive behavior from that which is moulded by the influence of parents and companions. The study of the solitary wasps is almost entirely free from this complication. In each of the species we are to consider, the female wasp emerges full-grown from the grub and proceeds forthwith to lead her solitary life. Alone and without the example or assistance of any companion, she sets about her task of perpetuating her species. This task is accomplished by a cycle of behavior of several phases: she makes, or finds, a suitable nest for her eggs, lays one or more eggs in it, and deposits beside them a store of animal food, which she secures by hunting with much and varied activity. The grub which hatches from the egg feeds upon the prey deposited beside it, and grows; until it in turn emerges a perfect wasp, almost ready to enter upon a similar cycle of activity. Unlike the Yucca moth and many other insects, each wasp performs, or may perform, the cycle of egg-laying many times. After depositing her egg with the supply of animal food, she leaves the nest (generally having first securely closed it) and never returns to it; she proceeds to find or make a new nest and to repeat the cycle. It seems clear, therefore, that the wasp never learns by individual experience the issue of her labors, namely, the birth of offspring like herself. And it seems fairly safe to assume that she has no knowledge and no foresight of this issue of her untiring activity. Her parental care is certainly not to be attributed to an intelligent anticipation of benefits to be received; whether in the form of the pleasures of contact with her young, or of a proud contemplation and display of her offspring, or of care and attention from them in her old age. It is safe to assume that the institution of old-age pensions among these wasps would have no appreciable effect on their birth-rate.

Such lack of all knowledge of the ultimate issue of action on the part of the performer is sometimes made a part of the definition of instinctive action; but this also is an extrinsic and unessential mark. But when it can be confidently inferred, whether in human or animal behavior, it is a sure indication of an instinctive basis or factor.

Various holes are used by the solitary wasps as nests; but

each species makes use of only one kind, or at most a few similar kinds. Some dig holes in the ground; and the form of the hole so dug is characteristic of the species. Some choose holes in timber, or the cavities of straws, and so on. And the prey hunted by the wasps, to be stored in their nests as provender for the grub, is equally various; but is more strictly peculiar to each species. One species makes use of caterpillars, another of spiders, a third of grasshoppers, and so on. Here the limitation of their intelligence is strikingly displayed; for it is probable that the grub of any species might thrive upon the flesh of many different kinds of prey. Yet each species of wasp is so narrowly limited in its choice of prey that, if prey of its proper kind were to be suddenly destroyed by a plague, that species of wasp would, it seems, inevitably die out also.

The wasp, emerging from the shell within which the metamorphosis has taken place, spends some days or weeks in flying about within a limited area, finding her proper nourishment, and making herself acquainted with the geography of her neighborhood. Is this last expression unduly anthropomorphic? To the mechanist, who can see in animal behavior nothing but responses to "stimuli," it will seem so. But the statement is, I think, fully justifiable; for the success of the whole cycle of instinctive activity depends upon this detailed acquired acquaintance with the locality. Consider the following facts: A wasp digs in the ground a burrow of suitable shape, and then departs in search of prey to deposit in it. She wanders freely throughout a considerable area, certainly some hundreds of yards in extent. At any point in this area she may come upon her prey. Having seized and mastered her prey, the wasp returns to the nest she has prepared; and she does not achieve this by travelling hither and thither at random over the whole area until she blunders upon the nest. That procedure would seldom be successful; the wasp would be worn out by her labors in dragging her prey over vast distances. It might have been supposed that Nature would have solved the problem by endowing the wasp with the instinct to find her prey first, and then to choose or make her nest close beside it. But, no! Nature, working through Mind and not merely through mechanical reflexes, has endowed the wasp with an instinctive tendency which requires for its success the co-operation of intelligence, and intelligence of no mean order; an intelligence utterly different from any system of "conditioned reflexes." For, in order that the wasp shall return to her nest, it does not suffice that she should in some sense recognize landmarks within the area of her explorations and react to them with this or that movement. Given a power of recognizing landmarks, something more is required, something much more intellectual, something higher in the scale of intelligence. Namely, these landmarks, if they are to guide the wasp back to her nest, must each be recognized not merely as a detached object, but also as an object spatially related to others in more or less definite fashion.

We are compelled, I say, to believe that in some sense the wasp constructs and *carries with her a map or plan of the locality*, for her behavior shows that she perceives and recognizes objects within this area as parts of a geographical whole of which the nest is also a part.

If any thoroughgoing behaviorist should read the foregoing passage he will, I know, hardly refrain from laughter at this point. But that is only because he has not thought out the problem in view of all the available facts. Here are some of the facts which have to be taken into account. It has been observed that it is the practice of many of these wasps, when they leave the nest to search for prey, to circle round and round it many times in an enlarging irregular spiral course. This is described by the Peckhams as the making of a locality-study; and there can be little doubt that the terms are well chosen. This behavior would seem to serve no other purpose; it is meaningless and otiose, if the wasp does not find her nest by recognition of its surroundings.[1] We know that other animals, which find their way home from distant regions—for example, homing pigeons—behave in a similar fashion. The days or weeks of wandering

[1] Some wasps will sometimes lay down their prey after carrying it part way to the burrow, depart from it (apparently in order to make sure of their topography), and return after a short interval. Before leaving the prey, they are apt to make a "locality study" as on leaving the nest.

over the area, before making or choosing a nest, seem to have no other biological value or function than the facilitation of the return to the nest within the area thus made familiar. Again, if during the absence of the wasp in search of her prey, objects surrounding the nest are moved or otherwise changed, the wasp on her return is apt to wander about uncertainly for some little time, instead of proceeding directly to the nest, as she more usually does.

Further, it seems to be impossible to suggest any other explanation of the wasp's power of finding her nest than the assumption that, like ourselves, she learns to recognize landmarks in their relation to the whole area and to one another. Let the reader imagine himself set down in the midst of a dense forest of vast trees in hilly country.[1] He is provided with a hut and has to find his way back to this for shelter, after every expedition in search of food. He will proceed just as the wasp does, if he is wise; he will make locality studies of its immediate neighborhood, and he will wander about, extending his range gradually, noting various landmarks, until he is familiar with a sufficient area; and then he will conduct his searches for food within this area. And, when he wishes to return to his hut, it will not suffice to find one of his landmarks and to recognize it as an object that he has seen before. That in itself would not help him. He must also remember the relations of this to other landmarks or to his hut.

The Tropic Theory Unable to Account for Homing

But does not the principle of tropism make possible a simpler interpretation? A leading mechanist has made a valiant attempt to apply the principle, not to the nest-finding of the solitary wasp, but to the return of bees to the hive. This problem of "homing" is so important that it is worth while to examine this attempt[2]; if it is successful for the bees, it will no doubt apply to the wasps. Bethe's argument and conclusion may be

[1] Cf. the Peckhams' description of the return of a wasp on foot through a patch of corn. *Op. cit.*, p. 18.

[2] "Dürfen wir den Ameisen u. Bienen psychische Qualitäten zuschreiben," A. Bethe. Archiv für die Ges. Physiologie, Bd. 70, 1898.

briefly stated as follows: It is impossible to admit that a bee can find its way home as a man does, by intelligent recognition of familiar objects and places; and it is clearly impossible to regard her return to the hive as a long chain of mechanical reflex movements; therefore, the bee must be guided by "tropism"; and, since no other explanation is possible, we are compelled to believe that energy of some unknown form radiates from the hive and acts upon the bee tropically.[1] We must suppose that the bee, so long as she is unladen, is indifferent to, or negatively tropic toward, this mysterious X-ray; and that she, so soon as laden with honey or pollen, becomes positively tropic toward it; so that, as she flies, this radiant energy turns her always toward the hive.

What facts does Bethe adduce in support of this hypothesis? He shows that the return of bees to the hive is little disturbed when the appearance of the hive is disguised by screens of paper or leaves; and that, if the hive be moved, the bees return to and hover about the place occupied by the door of the hive, before it was moved. These and other facts of the same order show, Bethe argues, that the bees do not guide themselves by vision, in the way that a man seeking the hive would do. And Bethe hastily concludes that they are not guided by vision. It seems clear also that they are not guided by smell. Hence, says Bethe, we are compelled to postulate an unknown form of radiant energy which guides their return.

What facts are there which make this hypothesis unnecessary and improbable?

1. Other forms of behavior of the bees and wasps imply a high degree of intelligence, as we shall presently see; and, though the return to the nest perhaps implies a higher level of intelligence than any other of their actions, it is in accordance with many other facts that just this capacity (this specialized form of intelligence, the capacity to acquire and use knowledge of or familiarity with a locality), which is essential to the achievement of their principal task in life, is found to be possessed by these insects in the required degree.

2. If, while the bees are out foraging, the hive be removed some little distance from its place, the bees return to the place where the hive previously was

[1] "The bees follow a force (einer Kraft) which is quite unknown to us, and which compels them to return to the position in space from which they have flown forth." *Op. cit.*, p. 82. Fabre, who, while denying intelligence to the insects, credits them with a certain power of "discernment," would explain their "homing" by the postulation of "un sentiment topographique," which remains merely a phrase, a form of words comparable to "the homing instinct," the utterance of which phrase suffices for the popular mind as an explanation of all facts of this order. Such use of the word "instinct" as a mere cloak for ignorance is, of course, regrettable.

standing; and they will even hover about the spot where they were accustomed to find the landing board. Bethe meets this fact by supposing that his hypothetical X-ray radiates, not from the hive, but from the spot where it had previously stood—thus piling one wild improbability upon another. The fact serves to negative the least wildly improbable form of tropic theory, namely, that the bees are guided to the hive by the odor of the queen bee, or of the hive in general.

3. It is a well-known fact, established by simple observation as well as by experiment, that bees commonly do not travel more than about two miles from the hive, and that, if they are carried beyond this limit, many of them fail to return.

4. If bees are overtaken by the dusk while at some little distance from the hive, they fail to return.

5. But far more conclusive is the following observation: Bees dwelling in hives which adjoined an arid district naturally foraged much in the fertile region on one side of the hives, and little or not at all in the arid region on the other side. It was found that, while bees carried to any point within the two-mile limit in the fertile zone did not fail to return, of those carried to similar distances in the unexplored arid zone many failed to return.[1] Bethe, of course, would meet this by pointing out that in the arid zone the tropism of the bees was not reversed by the finding of pollen or honey. It is regrettable that the bees released in the arid zone were not fed before release. Here is a beautiful and conclusive experiment still to be made.

6. In New England, wild-bee hunting is a sport ardently pursued by some experts, whose method of locating the hives is very instructive in the present connection.[2] The hunter captures a bee, and, having marked her with a spot of paint, puts her into a small box; where she feeds on syrup. When the bee has taken her fill she is released and, having (like the wasps) flown round a little,[3] disappears in the distance; and the hunter sits down beside the box confidently awaiting her return. He is seldom disappointed. Under favorable conditions the bee usually returns (identified by her paint-spot) accompanied by others; and these also fill themselves with syrup and depart to the hive, to return again and again until the syrup is all harvested. By studying the line of flight followed by the bees, the hunter discovers the locality of their hive. Here, then, is a new difficulty for the tropic theory. It must assume that yet another form of unknown energy radiates from the syrup, and that toward this the bees are positively tropic when they are unladen.[4]

[1] Cf. Van Buttel Reepen, a high authority, who criticises and rejects Bethe's hypothesis as utterly impossible. "Sind die Bienen Reflexmaschinen?" Leipzig, 1900.

[2] Article in Boston *Evening Transcript*, June 4, 1921, on "The Technique of Bee Hunting," by Mr. E. K. Vaughan, an expert of large experience.

[3] When a bee has made several journeys to and fro between the hive and the box, she omits this spiral "locality study."

[4] Bethe himself has described similar facts, which in themselves suffice to refute his hypothesis. He describes how, when bees are carried some distance from the hive in a box and released, some, after flying about, will return to the box; and how, if the box be removed, some will return to the spot at which they made exit from the box, even though this is situated six feet above the ground. The farther from the hive was the place of release, the larger the proportion of bees which returned

7. Each hive must have its own peculiar form of radiant energy to which the bees of that hive are sensitively tropic, while they remain indifferent to the X-rays of other hives; for bees are in general faithful to their own hive.

8. The experiments of Lubbock and others on bees (some of which I have repeated on social wasps with similar results) show clearly that bees are guided by vision; for, when the appearance of the objects about the hive is altered in form or color, the return of the bees to the hive is no longer so unerring as it normally is.[1]

9. The difficulties of applying the tropic theory to the case of the solitary wasps returning to their nests must, one might suppose, make even the most determined behaviorist pause a moment to think. The theory would have to assume (1) that each wasp deposits in the nest she makes a source of radiant energy peculiar to herself (for hundreds of wasps sometimes have their nests within a small space over which they all wander freely); (2) that the wasp is negatively tropic to this form of energy so long as she has no prey; (3) that the possession of the prey reverses the sign of her tropism; (4) which is again reversed as soon as the prey is deposited with the egg in the nest. Truly, the behavior of the behaviorists lends some color to their theory; for it might well be maintained that the "tropic" theory of the "homing" of insects is the product, not of thought, but of the play of language mechanisms only.

The tropic theory is, then, impossible as an explanation of the homing of bees; it would therefore be obviously absurd to attempt to apply it to the solitary wasps. We have to reconcile our views of the mental powers of animals with the unquestionable fact that very many (even some as low in the scale as the

to that place. Bethe is, then, logically committed to the supposition that his unknown energy radiates not only from the spot where the hive has stood, but also from the place momentarily occupied by the box from which the bees are released. But he prefers even this wild absurdity to the supposition that the bees have a spark of intelligence of like nature with our own.

[1] In considering the facts, including those cited by Bethe, which he interprets as showing indifference to optical impressions, we have to remember that the vision of the bee with its faceted eye is very different from ours, lacking a focal area of foveal vision, and that the bee is probably guided by large areas of the visual field rather than by small features singled out of them. The question of the degree to which insects are guided by color and form (especially of flowers) has been much debated, and a vast amount of careful observation has been made. Professor Bouvier ("Vie Psychique des Insectes") sums up the results by saying: "Visual sensations of color and of forms certainly play a role of the first order in directing the anthophilous insects to the flowers." Again, he writes: "They know how to profit by acquired experience. When, in course of their researches, they have been led by chance or by their senses, either to sweetmeats on which they regale themselves, or to deceptive flowers [*i. e.*, flowers without nectar], they make use of memory of the places and appearances in order to return to the former and to avoid the latter." And: "Evidently the aerial insects have excellent and quicker topographical memory, to which without doubt the mosaic vision of their composite eyes contributes."

Limpet) have the power of finding their way home from greater or less distances, and that in the main this depends upon acquired familiarity with the area in which they wander, as does a man's power of returning home.[1]

This capacity for "homing" is one which, before all others, the mechanists are under obligation to deal with. We have seen how hopelessly Bethe's bold attempt has failed. To the best of my knowledge it is the only mechanistic attempt on the market. The return of the solitary wasp to her nest is rendered possible only through familiarity with its surroundings, acquired by the wasp in the course of her wanderings. It involves on a great scale *the application of past experience to the guidance of present action;* it is therefore intelligent behavior according to the almost universally accepted usage of the words "intelligent" and "intelligence." I do not suggest that the wasp, on leaving her nest, says to herself: "I must fly round about and take careful note of the position of this nest, so that I may be able to find it when I shall have caught the caterpillar I want for my grub to feed upon." The return to the nest is highly intelligent

[1] Messrs. L. B. Arey and W. J. Crozier have recently made a careful study of the "homing" of Onchidium, a mollusc which stands in the scale of organization at about the lowly level of the common limpet, and which, like the limpet, wanders over the rocks when the tide goes down, leaving exposed the homes or nests of the animals, which always occur between the high and low water marks. They report: "Onchidia return each to its own particular nest, even on much eroded rocks and where the nests are many and close together, and that in spite of the fact that the individuals emanating from different nests frequently mingle during their wanderings . . . over an area a metre in diameter." Further: "An individual taken from one side of its nest and placed on the opposite side, at a distance of a metre or slightly more, frequently exhibits little or no hesitation in turning and moving directly toward the nest." After considering all possibilities of explanation of these facts, including the tropic principle, they conclude: "We are therefore forced to the provisional opinion that an Onchidium returns to its particular nest by virtue of some internal condition simulating memory of the position of the nest in terms of its surroundings" . . . The homing "seems to depend mainly upon internal conditions akin to the remembrance of specific localities" (Proc. Nat. Acad. of Sciences, 1918). Doctor H. Piéron has made a similar study of the homing of limpets and comes to the conclusion that each limpet is enabled to return to its station on the rock surface over which it wanders when the tide covers it, in virtue of its acquired familiarity with the slopes and irregularities of the surface (C. r. Soc. de Biol., 1919). These observations refute completely the dogmatic assumption of Bethe and other mechanists that the limpet and its relatives must be supposed to be guided home by odor or other sense im-

behavior; and yet the intelligence is very strictly limited in its range and scope; it is Intelligence in bondage to Instinct. *Intelligence here serves Instinct, and its service is essential; without it Instinct would be of no avail.* This, as we shall see, is universally the relation of Instinct to Intelligence, and of Intelligence to Instinct. With the doubtful exception of those most machine-like instances of instinctive action (of which the egg-laying of the Yucca moth is the type), *we always find Instinct and Intelligence in intimate co-operation;* neither is effective without the other. If the further course of our inquiry bears out this formulation, we shall have to reject Professor Bergson's statement of their relation as a serious and very misleading error.

The wasp's circling about her nest before she leaves the spot is, we may feel sure, instinctive; it is a phase of a complex chain of instinctive action, each phase of which prepares for the next. But her noting of the features surrounding the nest is a mental activity which synthesizes the successively noticed details in some kind of a whole; and this experience produces in the wasp's mental structure some kind of change or development which persists and plays its part in guiding her return to

pressions from their own tracks. Lest my summing up of the facts of insect-homing may seem to be biassed, let me cite in support that of Professor S. J. Holmes, who is not a mere psychologist, like myself, but a zoologist of high standing. He writes: "The power of return exhibited by bees and wasps is shown pretty clearly by the experiments of Lubbock, Buttel Reepen, the Peckhams, Wagner, and others to depend upon the individual experience of these insects. The homing of insects takes place in essentially the same way as the homing of carrier pigeons, and involves an acquaintance with the locality gained by previous exploration." ("Animal Intelligence," p. 193.)

The problem of "homing" is by no means solved in all cases The homing of pigeons is still under experiment and discussion. Horses, dogs, and cats are commonly believed to have shown in some instances an inexplicable power of returning home over great distances in unfamiliar country. This possibly is a matter of the recording of the few fortunate successes among many random wanderings. The migration of birds still presents unsolved problems. If it be true, as often asserted, that the young birds of a species precede the older birds in migrating, none of the explanations suggested, except the hypothesis of what can only be called racial or inherited memory, would seem adequate to the facts. The golden plover oscillates between the extreme north and the south of the American continent, and follows entirely different routes when flying north and south respectively. This looks like racial memory. On the other hand, some individual birds have been found to return to the same spot after migration; this clearly implies individual memory.

the nest. And the preliminary exploring of the whole area of operations is a process of the same type, but of a more general, more varied, and more elaborate nature.

Other Instances of Intelligent Adaptation of Instinctive Action

Let us glance now very rapidly at some other actions of the wasps. Of all the solitary wasps *Ammophila* has been raised to the highest pinnacle of fame, owing to Fabre's fascinating description of her behavior and Professor Bergson's alluring interpretation of it.

Fabre has described how this wasp, which preys upon caterpillars, seizes her prey and, with marvellous precision, plunges her sting into the principal nerve ganglia, and thus paralyzes without killing her victim; how she then drags it to her nest and deposits her egg upon it, leaving it as a supply of fresh (because living) meat for the grub which will hatch from the egg. It is implied by both these eminent authors that, if the caterpillar were killed instead of being merely paralyzed, it would be useless to the grub, and that the whole cycle of instinctive activity would therefore fail to attain its natural goal.

Fabre would have us see in this behavior the direct intervention of the finger of God.[1] Bergson likens the powers displayed by the wasp to the skill of the surgeon, combined with the insight of the physiologist and the knowledge of the comparative anatomist; and he would explain this remarkable action by ascribing to the wasp an instinctive sympathy with the victim which teaches her just where the caterpillar is most vulnerable.

It seems to me that both of these eminent authors, in their enthusiastic admiration for the action of the wasp, have neglected to contemplate the action from the point of view of the caterpillar. However that may be, further study of this behavior has shown that neither Fabre's description nor Bergson's interpretation was strictly scientific; that the former was biassed by a theological conviction and the latter by a philosophical theory. For Mr. and Mrs. Peckham have observed and de-

[1] His language seems tc me to imply this very clearly.

scribed this behavior of *Ammophila* with minute care and admirable impartiality.[1] Their description shows clearly, (1) that the wasp does not always sting her prey precisely in the ganglia, but rather that, standing over her prey, she plunges in her sting at the joints between the segments where the cuticle is least resistant, and on the under side, where the sting most naturally comes in contact with the caterpillar (given the position of the wasp standing over her prey); and that she repeats the sting a variable number of times, in a somewhat irregular and variable series of spots; (2) that the caterpillar sometimes is not merely paralyzed, but killed; and in other instances is neither killed nor lastingly paralyzed, and that in either case the grub thrives upon its flesh, with seeming indifference to its putridity or its writhings.

The Peckhams' account is valuable also as refuting the theory of the chain-reflex. If Fabre's description were accurate for all cases, if the wasp always held and stung the caterpillars in exactly the same way, with the same sequence of movements, it would be plausible to interpret this series of movements as a series of chain-reflexes. But if (as the Peckhams' account shows to be the case) different individuals and the same wasps on successive occasions master the caterpillars by movements which are different in their sequence and direction on each occasion, the theory of the chain-reflex must appear less plausible; for this theory presupposes just such machinelike precision, regularity, and constancy of movements as Fabre has described.[2]

Consider another instance in which the Peckhams have supplemented the description of Fabre, with disconcerting results for him, for M. Bergson, and for the chain-reflex theorists.

Fabre has described how the wasp of a certain species, on bringing her prey near the nest in the ground which she has prepared, invariably lays it down near the entrance, enters the hole without it, and after a few moments emerges to seize her prey again, and drags it into the nest. On one occasion Fabre

[1] "Wasps, Social and Solitary," p. 25.

[2] The Peckhams write: "In this species, as in every one that we have studied, we have found a most interesting variation among the different individuals, not only in methods, but in character and intellect." *Op. cit.*, p. 22.

made the following experiment: As soon as the wasp had entered her nest, leaving her prey near the entrance, he removed the prey a short distance from the hole. The wasp came up, searched for her prey, and, having found it, dragged it once more to the mouth of her burrow, and again entered, leaving it at the mercy of the observer. Again he removed it to a little distance. Again the wasp emerged, sought and found her prey, and left it close to the entrance, while she performed the instinctive ritual of entering the nest "empty-handed." And this was repeated many times; until the patience even of Fabre was exhausted, and the wasp had her way. Oh, wonderful and inscrutable instinct! How radically different from and incompatible with all intelligent action! Shall we call it, with Fabre, the working of the finger of God; or, with the mechanists, an illustration of the chain-reflex principle? Or shall we, with Bergson, see in it an example of the complete divorce in the insects of Instinct from Intelligence? But wait! the facts are not all in.

The Peckhams repeated the experiment with a wasp of the same species. At first the result was the same. But the observers persevered again and again; and, after many repetitions of the comedy, the wasp at last omitted the "ritualistic" act, dragged her prey to the opening and, without laying it down, drew it into the nest. Oh, admirable co-operation of Intelligence with Instinct! After so many repetitions of the unintelligent instinctive routine, a little spark of Intelligence at last stirs, breaks through, and gives to Instinct just that help without which Instinct so often would fail. Was it that the American observers were more patient? Or that the wasps of the New World have gained a little in "cuteness" over their relatives in the Old? Or was it a matter of individual difference of endowment, or of happy chance? Who shall say? In any case the incident is but the most striking of many reported, which show that the sequence of actions of a typical chain-instinct is not absolutely fixed and invariable, as the theory of the "chain-reflex" requires that it should be. In this, as in so many other instances, the animal shows itself capable of omitting a phase, or of going back and repeating a phase, of varying in many other ways the usual sequence of actions and of adapting them to unusual circumstances; the wasp's intelligence enabled her to solve the unprecedented problem set her by the insatiable curiosity of Man.[1]

A few more instances of intelligent action, out of a multitude, must suffice. Wasps of a certain species choose for their nests the cavities of cut straws protruding from a straw stack. The straws they use are by no means always of the same diameter. The wasp (we are told by the Peckhams) which has chosen a straw of a particular diameter invariably chooses for her prey, among insects of very many sizes, one which is not too large to be dragged into the rigidly bounded nest. Does not this imply comparative judgment of size? Any one who has bought shoes for his children in their absence will appreciate the difficulty of the wasp's achievement.

Wasps of another species prey on spiders and always draw their prey into the burrow by walking backwards, with the spider held in the jaws. One such wasp, holding her spider by the ventral surface, was prevented from drawing it into her burrow by the resistance of the spider's spreading legs. She tugged hard and long, but in vain. At last she released the spider, took a new grip of it, this time by the dorsal surface, and then backed easily into her hole, the legs folding up like an umbrella.

One more example from the repertoire of the admirable *Ammophila.* This wasp makes her nest at the bottom of a sloping burrow dug in the earth. When she has deposited in it her egg and the necessary caterpillar (dead or alive, paralyzed or writhing), she proceeds to fill up the hole by tearing down loose earth from the walls and raking particles from the surrounding surface of the ground. When she has thus filled the hole flush with the surface, she smoothes it off neatly, so that neither mound nor hollow remains, stamping down the loose earth. On one

[1] Other evidence that the instinctive actions of the wasps are by no means rigidly prescribed, limited, and uniform is afforded by certain species which are parasitic upon allied species, in that, instead of hunting prey for themselves, they are content to lay their eggs upon the prey captured by their allies. whom they may drive away from it by a lively attack. But the most interesting in this respect are members of a species which (as described by Ferton) sometimes capture their own prey and sometimes make use of prey which has been captured by wasps of an allied species. (Cf. Bouvier's "Vie Psychique des Insectes," p. 162.)

occasion the Peckhams observed the following behavior: *Ammophila* had filled her hole, and the operation, the last of the cycle of activities, seemed to be nearly completed. She seized in her jaws a tiny pebble and with it pounded down the loose earth filling the mouth of the hole, repeating her strokes many times. Oh, wonderful *Ammophila!* What shall Fabre, or Bergson, or the mechanists say of this most irregular behavior, so upsetting to every theory—except the common-sense theory that Instinct and Intelligence co-operate most intimately and that, while the wasp has much Instinct, she has also some Intelligence. Here is *Ammophila* using a tool! A mode of behavior commonly regarded as the exclusive prerogative of man, and sometimes proposed as the defining mark of his species.

If the Peckhams' instance stood alone, perhaps it would be wise to dismiss it as a joke, a hoax, or an error of observation or of memory. But, unfortunately for the theological, the philosophical, and the mechanical theorists, it does not stand alone. Closely similar behavior, on the part of another member of the same species, has been minutely observed and described by an independent observer in a distant part of America. Are we then to regard each of these two wasps as a lively "bahnbrechende" genius, leading their species onward to the use of tools; individual sports comparable to the man, or ape, who first took a stone in his hand to crack a nut and so foreshadowed the genius of Nasmyth? I see no other plausible interpretation of the facts.[1]

I must pass over with only one comment the marvels of the social life of the bees and ants; for, as I said above, these are not yet sufficiently analyzed to be profitably discussed here. I would only point out that those who have studied them most

[1] Professor E. L. Bouvier, a most impartial and well-informed authority, writes as follows: "With their tropisms, their rhythms, their adapted manifestations of differential sensibility, above all, with power of transforming habits into automatisms, the insects are essentially animals of instinct whose activity is composed above all of automatic acts, but automatic acts dominated by the power of the brain. One may not see in them mere "reflex machines," for they know how to adapt themselves to circumstances, how to acquire new habits, how to learn and retain, how to manifest discernment; they are, one might say, somnambulists, whose mind awakens and gives proof of intellect when the need arises, and that removes them far from the mechanism of which Bethe is the protagonist." ("La Vie Psychique des Insectes," 1918.)

intimately are not to be found in the ranks of the mechanists. Lubbock, Fabre, Forel, Wheeler, Wasmann—these are lifelong students of the behavior of these insects; and though their interpretations differ widely, they are at one in rejecting the strictly mechanistic view.

Instinct and Intelligence Not Separable

The chief lesson I would have the student learn from the behavior of insects is that Instinct and Intelligence are not two diverse principles of action or of guidance of action. Instinctive behavior is indistinguishable from intelligent behavior by any outward mark. It is true that, when the same favorable conditions of the animal and of the environment are repeated, instinctive behavior is apt to be repeated with a regularity which gives it a machinelike air. But the same is true of intelligent behavior. If we have found the best way of dealing with a particular situation, then on its recurrence, if we are intelligent, we deal with it by the repetition of the same series of movements; as when we roll a cigarette or brush our hair. To do these things differently upon each occasion would add nothing to the evidence of our intelligence. When the circumstances of the creature are such that its instinctive actions do not immediately reach their goal, we see variation of direction and of mode and sequence of actions, with persistent effort. The behavior of the solitary wasps abounds in such variation and persistence in face of difficulties and failures to attain immediate success; for example, the varied modes of tugging, biting, and stinging the prey displayed by individual wasps, according to the size and shape of the prey and other circumstances of the task in hand. In some instances these variations astonish us by their effectiveness, their nice adaptation to the particular and unusual circumstances; for example, the seizing of the spider by the back, the omitting of the "ritualistic" act, the use of the pebble as hammer. These isolated acts are hard to interpret, though it is difficult to deny them the quality of intelligence.

More important are those forms of intelligent behavior which are displayed by all members of a species, and in which the past experience of the individual is unmistakably brought to bear in the guidance of present action. The return to the nest is the most striking and most abundantly illustrated of such actions. The tendency to explore the area for some days before making a nest; the tendency to make a particular study of the immediate neighborhood of the nest; the highly specialized capacity of all these species for organizing such experience in a systematic whole of knowledge of the area such as is implied by their return to the nest—all these tendencies and capacities are innate in the species. On the other hand, the knowledge of the locality which they acquire is not innate, but built up by many successive acts of perception.

How then shall we separate instinctive from intelligent behavior? We might perhaps say that the making of the locality study is instinctive, and that, when the wasp seeks her nest, the application of the knowledge so acquired is intelligent. But even this is an arbitrary distinction; for, in returning to the nest with her prey, the wasp is impelled by an innate tendency which is only awakened when the prey is secured, by an instinctive impulse of whose ultimate goal she perhaps has no foresight; yet this instinctive innate impulse can attain its end only when aided and guided by the acquired knowledge of the locality. Here, clearly, Instinct requires and implies the cooperation of Intelligence, and without its aid can achieve nothing of value to the creature or the species. And Intelligence operates only and always in the service of the instinctive impulses to action. This, then, is the relation of Instinct to Intelligence among the insects, which by common consent display Instinct in its purest and most typical forms. We shall see that the same relation obtains throughout the vertebrate realm, the human species not excepted.

CHAPTER IV

BEHAVIOR OF THE VERTEBRATES

The fishes are at the bottom of the vertebrate scale. Their behavior is predominantly instinctive; and, accordingly, it seems in many cases quasi-mechanical and unintelligent, as when the fish which has escaped from the angler's hook seizes the same bait and the same hook a second time after a brief interval. Yet every angler knows how wary are the trout in a much-fished river; and it does not seem possible to attribute this wholly to selection. And that fish are capable of "learning" is shown by those instances in which they learn to come to be fed at the sound of a bell Some fish have in some degree that capacity for returning to a particular spot which we have seen to be so highly specialized in the wasps; as those which deposit their eggs in some rude nest and then hover in the neighborhood keeping guard over them; and in those more doubtful but more striking instances in which fish are said to return to the same stream after migration to the sea, even sometimes to a stream, one of many, opening into a lake far from the sea.

The amphibia and the reptiles come next to the fishes in the evolutionary scale and lead on from them to the birds and mammals. In the mental scale they seem to rise but little above the level of the fishes.

In the birds Instinct is prominent. Their migrations, their nesting, their mating, their song, their modes of feeding and of seeking their prey or food, all these modes of behavior are in the main peculiar to each species; and they are closely alike in all members of the same species; sure indications of their strong instinctive basis. Yet striking instances of great modifications of all these modes of instinctive behavior in the light of experience are well established. The specific song is sometimes greatly modified by example; the parrot and other birds can even learn to utter words or human melodies.

Sea-gulls learn to follow the plough or the steamship; and in the severe winter of 1894 they learned to come up to London Bridge to be fed by the passers-by—an acquired behavior which has become traditional among them.

The carrier-pigeon, if released on successive occasions farther from his home, can be taught to return over great distances. In the presence of an abundant supply of some strange but suitable material, some birds have been known to use it in the construction of their nests, in place of the more usual matter supplied by nature. And almost all birds make nests in places to which they return after wandering freely over more or less extensive areas, sometimes after travelling immense distances; that is to say, they have that power of "homing" which among the wasps is so highly developed and which involves, as we have seen, the intimate co-operation of Instinct with Intelligence, of innate or instinctive impulse common to the species with knowledge acquired by and peculiar to the individual. M. Bergson has not told us to which of his two supposedly divergent lines of evolution the birds belong; to ask him the question is to refute his theory.

Recognition of Species, of Sex, and of Individuals by Birds

The problems of bird-behavior are innumerable. I will draw the student's attention to one of peculiar interest. How do birds recognize the members of their own species? And how do they single out their mates, to whom so many of them remain faithful for life? The second problem includes the former; we may concentrate upon it. Peculiarities of voice and of shape and of coloration are the main guiding marks for the recognition of species, sex, and individuals. Voice and plumage are in this respect more or less complementary; where the one is highly peculiar, the other is in general but little specialized.

Consider the case of the nightingale, the little brown bird, so insignificant to the eye, which, when it opens its throat, pours out a melody that enraptures the poets of every age. There can be no doubt that the biological function of this song is the attraction of the female to the male. In the spring of the year, the male birds arrive in the south of England from distant southern haunts, where they have passed the winter. Each chooses some dense coppice and there spends a large part of both day and night pouring out his song.[1] Some days or weeks later, the females arrive. Consider the behavior of a young female. Probably she has never yet heard the song of the male; or, if she has, it was when, as a fledgling, she was indifferent to it. When she comes within range of this sound, it affects her as no other sound can do. Among all the chorus of bird-song and the multitude of other sounds, this sequence of sounds alone attracts her. If she were guided to the male by odor, we might plausibly speak of "tropism." If she were guided by the monotonous repetition of some single peculiar note, we might try to explain her approach as a series of reflex reactions; and, if she might be supposed to have heard the note before, we might invoke the aid of "the conditioned reflex." But the song, the specific object to which she responds, is no simple sense-stimulus; it is rather a sequence of sounds (or vibrations) which, by the specificity of their temporal and harmonic relations, constitute a specific complex object. The specific response to this complex series of impressions implies just such synthetic appreciation of the series as is implied in that appreciation of a complex of spatially related visual impressions by which the wasp is guided to her nest. It implies *a synthetic activity of perception*, which alone, and not any mere sense-stimulus, can initiate the instinctive behavior of approach to the male. If it should be shown that any previous hearing of the song plays any part in determining this behavior, that would only illustrate once more the intimacy of co-operation of Intelligence with Instinct.

In many species of birds the male is distinguished from the female by splendor of color or by peculiarities of form, such as a crest or tuft or a great tail; or by both, as in the peacock. It seems as though, in such instances as the nightingale and the peacock, what began as a necessary recognition mark of sex had been developed into a display of beauty which allures the female more effectively than more simple notes or colors. And, though the evidence in such instances as the peacock is less clear than in the case of the nightingale, there can be little

[1] It is a common error to suppose that the nightingale sings only by night.

doubt that the pea-hen is prepared by Nature to perceive the splendors of the male and to be stirred by them. That again implies that, in spite of her very limited intelligence, she has at least this one capacity for complex perception. For the peacock's tail is anything but a simple "stimulus."

It seems to me that to speak of such complex objects as "stimuli" in the physiological sense is as seriously misleading as to speak of the responsive behavior of the female which they evoke, or the activity of the male which sets these objects before the female, as reflex actions, comparable to the knee-jerk. Their effect upon the female may be likened much more truly to the experience of a young man "bowled over" for the first time by the beauty of a maiden. The biological function of the nightingale's song can be understood far more fully and truly by him who has survived that strange experience than by one who has never suffered it.

In some species, notably among the pigeons, the cock-bird is not distinguished from the female by any marks perceptible to our senses; we find accordingly that the birds have the same difficulty as the pigeon-fancier in distinguishing the sexes.[1] The most expert fancier can distinguish the sexes only by observing their behavior, and not rarely he is deceived or in doubt for some time. The same is true of the birds themselves.[2] If two unmated pigeons be placed in a cage where they are separated only by a wire screen, the process of mutual recognition of sex may sometimes be observed to be tentative, gradual, and cumulative; and sometimes a hen-bird will play the male so exactly as to deceive for a time all observers, human and avian.

Among the birds, then, there are three principal kinds of sense-impression by means of which the male evokes in the female

[1] This fact is of interest as showing that birds do not distinguish the sexes by any occult sense-impression of a simple kind, such as an odor, which might escape our senses, and such as the tropists and the reflexists are bound to postulate.

[2] This difficulty has arisen again and again in the course of my large experience of pigeon-keeping. But I refer to Professor Wallace Craig's excellent study of doves ("Appetites and Aversions as Constituents of Instincts," *Biol. Bull.*, February, 1918, and a long series of papers in the *Journal of Animal Behavior* and elsewhere) for this and many other instructive observations. The keeping of domestic pets of various kinds should be recognized as an essential part of the education of a psychologist.

the train of instinctive behavior which culminates in her submission to impregnation by him; the vocal display, the display of plumage, and the display of antics. In all cases the display involves some activity on the part of the male; and in many species, as notably among the pigeons, the male is active in all three ways: he struts and bows and spreads his tail; at the same time he swells his splendid breast and from time to time coos in the manner peculiar to the occasion.

The female is prepared by nature to be affected in a specific manner by these displays of the male; they normally evoke in her the submissive attitude and behavior which are her instinctive role in the business of pairing; but not suddenly and fatally; her response is as unlike the knee-jerk or the scratch-reflex of the dog's hind leg as any action well could be; it exhibits all the marks of behavior in the highest degree. Only after many hours or days of active courtship by the male, does she at last yield to him. The peacock's tail or the nightingale's song may be called the "stimulus" to the pairing instinct of the female; but, if we so describe it, we are using the word in a sense very different from the physiologist's usage; as we might speak of the stimulus that comes to a man from a great example, from an ideal, from prizes, or from rivals.

Such a specific object, any object that evokes an instinctive response, may be likened more profitably to a key that unlocks a door. The key and the lock are unlike one another, but they are made for one another; each implies the other and is useless without it. The pairing instinct of the female bird is provided by Nature with a lock which can be turned only by a key of one specific pattern; the male is provided by Nature with that key. And the key is no magic formula, no mere "stimulus," that needs only to be presented in order that the door may swing open. The male must use the key with skill and persistency, adapting his actions to the various circumstances of the successive phases of his courtship. Nor is the opening of the door a simple process, like a reflex movement; the opening of the door lets out a flood of energy which impels the female to a train of activity of many phases, in all of which the male continues to co-operate.[1]

[1] Cf. Craig, *op. cit.*

In the case of the pigeons we see how complex is the pattern of the key used by the male, involving, as it does, the antic display, as well as the display of plumage and of voice, presented to both eye and ear of the female. The lock of the female's pairing-instinct is no simple one; it is comparable rather to one of those vastly complicated locks we sometimes glimpse in a banking house, the successful working of which implies not only the possession of the key but also the knowledge of its usage with a due sequence of actions.

These facts illustrate a fundamental truth which has been overlooked by very many of the writers upon Instinct. Instinctive activity is normally initiated by an activity of perception, more or less complex; the capacity for this activity is given in the innate constitution of the animal and is as essential a part of the total instinctive disposition (or instinct) as the capacity to execute the train of bodily movements which catch our eye. The first part of the instinctive response of the female is actively to perceive or appreciate the pattern of the key. If she were not endowed by nature with a lock of the required pattern for its reception, she would remain indifferent to the blandishments of the male, no matter how precisely the appropriate bodily movements might be laid down in her constitution, and no matter how strong her potential impulse to execute those movements. It is only because the store of energy and of movements has a lock which fits the key that that energy and those movements are set in train on the appropriate occasion; that is, when the key is skilfully applied to the lock.

This feature of instinctive behavior appears clearly among the solitary wasps. I did not insist on it in that connection, because the birds illustrate it more clearly. Since the wasps of each species prey only on animals of one kind—spiders, grasshoppers, caterpillars, or what not—it is obvious that the train of instinctive activity, which consists in seizing and mastering the prey and dragging it to the nest, is only to be set going by the specific object, namely, prey of the kind proper to each species of wasp. We cannot be sure what sense-impressions play the chief role here; but it seems probable that visual impressions are all-important, and that the key to this instinct in each species of wasp is the bodily form and characteristic movements of the specific prey, as appreciated by the vision of the wasp.

To return to the pigeons: the instinctive activity of courting culminates after some days in the act of sexual union (generally repeated several times) which results in the impregnation of the female. Then begins a new phase of activity, that of preparing a nest. This in turn presents two minor phases, the choosing of a suitable spot and the construction of the nest. When, after some days, this work is completed, the eggs are laid in the nest, and a third phase begins, the brooding or sitting, which continues until, after some three weeks, the young hatch out. Then begins the fourth major phase, the task of feeding the young, which continues for some weeks. This completes the cycle; after a short time courtship begins again, and the whole cycle of four major phases and of many minor ones is repeated. During each of these phases the two birds co-operate most fully. For example, during the sitting phase, about the middle of each morning the male bird approaches the nest, on which the female has been sitting continuously since late afternoon, and gently coaxes her to give place to him. She rises, steps out, stretches herself, seeks food and drink, and for some six hours leaves the business of sitting wholly to her faithful partner, while she enjoys her freedom.

There is something extraordinarily touching and beautiful in the partnership of such a pair of pigeons. In some cases it continues for many years and is ended only by death: a perpetual round of gentle, tender, graceful actions, all directed by the partners to one another and to their successive broods of young. It is disturbed only by occasional outbursts of fury, when either bird will fight in defense of their home, or the male will fight to the death in defense of his partner against some other aggressive male. But here we are not concerned with the æsthetic and moral implications of these forms of behavior. I will only say that, unless the angels are constituted very differently from ourselves, there must be more rejoicing in heaven over the life of one faithful pair of pigeons than over the human sinner who repents him of his vileness and cruelty.

Appetite as a Factor in Instinctive Behavior

Professor Craig has rightly drawn attention to the evidences of appetite in the instinctive behavior of pigeons. We know what we mean by the experience of appetite when we are hungry or thirsty or lustful. But at present we are seeking the objective evidences of appetite and some understanding of its conditions. The word "Appetite" as applied to animals, like the word "Instinct," denotes a general fact of their behavior; namely, that instinctive behavior of a particular kind cannot always be evoked even by the most perfect application of the specific key. A small boy may lead the horse to the water; but the most expert horseman cannot make him drink—or can do so only by keeping him under such conditions as will induce in him an appetite for water.

Hunger and thirst are the types of Appetite, as the common usage of the word implies. But it is probable that all instinctive action depends in some degree on Appetite. The beast of prey hunts only when he is hungry. The sated cat may allow the mice to play over her tail. The true dipsomaniac is indifferent to alcohol, until the fierce appetite springs up within him. In a similar way each major phase of the pigeons' cycle of reproductive activity seems to depend upon a corresponding appetite. An appetite for pairing comes upon them in the spring, and recurs on the completion of each cycle during the summer. At other times the female cannot be moved to respond to the approaches of the male; and the male does not normally make such approaches. When the pairing is completed, a new appetite begins to dominate the scene; sheltered corners and bits of stick and straw, which evoked no response during the first phase, are the keys which unlock the activities of the second phase. The nest and the eggs are the master-keys to the activities of the third phase; and the scene is dominated by an appetite for "sitting." With the hatching of the young, this slowly gives place to yet another appetite, namely, that for being pestered by the young and yielding to their clamor for "pigeon's milk." If in any phase of the cycle, owing to disease, old age, cold weather, or other untoward circumstance, the appetite fails, the whole cycle is deranged and fails to attain its goal.

How then do we judge of the presence of the appetite? What are its external or objective marks? First, the fact already indicated, namely, that only at certain appropriate times do the specific objects (the keys to the locks) excite the instinctive responses; the mechanism is there, but the driving power is lacking, the energy without which the turning of the key cannot set the wheels in motion.

Secondly, an appetite is apt to manifest itself in the absence of the key, the specific object, in a more or less vague restlessness; a wandering which, in the absence of prior experience of the object, is usually of a more or less random character, but which nevertheless seems to be vaguely purposive, a search for an object which is not definitely anticipated. It is as though the spring of energy which drives, or actuates and sustains, the train of activity of each phase of instinctive action were liable to bubble over among the motor mechanisms and to keep them in random activity, until the animal encounters the specific object; this object alone can direct the energy in the courses proper to the securing of the instinctive goal, by unlocking the door and allowing the overflowing energy to escape in the appropriate channels.

There can be no doubt that the appetite, the welling up of the energy of the instinct, is largely determined by the bodily metabolism and the various external and internal influences which affect it: temperature, food, chemical substances, especially those complex internal secretions that are called *hormones* or *endocrines.* And there can be equally little doubt that the evoking of the instinctive action, the opening of the door of the instinct on perception of its specific object, increases the urgency of the appetite.

In some instinctive behavior Appetite is a very prominent fact, notably in food-seeking. In other types it is less clearly manifested and is liable to be overlooked; as, for example, in the case of the combative instinct, which in some species seems to be always ready for action, though in others it clearly is subject to Appetite, at least to the extent that at certain seasons it is much more readily and intensively brought into play than at others.[1]

Some General Principles of Instinctive Activity

We have now reviewed so much of instinctive behavior that we may attempt to formulate some general principles.

First let us ask whether anything is to be gained by the use of the expression "an instinct"; and, if so, how the term is to be used and understood.[2] I have used it in the immediately preceding pages in writing of "the pairing instinct." And I have already tried to suggest the essential features of "an instinct." As I conceive it "an instinct" is a concrete fact of mental structure, which in the main we infer from facts of behavior and of experience. As we are dealing now with animal behavior, the facts of experience are also inferential; but, as I shall show, we have good ground for inferring them by analogy from human experience. I have already insisted upon the importance of this distinction between facts of mental structure and facts of functioning or activity. The use of the term "an instinct" or such a term as "the pairing instinct of this pigeon" enables us to observe this distinction faithfully. The critics of this usage object—But what do you gain by it? You say that the behavior of this pigeon during courtship and mating is due to the possession by the pigeon, and to the operation within it, of "this instinct"; but "this instinct" is nothing but a direct translation into static terms of the observed facts of behavior; the use of the word tells us nothing new about the behavior, throws no further light upon it.

My reply to this is: (1) The instinct does not reveal its whole nature in any one action, or in any one train of behavior. We build up our description of "this instinct" by observing the behavior of the same animal on a variety of occasions. This fact would provide some justification for the expression "this instinct." But (2) "this instinct" in this particular pigeon is only one example of the large class of similar concrete things, similar instincts each one of which resides in the constitution of one of the many pigeons of this sex and species. And we enrich our description and understanding of "this instinct in this pigeon" by studying the similar instinctive behavior of many other pigeons; just as we may build up our description of the structure of a

[1] Some authors, *e. g.*, Professor Drever ("Instinct in Man"), propose to separate appetites from instincts, as two distinct kinds of innate organizations. What I have said above may serve to show how impossible is this disjunction. Cf. on this W. Craig, *op. cit.*

[2] This is in accordance with popular usage, and there are good precedents for it among psychologists. William James, *e. g.*, among many others, adopts this usage. In my "Introduction to Social Psychology" I have used the expression and have attempted to give it a more definite meaning. The usage has been severely criticised of late, *e. g.*, by Professor J. R. Kantor (*Psychological Review*, January, 1920), and in a manner more intelligible to me by Mr. G. C. Field ("Instinct Psychology and Faculty Psychology," *Mind*, July, 1921). The principal point of his criticism is the assertion that to ascribe an action to "an instinct" throws no more light on it than to ascribe it to "a faculty."

particular flower by studying many specimens of that species. (3) We gain further light upon "this instinct" by a comparative study of the pairing behavior of pigeons of this species with that of birds of other species, and that of other animals and, not least, with that of the human species; where we are further helped by our own experience during courtship and by the experiences of other human beings, reported more or less indirectly in innumerable novels, romances, and poems. (4) We gain further light upon "this instinct" by a comparative study of instinctive behavior and experience of all varieties. Such study enables us to formulate some empirical laws or rules about instincts in general, which we can then apply to this particular instinct, with a view to discovering whether it does or does not conform to the rules; and we may use such general rules as hypotheses to guide our observations and experiments upon "this instinct." (5) We may gain further light upon "this instinct" by the purely biological study of Instinct, especially the study of heredity. For example, it has already been shown that some simple instincts seem to be transmitted according to the Mendelian laws; and it seems highly probable that, as these studies are carried further, we shall find that "an instinct" is a Mendelian unit-factor in the make-up of the constitution of the individual. If this probability should be generally substantiated, it would in itself justify and require the use of the term "an instinct." (6) Closely allied with the last is the light thrown upon "an instinct" as a unit factor by the comparative study of "strains" within the same species. For example, we find that some strains of the domestic fowl are good "layers"; while others are noted as good "sitters," and are not liked as "layers" because they so quickly and obstinately "go broody." Other strains again are distinguished as excellent mothers; while some of the good "laying" and good "sitting" strains are such poor mothers that their broods are in constant danger of disaster. These three phases of instinctive activity in the fowl, laying, sitting, and mothering, would seem to be independently variable in the species; and this goes far to justify us in ascribing them to three distinct "instincts"; and if it were found that each of these is transmitted as a Mendelian unit, it would be difficult to see how the most captious critic could continue to gird at "an instinct." (7) "An instinct" is an enduring feature of the constitution of the individual animal which has a life-history of its own. It comes into action (or readiness for action, waiting only for the appropriate circumstances, external and internal, for the turn of the key combined with the presence of appetite) only when a certain stage of the general development of the individual is reached; it undergoes further change and development in the course of its functioning; and it enters into enduring functional relations with other features of the mental structure; and, whether it comes into play or remains dormant, it eventually (in some instances at least) seems to fade away, or undergo involution, to the point where it cannot be brought into action by the most favorable conjunction of circumstances. (8) The physiologists also have something to tell us about instincts. They have shown reason to believe that each kind of instinctive activity of any species is bound up with and dependent upon the normal development and integrity of certain parts of the nervous system. It has, for example, been shown that instinctive actions of the mammalia are chiefly dependent on the basal ganglia of the brain (especially the *optic thalamus*); and there is good evidence that each of the principal forms of instinctive activity is especially dependent upon a particular small mass of nervous tissue within the basal ganglia. Further, the physiologists are showing us how certain forms of instinctive activity are favored and facilitated and supported by internal secretions or hormones; and it seems probable that each instinct is served in this way by one or more hormones which have no such specific effect upon other modes of instinctive behavior. (9) Therefore, when I speak of "this instinct in this individual pigeon," I am not merely translating into static terms the facts of its behavior which I have observed; I am rather implying a large body of knowledge built up by observation and experiment in many different fields. (10) It results that, when I point to some action of a particular animal and say "That is an expression of its pairing instinct, or of its fighting instinct, or of an instinct named in any other way"—I am not, as some critics suggest, merely using a circumlocution for the expression "that is instinctive behavior" or "that is due to Instinct." For my sentence implies far more, and to any one who has made any study of Instinct conveys much more meaning than the other sentences. Among other things, it implies on my part a considerable power of prediction about the further course of this behavior, which, like all scientific prediction, may prove to be faulty, but which attains greater probability the more our knowledge of Instinct in general, and of this kind of instinct in particular, is enriched by further observation and reasoning. I add the word "reasoning," because some of the critics of "an instinct" seem to be under the delusion that the science of behavior can be effectively built up by the mere accumulation of printed reports of observations of concrete facts of behavior.

Instincts as Springs of Energy

We may properly say that a particular instinct, such as the pairing instinct, is a feature of the innate mental constitution of a particular animal. We can infer the instinct with high probability, even though we know nothing more of the animal than its species and sex; just as the botanist, on recognizing the species of a flower, can tell us something about the structure and arrangement of its invisible parts and can predict with some confidence how they will grow and develop. For each animal species is endowed with certain instincts, just as each flower of a given species has certain parts or organs which characterize the species.

"An instinct" is a fact of mental structure, and we need some most general term to denote such distinguishable features of mental structure. We have rejected "idea" and "sensation" and other terms which are ambiguously used to denote facts of structure as well as facts of activity or functioning. The best word available, though it is clumsy, seems to be the word "disposition." In adopting this word as the most general term to denote all the functional units of mental structure, I am following good precedent, and am merely specializing for psychological usage a term of common speech, without seriously distorting its common meaning. And this is what we are compelled to do with many words of the common-sense and literary traditions, in order to build up our psychological terminology.

"An instinct," then, is a mental disposition, whose nature is revealed to us in, and inferred by us from, the modes of behavior and of experience which it determines. And we can confidently infer that the typical instinct is a complex disposition in which we may distinguish at least two principal parts. There is the part which renders possible the perception of the specific object (the key to the instinct); this part is the lock into which the key fits. Secondly, there is the part which determines the outflow of energy into all the bodily organs that take part in the instinctive activity.

Should we distinguish a third part? This is a very difficult question. We have seen how, when an instinct is excited in an animal, its behavior may involve a great output of energy and may exhibit great persistence; so that in extreme cases the animal perseveres to the point of exhaustion and even to death.[1] When the sense-organs of any animal are brought within range of the specific object of any one of its instincts an outburst of energy, of energetic action, even if it be only the maintenance of an attitude of alertness, is the general and characteristic result. Often there is an output of surplus energy, manifested in an excess of more or less random movements, in addition to the more specifically directed movements; as when the wasp buzzes excitedly about her prey or her nest; or when the terrier strikes the trail of a rabbit; or an unmated cock-pigeon is brought into the presence of a hen-bird. This excess of movement brings, no doubt, certain advantages, in the way of trial and error, which may lead to improved modes of behavior. When the conditions

[1] Many instances might be cited. I well remember a fine old pouter pigeon of my own, who, when his partner had been accidentally killed shortly after the hatching of a pair of young, persisted valiantly in the heavy task of feeding them. In spite of all efforts to assist him, the task proved too much for his declining strength and, before the young could feed themselves, he died, a mere mass of skin and bone.

are favorable for specifically directed actions, we commonly see such behavior sustained with all the energy which the organism has at its disposal. The creature seems to become wholly absorbed in the task in hand, in the pursuit of the natural goal of the instinct, and so continues until the goal is attained, or exhaustion supervenes, or some strong appeal to some other and perhaps stronger instinct is made. How are we to conceive this output of energy? Whence does it come? And how is it liberated?

The essence of instinctive activity seems to be such liberation and direction of energy, which perhaps we may best speak of as psycho-physical energy. We are naturally inclined to suppose that it is a case of conversion of potential energy, stored in the tissues in chemical form, into the free or active form, kinetic or electric or what not; and probably this view is correct. And we may legitimately speculate on the sources, the seat of storing and of liberation, and the mode of direction of the liberated active energy, in purely physiological terms.[1] But, since we are still so ignorant of the deeper secrets of the nervous system, it is best to formulate our description in the terms most consistent with the known facts and most serviceable for our psychological purposes. Two alternatives then present themselves. First, we might regard each instinct as containing a store of potential energy, which is liberated and directed into the appropriate channels when the instinct is excited, and which leaks or overflows in that restlessness which we have seen to be characteristic of Appetite. Secondly, we might regard the several instincts of an animal as somehow drawing upon a common store of reserve energy. There is much that requires or justifies the second view; and yet, if we accept this, we have to recognize that the several instincts do not draw upon this common store with equal

[1] I have put forward such a hypothetical description of the nervous conditions of this process ("The Sources and Direction of Psychophysical Energy," *American Journal of Insanity*, 1913). My suggestion was that each instinct is in part a sluice-gate in the system of barriers which dams back the energy liberated in the afferent side of the nervous system; that on stimulation of the instinct, on turning of the key in the lock, the sluice-gate swings open and makes the efferent channels of the instinct the principal outlet, "the final common path," for all available free energy. These sluice-gates are in the main situated in the *optic thalamus* of the vertebrate brain. This seems to me the most acceptable of any views suggested; but, like any other view, it is very speculative.

facility and freedom. For, some forms of instinctive behavior seem to involve as a rule a great, perhaps a maximal, output of energy; while others seem to be relatively feeble in this respect, and to be incapable of being excited to a degree which would involve any great output. Such a relatively feeble instinct is the "curiosity" of many species; while in very many species the mating instinct, the fighting instinct, and the instinct of escape seem capable of determining a maximal output of energy.[1] Some combination of these two views seems to be required, or something intermediate between them. We may best express the facts we are considering by saying that the excitement of "an instinct" evokes "an impulse" to action; that this impulse is variable in strength with any one instinct, according to the conditions (internal and external) of its excitement; and that the impulses of the several instincts of any animal are not capable of the same maximal strength. For we may observe how one instinctive impulse may overcome another, when they are simultaneously excited.[2]

Whether we conceive of each instinct as an independent store or spring of energy, or of all the instincts of an animal as drawing in various degrees upon a common store of energy and merely liberating and transmitting some proportion of this energy, when each in its turn comes into action, we may speak of the energy of the instinct, or of the energy derived from the instinct; and we may regard the felt strength of the impulse to action as in some sense a measure of the flow of such liberated energy.[3]

[1] Doctor W. H. R. Rivers suggests that every instinct obeys the "all or nothing" principle, *i. e.*, if it is excited at all it is maximally excited. This seems to me to be obviously untrue of many. (Cf. symposium on "Instinct and the Unconscious," *British Journal of Psychology*, 1919.) In his more recent book, "Instinct and the Unconscious," Rivers has modified his view by suggesting that the "all or nothing" principle holds good for some instincts, but not for others.

[2] Another way of expressing the same facts is to speak of the relative strengths of the several instinctive "tendencies"; but "impulse" seems the better word; impulse to action being something that we experience in ourselves as well as observe at work in others; and it denotes essentially a fact of activity; whereas "tendency" has the objectionable ambiguity, so beloved of psychologists, which enables it to be used to denote both facts of structure and facts of functioning.

[3] Though we have no guarantee that the correlation between the felt strength of the impulse and the flow of energy is a close one, our experience justifies us in assuming that it is in the main a positive correlation.

Those who like mechanical analogies may find some help in the following one. We may liken the dispositions which are the instincts of any individual organism to the following mechanical arrangement: Each instinct is represented by (1) a chamber within which a process of fermentation or other chemical change constantly liberates a gas, which accumulates under pressure. The several chambers communicate with one another by fine channels through which the gas can pass against considerable friction, when the pressure in any two chambers is different. (2) Each chamber has an outlet which branches into a complex system of pipes leading to a group of executive organs (nerves leading to muscles and glands). (3) This outlet is closed by a door or sluice-gate provided with a lock of more or less complex pattern peculiar to itself (in some cases it is a series of locks rather than a single one). This door is never quite gas-tight; gas leaks through, and leaks in larger quantity the higher its pressure in the chamber (appetite and the restlessness in which it is expressed). When the key is turned, the door swings open and the gas, issuing along the many channels, sets in action the various mechanisms to which it is led; and at the same time the relief of pressure in the chamber leads to a more rapid evolution or liberation of gas within it and to some drainage into it from other chambers. The key is the sensory-pattern presented by the specific object of the instinct (*e. g.*, the nightingale's song, the peacock's tail). The turning of the key is the act of perceiving the object. Such a mechanical model is inevitably inadequate in many respects to represent the psychophysical disposition. It might perhaps be improved by replacing the locked door by a spring valve, which is opened by the short arm of a lever, in proportion as the long arm of the lever is depressed by a strong spring attached to its free end. Such depression is prevented, when the mechanism is at rest, by a series of stops, each of which can be drawn back by touching a key on a keyboard (like the keyboard of a piano). The complete depression of the lever and the fullest opening of the valve occur only when a certain combination of keys is struck; the striking of some of these keys will permit a partial depression of the lever. The keyboard is the array of sensory-organs; the key is any natural object which will strike the appropriate combination of keys. To complete the analogy, we should have to suppose that the mechanisms actuated by the pressure of the released gas are such as will, under favorable conditions, change the set of affairs which determines the striking of the keys, so that a new combination of keys is struck; the new combination releases the lever from its spring and so allows the spring valve to return to the closed position, and perhaps actuates another lever opening another valve (as in the case of chain-instincts), and so sets a different mechanism in action.

This rude analogy, which likens the organism to an organ whose keys and stops are played upon by Nature, is, I repeat, wofully inadequate; but certainly less inadequate than the description of instinctive behavior as a series of simple reflexes and tropisms.

When an instinctive impulse is liberated or evoked, the organism becomes absorbed in the endeavor toward the goal of the instinct; its reaction to the exciting object is a total reaction; its energies are concentrated on the task in hand and the functioning of the various organs is subordinated to and harmonized with the dominant system of activity. This absorption of the organism in any particular task or mode of activity is what we call in ourselves "attention"; and that general excitement whose indications we observe in the animals, when their instincts are strongly excited, is what we call in ourselves "emotion." We may therefore define "an instinct" as an innate disposition which determines the organism to perceive (to pay attention to) any object of a certain class, and to experience in its presence a certain emotional excitement and an impulse to action which find expression in a specific mode of behavior in relation to that object.[1]

This formula will hold good generally only if we take the word "object" in the very widest sense, namely, to include not only material things and organisms, but also various situations in which the creature may find itself, consisting in conjunctions of internal and external conditions: for we must remember always that a large part of the sensory stimuli that play upon the sense-organs come from within the organism; and these constitute an important and constantly changing part of the total complex of sense-stimuli.

I shall illustrate and further justify this definition of "an instinct" on later pages. It may be, and often is, difficult to mark off a particular action or train of behavior as the expression of one instinct. But the difficulty is not one of principle, but rather one of practice. In principle it is legitimate to ask How many instincts has this species of animal? and to endeavor to define the objects or situations which will bring each one into play, the kind of behavior which each one will determine, and the kind of goal (or change of situation) which will satisfy the impulse and bring the train of activity to a close.

[1] We might attempt to enrich the definition by placing before the word "disposition" the adjective "mental," "physiological," "neural," or "psychophysical." Of these the last is, perhaps, preferable to the others, because it clearly implies that the disposition plays a part in determining both bodily action and the course of experience. If we use the adjective "physiological" or "neural," we should do so with the explicit understanding that it is not meant to imply the mechanistic interpretation of instinctive action.

The Life-History of an Instinct

Each instinct develops in the organism gradually and may express itself in partial and incomplete fashion before it is perfected. This hardly occurs in the insects, because they emerge from the chrysalis fully developed (or very nearly so). In other words, the insects have but little youth, that period of development in which skill and knowledge are acquired while the instincts are still slowly maturing. Such a period of youth, however, is not entirely denied to all insects. We have seen that the solitary wasps enjoy a period of free wandering before they begin their principal life-task, that of laying the eggs under conditions suitable for their development. This is their youth; during this period the instincts which determine the cycle of egg-laying, with its several major phases, are not yet mature, or they would begin to function. For the beginning of this cycle of activity is, so far as we can see, determined by no change in the environment, but only by the maturing of the instincts. During this period of youth the wasp is actuated in the main by the instinct of self-nutrition; she feeds herself and is indifferent to the small animals which later she will hunt on behalf of her grub; and during it she lays up that knowledge of the locality which is an essential aid to the operation of the system of reproductive instincts when they become mature.

In some few cases it appears that an instinct, if it is not excited or brought into play soon after the date at which it normally matures, fades away, or at least becomes incapable of being excited. A few such instances have led to the statement of a "law of transitoriness of instinct" alleged to hold good of all instincts. James taught that every instinct is essentially transitory; that it endures but a little while, during which it may determine the formation of "habits" of action; that, as the instinct decays, these habits take its place; and that, if no such habits are formed, the instinct passes away, leaving no trace behind. Assuming this theory to hold good of the human instincts, he based on it certain precepts for educational practice.

There seems to be no foundation for this theory, beyond a few striking instances in animal life, such as the instinct which leads the young lamb to follow its dam. And James's doctrine seems to involve a radical misconception of the nature and function of habit in human life. There are many instincts which clearly do not conform to this law of transitoriness. Wild birds, for example, hatched and brought up in captivity, kept perhaps in a narrow cage where they cannot even fly until long past their youth, will, when released, show all or most of the instinctive behavior proper to their species.[1] If James's generalization were true of all the human instincts, it would indeed be of vast practical importance. But all the great development of psychotherapeutics which has been achieved since he wrote tends to show its falsity. The element of truth which it contains is a very modest one, namely, that in the main the repeated exercise of any instinct seems to render it more easily excitable and to strengthen its impulse to action.

It is probably true to say in general terms that the exercise of all its instincts in normal degree is essential to the fullest vigor and health of any animal. The absence of such conditions as evoke or give scope to any one form of instinctive activity is probably detrimental in some degree to the organism's health and development; and we may infer that, if it were possible to prevent the excitement of every instinct, the young animal could not develop and the adult animal could not live. This is the ground of the difficulty of keeping and raising some wild animals in captivity. We have to recognize that the instincts of an animal are, as it were, its very essence and central core, all its bodily organs and functions being merely the servants of the instincts. A species is most completely characterized by its instincts, all its peculiarities of form, color, structure, function, and habit being subservient to and determined by them.

[1] In my own experience wild ducks, hatched and brought up in the poultry-yard with closely clipped wings, show a remarkable tendency to find any patch of water; and, when the wing feathers are allowed to grow in adult life, the birds will take to the wing and disappear into the wild, the habits of half a lifetime passed in the poultry-yard notwithstanding. Some domestic animals will display terror and violent efforts to escape at the smell of the lion or at the sound of his voice, encountered for the first time at a mature age. The pairing instinct in many species seems to survive all denials of opportunity. It is well known that many domestic animals will readily "run wild" or become feral, reverting to the life of instinct denied them in large part under domestication.

This is a fact too often overlooked in discussions of biological evolution. The evolution of the animal world is primarily a process of differentiation and specialization of instincts; this much-neglected truth is obvious when we reflect on such facts as the following: Horned cattle or antlered deer do not fight because they are provided with horns or antlers; the species develops these weapons in the service of the instinct of combat. The carnivore does not prey on animals because he has large teeth; his teeth and claws have been evolved, because his food-seeking instinct has become specialized in this direction. The seal did not take to the water because his legs were flipperlike and his body fish-shaped; he acquired these peculiarities of structure in consequence of his food-seeking instinct having become specialized for the pursuit of fish. The same is true of a thousand instances of shape and form and coloration, of bodily structure and function, down to the minutest details. The evolution of the animal world may properly be conceived as primarily and essentially the differentiation of instinctive tendencies from some primordial undifferentiated capacity to strive. It is this undifferentiated capacity to strive, this primordial energy, which M. Bergson has named *l'élan vital*, which others (notably Doctor C. G. Jung) speak of as the *libido*, and which perhaps is best named *vital energy*. We may regard the instincts as so many differentiated channels through which the vital energy pours itself into or through the organism.

Two (or more) instincts may be simultaneously excited. If their tendencies are not incompatible, behavior is then a blend of the actions characteristic of the two instincts, each being modified by the other. If their tendencies are opposed, we may witness a struggle, with alternation of the movements of opposite kinds, until one gains the upper hand. Or, when one instinct is in operation, an opposed instinct may be excited (although this is not so easily excited as when the animal is at rest) and may cut short more or less suddenly and completely, may inhibit, the other mode of behavior; in which case we may assume that the impulse of the second is stronger than that of the former.[1]

Degrees of Specificity of Instincts

The specificity of instincts, both on the receptive or perceptive side and on the executive side, is of very different degrees. An understanding of this is of the first importance, and to the lack of it is due much of the prevailing confusion about instincts. It is when an instinct is highly specific, or of highly specialized

[1] This seems to be an instance of the general law of reciprocal inhibition of incompatible movements.

structure on both sides, that instinctive action appears in its most striking forms, striking because relatively machinelike and unintelligent. This specialization is carried to the highest degree in many of the insects; it is for this reason that they are commonly regarded as the exponents of instinctive behavior *par excellence.* An example is that chain-instinct of the Yucca moth which prescribes minutely the series of actions by which the egg is deposited, actions which only occur when the required conditions (the specific characters of the flower) are present. It is clear that *the more highly specialized the instinct on both sides, the less scope is there for the play of Intelligence.* If it is very highly specialized on the receptive side, it can be excited only by the presence of just one particular kind of object; and any abnormality in the object results in failure of the instinctive behavior. And, in a similar way, a high degree of specialization on the executive side renders the animal incapable of attaining its natural goal, if in the course of its train of instinctive action it meets with unusual conditions; as when, for example, Fabre's scientific curiosity led him repeatedly to withdraw the prey from the entrance of the wasp's nest.[1]

On the other hand, *the less specialized the instinct, the greater the scope for and the demand for Intelligence to supplement Instinct.* In this respect the solitary wasps are intermediate between those insects of very highly specialized instincts (such as the Yucca moth) and the higher vertebrates. The instincts of the latter are so little specialized that to the undiscerning eye these animals may seem to have no instincts at all; because Intelligence plays so large a part in modifying instinctive behavior.

The instincts of the birds are in the main less specialized than those of the wasps; therefore their operations are more modified by Intelligence. But the modes in which Intelligence modifies instinctive action may be best studied in the behavior of the mammals.

Instincts and Motor Mechanisms

One other feature of instinctive action, one very difficult to understand, may be touched on at this stage. When a young

[1] F. 88.

bird becomes fully fledged, it takes to the wing and flies and perches with considerable accuracy. Commonly its first flights show some lack of the perfection shown after some little practice. It is probable that this is chiefly due to the bird undertaking its first flight, before the spontaneous development of the power of flight is completed. If it be prevented from flight for a few days longer, it exhibits on the first occasion a skill but little inferior to that of the much practised adult. In a similar way a young ground bird hatched but an hour or two will run about, preserving its balance and using its legs effectively; and equally early it will peck at small grains on the ground and pick them up with astonishing accuracy. Or a newly hatched duckling or water-fowl will take to the water and swim or dive in a manner that hardly permits of improvement by practice. Only birds that are hatched in nests built in safe places are nearly quite helpless in the first days after hatching; but even these will rise up in the nest, stretch out their necks, open wide their bills and squeak, when the parent approaches or the human observer roughly imitates the sounds of the approaching parent. All these actions are complex and involve the nice co-ordination of the contractions of many muscles. The mechanist naturally inclines to regard these as the very types of instinctive action and to concentrate his attention upon them to the neglect of all others. For they may easily be conceived as complex reflexes. The question we have to consider is, whether they are merely reflex, or are properly regarded as instinctive actions. In either case—What is their relation to the more complex forms of instinctive behavior, of which such bodily activities as walking, flying, swimming, and diving are partial constituents? For it is clear that, in such instinctive activity as the pairing or the combat of pigeons, or the capturing of its prey by a wasp, almost all the forms of bodily movement proper to the species may be brought into service; and that each major phase of instinctive activity may involve many of the same kinds of co-ordinated bodily movement as other phases. If we regard each distinct kind of innately co-ordinated movement as the expression of a corresponding instinct, we shall have to say that the major instincts somehow make use of the minor instincts.

Some writers, notably Mr. A. F. Shand,[1] have taken this line, regarding each form of co-ordinated bodily movement that requires little or no practice for its execution as the expression of "an instinct." Shand's position has this further peculiarity that he confines the term "instinct" to these innately organized motor dispositions and describes as "emotional dispositions" what I am describing as the major and typical instincts. Shand has kept in view chiefly the behavior of men and mammals; I think that, if he would turn his attention to the birds and insects, he would see that his position is untenable. Professor Lloyd Morgan has taken a similar line in face of this problem.[2] He proposes to recognize instincts of at least three levels. He would call "lower-level instincts" all the innately organized nervous structures, concerned in the production of co-ordinated bodily movements, which I propose to distinguish from instincts as mere motor mechanisms. Secondly, all the instincts that I recognize as such he would call "mid-level instincts." And he would recognize a third class of instincts of a higher level, of which class he names two only, namely, "self-preservation" and "race-maintenance." I venture to think that these alleged "higher-level instincts" are fictitious; each of them is in reality a group of instincts, and neither group is in any sense a functional unity. All that is common to the instincts of either group is that they contribute to self-preservation or to race-maintenance. Clearly both food-seeking and escape from danger are activities that contribute to self-preservation. I can see no justification for lumping them together to make a single "high-level instinct." Both of them contribute directly to race-maintenance also; as when the parent seeks food for her young, or leads them to take cover.

But that way of stating the facts seems to me erroneous. I see no reason why these complex co-ordinated movements should be regarded as the expressions of so many distinct instincts. In my view they are essentially the expressions of motor mechanisms; the execution of each such movement presupposes a complex motor mechanism in the nervous system, comparable to that which in the brainless dog may determine "progression" movements of the legs, or the scratching movements of the hind leg, so long as suitable stimuli are applied to certain sensory surfaces. Possibly each such motor mechanism[3] is connected with sensory nerves and sense organs, by stimulation of which it

[1] "The Foundations of Character."

[2] "Instinctive Dispositions," *Scientia*, October, 1920.

[3] These motor mechanisms are made up of nervous elements which reside very largely in the cerebellum; and all the evidence we have goes to show that the cerebellum is immediately concerned neither in impulsive action nor in experience. On the other hand, the cerebellum is always found to be large in proportion to the number and complexity and delicacy of co-ordination of the motor mechanisms of which the species normally makes use, and especially so when these involve delicate adjustments of the balance of the whole body, as in flying and swimming; thus it is proportionally large in the birds that catch insects on the wing and in the porpoise,

may be thrown into action (as in the case of the scratch-reflex mechanism); though we have evidence of this in a few instances only, which possibly are exceptional.

We have to regard such motor mechanisms not as instincts, but merely as the instruments of the instincts. Each one is what the physiologists call a "final common path," and as such may serve as the channel of outlet for the energy liberated from any one of the instincts. No doubt each instinct discharges more readily into some one motor mechanism than into others; but it is capable of discharging into others, and under appropriate circumstances will do so. Thus the combative instinct of the pigeon most immediately discharges itself into motor mechanisms which effect an aggressive approach to the enemy on foot, followed by pecking and striking with the wings when he comes within range. But, if the enemy takes to flight, the angry bird may pursue him on the wing and renew the attack on alighting. In a similar way, the pigeon startled when on the ground takes immediately to the wing; but, if startled when perched in or near the nest, he merely assumes an alert attitude and utters a subdued warning note; and he takes to flight only if the startling object becomes more immediately and powerfully threatening. These seem to be instances in which the same instinct makes use under different circumstances of different motor mechanisms; and they are typical of all instinctive behavior.

Observation of the ways in which the various motor mechanisms are first used by young creatures bears out, I think, this view that they are not to be identified with instincts, but rather require some instinctive impulse for their actuation. In other words, they are in themselves inert mechanisms which require to be "driven" by some impulse, by a stream of energy derived from some instinct; just as an electric motor is an inert mechanism which requires to be driven by a stream of energy generated and directed elsewhere (though by turning its wheel by hand the whole mechanism may be put in movement—a case comparable to the reflex excitation of the scratch-reflex).

If you watch a young pigeon almost fully fledged, you may observe that its first flight, the first actuation of the motor mechanism of flight, is undertaken not for its own sake, but in the course of its clamorous pursuit of its parent; that is, in the service of its food-seeking impulse; or perhaps when it is escaping from the attack of some hostile cock-bird. In a similar way, the first pecking of the newly hatched chick seems to be not a mere reflex in response to the optical stimulus of a small grain, but rather the actuation of this particular motor-mechanism by the impulse of the food-seeking instinct: this impulse may express itself by means of other mechanisms also; as when the chick runs to and fro, and especially when he runs to his mother as she scratches the earth and gently calls him with a specific note.

This principle, that *any one instinctive impulse may make use of a variety of motor mechanisms*, according to the circumstances of the moment, is no doubt difficult to understand or interpret in terms of the mechanistic hypothesis, *i. e.*, in terms of reflex mechanism; but it seems to be a fact, nevertheless, and unless we recognize it and take it fully into account, we meet with insuperable difficulties in attempting to interpret instinctive behavior.

How Is an Instinct Defined If Not by Its Motor Expressions?

We may raise at this stage, also, a still more difficult question. If one instinct does not always express itself in the same kind of bodily activity, but rather may actuate or make use of several different motor mechanisms in succession, according to the circumstances of the moment, how are we to recognize the goal of the instinct, and how define the instinct and mark it off from others? Obviously, if every instinct always expressed itself by setting in action some one motor mechanism peculiar to itself, or several in a given order, there would be no difficulty in defining the instinct; and also the path of the "mechanist" would be made comparatively smooth, for one of the principal distinctions between instinctive and reflex action would be lacking. Is there, in fact, any stable position between the mechanist's identification of instinctive with reflex action and the mere attribution of actions to "Instinct" written with a capital letter? I think there is. "An instinct" is to be defined and recognized, not by the kind of movements in which it finds expression, but by the kind of change of the animal's situation which its movements, whatever they be, tend to bring about and which, when it is achieved, brings the train of behavior to a close. Thus the nature of the instinct at work in an animal cannot be recognized by simple observation of its movements. You may see one pigeon pursuing another assiduously from place to place; but these varied movements of locomotion and pursuit may express either the combative instinct, or the pairing instinct, or the food-seeking impulse of the young pigeon. Yet there can be no doubt that these are distinct instincts, whose operation is attended by appetites requiring very different situations for their satisfaction. Unlike reflex action, instinctive action strives toward a goal, a change of situation of a particular kind, which alone can satisfy the impulse and allay the appetite and unrest of the organism. We must, therefore, define any instinct by the nature of the goal, the type of situation, that it seeks or tends to bring about, as well as by the type of situation or object that brings it into activity.

We shall see that this principle requires very careful handling in connection with some problems of human instinct. For example—What degree of generality may be assigned to the goal of an instinct. The majority of the psychologists who recognize any human instincts postulate "an instinct of imitation"; and they continue to do so in spite of the fact that no such instinct has been shown to exist in any animal species, and in face of the fact that, if this instinct exists in man or any animal species, its goal can be defined only as the performing of any action witnessed by the imitator. In the same uncritical way, many psychologists continue to postulate "an instinct of play" in man and many animals. This kind of "instinct psychology" may fairly be likened to the "faculty psychology" which we all profess to repudiate with scorn. So far as I can see, to say that play (or imitation) is due to an instinct of play (or imitation) differs not at all from saying that it is due to a faculty of play (or imitation); whereas to say that the wasp's pursuit of her prey of a particular kind is due to an instinct to provision her nest with that kind of prey is very much more than to say it is due to a faculty for pursuing prey. If the reader cannot at first glance see any distinction between the two cases, I would advise him to ponder the problem; perhaps after some years of psychologizing the distinction may become clear to him.

CHAPTER V

THE INSTINCTS OF THE MAMMALS AND OF MAN

Few will deny that the lower mammals are largely governed by Instinct; but, when we consider the behavior of an intelligent house-dog, the role of Instinct is not so obvious. We are apt to discern Instinct when we see him performing some utterly useless action; such as scratching the carpet and turning round and round, before lying down to sleep in a familiar corner. But most of his actions seem so intelligent that the instinctive factor in them does not clearly appear; and, reading our own experience into him, we are apt to interpret and explain his actions in terms of emotions, or emotional experiences, which we attribute to him. Thus we say that he is barking loudly at the intruding stranger, because he is angry; or that he is running away with his tail between his legs, because he is afraid; or that the mother-dog tenderly licks her puppies and anxiously watches over them, because she loves them; or that the hound crouches humbly at a word from his stern master, desisting from the wildest pranks or the most absorbing pursuits, because he stands in awe of him. And in all such cases we rightly feel that we have in some sense explained the dog's behavior and that, if we are right, we in some sense understand it.

Motives and Intention

Notice that we interpret human behavior in a similar way. Suppose that you are sitting in a concealed spot near a lonely road, and that you observe an acquaintance, X, walking alone along the road. Suppose, further, that you see a needy-looking man coming in the opposite direction; that, when the two meet, they stop and exchange some words; and that X puts his hand in his pocket, hands some money to the other man, and passes on. How will you interpret that behavior of X? If he is well known to you, you may interpret his behavior with some confidence. But, if he is a stranger or a casual acquaintance, and if you have observed nothing more than the facts described, you will be at a loss. You will be able to infer that the man begged alms of X, and that X gave them; further, you can infer that X, when he put his hand in his pocket, intended to find a coin and to give it to the beggar. About his intention, then, you are clear. But what about his motive? That remains problematic. Here we have a clear illustration of the obvious fact that motive and intention are entirely distinct facts. Yet many psychologists and some lawyers deliberately confuse them, or assert that a motive is merely an ulterior intention. There is no distinction of more importance for the understanding of behavior; and he who has not grasped it can be neither a good lawyer nor a good psychologist.[1] If X, when he put his hand in his pocket, had pulled out a pistol instead of a coin, and had put a bullet through the other man, the question of motive would have become a matter for the lawyers to discuss. The intention to shoot at the other man might be confidently assumed, though the motive remained absolutely unknown.

On seeing the coin given, at least three possible motives might be guessed with equal plausibility. You might guess that X was a timid person and that he gave the coin because he was afraid of the other man, afraid of being assaulted by him if he refused to give. Secondly, you might guess that X was a pitiful or kindly man, and that he was moved to give by pity. Thirdly, if you were "inclined to be cynical," you might guess that X is a man who likes to feel himself superior to others and who enjoys any situation that enhances his feeling of superiority to others and their sense of his power over them. You might formulate your interpretations by saying, in the first case, that the act of almsgiving was due to fear; in the second, that it was due to pity; in the third, that it was due to pride: that is to say, you would explain the action by attributing it, not to an instinct, but to an emotion—just as in the case of the dog. In each case you would be assigning an emotion as the motive of the action;

[1] Of course, for the consistent mechanists motives are fictitious or illusory; there are only physical and chemical stimuli and mechanical responses.

and, in so far as your guess was a good guess, you would have explained the action as completely as the psychology of the common-sense tradition can pretend to explain it. Of course, your explanation might be less simple; you might guess that all these three emotions were at work together, that X was a little bit afraid, a little bit compassionate, and a little proud, all at once; and, if he were a stranger to you, it would be safest to assume some such mixed motives or emotions.

Now, if you had observed from a distance only the outward action of X, your guess would be a mere guess; you would merely be naming one or more of the emotions which your general knowledge of human nature would lead you to suppose might be evoked in any man by the appeal of the beggar. But, if you were in a position to observe X closely during the incident, you might be able to make your guess with much greater confidence. If, for example, you had observed that, as the beggar approached X, the latter looked up and down the road and all around, that his hand shook a little as he handed out the coin, that his voice trembled, his face paled, and that he walked on at a faster pace afterwards, you would feel pretty confident in assigning fear as the dominant emotion of the moment and the chief motive of the act. If X's face had assumed an air of kindly interest, if his voice and gestures were gentle, if he moved on slowly, looking back again and again at the beggar, your diagnosis of pity would be confidently made. If X had pulled out his coin and handed it over with an air of condescension and had walked on with his nose in the air and a cheerful complacency reminiscent of Jack Horner, your diagnosis of pride or vanity would be assured. Or you might have detected symptoms of all three emotions in X; a shaking of the hand, a tear in the eye, and an air of condescension and complacency; when you would feel that his motives and his emotions were mixed. If now you approached X and asked him—"Why did you give a coin to that beggar?" you might get any one of several answers. He might say—"I think it right to give alms to the needy," or give some still more sophisticated reply. But, if he were a child or a blunt honest man, he would possibly say: "Because I was afraid of the beggar; he looked capable of any desperate act", or, "Oh, I couldn't help feeling sorry for the poor devil. I know it's not right to give money to wayside beggars, but I couldn't help it." Or, if he were a person quite unusually honest and interested in self-analysis, he might say—"Well, do you know, I really believe the humble way he came up and cringed to me made me feel so big and rich and benevolent and lordly that I just had to do it." In each case, if the statement agreed with your observation of symptoms of emotion, you would feel that the question of motive was solved. If the reply did not so harmonize, you would feel sure that it was at best only partially true. And, if you felt so convinced, you would not, unless you were a very naïve and ignorant person, necessarily infer that X was a liar or that he intended to deceive you. For you would know that it is very difficult to be sure of our own motives, at least as difficult as it is to give just the right name to our emotion at any moment.

When you had extracted some such answer from X, you would have gone as far as common sense ever goes in the pursuit of motives. If you were a lawyer examining X in court, you might try to show that his statements were untrue, by catching him in some inconsistency; or you might try to discover what sort of character and reputation the man bore. If you could show by an array of testimony that he was a notoriously timid man and one who had never been known to perform a kindly action, you would establish a presumption in favor of fear as the motive, and against pity—and so on.

What could psychology contribute to the solution of this psychological problem, one of a type with which we all have to deal in practical life, and with which we do deal more or less successfully on the whole? Well, in face of the concrete problem, it could not do very much. If you had studied psychology, you might have observed the indications of X's emotions a little more fully, accurately, and analytically; and, when you put your questions to him, you might have formulated them a little more searchingly. And, if at the critical moment you could have examined him closely, with the aid of a laboratory full of apparatus, you might have counted his pulse and respiration, noted other peculiarities about them, recorded his blood-pressure curve, determined the amount of adrenalin or sugar in his blood, and so on; and in these ways you might have made the diagnosis of some particular emotion a little more surely.

The psychologist could do little more than any intelligent man, in face of the concrete problem of behavior. But let it not be inferred from this that psychology is a useless purely academic game. The professed student of any other science would be in much the same position, when confronted by a concrete problem. Suppose, for example, you show to a geologist a volcano in eruption, and you say to him: "Now, you are a geologist, you know all about volcanoes. Tell us just exactly why this volcano is erupting at this moment." Your geologist would not be able to answer your question forthwith. Yet that would not prove him incompetent nor his science utterly useless. It would only seem so to the "practical" man. The geologist could tell you much about the general principles of volcanic action; and he could set about the study of this particular volcano and, after much labor, arrive perhaps at some probable explanation of the immediate causes of this eruption and, perhaps, predict with fair degree of confidence the further course of its eruptions.

The limitations and the possibilities of the psychologist in face of any concrete eruption of human nature are similar. He can give some statement of the general principles of human nature and action; and, after studying the individual, he can exhibit the particular action as an instance illustrating and conforming to those principles.

Common Sense and Motives

The cases of canine and human behavior we have imagined illustrate a very important fact, namely, that common sense identifies emotions with motives. Common sense, when it has named correctly the emotion dominant during any man's action, holds that it has explained the action, made it intelligible, in general terms. If any further explanation is required, it must take the form of explaining why that man experiences and displays that emotion under the circumstances of that moment. This stage of the explanation involves the description of his "character"; and an adequate understanding of his character can be attained only by considering both his hereditary constitution and the course of his development. It is in this second stage of the explanation that psychology should be of service.

It is a principal feature of this book that, in this all-important matter of the explanation and understanding of human behavior or conduct, it holds "common sense" to be in the right; and it holds many of the psychologies and philosophies of the past to be in the wrong, because they have rejected the common-sense procedure and offered in its place a variety of fantastic theories. We have seen already what some of these theories are. There is (1) the theory of reflexes and "conditioned reflexes," which was elaborated by Herbert Spencer and has recently been furbished up again as "behaviorism." There is (2) the theory of "ideas," which, when applied to the explanation of conduct, takes the form of the "ideo-motor" theory, and asserts that this mysterious unintelligible something called an "idea" is a motive force as well as a mosaic of bits of "consciousness." There is (3) the pleasure-pain theory which dominated British psychology and social philosophy for several generations, under the name of "psychological hedonism." It asserts that pleasure and pain, or the desire for pleasure and the aversion from pain, are the motives of all human conduct. And, not content with the utter inconsistency of this theory with a thousand obvious facts, many of its exponents have combined with it the obscurities and absurdities of the "idea theory" and have asserted that "the idea of pleasure" or "the idea of pain" is the motive of all action. Then (4) there is the theory which explains all human action by saying it is due to "The Will;" though what "The Will" is and what is the relation of the "willed" acts of human adults to the behavior of animals and children it has never made clear. There is (5) the theory that all human conduct is the expression of "Reason"; and this theory is in the same position as the theory of "The Will"; and both are remnants of the Faculty Psychology of the eighteenth century. Lastly, there is (6) the theory that all human conduct is determined by "The Unconscious." This, the latest and most fashionable fad in psychology, is a new development by medical psychologists of the theory of Schopenhauer and Ed. von Hartmann. All these are interesting exhibits in the museum of psychological antiquities and curiosities. The beginner may safely stand at a little distance and view them with the respectful curiosity due to every historically interesting object, while still preferring explanations of the common-sense type. In this book it will be my chief endeavor to show him how the common-sense explanation may be refined and made more definite and systematic

Instincts and Emotions

We have seen that, in face of the behavior of such an animal as the dog, we are apt to invoke explanations of two kinds. When his behavior is like our own, and seems to express any emotion such as we ourselves experience, we are content to ascribe it to that emotion; as when we say that the animal is impelled by anger or fear or curiosity or disgust. When it is very unlike our own and expresses no emotion that we can recognize by its expressions, we ascribe it to Instinct. And, in either case, we recognize that a little dose of intelligence may modify the impulsive power of emotion or of instinct. On contemplating the behavior of birds, we are more ready to invoke Instinct and less ready to infer Emotion; for the greater difference of bodily structure and mode of life renders our recognition of their emotions more difficult and ambiguous than in the case of the mammals nearest to ourselves. Yet common sense and the literary tradition do not hesitate to ascribe to the birds emotions not utterly different from our own. The insects being still more remote from us in structure and mode of life, common sense invokes Instinct only; for, though it does not fail to see signs of emotions in insect behavior, it rightly judges these to be so unlike our own that they cannot safely be given the same names and cannot profitably be assigned as the motive powers of their actions.

What, then, is the relation between these two principles of action that we invoke to explain animal behavior, so long as we are not sophisticated by psychological theories? Are Emotion and Instinct two distinct principles of action; impulsive powers of two different orders? Common sense hardly seems to think so; for in some instances it seems to identify an instinct with an emotion, by giving them the same name; notably in the cases of fear, curiosity, and disgust.

Suppose that psychology, instead of turning away with scorn to devise fantastic theories which cannot be brought into any intelligible relation with the common-sense type of explanation, should accept this clue offered by common sense and work it for all it may be worth. Might we not hope to find that common sense, the wisdom of the ages, is fundamentally right, and that its practice is capable of being developed into a consistent and useful theory?

This was the line taken in my "Social Psychology." [1] For the first time the cue offered by common sense was frankly accepted as a working hypothesis. Emotion was regarded as a mode of experience which accompanies the working within us of instinctive impulses. It was assumed that human nature (our inherited inborn constitution) comprises instincts; that the operation of each instinct, no matter how brought into play, is accompanied by its own peculiar quality of experience which may be called a primary emotion; and that, when two or more instincts are simultaneously at work in us, we experience a confused emotional excitement, in which we can detect something of the qualities of the corresponding primary emotions. The human emotions were then regarded as clues to the instinctive impulses, or indicators of the motives at work in us. Guided by this hypothesis, I attempted to sketch the instinctive basis of our active nature and its development, under experience and education, into character. Some psychologists have explicitly accepted this scheme for the development of common-sense psychology; but very many, in view of difficulties that arise in the course of its detailed application, have rejected it. Yet I hold fast to the scheme as essentially on the right lines; my confidence in it has been strengthened chiefly by two facts. First, it has been found useful in several fields of practice, notably in education, medicine, and industry. Secondly, its critics have nothing to put in its place but one or other of those six theories (enumerated

[1] "An Introduction to Social Psychology," first published in 1908.

on p. 126), all of which I find to be obscure and unintelligible or grossly inconsistent with many facts of observation.[1]

The Common-Sense Cue Justified by the Theory of Evolution

We return now to the study of mammalian behavior with this clue in our hands. Whenever we observe in an animal signs of emotion which we feel able to interpret with some confidence, we may accept that as an indication of the working of a corresponding instinct. And, whenever we see an animal aroused to some train of instinctive activity, we may assume that it experiences some emotional excitement; and we may endeavor, though often with little success, to interpret the action sympathetically in terms of emotion.

That we may thus interpret the behavior of the higher animals with considerable confidence is shown by the fact that those who practise such interpretation and rely most upon it achieve the greatest success in their practical dealing with animals; the hunter, the herdsman, the horseman, the trainer of dogs, and the tamer of wild beasts, all proceed on this principle, however little they may have formulated it in explicit propositions. The success of this practice is the best evidence of our near relation to the animals; better even than the discovery of morphological homologies of their parts and organs with ours. If the behavior and the emotions of the dog and the horse and the ape were as obscure to us as those of the bees, we should, in spite of all morphological homologies, hesitate to accept the theory of the continuity of human with animal evolution. But, in face of this success, we cannot deny our continuity of nature with our humble relatives; and the theory of evolution affords the best explanation of that continuity.

In the days before Darwin, when evolution was merely a wild speculation accepted by few, it was not unreasonable to assert that animals are guided by Instinct and man by Reason; for each species was regarded as specially created and independently endowed with such faculties and organs as seemed best to its

[1] I do not stop to criticise each of these theories in detail. I shall point out incidentally on subsequent pages some of their shortcomings.

Creator; and Man was endowed with Reason, in place of all the many different instincts with which the various animal species were endowed.

It is strange that this view should have survived the Darwinian revolution and that to-day it should still be necessary to argue against a mass of professional students of human nature who, while not denying that animals are guided in the main by instinct, fail to see any evidence of the part played by instinct in human life.[1] For it would be strange indeed if Nature, after successfully evolving through many millions of years all the wonderful varieties of nicely adapted animal behavior on the principle of Instinct, had suddenly deserted this principle for another, had thrown the instincts of our prehuman ancestry on the scrap heap, and had made a new start on a new principle. And such a reversal of policy by Mother Nature would seem the more strange, when we see how, even far down the scale of animal life, Intelligence co-operates so beautifully with Instinct, remedying its defects and supplementing its inefficiencies, widening its scope and range of application; and how, as we approach Man in the animal scale, the evidence of this supplementing of Instinct by Intelligence and of their harmonious co-operation becomes ever clearer and stronger.

The Parental or Protective Instinct

In reviewing mammalian behavior, we must begin by considering the role of one great instinct, Nature's brightest and most beautiful invention, the *parental instinct.* The systematic zoologists have rightly seen that the suckling of their young is the all-important and characteristic feature of the life of mammals. Not the anatomical fact of the possession of milk-secreting

[1] During the past few years there have appeared many articles which attack the view that human nature comprises instincts, or maintain that any human instincts are of little or no importance for adult life. I have replied to some of these critics in an article in *The Journal of Abnormal and Social Psychology*, 1922 ("The Use and Abuse of Instinct in Social Psychology"), pointing out that this adverse negative attitude toward human instincts arises in the main from the confusion of instincts with mere motor mechanisms. The distinction between them is all important. It will be developed in the following pages.

glands, but the psychological fact of the use of them, is all-important.

It was this "invention" which alone rendered possible the development of a highly intelligent species, such as *Homo Sapiens*, and which also gave to his nature, conduct, and institutions all that is truly admirable in the moral sense. And if, as has been claimed, the birds contain the potentiality of a mental and moral development rivalling that of man, it is only because they also (or most of them) are endowed with the parental instinct. It is no exaggeration to say that this one instinct is the mother of both Intellect and Morality. For, without it, Intellect could not have been evolved; and its impulse is the only truly altruistic element in Nature; and, though many philosophers have ignored the fact, the moral tradition, by which all moral character is shaped, could never have been built up without this altruistic factor.

Among the mammals this instinct is part of the natural endowment of the female sex in all species; for the suckling of the young is its simplest and primary expression, without which the mammary glands would be useless and the young could not live. So much activity on the part of the mother as is necessary to the suckling of the young is an expression of the instinct common to all species. The particular movements and attitudes by which suckling is achieved vary from species to species, according to the bodily form of the species and the degree of activity of which the young are capable. But more than suckling is necessary in most species. The mother wanders in search of food; and either the young wander with her, as in most herbivora, or they lie snugly in some hidden nest or lair, awaiting her return. In the former case the mother and young must keep together. They achieve this by the aid of special powers of vision, hearing, and smell, and of recognition marks, visible, audible, or olfactory, which are so many locks and keys to the instincts of parent and offspring. In the other case, the mother must return to her nest after all her wanderings in search of food; and so she shares with the wasps the capacity for "homing," that is, for acquiring familiarity with, or knowledge of, the wide area in which she roams; her maternal instinct thus requires the large co-operation of intelligence, of acquired knowledge. This is one chief reason for the superiority of the carnivores to the herbivores in respect of intelligence, a superiority only partially offset by the requirements of the gregarious life of the latter. The carnivorous mother's instinct commonly impels her to bring home her prey to her young; in this work the male of some species co-operates, and then the family is founded.

It is from the apes that we may hope for most light on the instincts of the human species. Unfortunately, we know little about them. Yet we do know that in some of them the parental instinct is very strong, prompting the mother to carry her young with her in almost all her roaming through the trees, and on occasion to defend it with the utmost fury and desperation. Thus the arboreal life demands of the mother-ape more continuous contact with her young and more unremitting care and toil than any other animal-mother displays. This, rather than any structural peculiarity, such as the prehensile tail or paw, was the prime condition of the evolution of Man.

The external skeleton of the insects compelled their ontogeny to take the form of the grub, the chrysalis, and the metamorphosis which launches the fully formed insect on its independent life with all organs complete. It was necessary, therefore, that, when so launched, the insect should have matured all the instincts of self-maintenance, and that these should at once come into play. And this, as we have seen, is the rule among the insects. This inevitable consequence of metamorphosis is very prejudicial to the development of Intelligence. For instincts which are to operate before the animal has had time and opportunities to accumulate experience must be fully, precisely, and more or less rigidly organized, on both the receptive and the executive sides; a condition which permits little scope for the modification of instinctive dispositions by experience. In other words, this necessity for precision of instinctive behavior, independently of prior experience, prevents the insects from enjoying a period of youth; except in a very limited degree, such as that of the short period in which the solitary wasp wanders freely, before beginning her major task of egg-laying.

Youth is essentially the period of free development during

which the young creature, freed by parental care from the full responsibilities of self-maintenance, can afford to play and to experiment and, by so doing, to build up a rich body of experience. Only the young creature whose prime needs (food, shelter, warmth, and protection) are cared for by the parental instinct can enjoy such a period of youth in any full sense. The young so cared for have no need for instincts mature at birth. Their instincts may ripen at leisure and come into operation at such intervals after birth as may be most conducive to a rich and varied experience. And they do not require instincts precisely organized and nicely fitted to the various objects and situations with which the adult animal will have to deal. Rather, the young animal that enjoys a protected period of youth requires instincts which, though capable of generating powerful impulses to action, are relatively general or non-specific on both the receptive and the executive sides. The type of instinct that is most serviceable to them is one which can be brought into play by a wide variety of objects or situations conforming to one general type or presenting some feature in common, though widely different in other respects; one which impels them not to actions precisely adjusted to deal with one type of object alone, but to actions conforming to a general type.

Instincts of just this general or non-specific type we find among the mammals. The carnivore, unlike the solitary wasp, does not prey on one species of animal only; rather his instinct is so generalized that it impels him to pursue any living moving thing of suitable size. And, when he has seized it, he does not master it by means of any one series of narrowly prescribed movements, which would be suitable to one form of prey only; rather, he displays a great range, variety, and freedom of movement, adapting his actions to the form and behavior of each kind of prey. Instinctive behavior of this kind is clearly rendered possible only by the period of youth, passed under parental care. For such relatively general or non-specific instincts absolutely require the co-operation of a considerable body of accumulated experience, if they are to subserve the serious tasks of life. And the longer the period of youth, that is, of relative incapacity under parental care, the richer the experience which co-operates in the pursuit of the goals prescribed by the instincts.

Accordingly, we find that the longer the period of youth the higher is the development of Intelligence, and the more obscured by Intelligence is the operation of Instinct. And in Man, in whom youth is prolonged for so many years, the generality of instincts and their dependence upon and overlaying by Intelligence reach such a point as to obscure the existence of the instincts from the eyes of Man himself, especially those of sophisticated men.

But Man, though he is Nature's most favored child, was not constructed by her upon any new principle. He is only one among her many marvels, though the greatest of them; and in the structure of his mind, as in his body, there are no elements and no principles that she has not used again and again in those less exalted achievements which we call the animals. In making Man she did but compound the same elements more subtly and with greater skill and success; and especially she pushed her greatest invention, the parental instinct, for all it was worth. And behold! Man slowly diverged from the animals, stood up, looked round on the world, and saw that it was both good and bad—and the moral conflict began.

And when the college student of the twentieth century pockets the harmless necessary check, and with patience and good-humored tolerance accepts the accompanying admonitions, he is but co-operating in Nature's most successful experiment, the development of Intelligence by the agency of the parental instinct. So let him not be too squeamish in accepting that parental aid; if a post-graduate course of study will really further his intellectual development, let him feel that Nature bids him pursue it, even at the cost of continuing to accept parental care in the sublimated form of a check.

Among the lower mammals, the development along this new path has gone but a little way. Instinct still rules and Intelligence halts. Such a creature as a rabbit is still obviously but a bundle of instincts; and the parental instinct does little beyond providing food and shelter for a little while. But, when we come to the carnivores, we see a considerable advance; the young are more helpless, youth is more prolonged, parental care more diversified. And the instincts themselves are so modified as to aid in the development of Intelligence; as when the parent, instead of providing merely milk or dead meat, brings home the living prey on which the young may feed, acquiring, in so doing, experience which later will supplement in a hundred ways their highly general instincts.

We cannot attempt a complete examination of the mammalian instincts. We must be content to notice some which are of greatest importance and widest distribution, to try to assign the natural goal and the natural occasion of the activity of each of these, and to note the principal ways in which these instinctive reactions are modified by experience. Let us begin with the parental instinct itself.

The Working of the Parental Instinct

The litter of young is the natural object that evokes the parental activity; but not the young as inert objects merely. Doubtless their odor plays a part, but far more important is their behavior. The instincts of the parents and of the young are reciprocally adjusted, as we have seen so clearly in the pigeons. The mother offers her teats, and the young respond by actively seeking them (aided no doubt by smell) and by actively sucking. The mother calls for silence and immobility, and the young lie still. The young cry in distress, and the mother rushes to them. As they grow stronger and begin to stray, she lifts them in a way which does no harm, and, in spite of protesting squeaks, lays them back in the nest. And, when she herself enters the nest amidst the writhing mass of young, she so regulates her movements as to achieve the apparently impossible and avoids hurting any one of them. In all species it is, above all things, the cry of distress from the young which most powerfully and certainly evokes the maternal response; a response which is no mere reflex (conditioned or unconditioned), but which from the first adjusts itself to the circumstances of the moment, and may consist in offering the teat or licking clean the young, in carrying it back to the nest, or in driving off the intruder with fierce threats or actual attack.[1] Shall we, on contemplating this behavior, follow the behaviorists in refusing to speculate on the nature of the mother's experience while she performs these offices? It is true that we can never know with certainty what exactly that experience is; just as you can never know with certainty the nature of the experience of another man. The difference is only one of degree, and the justification for attempting to understand that experience is the same in both cases; namely, that *the more fully and accurately we understand it, the better we shall understand the accompanying behavior, and the better we shall be able to foresee and to influence both the experience and the behavior that must ensue.*

When a human mother sees another suckling or comforting her infant, she knows, with as good warrant perhaps as any human knowing, what that other woman feels. When we see a mother-animal gently moving among her young, feeding them, guarding them, responding to their signs of distress, patiently suffering many things and laboring incessantly on their behalf; always showing signs of complete satisfaction, as each phase of her activities completes itself, and acute restlessness and anxiety when her efforts fall short of success; then we may infer with a high degree of probability that the human mother who "sympathizes" with her is not altogether mistaken. And, when we notice how in so many ways the behavior of the human mother most closely resembles that of the animal-mother, can we doubt that the principles of explanation required for the two cases are essentially similar? That, if the animal-mother is moved by the impulse of a maternal instinct, so also is the woman? To repudiate this view as baseless would seem to me the height of blindness and folly; yet it is the folly of a number of psychologists who pride themselves on being strictly "scientific."

[1] The specific effect of the cry of distress is well illustrated by the following description by Professor W. Köhler of the response evoked by the distressful cry of a chimpanzee separated from his fellows: "It happens often enough that, if the cage of the isolated animal can be reached, one or other of the group will quickly spring to it and embrace the complaining one through the bars. But the latter must actually cry and howl (*heulen*) in order that this friendliness shall be shown him; as soon as he becomes quiet the rest of the group remain unconcerned." ("Zur Psychologie der Schimpansen," *Psychologische Forschung*, 1921.)

Among many carnivora the parental labors of the mother are shared by the male. Where he plays an essential part, there the family exists. In all species in which the male does not share in the parental labor, he seems to be entirely devoid of the parental instinct; and in almost all such species he shows no particular attachment to or constancy to one female. But in those species in which the males co-operate, they must be credited with some share of the parental instinct. In almost all cases, and even among such birds as the pigeons, the care given by the male is less intimate and less constant than that of the mother. These facts in themselves serve to show that the parental instinct is entirely distinct from the pairing instinct; although of course the two instincts have that kind of dependence which consists in the necessary precedence of pairing to the exercise of parental care. But the behavior of the two instincts has nothing in common; and in their strength and distribution they are independent variables.[1]

The parental instinct of the higher mammals shows that lack of specificity which characterizes all their instincts, and whose importance we have seen. A female cat or dog will feed and cherish, not only her own offspring, but even those of widely different species; a fact which implies lack of specificity of the instinct on both the receptive and the executive sides. But no one, I think, has reported a case of a rabbit mothering a kitten, or of a sheep adopting a kid, or a cow a foal. And this lack of specificity is carried a stage further by the monkeys and apes; and to the highest level by the warm-hearted woman in whom the maternal instinct responds most delicately to any young and helpless creature, especially if it shows signs of distress

This extension of instinctive responses to objects other than the specific or natural object of the instinct implies something more than the lack of specificity mentioned above. The lack of, or low degree of, specificity is merely a permissive condition of such extension. The extension involves a positive mental function or capacity of the utmost importance, namely, the

[1] I can see no slightest justification for that confounding of the parental with the pairing instinct which is one of the foundation dogmas of the Freudian psychology. If I am right in regarding these two instincts as separate and distinct units of our constitution, at least half of what has been written by the Freudians falls to the ground.

capacity of being affected by one aspect or feature of a complex whole in the same way as by the whole itself. We shall see in a later chapter that this function is essentially involved in all the higher flights of the mind, and is of the essence of all that we call reasoning. At the level with which we are now concerned, its exercise does not involve a conscious singling out or discrimination of the aspect, quality, or feature of the object to which response is made.

In my "Social Psychology" I have maintained that the protective impulse of the parental instinct is a truly altruistic factor and the only altruistic factor in human nature; that from its prompting all truly altruistic striving, directly or indirectly, proceeds. The proposition is so important for social and ethical theory, and the reality of any altruistic factor has been so frequently denied or ingeniously explained away, that it is worth while to cite evidence of it in the anthropoids. Köhler (*op. cit.*) writes as follows of a sick young chimpanzee and a female not his mother: "One day when he seemed to be rather better, the young one was allowed again into the open place where the others were eating green stuff. With difficulty he crawled towards them, and after a few steps he collapsed on the ground with a piercing cry of distress. Tercera was sitting chewing, a little to one side. She sprang up; all her hair stood out with excitement; with a couple of great bounds in the upright position she sprang to his side, her face all anxiety, her mouth distressfully pouting, and uttering cries of sorrow (*Trauerlaute*); she seized the prostrate little one beneath the arms and labored strenuously to bring him to the erect posture. No one could behave in a more *motherly* manner than this chimpanzee on this occasion, and I give these words expressly their full significance." Further, Professor Köhler describes how, when one animal is punished, others will display a tendency to interfere: "It was especially the feeble little Consul who would come hurrying up and (in the way in which young chimpanzees express all urgent wishes) lift up one arm to the attacker with beseeching mien; if one still did not release the chimpanzee undergoing punishment, he would seek to hold one's arm with all his strength, and finally would begin, with angry gestures, to beat the big human." [1]

A very striking fact, which reveals the predominantly instinctive nature of all parental care among the animals, is the indifference shown by the parents as soon as the young cease to need and to demand their care. It seems probable, though so far as I know the experiment has never been made, that, if the young could be kept young and helpless and clamorous for food and care, or if, for example, young birds in a nest could be constantly substituted by others of the same species a few days

[1] It is necessary to point out that Professor Köhler is not merely a hunter or trainer or lover of animals, but an academic psychologist of the highest standing, and that he writes his description with full sense of responsibility and of the meaning of his words. Further, he has enjoyed opportunities of studying a group of chimpanzees in captivity such as no other trained observer has had.

younger, the parents would continue to respond indefinitely.[1] It is the key operated by the young which keeps open, or repeatedly opens, the door of the parental instinct; and, when the key is no longer applied, the instinct sinks into quiescence; though in rare instances some appetite may be displayed, as when an animal that has no offspring seems to make efforts to adopt those of another.[2]

The Instinct of Combat

Let us consider now the notorious fact that a mother will fight in defense of her young. There are, I suppose, exceptions to this rule. I have never observed any indication of this tendency in the mouse or the rabbit; and among birds some mothers seem to be innocent of it. But, among all animals that display pugnacity under any conditions, any threat to the young seems to be the surest excitant of such behavior; and many animal-mothers, like some human mothers, will fight with the utmost fury against overwhelming odds and in face of the most certain destruction from which they might easily escape by flight.

Some species are provided with special organs of combat; and in each species the movements and attitudes of combat are common to the species and often are characteristic of the species. Many animals assume a specific threatening or warning attitude, or utter cries of the same nature, before actually attacking.[3] I make no distinction between attack and defense. Nature knows well that attack is the best mode of defense; and the two cannot be distinguished in animal behavior. The threatening attitudes and cries obviously serve to warn off intruders, or to intimidate them. These attitudes and the modes of attack are clearly, in the main, unlearned and innately prescribed; but they are not the mere reflex agitations of as many motor mechanisms.

[1] We have an approximation to this in the way a hen continues to lay eggs when the eggs laid are removed day by day, and in the way a cow continues to give milk when her udders are regularly emptied by "milking."

[2] It has often been remarked that among the laboring classes a similar indifference on the part of the parents often supplants their tender solicitude, when the children no longer need their constant care. This is a perfectly natural consequence of the fact that, as the child grows up, he gradually loses those qualities which appeal directly to the parental instinct.

[3] Cf. W. Craig, "Why Do Animals Fight?", *International Journal of Ethics*, 1921.

The train of action, once initiated, exhibits in the highest degree the characteristic marks of behavior or purposive action. It is spontaneous, persistent, varied, total, directed, anticipatory, and perceptual. Such combative behavior seems, then, to be instinctive. But, if so, are we to regard it as one of the expressions of the parental instinct? That would, I think, be improper. Similar combative behavior may be displayed on many occasions, when the young are not concerned; and it is displayed more readily by the male of many species than by the female, and by males in which the parental instinct seems to be entirely lacking. Notably, any interference with the food-seeking impulse, or with the pairing impulse, is liable to evoke this behavior. And the behavior generally expresses, in an unmistakable manner, an emotional excitement as different as possible from the tender feeling that seems the proper accompaniment of all operations of the parental instinct; namely, the animal displays anger, rage, or fury—these being three names for three degrees of intensity of this emotion.

If we try to enumerate and describe the various objects or situations which provoke the combative behavior of such an animal as the dog, in which the impulse is strong and lively, we shall find that they are extremely various. Yet they all have this in common: the combative behavior and signs of anger are evoked by the behavior of any other creature that tends to thwart or obstruct him in the pursuit of any natural goal, that is, in the working out of any instinctive train of behavior. Whether it be the pursuit of his mate or of his prey, the gnawing of his bone, the guarding of his home, the assertion of his superiority over his fellows, or, most striking of all, the effort to escape by flight from a superior aggressor, single or collective, the dog will fight angrily if hindered or obstructed in any of these instinctive activities. Wherever we look in the animal kingdom, the same rule seems to obtain: in general terms, the stronger the impulse at work in an animal, the more readily is the angry combative behavior evoked by any obstruction from other creatures, if the species is at all capable of this response.

Combative behavior is, then, the expression of an instinct which is peculiar in that it has no specific object; the key that opens its door is not a sense-impression or a sensory pattern of any kind,[1] but rather any obstruction to the smooth progress toward its natural goal of any other instinctive striving.[2]

The natural goal of the combative impulse, toward which it tends and the attainment of which alone allays it, may be adequately defined as the getting rid of the obstruction which evoked it. This it does most commonly by driving away the obstructive intruder; it goes on to destroy him, only if he does not yield to the threats or the first attack.[3] The instinct is, then, one which, like so many others, normally operates in two successive phases, involving different bodily attitudes and movements, the phase of threatening and the phase of attack. It is true that the actions of the two phases are often intermixed or blended in some degree; yet, though the attitudes of the threatening phase are largely of the nature of preparation for attack, they commonly include certain features proper to this phase and of no direct value in the second phase. Swelling of some part of the body, the erection of hair or bristles, lashing of the tail, are among the actions peculiar to the threatening phase. But the most widely used are sounds produced by the voice or other means;[4] the noisiness of the first stage of combat contrasts dramatically with the silence of the second, when the combatants are locked in deadly struggle.

Shall we say, then, that the normal course of combat involves the successive operation of two distinct instincts, one of threatening and one of actual struggle? This question is of much importance; for a similar one arises in connection with many forms of instinctive behavior. Especially the instinct of escape presents the problem in an acute form, so that some authors speak of

[1] If it be true that the mere display of a patch of red color before a bull will provoke him to rage, this would seem to be an exceptional instance.

[2] We may perhaps interpret this relation physiologically by imagining the disposition of this instinct to be related to all other instinctive dispositions in such a way that it is a channel of overflow for energy banked up in any one of them.

[3] As Craig (*loc. cit.*) points out, the instinct is satisfied by the retreat of the intruder in almost all instances. This is true of beasts of prey, as well as of the herbivora; but in their case it is often difficult to distinguish the working of the combative from that of the preying impulse. To this peculiarity of the combative impulse is due the success of the precept to lie perfectly still when escape from an angry beast is impossible, and also the truth of the saying "A soft answer turneth away wrath."

[4] In accordance with the principle, to be noted below, that a sudden loud noise is the most universal key to the fear instinct.

a group of "danger instincts,"[1] rather than of a single instinct. Of course, if we regard an instinctive action as nothing more than a reflex action, and "an instinct" as nothing more than a sensori-motor reflex arc in the nervous system, we shall have to recognize in every train of instinctive behavior the operation of a multitude of instincts. It is this way of thinking, adopted more or less explicitly, which has led several authors to recognize far more instincts in man than I am prepared to admit. Professor Thorndike's discussion of the human instincts illustrates the consequence of accepting that principle.[2] He recognizes some forty human instincts; and the consistent application of the principle would compel us to recognize a much larger number. On the other hand, Mr. Shand's[3] acceptance of that view of instincts (the identification of instincts with motor mechanisms) is combined with the recognition of the fact that we cannot explain human behavior as the mere conjunction and succession of such a multitude of reflex actions; he sees that we must recognize some larger purposive co-ordination of the motor mechanisms which he regards as instincts; and so he is led to the peculiar view that the innate constitution of man comprises, besides a multitude of these so-called instincts (motor mechanisms), certain innate dispositions which he calls "the emotional dispositions." When we attempt to apply this way of thinking to animal behavior, we see at once how unworkable it is. For example, applying it to the pigeons, we should have to say that many instincts displayed during the first phase of their reproductive activities are governed by a "pairing emotion"; those of the second phase by a site-choosing emotion and a nest-building emotion; those of the third phase by a "sitting" or "brooding" emotion; those of the fourth by a "nutritional emotion" or a "feeding-of-the-young emotion." And, applying it to the solitary wasp, we should have to say that, in securing her prey, she is governed in turn by a "prey-seeking emotion," a "prey-seizing emotion," and "a return-to-the-nest-laden-with-the-prey emotion." To do this would be to fly in the face of all common usage of the words, without bringing any advantages, but rather confusion only. We have to recognize two distinct types of bodily movement among the higher animals, namely, the mechanical or quasi-mechanical reflex and the purposive instinctive action; and I cannot see that anything is to be gained by introducing a third category of actions, the emotional. Mr. Shand, if he would consistently carry through his scheme, should cease to use both the terms, instinct and reflex, since he identifies the things denoted by them. He would agree with me in recognizing only the two categories of action, which he would call reflexes and emotions, but which I prefer to call reflexes and instinctive actions.

The Instinct of Curiosity

A succession of phases of action is common to the operation of all instincts, save perhaps the very simplest. Let us consider this fact in connection with an instinct which in most of the mammals operates in relatively simple fashion, namely, the instinct

[1] *E. g.*, Doctor W. H. R. Rivers, "Instinct and the Unconscious."
[2] "Educational Psychology."
[3] "Foundations of Character."

of *curiosity*. This instinct is in a sense the opposite of the combative instinct; for, whereas the operation of the latter normally supervenes upon that of some other instinct, curiosity is commonly displayed as a prelude to some other mode of action. Yet, in another way, the two instincts are of similar type; namely, in that curiosity, like the combative instinct, has no specific object, is not called into activity by objects of any one type only, but rather by any object or situation which involves a certain feature, namely, imperfect apprehension or perception insufficiently clear to invoke any other instinct.

The goal toward which this instinct strives is fuller apprehension or clearer perception, perception definite enough to determine some other instinctive reaction.

The object (using this word again in the widest way to include every kind of perceptible situation) that is to excite curiosity must have some degree of resemblance to objects that normally evoke some other instinct, or it will fail to draw the attention of the animal; but, under the particular conditions of the moment, it must present so much of novelty, or of the unusual, as not to excite that other instinct or to fail to excite it in full strength.[1]

The service to the animals of this instinct is obvious; namely, it determines fuller perception and so leads on to appropriate action. It is naturally through the distance-senses, eye, ear, and nose, that curiosity is chiefly, perhaps always, evoked. And the sense on which an animal chiefly relies for discovery of its food or avoidance of its enemies is that through which its curiosity is most readily evoked. The display of curiosity normally proceeds in at least two phases—a phase of approach to the object and a phase of closer examination by one or more channels of sense. During both phases the specific reactions which more definite perception may evoke are apt to show through, as it were, complicating the behavior proper to curiosity. The horse approaches the strange ill-defined object on

[1] Cf. Mr. W. T. Hornaday's description of a mountain sheep which stood for some twenty minutes fixedly gazing at the spectacle of a horse bearing on its back the horns and skin of a large sheep. ("The Manners and Habits of Wild Animals.")

the ground, circling round it, with eyes, ears, and nose on the alert, starting away in retreat and again approaching. Movement of ill-defined objects makes perhaps the most universal appeal to this instinct. Hunters and trappers learn to play upon it, studying the responses of the various species they have in view. The omnivorous monkeys, preying upon and preyed upon by so many other creatures, display this instinct in great strength and versatility; and this feature of their constitution was probably of the first importance in leading them on in the scale of intellectual development. For no other instinct gives so great scope for the exercise of discrimination and the co-operation of reflective judgment. The attitude of curiosity is essentially one of suspended judgment; and that is the beginning of wisdom, of questioning, of further examination, and of explicit judgment.

The Food-Seeking Instinct

That animals seek their food instinctively is a fact generally recognized. In all cases their organs are adapted to the intake and digestion of food of the kind they instinctively seek. It is a fair assumption that all forms of the *food-seeking instinct* are differentiations from one most primitive and fundamental of all instincts. The impulse to wander in search of food seems to have led to the differentiation of animals from plants. In most of the insects the instinct has become highly specialized, so that each species seeks and thrives upon some one narrowly prescribed kind of food only. In the mammals the instinct is less specialized, conforming in this respect to the general rule; but in the lower mammals and in many birds we observe such a degree of specialization that the animal may starve to death in the midst of plenty, through lack of adaptability of this instinct. The higher mammals show but little specialization and hence considerable adaptability. Most grass-eating herbivora will on occasion browse on leaves of bushes and trees. The stupid sheep hardly attains to this; but to the more intelligent goat almost all green stuff is fair game Some carnivora are very selective; but others will prey upon and devour almost every kind of animal.[1] All animals are alike in this—that when the impulse of this instinct is aroused in great strength, it overrides every other tendency, subduing or preventing even fear itself. Both in this sense and in that it was presumably the first tendency to be differentiated from the primal purposive energy or *élan vital*, the food-seeking instinct may claim primacy over all the others.

The most interesting problem presented by food-seeking is this: Are the various activities involved in the unlearned search for food by any one creature to be attributed to one instinct or to several? That such activities are instinctive is shown by their peculiarities proper to each species and common to all members of the species. In herbivora, such as the sheep, the problem appears in its simplest form; for the food-seeking of the adult animal is monotonous and simple in the extreme; though even here there are the two phases, first, of wandering in search of pasture (which on a barren mountainside is of some importance), and, secondly, the actual cropping of herbage when found. Those who identify instincts with reflexes must attribute these two phases to two distinct instincts. Others will confidently assume that the same appetite, the same impulse, sustains both phases. But what shall we say of the relation between the food-seeking of the young and that of the adult animal? The young animal satisfies its food-appetite by sucking the udder of its dam; and this also is a two-phase activity, the running to the dam and finding of the udder, and the actual sucking; both phases are clearly dependent on the same appetite; both are inexcitable when the appetite is stilled. Shall we say that at a certain age a new instinct ripens in the lamb, an instinct to nibble the grass, and that this gradually supplants the sucking instinct? Surely not; surely it is the same appetite that seeks and attains satisfaction in these two ways, by means of these different motor mechanisms. Smell is probably the guiding sense in both cases, and presumably the same odors operate in both cases. The milk of the dam is odorous of the herbage on

[1] The dog under domestication becomes almost omnivorous. One of my dogs spontaneously learned to regale himself on peas, beans, marrows, and other vegetables growing in the garden.

which she feeds; it is, then, not difficult to see how the transition from the one kind of activity to the other is made, and how, once begun, the more satisfying form of feeding supplants the other. There can be little doubt that the lamb, if it were prevented from grazing and if the dam continued to yield milk, would continue to feed from the udder indefinitely. This problem, which is presented by all mammals, seems capable of a similar solution in all cases.

More difficult is the relation of thirst to hunger in those animals that drink water. The problem may be stated in this way: Is thirst the same appetite as hunger, or are they distinct appetites rooted in two instincts? Here the best indication is afforded by one's own experience. For myself, I can confidently say the two appetites are not distinct. Frequently I am at a loss to know whether I am hungry or thirsty; and I can then decide the question only by taking a drink of water. If this allays my craving, my appetite was thirst; if not, it is hunger. The true statement seems to be that in ourselves, as in all drinking mammals, the one appetite requires both food and drink for its satisfaction. We see this clearly in the carnivora, which normally eat and then drink, before lying down in satisfied repletion.

The food-seeking instinct is variously specialized among the carnivora. In those that hunt game on the ground, this specialization expresses itself in following the scented spoor, in cautious approach, making use of cover and avoiding all unnecessary movements, and in lying in wait. In others it leads to the climbing of trees, and in others again to swimming and diving in pursuit of fish; in both cases the bodily form and organs have become adapted to these modes of pursuit. Thus, all the behavior which is sometimes attributed to a "hunting instinct" is in reality the expression of this one most fundamental impulse. And I see no reason to doubt that this is true of man, who seems to find in hunting a satisfaction that implies an instinctive basis; he readily turns to hunting when other forms of food run short; and he finds the most complete satisfaction in hunting, only when the successful hunt is followed by the devouring of his prey, and when the hunting itself is accompanied by anticipation of this consummation of the activity. Hence the significance of the phrase, "as hungry as a hunter."

Odors seem to play a large part in guiding all mammals to their food; while taste proper seems to have the function of further stimulating appetite and the digestive functions and of carrying to a further stage the discriminations effected by smell between the edible and the noxious. The low degree of specialization of the instinct on its receptive side among the higher mammals gives large scope for profiting by experience and the exercise of intelligent discrimination.

The Instinct of Repulsion

In order to understand how such discrimination is effected, we must take account of another instinct, namely, the *instinct of avoidance, repulsion*, or *disgust*. This is perhaps the simplest of all the instincts. Its end is merely the avoidance of noxious things, or their rejection, if they have been taken into the mouth. Among the animals in which the food-instinct is highly specialized on the receptive side, an instinct of avoidance and repulsion is hardly required. But in the higher mammals, in which the food-instinct is but little specialized on the receptive side, the utility of the instinct of disgust is obvious. It permits them to experiment with safety upon a large variety of edible substances.

I may illustrate the complementary working of these two instincts by describing very shortly an experiment made with one of my dogs who had long been accustomed to eat cubical lumps of sugar with every sign of gusto. My design was to investigate his power of color-discrimination. With this end in view, I dyed a large number of cubes of sugar with a variety of bright colors. The dyes were vegetable, harmless, and tasteless. The dog ate the colored cubes as readily as the white. All the cubes of one color, red, were then impregnated with a solution of quinine. He took the first red cube and mouthed it, then speedily put it out, and gazed upon it from a respectful distance. After a little encouragement he ate cubes of other colors, and then again took a red cube and rejected it. After several repetitions of this experience with the red cubes, he showed reluctance to take any cube, white or colored; but after an interval of some days he again took the cubes of all colors, and now, although he hesitated in crumbling the red cubes, he finally swallowed them. My experiment failed to achieve its purpose[1]; but it brought

[1] I am nevertheless inclined to think that the method is a sound one for the investigation of color-discrimination in animals and infants; the same method might be used for investigation of the discrimination of form and size.

out in an interesting way the conflict between the two opposed impulses of gusto and disgust, the former eventually getting the better of the latter; so that the dog may be said to have acquired a new taste, just as we learn when hungry to like, that is, to eat with gusto, things that at first and when we are not very hungry excite disgust—such as tomatoes or strong cheese. There can be no doubt that, if all the cubes had been impregnated with quinine, he would quickly have learned to avoid all such objects.

It is obvious that the wild animal may learn in this sort of way to discriminate between the harmless and the noxious among a wide range of substances: for those substances that are noxious have in the main odors and tastes that excite disgust; for example, putrescent things and those vegetables that contain the bitter and poisonous alkaloids.

To say that the instinct of disgust generates an appetite would do violence to common usage; but we can properly say that its operation is accompanied by aversion. Aversion is striving away from the object, just as appetition is a striving toward it. As a technical word we may perhaps use "appetite" to include aversion, which then may be classed as a special variety of appetite. It is worth noting that our own reactions toward food-substances are determined very largely by our bodily condition. If we are hungry, the odors from the kitchen attract us, excite our appetite. If we are replete, the same odors may excite our disgust. We may sit down to a feast of sweet things with keen appetite, which, as repletion supervenes, gives place to disgust. And we know how a single experience of this sort may have a more or less lasting effect in changing our attitude toward the substances concerned. Again, nausea, which is only disgust in an acute form, may be induced by physical causes, such as the motion of a ship or by drugs; and we know how, when in that condition, to perceive or in any way to think of food does but excite or intensify our aversion.

Under the guidance of disgust and of the food-seeking instinct, animals in which the latter is not highly specialized acquire a large range of likes and dislikes, that is to say, they learn to avoid on sight or sound or smell (*i. e.*, from a distance) those things which, when first taken into the mouth, excite disgust, and to be attracted by the sight or smell or sound of things to which they are natively indifferent. This acquirement of "tastes" for a variety of objects is carried furthest by the monkeys; and it is probable that in them, as also in some degree in other animals, the process is greatly aided by the impulse of curiosity; for the monkey, like the young child, usually carries to his mouth, nibbles, and tastes whatever small objects excite his curiosity.

Instances of perversion of the food-appetite are not unknown among animals; in the human being such perversions become of great importance. Many things are found to yield a partial satisfaction to the food-appetite, when they are taken into the mouth and chewed or tasted and swallowed. A large part of the machinery of civilization is devoted to the preparation and distribution of such substances—chewing-gum, tobacco, candy, betel-nut, soft and strong drinks of all kinds, and all the array of condiments from pepper and salt to the most refined spices and flavorings. It is true that some of these, such as salt, alcohol, tea, coffee, cocaine, and opium, owe their attraction largely to further and more subtle chemical effects produced after their absorption into the blood; but the immediate satisfaction of the food-appetite which they yield remains the foundation of their charm. I see no reason to doubt that the craving for such substances, which is apt to become established after much usage of them, may be identified with the food-appetite working in a perverted manner. In no other way can we explain the great power of such cravings. This identification is borne out by three considerations: First, such cravings may be arranged in a series of increasing perversity; the less unnatural cravings of the series are obviously but slight specializations of the food-appetite, such as the idle woman's craving for candy; and these connect by steps, such as the quid of tobacco, with the most unnatural of such cravings, as that for cocaine or opium. Secondly, it is noteworthy that the indulgence of such cravings always tends to disturb the normal appetite, to substitute for natural food the substance craved for, so that the drug-addict always suffers from loss of appetite for food. Thirdly, the use of these substances, from chewing-gum, betel-nut, the cigarette, and the quid of tobacco to opium and cocaine, does as a matter of fact relieve both hunger and thirst; and often, when food and drink cannot be obtained, they are deliberately used for this purpose.[1]

The Instinct of Escape

Avoidance of and escape from danger are instinctively achieved by almost all mammals. Even the lion will on occasion slink away with his tail between his legs. The hedgehog and the porcupine are so well defended by their quills, and the skunk by his

[1] A wise treatment of these perverted appetites gives practical recognition to this view of their nature. The almost universal use of such substances, among peoples who have learned to eat full meals at regular intervals, is to be connected with the fact that primitive men, like the apes, nibble and chew almost continuously such things as sugar-cane and raw fruits.

odor, that they do not need this instinct; and they seem to remain calm in all situations. The more defenseless the species, and the more it is subject to be preyed upon by others, the more sensitive is this instinct and the more powerful its impulse; as in the deer, the rabbit, the sheep, and the mouse. The most difficult question in regard to the behavior of escape is this: Is all behavior of escape the expression of a single instinct, or have we to do with a group of instincts of allied function? Having recognized the avoidance of disgust as the expression of a distinct instinct primarily concerned in correcting the food-seeking impulse, we may, I think, recognize all other forms of aversive behavior as expressions of a single instinct.

Some influential writers have taken the other view, notably Doctor W. H. R. Rivers.[1] He recognizes in Man a group of five "danger instincts," as follows: (1) flight or escape proper, (2) aggression, (3) manipulative activity, (4) immobility, (5) collapse with tremor. This multiplication of instincts, all subserving a common end and all evoked by threatening situations is, like so many other confusions in this field, largely due to the failure to distinguish between motor mechanisms and instincts. The student will see that, if we observe this distinction, this array of alleged danger-instincts is unnecessary; because these various modes of reaction to danger can be adequately accounted for without postulating more than a single danger instinct.

What name should we give to this instinct? It is sometimes spoken of as "the instinct of self-preservation"; and there is no serious objection to this name, though it has the drawback that it may seem to imply self-consciousness and a higher level of intellectual development than we can legitimately attribute to most of the animals; and it is a clumsy name. Common sense has in this case recognized the essential relation of emotions to instincts by using the word "fear" to name both the instinctive behavior and its characteristic emotional accompaniment. And I see no reason why we should not follow this usage. But, if we must have a separate name for the instinct, we may best call it the *instinct of escape*. In man and many other mammals it is distinctly a two-phase instinct. In the young of the human and of many other species it determines, first, a running to shelter; secondly, a lying hid when the shelter

[1] In his "Instinct and the Unconscious," Cambridge, 1920.

has been attained. The shelter may be the nest or the body of the mother. For the adult, the shelter may be the lair or any other cover; for the gregarious species, it may be the mass of the congregated herd. The fainter manifestations of this instinct we commonly speak of as caution or timidity; in its most intense expression we call it terror. When strongly excited, this instinct impels to extreme efforts to which every bodily organ is attuned. The flight to cover requires extreme bodily exertion, if it is to attain its maximum efficiency; and, when cover has been found, a continued readiness for further exertion, either of flight or combat, is needed, as also a continued alertness of all the senses.

One expression of terror common to man and many animals is difficult to understand, namely, the trembling of the limbs, which goes so far, in some men at least, as to incapacitate them for steady effort. I think that this well-known symptom of fear may properly be regarded as one of Nature's disharmonies, a fortuitous by-product; it seems to express an incoordination of muscular action consequent upon the conflict of incompatible impulses. In man this symptom is most apt to appear when, in the presence of threatening danger, escape is impossible, either for moral or for physical reasons, and the man therefore makes an effort, only partially successful, to control his fear. And in animals the same seems to be true. The terrified horse does not tremble, if he can gallop wildly away; but only if his master restrains his efforts and compels him to face or to approach the terrifying object.[1]

In the gregarious animal the first reaction of this instinct is commonly the giving out of some signal which serves to warn its fellows, and to bring them together for defense or escape. Stamping on the ground is one such signal. The bobbing of the rabbit's white tail in the dusk achieves this function, while he bolts to his hole. But a cry, symptomatic of fear in each species, is the commonest danger signal; and in this respect man reveals clearly his community of nature with the gregarious mammals.

In the more defenseless mammals fear is very readily and frequently excited. And the objects which are capable of exciting

[1] This was the history of the persistent tremors which during the war were the most common symptoms of "shell-shock." We observe trembling in ourselves and in animals on conflict of impulses in which fear is not involved, as when we strive to restrain our anger; or in the dog or cat excited to spring upon a rabbit, yet restrained by his master's prohibition.

it, which serve as keys to the gates of fear, are many and highly general. A loud and sudden noise is perhaps the most nearly universal key. The sudden movement of a large object is perhaps as nearly a universal key. More specific is the danger-cry (or other danger-signals) emitted by members of the same species; for this, as we see best in the case of birds, may evoke the behavior of fear even when the sound is of low intensity. Still more specific are certain odors, if it be true that the scent of man, or of other beasts of prey, drives some animals to headlong flight on their first encountering it.

The instinct of escape has many locks; and its gate may be thrown open by the application of the appropriate key to any one of these locks. Another universal excitant of fear, another specific key to the instinct, is bodily pain. In the healthy wild animal, pain normally is excited only by violence from without. The behavior of the fighting animal, as soon as it goes beyond the preliminary phase of threatening, is an endeavor to inflict pain; if he succeeds in inflicting sufficiently intense pain on his foe, he evokes fear in him and so drives him to flight. It is because bodily pain excites fear that it is capable of so strongly inhibiting all forms of activity other than efforts to escape. In ourselves, the distress we suffer from bodily pain, both in anticipation and in actual endurance, is the distress of fear which cannot achieve its goal. Let any one who doubts this consider his experience in the dentist's chair. The child especially is full of instinctive fear in such a situation. If we can feel absolutely assured that no harm, but only good, will be done to us by the painful operation, it is easy to support the mere pain. So, when the child cuts his finger, feels the smart, and sees the blood flow, his physical pain is slight, but his fear and, therefore, his distress are great.

One other very general excitant of fear is especially interesting, namely, *the mysterious*, the uncanny. In this respect curiosity and fear are closely allied. The object that is to excite curiosity must have a certain similarity to familiar objects in order to attract attention; and yet it must be so far different as to fail to produce the reactions that are usual in the presence of the familiar object. It would seem that a higher degree of this difference-in-spite-of-similarity provokes fear. Hence we may see animals or children, in the presence of such objects, alternating between the attraction of curiosity and the aversion of fear. Professor Köhler's chimpanzees displayed much and long-sustained curiosity in the presence of a mirror, and learned to study reflections in pools and various polished surfaces. But, in the presence of rudely made toys representing various animal forms and on the approach of a familiar man disguised by a face-mask, they displayed fear.

"Large, unusual animals need only come near the chimpanzees and at once they are thrown into panic. When it happened that a pair of the huge oxen of Teneriffe dragged a plough to and fro before the cage, the whole group flew to and fro like hunted creatures, always to the spot remotest from the terrifying object, and there hid their blanched faces, trembling, only to flee again with incredible swiftness when the oxen came nearer." Rude toy models of oxen and donkeys about 40 cm. high were prepared. "It was quite impossible to bring Sultan (who could be led about in the open by the hand) near to these small and unnatural beings; at a distance of many meters he fell into extreme fear. . . . One day I entered the animals' room unexpectedly with one of these stuffed models under my arm. . . . In a moment a dark cluster, composed of all the chimpanzees, hung from the remotest corner of the roof; they sought to push one another aside, each trying to bury his head as deeply as possible in the mass of the others. . . . One makes too easy an explanation if one assumes that the novel, the unknown, is in itself terrifying. . . . Not every new thing is uncanny to the chimpanzee. . . . Nor is any appreciable similarity to the living foes of the species a necessary condition [of fear]. . . . One day, when I suddenly put on a hideous face mask . . . the chimpanzees disappeared in a moment. They dashed as though possessed into a box." (*Op. cit.*)

The Gregarious Instinct

Many species of mammal are gregarious, grazing, roaming, or hunting in herds, flocks, packs; or dwelling in colonies of burrows. In all such species we may infer the presence of an instinct whose function is to keep the members of the group together. For, without the operation of such an instinct, the young, on becoming capable of foraging for themselves, would soon become detached from the parents in the course of their search for food, and no enduring group would be formed. Adhesion to the group brings three principal advantages, which offset the greater difficulty of foraging involved by membership in the group; namely, collective attack and defense, mutual warnings of danger, and in various degrees the sharing in a traditional knowledge and in the benefits secured by the keener senses or by the superior intelligence of other members of the group.

The lack of cohesion among such animals as the solitary carnivores illustrates the all-importance of Instinct and the small importance of Habit among the animals. For most of these carnivores spend the first months or years of life as members of a family group; and, if Habit were the enduring and all-powerful factor in human and animal life that it is so often said to be, we should expect them to form during this period an enduring gregarious habit. But we find nothing of the kind. A species is either gregarious or non-gregarious by nature; and in this respect Habit modifies its members but little or not at all. We see the fact illustrated also in the inverse manner by individuals of gregarious species brought up in solitary captivity by man. Such an animal, as soon as released, seeks and merges himself into the herd or other group; as with horses that run wild on the pampas.

This instinct is best called the *gregarious instinct*, though "herd instinct" is perhaps a neater term.[1] It is sometimes spoken of as "the social instinct"; but this is undesirable, for it is not clear that it is the root of all social life—the carnivorous family of some species, for example, enjoying a social life without, it would seem, any such instinct; though it remains a question whether in such cases some rudiment of the instinct be present. The goal of the instinct is merely the near presence of other members of the species; its impulse is to approach others, especially a group of others. The outward form and coloring of the species, its specific cries, and probably the specific odor are the keys to which the locks of the instinct are adjusted. The appetite of this instinct seems to be strong in many species; when absent from the group, such a creature grows uneasy and

[1] This term has been popularized by Nietzsche and by Mr. W. Trotter's book, "Instincts of the Herd in Peace and War." This brilliant and very readable little book is pervaded by the error of attributing to the "herd instinct" every form of social relation and influence, in a quite undiscriminating manner.

roams restlessly; until some one of the recognition-marks of the species guides it back to company and the craving is satisfied, the impulse allayed. It would be an error to suppose that, in the mammals generally, this impulse prompts to behavior that could be called altruistic. The only doubtful exceptions are the protective behavior of the leader or patriarch of a herd, and the keeping watch in turn by members of a herd or flock. This last form of behavior has often been reported; but it is very difficult to interpret.

We can hardly doubt that the human species is endowed with the gregarious instinct. The gibbon is distinctly gregarious. One who has startled a troop of these animals, and caught a glimpse of them swinging swiftly through the forest with loud musical cries, can hardly doubt it. In the chimpanzee the same impulse seems to be strong. In evidence I cite the following passage from the recent report by Professor W. Köhler.[1] "One hardly exaggerates if one says that an isolated chimpanzee is not a true chimpanzee. . . . The specially characteristic qualities of this species only reveal themselves to observation, when one has a group of the animals before one. . . . The observation of several peculiarities of the chimpanzee can only be clearly interpreted when the behavior and counter-behavior of the individuals in the group are regarded as a total process. . . . The hanging together of the group of chimpanzees must be regarded as the expression of a very real force, sometimes of astonishing strength. One sees this clearly at every attempt to isolate an animal from a group well accustomed to be together. If this has not happened before or not for some considerable time, the separated individual becomes wholly absorbed in the striving to unite itself with the group. Very small animals display fear (*Angst*) . . . Larger animals, by which no symptom of fear is displayed, cry, howl, and rage, throw themselves against the walls of the confining chamber and, if there appears even a most improbable route by which the others may be reached, will forthwith launch themselves upon it at the risk of life, in order to return to the bosom of the group. Even when they are quite exhausted by desperate efforts, they crouch whimpering in a corner, until they have regained strength for a new effort."

Primitive Passive Sympathy

In connection with the gregarious instinct, we should notice a fact of primary importance for all social psychology; namely, among the gregarious animals, where concerted action or, rather, community of behavior, is necessary for securing the full benefits of group-life, each of several of the instincts seems to be specially

[1] "Zur Psychologie der Schimpansen," *Psychologische Forschung*, 1921.

adapted on the receptive side, in such a way as to be played upon by the expressions of the same instinct in other members of the species. We see this clearly in the familiar response of dogs to the specific cries of other dogs. The yap which the dog utters, when he starts a rabbit or other prey, was designed by Nature to bring his fellows to his aid; it is one of the keys of the hunting instinct. But the key would be useless without a lock into which it may fit; and this lock is to be found in the perceptual organization of the same instinct of every member of the species. Hence, when this yap resounds, it fits into all such locks and arouses the impulse of pursuit in all dogs within hearing. The same seems to be true of the bark of anger; it brings to the scene of combat all the dogs within hearing, all tensely prepared to take part in the struggle.

Perhaps the most generally manifested response of this sort is the behavior evoked by the cry of fear; for among the more timid animals a cry is in nearly all cases the first expression of fear. The cry of fear and other expressions of fear, such as headlong flight, are specific excitants of fear itself.

The instinct of curiosity and seemingly in many species (especially among gregarious birds) the pairing instinct are adapted in a similar way; each has a lock which is adjusted to the key formed by the expression of the same instinct.

This liability or capacity, so wide-spread among gregarious animals, the liability to be stirred to that kind of instinctive behavior whose signs are displayed by other members of the species, I have proposed to call *primitive passive sympathy*. For subjectively it involves the sharing of the emotional excitements that accompany instinctive behavior. It seems to be very general in the human species; that is to say, most of the human instincts have this lock or specific adjustment on the receptive side. It is the source of many of the phenomena of crowd behavior, such as the panic, the frenzied applause and frenzied anger of the mob. And it is the essential basis of the higher forms of sympathy. If the gregarious instinct is the cement without which the group could not come into existence or grow beyond the very simple form of the family, it is primitive sympathy that renders group-life advantageous to all members of the group and is the basis of all higher developments of sociability.[1]

The Instincts of Self-Assertion and Submission

Among the gregarious animals some kind of social order within the group is commonly preserved. The lowest form of such order exists where certain individuals that are endowed with more strength or initiative than others lead the way in all collective locomotion and are followed by the rest. But in many cases social order attains a higher level, through the recognition by the group of some one leader, master, or chief. This is commonly an adult male who may, or may not, tolerate the presence of other adult males in the group. It is clear that, in the latter case, the group must remain much restricted in size, and must thereby forego many of the advantages of group-life. Hence, we commonly find the former state of affairs, namely, a male who is the recognized leader and other adult males who submit to his domination. How is this domination effected? In part, no doubt, it is through fear. In groups of many species, the leader of the group must be prepared to assert his superior-

[1] Cf. my "Group Mind," London and New York, 1920. The same principle seems fundamental in the life of the social insects. When the queen bee is removed from a hive, all the bees set up a peculiar cry (the so-called *heulen*) and, as Professor Holmes says (*op. cit.*): "Among bees, ants, and termites signs of anger by one individual may awaken the whole community to a high pitch of excitement. Each individual then serves to arouse the others, and the larger the community the greater the mass effect." Köhler (*op. cit.*) describes this process in the group of chimpanzees as follows: "At times the slightest falling out between a man and a chimpanzee which leads the latter to angry cries and attack upon the foe suffices —immediately a wave of anger sweeps over the group and from all sides they hasten to the common attack. In this instantaneous spread of the cry of anger through all the animals a dæmonic power wells up from the depths of these organisms. . . . The whole group is thrown into blind rage, even when most of the members have not seen what was the occasion of the first outcry, or what the trouble is about. The outburst follows simply upon the resounding of the peculiar exciting cry. I have experienced that the good-tempered Diana has on such an occasion suddenly sprung upon my neck in senseless fury, although in the previous moment she was playing gaily with me." I would specially commend this account to the attention of those who doubt the principle of primitive passive sympathy and to those who deny that the primary emotions indicate the workings of the instincts. I would also especially beg my readers to notice that I do not describe primitive passive sympathy as an instinct, nor as the expression of any one instinct.

ity in combat at any moment; and punishment in such combat does, no doubt, inspire in the vanquished a more or less enduring fear of the victor, a tendency to approach cautiously and to flee at any sign of anger. But the maintenance of social order in this way alone would be wasteful of energy and of life itself, and little conducive to harmonious social existence. Hence we find evidence in many gregarious animals of two other instinctive modes of behavior, complementary to one another, the interplay of which secures social order in a less wasteful and more comfortable manner.

We are here dealing with intimacies of the life of animals which in the natural wild condition remain hidden from us for the most part. We have to rely mainly upon such indications as the enfeebled and perverted instincts of the domesticated animals afford us. We observe how a young dog will approach an older one in an attitude and with movements which we can describe only as deferential, conciliatory, deprecatory, or submissive. He crouches, his ears and tail hanging loosely, his back smoothed and hollowed, every detail expressing the absence of all defiance, an acknowledgment of the superior power of the other. The bigger or older dog, on the other hand, receives him in an attitude which we can hardly describe without such words as dignity, pride, condescension, sense of superiority or power. We see indications of similar reciprocal modes of behavior among horses at pasture. In the chaos of the farmyard or of the monkey cage at the zoo, where all natural relations are disturbed and perverted, it is, no doubt, difficult to discern the reciprocal play of these two instincts; but we may infer that, in many animal groups, it conduces greatly to the preservation of social order, by the due subordination of all to the natural leader of the group, and by regulating precedence among the other members.

We may attribute these two opposed and complementary modes of behavior to *the instincts of self-assertion and of submission*, respectively. They are present in the gregarious human species and play an immense part in the social life of mankind. We must return to say something more of them, after a few words about the pairing or mating instinct in mammals.

The Mating Instinct

That mammals mate or pair instinctively is quite clear. Take two young white rats approaching maturity, male and female, which have been brought up in isolation from the earliest moment at which they could be weaned; and put them in the same cage. At once the play of courtship begins in the prettiest manner: the pursuit and retreat and the mutual exploration; and soon it culminates in the natural manner. The same is true of two young pigeons, and probably would be found to be true of all young mammals with which the experiment could be made. Although the movements and attitudes in which the train of behavior culminates are more or less specific or peculiar to this instinct, the preliminary behavior of courtship may involve all, or nearly all, the motor mechanisms possessed by the animals; but they are none the less actuated by the impulse of the pairing instinct. The natural goal of this impulse, which alone satisfies and allays it, is the act of union. The natural object is the individual of the opposite sex; the sex-characters of the one sex are the natural keys that unlock the door of the instinct in the other sex. But the element of appetite is strong, especially perhaps in the male of most species; its importance and its dependence upon bodily factors, such as hormones, or internal secretions and stimuli, are shown by the periodicity and seasonal variations of the appetite.

There is undoubtedly some considerable difference between the male and the female of most species, as regards not only the receptive but also the executive side of the instinct. The male is more aggressive and active and usually takes the initiative. We have seen how among the pigeons these peculiarities of behavior are the only clear recognition marks of sex; and how, among birds endowed with special sex-characters, such as plumes and special colors and patterns, the male actively displays these before the female. The same is true in a less degree of the mammals. The male, in subduing the female to his "will," makes use of his voice and a display of his size, strength, and agility. The stallion arches his thick neck, waves aloft his tail, steps high and prances proudly. The bull bellows: the lion roars; the cat caterwauls; and the young man curls his mustache, strokes his beard, raises up his voice, and displays his strength and agility in leaps and bounds and his prowess in real or mock combat or in a hundred different dances, games. or sports, more or less organized, from the corroboree and the head-hunting expedition to the mediæval tourney, the duel, the minuet and gavot of the eighteenth century, down to the "jazz," the "shimmy," and the "speed stunt" of the present day.

A very difficult question arises at this point. Is all this behavior of self-display on the part of the male, to which the female responds by a similar but less active and aggressive display of the peculiarities of her sex—is all this self-display to be regarded as the work of the mating instinct alone? Or is it the expression of the instinct of self-assertion? I do not think that we can hope to distinguish sharply here. The self-display of courtship is perhaps largely and directly due to the mating instinct. But, as in all social situations, the assertive and the submissive impulses are constantly at work, complicating the behavior of the pairing instinct.[1] Among many of the mammals and birds such complication would seem to occur in various degree.

In all mammals the mating instinct matures relatively late, and generally first expresses itself unmistakably about, or shortly before, the time at which physical growth is completed. There is much difference of opinion as to the age at which the mating instinct of the human species normally begins to influence experience and behavior. The view most commonly held, perhaps, is that it remains entirely latent until puberty, a period of development marked by bodily changes, which consist in the main of the development of the secondary sex-characters. Professor Freud and his disciples, on the other hand, teach very confidently that the instinct normally plays a very important part from earliest infancy. The truth seems to lie about midway between these extremes. It is probable that in this respect individual differences are very great, and that some extreme instances of precocity conform to and give color to the Freudian teaching. But there is good reason to believe, as I have shown,[2]

[1] This fact affords some excuse, but no justification, for the Freudian confusion of the pairing instinct with these others.

[2] Cf. "The Definition of the Sexual Instinct," Proc. Roy. Soc. of Medicine, London, 1914. For a fuller discussion of the nature and development of this instinct in the human species see the supplementary chapter on "The Sex Instinct" in my "Social Psychology."

that, in the normal average child, the instinct first begins to play some part at eight or nine years of age.

The Acquisitive Instinct

Some of the mammals gather surplus food and hoard it instinctively. The food of the carnivora gives little scope for this tendency; but we see a rudiment of it in the behavior of the dog who buries his bone and returns after an interval to dig it up. Among those mammals which have fixed abodes and which feed on grain, nuts, and other such durable vegetable products, the tendency is wide-spread.

Are we to regard such behavior as one expression of the feeding instinct? Or should we attribute it to a distinct and separate instinct? It may be that it is an instinct in process of differentiation from the feeding instinct, and that various species illustrate stages of this differentiation. But there is an objection to this view, namely, that a tendency of the same or similar kind is manifested by many animals that do not hoard food. The birds gather sticks, straws, hair, and moss for their nests; and they defend their nests from intruders, especially against members of their own species who, in the absence of such defense, would rob them of these gathered treasures. And, in general, animals that have any kind of lair or home are apt to resent the intrusion of other creatures; and this defensive attitude is very commonly extended to a certain area surrounding the "home"; the dictum that "his home is his castle" is true not only of the Englishman, but also of many humbler creatures. This possessive behavior seems to be instinctive. It is certainly closely allied with hoarding. Have we to do here with two separate instincts, or with two rather different expressions of one instinct? The question, as all questions of animal instinct, is chiefly of interest in its bearing upon human nature. I am inclined to suppose that there are two distinct instincts, and that both are constituents of normal human nature. But it is so difficult to distinguish their influences in human behavior and experience that for the present we may with advantage content ourselves with the recognition of an *acquisitive instinct*; and we may attribute to it both hoarding and the defensive possessive behavior. Still, it is perhaps not entirely fanciful to point out that, while some men are content with few possessions, but guard them most jealously, others seem to find their chief satisfaction in the perpetual garnering of new gains and seem relatively indifferent to the fate of their treasure, allowing it to slip away from them without protest or effort in its defense. Perhaps the born gambler is the man in whom the garnering instinct is strong, the hoarding instinct weak, in whom, therefore, the satisfaction of winning far outweighs the pain of losing; while the miser is he in whom the hoarding instinct is unduly strong.

The Constructive Instinct

Among the birds and insects and spiders the construction of nests, homes, webs, combs, and so forth affords some of the most marvellous examples of instinctive activity, in which the nice co-operation of Intelligence with Instinct is often displayed. Among the mammals such constructive activity generally attains but a low level. The beavers alone rival the birds and insects in this respect. Yet rudiments of such constructive behavior are widely displayed. The rabbit digs his burrows, the mole his galleries; the rat and the squirrel form their nests. It might have been expected that the monkeys would exhibit a high development of constructive power; but in this respect they are disappointing. The quadrumana alone seem to build a nest, and this seems to be at the best a very rude affair.[1] But the fact indicates the existence in them of an instinctive tendency which we can only ascribe to a distinct instinct. And this supports the view that human nature comprises a similar instinct of construction of a very low degree of specialization. Constructive play of young children, their delight in making things, especially houses, caves, and shelters, and their satisfaction in being within such constructions, are perhaps the most direct evidences of the presence of this instinct in man.

[1] The fact was generally doubted until my friend, Doctor C. Hose, procured the nest of a Maias in Sarawak and sent it intact to the museum at Cambridge, England, where, I believe, this unique specimen may still be seen.

The Instinct of Appeal

The young of many mammals instinctively utter a cry of peculiar quality, when they are unable by their own efforts to attain some instinctive end. This cry is the master-key to the parental instinct and brings the parent promptly to the aid of the young. It is the instinctive cry of distress, and seems to be the expression of a distinct instinct, which bears to other instincts a relation similar to that of the combative instinct; but, just as the impulse of the latter instinct is secondarily evoked, when other instinctive stirrings are thwarted, so the instinctive cry of distress is evoked as a further reaction, when the combative instinct fails to attain its goal, or when the re-enforcement that it gives to other impulses proves insufficient. We observe this sequence of impulses if we pinch or prick a young animal, such as a puppy, and restrain his efforts to escape. First, he attempts to escape in fear; secondly, he turns and snaps and struggles in anger; thirdly, if still his efforts are unavailing, he whines in distress. A similar sequence is shown very frequently by young children. Withhold the breast, or the bottle, or any other object which the infant keenly strives to attain, and he displays anger and redoubles his efforts; continue to withhold the object with ruthless determination, and his anger gives place to the cry of distress with all its natural bodily accompaniments of tears and sobs, and, if he has attained to the age of standing and running, he casts himself to the ground, with relaxation of all other efforts. Of course, the stages of anger and of distress often overlap and commingle their signs and symptoms; but the natural order of sequence is nevertheless clear.

This behavior must be ascribed to a distinct instinct whose function is to obtain aid and comfort from others, primarily from the parent. We may perhaps best call it the *instinct of appeal.*

Some Minor Instincts

I have now enumerated and briefly discussed thirteen instincts which seem to be common to most of the mammals and to be constituents of human nature. The number is notoriously unlucky, and I should like to add to it. But I cannot see adequate grounds for the recognition in man of any other tendency or impulse properly to be called instinctive, unless possibly it be the tendency to laughter and certain tendencies which are so simple and constant in their motor expressions that they approximate to the type of the reflex. These are sometimes called "sensation-reflexes," in order to distinguish them from reflexes that involve only the spinal level of the nervous system and seem to occur independently of awareness of any sense-impression.

The chief of these are the tendencies to sneeze, to cough, to scratch any itching spot, to defecate, and to urinate. Of these, *scratching* any itching spot of the skin seems to conform more nearly than the rest to the type of an instinctive reaction. For it does not find expression through any one motor mechanism only, but may make use of a very wide range of movements; as we may see especially clearly in the contortions of a man who has an itching spot between his shoulder-blades. The rest of these tendencies express themselves very constantly through particular motor mechanisms. But this seems to be because there is only one kind of muscular action which is capable of achieving the natural end of the impulse. This in turn is due to the fact that the sense-impressions by which they are evoked, and those also by means of which they attain satisfaction, are (except in the case of scratching) in each case peculiar to certain parts of the body.

The principal grounds for attributing each of these reactions to a special very simple instinct are the following: (1) Each of them is the expression of a definitely felt impulse, which, if it cannot at once find expression, is capable of becoming a strong desire; and this impulse and the effort prompted by it may absorb the whole energy of the organism, to the exclusion of other instinctive impulses and reactions; or they may conflict with other impulses. (2) They conform to the same rules of satisfaction and dissatisfaction. (3) They are subject to the same kind and degree of voluntary control as the other instinctive impulses. If we contrast them in these respects with certain reactions which at first glance may seem to be of similar nature, we see more clearly their affinity with the typical instincts. Sweating and blushing and pallor are organic reactions which may be evoked reflexly, or as elements in certain complex instinctive reactions, such as fear and anger. But they do not express any independent impulse. We never become aware of an impulse to sweat or to blush or to grow pale; and we have no direct control of these reactions, as we have of all the impulsive reactions. It is true that we may desire to exhibit such reactions, as, for example, when we wish to simulate or display some emotion; but such desire is secondary to some other purpose. These reactions are not in themselves purposive. On the other hand, a particle lodged in the throat may, by irritation of the mucous membrane, generate a desire of extreme urgency and strongly purposive efforts for its removal.[1]

Laughter also expresses an independent impulse, which sometimes, as we know, is almost or quite uncontrollable. It belongs to this group of minor instincts, but is of special interest and deserves some special discussion.

A Theory of Laughter

Laughter presents problems with which philosophers have wrestled with little success. They have given us many ludicrous theories of the ludicrous. Man is the only animal that laughs. And, if laughter may properly be called an instinctive reaction, the instinct of laughter is the only one peculiar to the human species.

Almost all of the writers who have discussed laughter have regarded it as an expression of pleasure; and most of the so-called theories of laughter have been endeavors to explain the source of the pleasure which is supposed to be the cause of the laughter. Thomas Hobbes, for example, saw this source in the feeling of "sudden glory" which he supposed all men to experience on seeing another man cast down. Many others have vainly pursued this false scent in other directions. That it is false becomes clear at once, if we ask ourselves the simple question—Are we pleased by the things we laugh at? Is the ridiculous, the ludicrous, the absurd, essentially pleasing? Obviously not—the things and situations that provoke our laughter are not pleasing in themselves, but rather the contrary; they are things that would annoy us if we did not laugh.

Herbert Spencer's theory of laughter was that laughter is merely an overflow of surplus nervous energy. There is an element of truth in this view

[1] It has been argued with much force by Professor E. Claparède that falling asleep is an instinctive process. I am inclined to agree with him. But the question is one of great difficulty. It will be further discussed in Part II.

which I shall indicate presently. But it is not an adequate theory. Laughter involves a very complex and nicely co-ordinated system of movements, which complex co-ordination is provided for in the innate organization of the nervous system. We all laugh in much the same way, without instruction. Such a complex organization can have been evolved in the species only if it performs some service, secures some biological advantage. A mere overflow of nervous energy can be, and is, effected through any of the other motor mechanisms; as we see in the restless fidgeting of the child under restraint. Nature therefore had no need to devise and construct a special and highly complex nervous mechanism for this service.

The latest notable theory of laughter, that of Professor Bergson, merely tells us that laughter serves the ends of social discipline, because we naturally laugh at whatever in behavior is stiff, clumsy, or machinelike. This, no doubt, is true and involves an advance on the "pleasure theory" of laughter. But it also is very partial and inadequate as a theory of laughter. We can hardly believe that this complex co-ordinated reaction was evolved by Nature to perform primarily this social service. And that is the first and fundamental question to be answered by the true theory—namely, What biological service does laughter perform? What advantage does it bring? What is its survival value?

We find the clue to the true theory if we ask—What does laughter do for us? What are its effects or consequences? Well, obviously we enjoy laughter; it does us good to have a good laugh. The fact is notorious. When we feel depressed, we welcome or seek the situations, objects, or persons which will make us laugh. Laughter prevents (for the moment at least) gloomy thinking and melancholy brooding, no matter how it is induced. How does it achieve this beneficial effect? In two ways—one purely physiological, the other more psychological. Physiologically its immediate effect is to stimulate the respiration and the circulation, to raise the blood-pressure, and to send a fuller stream of blood to the head and brain; as we see in the ruddy face of the hearty laugher. Psychologically it works by breaking up every train of thinking and every sustained activity, bodily or mental. Here presumably Spencer's theory finds a partial and inverted application. The nervous channels of laughter drain off energy from all others; but they do not serve merely to get rid of surplus energy as a waste product; rather they were evolved in order that, by draining off energy, they might prevent its application in other directions. Laughter is essentially relaxation from all effort, a relaxation whose mechanical effects bring speedy recuperation of energy, and which enables us to start afresh on life's tasks briskly and undismayed, unharassed by the past. This being so, it is obvious why we seek the objects and situations that make us laugh; we seek the ludicrous, the grotesque, the absurd, the ridiculous, not because they are in themselves pleasing, but because they make us laugh, and laughter does us good, makes us feel better and brighter, frees us from depression, prevents our thinking of depressing things. The perfectly happy man does not laugh, for he has no need of laughter, though he may smile. Almost all writers on laughter have assumed without question that the smile is identical with the laugh, or have regarded it as a partial and incipient laughter. I suggest that this is an error. The smile is the natural expression of the satisfaction that attends the success of any striving. The victor smiles the smile of triumph; but he does not laugh. The mother smiles as she soothes and cherishes her healthy infant. We smile as we discover a long-sought secret or the solution of a problem with which we have wrestled. We smile as we contemplate any well-completed task in which we have been absorbed; merely to anticipate success makes us smile. Note one extreme and significant contrast between the smile and the laugh—the smile is beautiful, the laugh is ugly. Why, then, does laughter so often die away in smiles? A fact which is, no doubt, at the root of their false identification. The answer is that laughter, freely indulged, gives rise, like all other successful activities, to satisfaction which expresses itself in a smile. The smile into which laughter so often subsides is the smile of the satisfaction brought by laughter; and it is only when the smile is blended with the subdued laugh that laughter is redeemed from ugliness and may even be beautiful.

If, then, laughter produces these beneficial effects, how shall we define the ludicrous? What is it that is common to all ludicrous objects and situations, beyond the fact that the contemplation of them makes us laugh? Certainly it is not that they are in themselves pleasing. Consider the types of the ludicrous. The man sitting down on his own hat, or pursuing it down the street before the breeze; the clown who falls with a resounding thud, lets fall a pile of crockery, or whacks another with loud blows and slaps. These are basic examples of the ludicrous. Rather less crude are all the instances in which men fail in some stroke of skill; as the golfer who cuts up the turf and drives his ball but a yard or two; or the man who lands in the ditch, instead of clearing it. More refined are the instances of the ludicrous provided by those who "make fools of themselves" by lack of tact or social adroitness; by the man who "can't open his mouth without putting his foot in it"; by the man who boasts or lies without seeing that his hearers understand him. Another great class of things ludicrous are awkward, defective, or bizarre modes of attire, of address, of speech, of gait, of eating. We laugh at all these things, and our laughter serves, as Bergson says, the ends of social discipline. But do we usually laugh in order to discipline the fool? How about the clown on the stage? Do we desire to discipline him? Can we suppose that Nature has given us this strange ugly reaction for this purpose? And are these ludicrous objects pleasing to us? Are stupidity, clumsiness, tactlessness pleasing? Surely not. Hobbes would have it that they are secondarily pleasing to us when displayed by others, because they make us feel our own superiority. A far-fetched explanation indeed! Are we not sometimes filled with admiration for the clever clown, even while he provokes us to roar after roar of laughter by his grotesque antics and mishaps? If we look at the ludicrous situation or action more directly and clearly, we see that the ludicrous is essentially personal, human or quasi-human. An arrangement of inert objects may be ludicrous, but only in so far as it suggests some human relation or the human action which did or might have produced it. The behavior of animals is sometimes ludicrous, as when a dog plays wildly with children or with other dogs; but then it is only in so far as we sympathize with the dogs and appreciate their sudden evasions, their feints, their failures, their tumbles, their surprises and disappointments, as we should those of romping children.

There are, then, two features essential to the ludicrous. First, it always involves some maladjustment, something inappropriate, which, if we contemplated it without laughter (as do some persons who seem incapable of laughter) would displease us, as every lack of harmony and order in nature displeases us. Secondly, in every case, the ludicrous situation or action is one which, if we ourselves suffered it or performed it, would be mildly distressing to us, and one which is, as a matter of fact, mildly distressing to the person who suffers or performs it; except in the case of the clown, who acts the part and finds satisfaction in the success of his efforts to provoke laughter. Now, if we had no capacity for laughter, in virtue of the primitive sympathetic tendency, we should, on contemplating these disharmonies of action, share in some degree the distress, the embarrassment, the disappointment, or the humiliation—in short, the pain and depression which accompany all failure of action. That is to say, a human being, deprived of the capacity for laughter, but otherwise normally constituted and leading a normally social life, would suffer very frequently from sympathetic pain and depression. For the pain of every little embarrassment, disappointment, failure, and mishap of all those about him would be sympathetically shared by him. We are saved from this multitude of small sympathetic pains and depressions by laughter, which, as we have seen, breaks up our train of mental activity, prevents our dwelling upon the distressing situation, and provides an antidote to the depressing influence in the form of physiological stimulation that raises the blood-pressure and promotes the circulation of the blood. This, then, is the biological function of laughter, one of the most delicate and beautiful of all Nature's adjustments. In order that Man should reap the full benefit of life in the social group, it was necessary that his primitive sympathetic tendencies should be strong and delicately adjusted. For, without this, there could be little mutual understanding and only imperfect co-operation and mutual aid in the more serious difficulties and embarrassments of life. But, in endowing Man with delicately responsive sympathetic tendencies, Nature rendered him liable to suffer a thousand pains and depressions upon a thousand occasions of mishap to his fellows, mishaps so trivial as to call for no effort of support or assistance. Here was a dilemma—Whether to leave man so little sympathetic that he would be incapable of effective social life? Or to render him effectively sympathetic and to leave him subject to the perpetually renewed pains of sympathy, which, if not counteracted, would seriously depress his vitality and perhaps destroy the species? Nature, confronted with this problem, solved it by the invention of laughter. She endowed Man with the tendency to laugh on contemplation of these minor mishaps of his fellow-men, and so made of such mishaps occasions of actual benefit to the beholder; all those things which, apart from laughter, would have been mildly displeasing and depressing, became objects and occasions of stimulating beneficial laughter.

This, I suggest, is the true theory of laughter;[1] it assigns its biological function, its *raison d'être*, explains why we laugh and are pleased at that which is essentially displeasing; and it is capable of taking account of all the many varieties and occasions of laughter. Let us look at some of the more special forms of laughter and at some facts which, at first sight, may seem to be difficult to reconcile with the theory.

There is a form of laughter which conforms to Herbert Spencer's theory; that is to say, it is a mere overflow of surplus nervous energy; for the motor mechanism of laughter, having been created, serves on occasions, as any motor mechanism may, as a mere channel of overflow. Such is the nervous laugh which is merely a form of fidgeting. Closely allied to this is the laughter of

[1] I first proposed this new theory of laughter in a letter to *Nature* (Vol. 67, 1903), and later expounded it in more detail before the British Association in a paper published in *Psyche*, Vol. II, No. .

"high spirits," when our nervous energy is so abundant that it seems to spill over in a variety of movements, and laughter occurs without assignable cause or occasion; just as we may shout or leap or run. This is the most elementary form of play; we must consider it more nearly on a later page.

There is laughter at our own mishaps. This is the essential basis of all humor. It presupposes the development of the capacity to stand aside and contemplate one's self and one's minor mishaps in the same way that we contemplate those of our fellows. Humor is essentially laughter at ourselves, at one's own individual self, or one's self as included in humanity at large or some group or class; it is laughter "at our own expense," as we say; we turn our own minor misfortunes into benefits by laughing at them. Not every laugher achieves this level of detachment; and, by a subtle complication, lack of this power becomes itself ludicrous to the onlooker.

There is a strange type of laughter which has puzzled and shocked many who have experienced or witnessed it; namely, the laughter sometimes provoked by the recital of a catalogue of human disasters. This occurs when disasters are recited which are great and horrible, but which afflict persons so remote from us in time and place, so unfamiliar, that their great mishaps affect us only in the same mild degree as the minor mishaps of those nearer to us.

Why do we laugh when we are tickled? This is a crucial question for any theory of laughter. Note first that, though we can tickle ourselves, or can be tickled by a stray hair, or a fly, such tickling is merely disagreeable and does not provoke laughter. The tickling that provokes laughter is playful tickling by another person. This shows the essentially psychological, rather than merely physiological, nature of the process. I suggest that laughter on being tickled is the crudest and earliest form of humor; it is laughter at one's self; one's self appears ludicrous, because the trivial attack of the other person produces so much discomfort and disorder of movement. Normally both the tickler and the tickled laugh, and the occasion is the same for both; both laugh at the discomposure of the tickled one; and, by laughing together, they intensify and prolong their laughter. For laughter is no exception to the law of primitive sympathy, but rather illustrates it most clearly and familiarly; the infectiousness of laughter is notorious and as irresistible as the infection of fear itself. That is to say, the expressions of laughter are themselves keys which unlock laughter. This fact goes far to justify the ranking of laughter with the instinctive reactions, and the classing of the disposition to laughter as an instinct. If we class it with the instincts, we must recognize that it differs from all other instincts in that its impulse seeks no goal beyond itself, but secures its own satisfaction by means of bodily processes which effect nothing in the outer world.

What sort of persons are the great and ready laughers? If Hobbes's theory of "sudden glory" were true, they should be the proud, the disdainful, and the scornful. But, fortunately, the harsh and hideous laughter of such persons is comparatively rare, and we hate to be laughed at by them. The great laugher is the person of delicately responsive sympathetic reactions; his laughter quickly gives place to pity and comforting support, if our misfortune waxes more severe. The laughter of such persons is in little danger of giving offense; for we detect their ready sympathy and easily laugh with them; they teach us to be humorous.

Although the philosophers have failed to penetrate the secret of laughter, it seems to have been revealed to more than one poet. Lord Byron wrote: "And if I laugh at any mortal thing, 'tis that I may not weep." And Nietzsche said: "Perhaps I know best why it is man alone who laughs; he alone suffers so deeply that he had to invent laughter. The most unhappy and melancholy animal is, as is reasonable, the cheerfulest." ("Will to Power," § 91.) The true theory of laughter may be stated in one sentence—laughter is the antidote to sympathy. Here, if anywhere, the Lange-James theory is true. If we are pleased when we laugh, we are pleased because we laugh.

Play Not the Expression of "an Instinct of Play"

Though animals cannot laugh, many of them play, especially when they are young. The gambolings of lambs, of puppies, or of kittens are the purest examples of play. Is, then, play the expression of "an instinct of play," as so many psychologists, educationists, and popular writers assume? While recognizing the difficulty of the problem, I must affirm that in my opinion this is an error and will state tentatively the view which commends itself to me. It is clear that in play all (or almost all) of the motor mechanisms possessed by the creature may be brought into action. Watch two young dogs at play. They race to and fro, they leap and turn, they bite and bark, they seize one another by the throat, they roll one another over, they lie down and roll over on their backs, and they adopt a great variety of attitudes. If an instinct were merely a motor mechanism, play would have to be regarded as the expression not of one instinct but of many, or of all.

Professor Groos's well-known theory of play asserts that it is essentially the exercise of instinctive modes of action, for the sake of development and improvement of skill in movement. We have recognized that youth is essentially the period of accumulation of experience before the instincts are mature. But there are difficulties in the way of Groos's theory. We have to ask: Is there a special instinct which impels to this kind of exercise and somehow modifies the behavior proper to each instinct? If only young animals played, the problem would be simpler; for then we might suppose that the several instincts which find expression in play are incompletely developed, and that the incompleteness of the instinctive reaction is due to this immaturity. But this will not do. For sometimes mature animals play; as, for example, a grown dog with a puppy. The problem appears most clearly, if we consider the special feature of dogs' play which consists in one biting the other. The problem is: How are we to interpret the fact that, in such playful fighting, the biter never drives home his teeth; while the other often makes no effort to escape or defend himself, but, rather, lies on his back, presenting his undefended throat and belly to his fellow, in a way he will never do in real combat? Clearly, if the combative instinct is at work, it is working in a strangely modified fashion. Further, it is clear as daylight that the combative emotion, anger, does not accompany these activities. Playful struggling may readily turn to real fighting; but, as soon as one of the players displays anger, the play is at an end, giving place to real combat or, at least, to the preliminary threats. Thirdly, the circumstances which evoke the impulse and emotion of the combative instinct are lacking in play. Neither dog is pursuing an instinctive goal; and therefore there is no impulse at work the thwarting of which would provoke anger. The same is true of the playful actions which seem to be expressive of other instincts. The one dog flees and the other pursues; but the fleeing dog is not really striving to escape, and shows no signs of fear. And the pursuer is not really hunting him; does not attempt to seize him and devour him if he comes near him; does not yap as he would if pursuing game; and he experiences, we may feel sure, little or none of the emotional excitement proper to the hunt.

Since, then, neither the occasions, nor the symptoms, nor the movements of the playing animals, are those characteristic of the instinctive activities which the play simulates, we are driven to the conclusion that the corresponding instincts are not really at work (or at play). I suggest that the animals are merely exercising their various motor mechanisms in turn under the guidance of their sense-organs, and finding pleasure or satisfaction in so doing. Play is activity for its own sake, or, more properly, it is a purposeless activity, striving toward no goal. Whence, then, comes the energy that sustains it? The answer is, I think, that the well-fed and well-rested animal, especially the young animal, has a surplus of nervous energy which works through the channels of the various motor mechanisms. We see this in the caged beast which prowls round and round, or from side to side, or springs aimlessly back and forth; we see it in the chained elephant who sways from side to side for hours together. We see it in the school-boys, who, after growing more and more fidgety, spring out into the playground, running and shouting and laughing aimlessly and independently of any exciting objects. We see it in the sailor who paces the deck; and in the student who throws down his book and goes for a walk, or perhaps merely paces up and down his room, or twists his limbs to and fro. We see it most clearly in the well-fed young horse who, as soon as he comes out of his stable, begins to frisk, running, lashing out with his heels, neighing, shying, prancing, exercising all his motor mechanisms, but without sign of emotion or purposive effort. It is the primal *libido* or vital energy flowing not in the channels of instinct, but overflowing, generating a vague appetite for movement and finding outlet in any or all of the motor mechanisms in turn.

All human play, save that of young children, tends to take the form of games. A game is not pure play; it stands midway between play and work; and, in proportion as it is dominated and sustained by purpose, it approximates to work. Of all motives that sustain games the competitive motive is the chief: we play the game to win; and the more strongly this motive operates and dominates, the less playful and the more serious is the game. We so choose our sports and devise our games as to evoke other motives and, therefore, more energy; in this way we give greater zest to the game and attain greater satisfaction. We hunt or fish for the sport; but we introduce the competitive element by aiming at bigger fish or more points to the antlers. And, when we go rock-climbing or big-game shooting, we seek the added energy and zest given by the element of fear; as do children when they play at ghosts and bogies.

But in games the competitive motive is easily first. What, then, is this? Is it the impulse of a distinct instinct, an instinct of rivalry or competition? That view is temptingly easy; but there is serious objection to it. It is not clear that any wild animal displays competitive behavior. And to assume such an instinct would be to assume a higher degree of generality and abstractness, in respect both of the object and the goal, than any known instinct displays. Every instance of competitive behavior may be attributed to the instinct of display or self-assertion, and seems to be adequately explained in this way. Competition is an effort to assert our superiority to others, and, by so doing, to throw others into the submissive uplooking attitude which gratifies or brings satisfaction to our impulse of self-assertion. Unless it can be shown that this explanation is inadequate, the principle of economy of hypothesis must forbid the assumption of an instinct of rivalry.

Imitation Not Due to "an Instinct of Imitation"

Closely allied to the problem of play are the question of "an instinct of imitation" and the problem of explaining imitative behavior, if we refuse to admit such an instinct. The grounds for rejecting it are similar to, but stronger than, those which lead us to reject instincts of rivalry and of play; namely, (1) the very high generality of the object or situation which must be assumed to evoke such an instinctive impulse; (2) the extreme diversity of its alleged manifestations; (3) the absence of any clear evidence of such an instinct in animals; (4) the possibility of explaining all outwardly imitative behavior in other ways. It is in the monkeys, if anywhere among animals, that we might expect to find such an instinct; and to them an instinct of imitation is unhesitatingly assigned by the popular mind. Yet careful experiment[1] seems to have shown that monkeys are no more capable of general imitation in the strict sense than any other animal; that is to say, they are quite incapable of it. Imitation in the strict sense implies the perception by A of the bodily movements or attitudes of B, and the subsequent production by A of movements or attitudes similar to those of B, the reproduction being determined or conditioned by the previous perception. As we have seen, some animals are moved by the gregarious impulse to follow others of the same species. And all gregarious animals have in some measure the tendencies of primitive sympathy, which lead them to behave as they perceive their fellows

[1] Cf. Professor J. B. Watson, in "Animal Behavior."

doing, to flee when they flee, to approach curiously when they approach, and so on. These two modes of behavior (simple following prompted by the gregarious impulse and the primitive sympathetic reactions) include most instances of apparent imitation in animals.

There is a form of imitation displayed occasionally by the higher animals, and more especially by the monkeys, which depends upon the appreciation by the imitating animal, A, of the fact that the behavior of the imitated one, B, leads to a result desired by A. It has been shown, for example, that when a monkey, A, has failed to learn to obtain food by manipulating some simple mechanism, it may be aided to learn the manipulation by the example of another, B, which has already learned the trick.[1] It would seem that the example of B merely serves to direct the attention of A to the essential part of the mechanism, which A has then to learn to manipulate by his own series of more or less random efforts. If, for example, the essential act is the pulling down of one end of a lever, A's attention and efforts may be directed to that end of the lever by B's example; but there is no good evidence that A's perception of B's action may be sufficiently analytic to enable A to proceed at once to pulling the lever downwards, rather than to pushing and pulling it in a variety of ways. It is clear that such vaguely imitative behavior does not imply an instinct of imitation, but rather a vague understanding that some action upon the lever is a necessary step toward the desired goal.

One other important field of action seems to give some support to the assumption of an instinct of imitation—namely, the learning of vocal utterances. It seems to be proved that some songbirds will learn to utter the song proper to other species, if they are brought up with members of that species, and that others can be taught to whistle bars of a melody. That parrots and some other birds can be taught to utter words and phrases is notorious. How are these facts to be explained, if not by the postulation of an instinct of imitation? We must notice that the action of uttering a sound is unique among all actions in one very important respect; namely, whereas action of any other kind cannot be perceived by the actor in the same way in which it is perceived by his fellow-creatures and in which he perceives their bodily movements, the sounds he and they utter are perceived by him and by them in just the same way. Suppose, then, a creature, child or animal, endowed by Nature with a number of vocal motor mechanisms, which enable it to utter a variety of sounds expressive of various emotions or impulses. Whenever any one of these is set in action, the creature hears its own voice uttering corresponding sounds; in consequence, this sense-impression becomes associated with that motor mechanism, so that the hearing of the sound tends to innervate that mechanism—hence the tendency to monotonous repetition of sounds, common to young children and many animals.[2] Now suppose the creature to hear the same sounds uttered by another. The sound will have the same effect; namely, in so far as the creature responds by vocal utterance, it will tend, in virtue of the preformed association, to utter the same sound that it hears. If now

[1] Cf. M. E. Haggerty, *Journ. of Phil.*, Vol. IX, No. 10, 1912.

[2] This is a common kind of pure play.

the creature has a number of such vocal motor mechanisms, each will become associated with the sound which its own working produces; and if thereafter several of these sounds are repeatedly uttered in its presence in the same sequence, it will, when it is moved to vocalization, tend to utter this same sequence. That, in rough outline, seems to be the principle involved in the imitation of sounds, the principle which leads children and some animals to utter sounds in the same combinations and sequences that they frequently hear. Given a certain variety of vocal mechanisms and an impulse to respond to sounds by some vocal utterance, it is inevitable that the creature so endowed will tend to "imitate" the sound-combinations that are frequently repeated in its hearing. The difference between the animals that can "learn to talk" and those that cannot seems to be merely that the former are endowed with a considerable variety of vocal motor mechanisms, while the latter are not. And the human infant is endowed with a larger variety of such mechanisms than any other creature. It cannot be doubted that, if the dog possessed a considerable variety of such mechanisms, instead of being so poorly endowed in this respect, he would learn to "talk" far better than the parrot or the starling; in all probability we could then push his education considerably further than is actually possible.

Most instances of human imitation are of more complex origin than the simple forms of imitation exhibited by animals; and they issue from a variety of complex mental activities of which the process technically known as "suggestion" is the chief. This we shall have to consider on a later page.

I have now enumerated and defined all the instincts that seem to me to be comprised in the innate constitution of the human species. Many writers who repudiate the notion of human instincts make much of the fact that the lists of these instincts drawn up by different authors are very unlike, some enumerating many and others few. This criticism is unfortunately well founded; but it does not justify the rejection of the notion as illusory. It was only after much discussion and research that the list of chemical elements was generally accepted. The differences of opinion among chemists during that period of discussion would not have justified any critic in repudiating the notion of chemical elements. The hypothesis of human instincts is now in a position similar to that of chemical elements during that period of discussion. I have no doubt that it will become as generally accepted as the theory of chemical elements has been, and that it will prove as useful to psychology as that theory has been to chemistry.

The differences between the exponents of human instincts are chiefly due to that confusion of instincts with motor mechanisms which I have pointed out in the foregoing pages. I have to admit that, in my earlier discussions of Instinct, I fell a victim to that confusion. This all-important distinction has only recently become clear to me.

Another great source of confusion and difference of opinion is the common practice of classing together, as expressions of one instinct, whatever modes of bodily activity subserve the same general biological function. This practice involves the application of purely external or biological rather than psychological criteria. It results in classing together such distinct instincts as the pairing and the parental instincts, because they both subserve the perpetuation of the species; and the instincts of food-seeking, disgust, escape, and combat, because all these subserve the preservation of the individual. Even if such terms as "social," "reproductive," and "self-preservative" are used merely as names for groups of instincts of allied function, they are, I think, to be deprecated; for they inevitably lead to cross-classifications and confusions, and bring no compensating advantages.

Some authors who agree with me in regarding instincts as enduring innate dispositions, which generate impulses to action, and who agree also in regarding them as the mainsprings of human conduct, refuse nevertheless to attempt to distinguish, enumerate, and describe the several human instincts. This is the attitude, for example, of Doctor C. G. Jung, who is content to speak of the hormic energy of all the instincts as the *libido*, refusing to distinguish any distinct instinctive tendencies beyond the nutritive and the reproductive. Similarly, Professor John Dewey, in his "Human Nature and Conduct," recognizes the importance of instincts and their impulses in human nature, but strongly deprecates any and every attempt to distinguish or define the several human instincts. Neither of these distinguished authorities offers us any intelligible and weighty ground for this refusal to be interested in what seems to me the primary task of the psychologist. Their attitude is, I think, partly due to their neglect to make any serious study of animal behavior; but, though it may be explained, it cannot be justified. It is true that many writers on social phenomena have made a crude use of the theory of human instincts, and have drawn illegitimate deductions from it; as when, for example, they allege that warfare between nations can never be abolished, because the combative instinct is an enduring feature of our innate endowment. But such improper use of the theory cannot be prevented by condemnation of all attempts to refine our knowledge of the human instincts, but only by deepening and clarifying that knowledge and presenting it in an intelligible form.

CHAPTER VI

HABIT AND INTELLIGENCE IN ANIMALS

We have seen that the mammals are well endowed with instincts, which differ from those of the insects chiefly in being less specialized. We have seen that this lack of specialization of the instincts leaves the young mammal comparatively helpless; but that he is more than compensated by the period of youth, during which he is fed, sheltered, protected, and to some extent guided by parental care, while he develops his intelligence and acquires knowledge of "good and evil," or, at least, learns to discriminate between those things which are noxious or dangerous and those which are useful.

Habit Too Much Used as Explanatory Principle

We have now to consider more nearly the development of intelligent behavior. And in this connection we must inquire into the formation of habits. The word "habit" is commonly used very loosely. We speak not only of habits of movement, but also of habits of feeling and of thought. Wherever we observe the repetition of any intelligently adapted reaction, we are apt to speak of the reaction as habitual and to ascribe it to a habit.

Some authors use the word in an even wider sense, though with more definite connotation. Ever since the rise of the association-psychology, there has been a strong and increasing tendency to explain by the principle of habit all behavior that exhibits improvement or adaptation through individual experience. Modern "behaviorism," with its reflexes and conditioned reflexes, is the culmination of this tendency. For the conditioned reflex is a habit. And the program of this school is to interpret even the highest manifestations of human genius in terms of habit. When used by psychologists of this school, "habit" is no longer a merely descriptive term denoting the fact of repetition of acquired reactions under similar circumstances. It implies rather a most far-reaching hypothesis, the mechanistic hypothesis, according to which all development of intelligence and all acquisition of knowledge are merely the formation of habits. And all habits are conceived as nervous structures, and their formation as a mechanical building up of such structures.

The scheme in terms of which it is sought to effect this reduction of all the life of intellect and feeling and will to the mechanical formation and play of habits may be outlined as follows. The nervous system contains an array of innately organized motor mechanisms. Each of these consists of motor neurones connected to form a system such that, when it is stimulated in any way, currents of neural energy issue from it along the axons which connect it with certain muscles. Each motor mechanism is connected by sensory nerves with one or more points in one or several sense-organs, in such a way that, when the sensory point is stimulated, a nervous current, initiated in it, runs into the motor mechanism and so produces a reflex movement. (I leave aside all consideration of the "Consciousness" which may or may not be assumed to accompany or "run parallel with" the nervous currents, according to the particular school of the mechanist; for all these schools agree that it makes no difference.) The movements so produced are simple or more or less complex, according to the number of muscles into which the motor mechanism discharges itself. If two or more such motor mechanisms are thrown into action simultaneously (or in immediate succession) by the conjunction (or succession) of appropriate sense-stimuli, they become linked together by paths of low resistance in the nervous system, so that thereafter they tend always to function simultaneously or in immediate succession; and this linkage becomes stronger upon every repetition of this conjunction or succession. Such linkage is the formation of a habit; the habit is the conjoined motor mechanisms; and habitual action is the mechanical working of the conjoined mechanisms.

The difficulty with this scheme is, not that it is altogether false, but that it contains enough of truth to lead so many to believe that it is an all-sufficient principle for the explanation of intelligent behavior. I will not dwell upon its difficulties,

Some of them I have indicated on earlier pages. But I insist again on the highly speculative nature of the scheme. We have only the most uncertain guesses as to how habits are formed.[1]

Habits of Mind and Habits of Body

We shall do well, I think, in approaching this very difficult topic of Habit, to preserve the old distinction between habits of mind and habits of body. The term "bodily habits," taken in its widest sense, includes all kinds of bodily adaptation through use; such adaptations, for example, as take place when the organism comes into a changed climate, when it adapts itself to the low atmospheric pressure of high places, or to the heat of the tropics, or when it adapts itself to a changed diet or to abnormally much or little muscular activity. These instances show that the formation of a nervous habit is only a special case of a more general power, that of adaptation to circumstances, possessed in various degrees by all organisms and organs, and not always dependent upon nervous factors. But we may confine our attention to the habits of the nervous system; for these are of chief importance in the study of behavior.

Men do undoubtedly form bodily habits of the nervous kind. We learn by practice, by purposive effort oft repeated, to combine our more elementary movements in new ways, gradually achieving the new combination more easily, with less effort; until it is, as we say, "secondarily automatic," and requires for its production no effort, but merely the intention or will to produce it. By far the greater number of the new combinations of movements that we thus acquire are made in the service of special purposes, and are useful to us as facilitating the achievement of such purposes; we call them, therefore, skilled movements, and speak of the acquisition of skill. Now, in acquiring a skilled movement (or secondarily automatic combination of movements) we undoubtedly build up in the nervous system a new motor

[1] The fact that the manner of formation of neural associations and habits remains a very obscure problem seems to escape the notice of many psychologists. In my view the most plausible attempt to solve this problem is that embodied in my "Primer of Physiological Psychology," under the heading, "The Law of the Attraction of the Nervous Impulse," which in turn rests upon my *hypothesis of inhibition by drainage.*

mechanism similar to those motor mechanisms with which we are innately endowed. The process is not only one of combination of preformed mechanisms; some analysis or breaking up of innate mechanisms into more elementary parts is also involved, a process even more difficult to understand in purely mechanistic terms than the conjoining of mechanisms. But, assuming the new motor mechanism to have been built up, we have to ask:—What are its status and function in behavior?

Those who identify instincts with mere motor mechanisms of the nervous system claim that an individually acquired mechanism, or habit, is essentially of the same nature as the innately organized mechanism which they regard as an instinct. Some of them, therefore, speak of habits as instincts, and of instincts as innate or racial habits; the difference between the instinct and the habit being, for them, merely one of history or genesis.[1] And, recognizing that instincts impel to action, they assert or assume that habits have the same impulsive power, the same power of driving us on to action and of sustaining effort or activity. We have seen that William James adopted this view, in asserting that instincts are essentially transitory and merely serve to give rise to habits, by which in the adult they are, he said, supplanted. The clearest and most consistent exposition of this view, which attributes impulsive power to habits, has been given by Professor Woodworth.[2] He uses the convenient term "drive" to denote the impulsive energy of an instinct; and he maintains that, just as each instinct drives, or has, or is, a "drive," so also in the same sense a motor habit drives, or has, or is, a "drive." This is a view which I cannot accept. But it requires careful examination; for at first sight it seems that much may be said in its favor.

Let us notice first that secondarily automatic or skilled movements, implying motor habits, are almost peculiar to man. Few animals acquire any modes of movement beyond those provided for in the innate constitution of the species. It is only the most intelligent animals, and they only under the patient control and guidance of man, that acquire motor habits; as when a

[1] This was the practice of the late Professor Wundt, also of Herbert Spencer.

[2] "Dynamic Psychology," New York, 1919. I have criticised Woodworth's doctrine in some detail in an article in *Mind*, N. S., 1920, "Motives in the Light of Recent Discussion."

dog is trained to walk on his hind legs or a bear to ride on a bicycle. In all such cases the new movements (or acquired combinations of muscular action) are closely allied to the natural (or innately organized) movements, and involve but little recombination. The displays of circus animals which excite our wonder are achieved by much patient training of those motor faculties which are naturally, or innately, highly developed in them; as, for example, the marvellous balancing and catching of balls by sea-lions; in these creatures extreme nicety of balance and of movement of the head under guidance of the eye is required by their pursuit of fishy prey. Now we do observe instances in which such animals, when they have acquired some such trick, repeat it again and again spontaneously, as though the habit once formed were a "drive." But we have to remember that, in the training of such animals, great use is commonly made of the feeding-instinct. The animal is kept hungry and rewarded with a piece of food, when he has done his trick. And, when we see a dog, taught in this way, spontaneously and repeatedly walking on his hind legs, or a sea-lion pertinaciously balancing a ball, we may infer with some confidence that he is "playing up" for more food; in other words, that he is impelled, not by any "drive" from the acquired habit, but by the impulse of the feeding-instinct, which operates now through this newly acquired mechanism, just as it may and does operate through and "drive" various innate motor mechanisms.

This example may serve as an illustration of the relation between instinct and motor habit in general. Consider any instance of motor habit in yourself, the habit which enables you to use the typewriter, or to play on the piano, or to adjust your necktie, or ply the knitting needles, so smoothly that the action seems to require no effort, or but a minimum, and can be carried on while you talk or read or think of other things. Does any such habit, no matter how perfected and how much repeated, become in itself a drive? Does it yield a motive, an impulse to action that may be difficult to control? Does it generate, or is it sustained by, an appetite? Is it *in itself* a source of purposive activity? To all these questions the answer is clearly—No. *The habitual action is only purposive when performed in the service of a purpose with the origin of which it has nothing to do.* We perform such secondarily automatic or skilled actions, not for their own sake, but for some purpose, with some goal in view, from some motive. Like all the innate motor mechanisms, *habits are only instruments, which subserve our purposes, but do not determine them.* In myself the most practised habit is probably the repetition of the alphabet. I must have repeated it some thousands of times, since I acquired the habit; and I trust it: when I am looking up a word in a dictionary or a directory, I will often run through the sequence of letters from the beginning. But is there any type of situation or object which can evoke in me an impulse to repetition of the alphabet comparable to the impulse to strike an angry blow evoked by your stepping on my toe or openly insulting me? No—the habit has no motive power, is not in itself a "drive." It is mere mechanism, a servant of the driving impulses which come from the instincts.

In certain cases, you may say, the habitual action does seem to be performed for its own sake: as when we repeat it, just because we are perfect in it. But then our purpose is either to display our skill and so assert ourselves over against others, or to assure ourselves of our possession of this prized instrument, or to maintain it in perfect condition, in order that we may display it, or make other use of it, on some future occasion; just as a vengeful man may take out his sword or pistol and polish it, or a lady may try on her new hat in private. The motor habit is merely an instrument which may be brought into play in the service of our various purposive impulses. Certain tricks, such as twirling the mustache or toying with the watch-chain, may seem to be exceptions to this rule. In reality, such habits come into play as partial and inadequate expressions of impulses toward goals, quite independently of what is effected by the habitual movement. Take such a habit as scratching the head when puzzled; or putting out and contorting the tongue, or puffing at a pipe, when writing. Such habits are formed in the first place as features of a more or less diffused and random activity, which is apt to occur whenever an impulse cannot immediately attain its goal.[1] With repetition they tend to become part of the total expression of the impulse, of the effort toward that kind of goal. Thus, scratching the head or chewing the end of one's pencil may become an habitual part of the expression of an effort to solve a problem. And putting one's hands in one's trouser-pockets may become an habitual part of the effort to appear at ease or unconcerned. Some such habits become uncontrollable and are then known as "tics." The modern study of such uncontrollable habits has shown, in many instances, that the tic is the partial, often symbolical, expression of an impulse which is uncontrollable, because it forms part of a repressed or dissociated system; and that, when the repression is relieved or the dissociation resolved, the tic is abolished.[2] These morbid habits thus illustrate very clearly the principle invoked above for the explanation of the minor senseless habits which do not go beyond the limits of the normal.

It would seem, then, that the motor habit is always acquired and used for some end, in the service of some purpose, and is not itself a source of purpose or motive power or "drive."

Attachment of Impulses to New Objects

Animals, though they acquire but very few and simple motor habits, nevertheless do acquire through experience habits of another kind, a kind which, if we observe the distinction between bodily and mental habits, must be classed as mental. Consider a simple instance. A beaver, having chosen a tree for felling, works at it intermittently, and completes the felling in the course of some ten or more nights, according to the size of the tree. And the task is, apparently, always achieved without the co-operation of other beavers. It has been found in many instances that, if a beaver is disturbed, when at work on a tree, by a flash-

[1] Such surplus of random movement is a characteristic feature of the process of trial and error all down the scale of life.

[2] Compare Part II.

light arranged so that he discharges it in the course of his movements, he never works again upon that tree, but leaves his task unfinished.[1] We may infer, with some confidence, that the flash of light in the darkness strongly excites in him the impulse to escape; and that, when he approaches the same tree on a subsequent occasion, the perception of the tree (and perhaps of its immediate surroundings) evokes again the same impulse. We cannot know what his experience is; but we may suppose without extravagance that his retreat from the tree was accompanied by fear, and that some such emotional excitement recurs, if he again approaches it. In this instance the tree, which had attracted the animal and provoked in him the instinctive activity directed to felling it, now excites in him an aversion, an impulse to avoid it and retreat from it. This new reaction to the tree is what the mechanists call a "conditioned reflex." In reality, the changed reaction implies an enduring change in the mental structure of the animal, a change which consists in the linkage of the disposition to escape, retreat, or avoidance, with the perceptual disposition by means of which the tree is recognized or discriminated from other trees.

A very similar instance is that of the puppy who approaches in friendly fashion a strange boy and is maltreated in some way that drives him to flee in terror. Thereafter the puppy will be apt to avoid this boy, or perhaps all boys; and he may flee with signs of fear on perceiving him or any one nearly resembling him. Repetition of such an experience confirms the acquired tendency. In the absence of repetition, the effect left in the mental structure of the animal is apt to fade away, until no trace is clearly manifested. The discipline of animals is conducted by some trainers largely on this principle, and few can dispense with it altogether. In the training of a lively young dog in a household, we may see the principle nicely illustrated. His mistress perhaps takes endless trouble, coaxes, rewards, scolds, uses the whip frequently and makes a great display of it; and yet never achieves control: the dog continues to defy or ignore her commands, when he is keenly interested in other

[1] *National Geographical Magazine*, August, 1921. The flashlight is arranged in conjunction with a camera, which secures a picture of the animal.

things, that is to say, when any of his instincts are strongly excited. His master, on the other hand, may, quickly and with a hundredth part of the care and energy devoted by his mistress, secure a complete submission and obedience of a lasting kind. This effect he commonly attains by inflicting one or two or a few severe punishments; he applies the whip with sufficient energy to evoke fear; while the mistress, unable to harden her heart sufficiently, has never pushed her punishments to this point. The whipped puppy may learn to fear, not only the person who whips him, but the whip itself; so that the mere sight or sound of the whip, flourished by any hand, will evoke fear.[1]

Learning of this kind is of the first importance among the higher mammals; it is chiefly in such learning that their intelligence is manifested. In their youth they are largely occupied in learning of this sort, learning, that is to say, to discriminate between individual things, and classes of things, and to react to them with appropriate impulses. Some of those who have recognized the importance for animals of youth, as a period of learning, have attached too much importance to the mere improvement of bodily skill. This does, no doubt, occur in some degree; though it is always difficult to determine the extent of such improvement of the innate motor mechanisms. It is a peculiarity of muscular tissue that it does not develop without exercise; therefore we are precluded from making any pure experiment. But, if the experiment of preventing all bodily movements until maturity were possible, we should find, I think, that most animals owe very little of the nicety of their movements to improvement by practice.

It is a nice question whether the training of a dog can be achieved without evoking fear on one or more occasions. My own experience inclines me to suppose that it cannot. Nevertheless, I feel sure that the occasions of evok-

[1] In the effects of fear we have one of the simplest of all illustrations of the inadequacy of the stimulus-response formula. A stimulus that provokes a mere reflex response leaves no appreciable effect that outlasts the bodily movement; but, if a stimulus, no matter of how brief duration, excites fear strongly, the behavior of the animal is apt to be profoundly and more or less enduringly modified. For some minutes, or even hours, all his responses to other impressions may be quite other than they would have been, if the fear-exciting impression had not preceded them; and, on coming into a place or situation similar to that in which fear was excited, the animal may show unmistakably the enduring effect of the fear, even after a considerable interval of time.

ing fear should be as few as possible. If you wish to make of your dog a devoted friend, as well as an obedient servant, you should rely chiefly upon the instinct of submission, and as little as may be upon fear. In the training of many dogs, especially of those employed professionally, the master establishes and maintains his ascendancy chiefly through fear; as may be seen from the general attitude and bearing of the dog toward him. But it is doubtful if the appeal to fear alone could succeed in training the dog to be a useful companion. If, in training your dog, you use the whip too severely and the appeal to fear exclusively, you will find that, while you can effectively inhibit him from various actions, you have little power to induce positive or active co-operation. And, when you flourish the whip, your dog, instead of obeying you, will be apt to flee away, leaving you in a state of baffled anger; for which there is no remedy but a nicer judgment in the use of means for playing upon these two instincts. For the impulse of fear is inhibitive and prohibitive; but docility comes from the submissive instinct. This is borne out, I think, by the experiences of animal trainers. Any animal of a gregarious species may be trained to be friendly and obedient; because it is endowed with the submissive instinct, which we can evoke if we use the right means. But with the solitary carnivora the case is different. The story of Androcles and the lion is pure fiction. The behavior of the lion or tiger or leopard in the presence of his trainer is a perpetual conflict and compromise between the impulses of anger and of fear. Such animals seem to be devoid of the submissive instinct, and are therefore but little if at all docile. They can be inhibited from their various instinctive modes of behavior; and they can be driven to leap from this place to that through fear; but this seems to be all that can be accomplished with them by the most judicious, skilful, and daring trainers. In all gregarious species, on the other hand, the submissive instinct seems to be always present in some degree; accordingly they are docile, and can be truly tamed and trained to a degree which is limited only by their intelligence. In this respect the contrast between the cat and the dog is striking and instructive. The cat is attached to his home, the dog to his master. The cat can be induced to perform certain tricks in the pursuit of his own ends, especially the securing of tit-bits; but he cannot be made docile or obedient in the full sense. He may come when you call him, if he has "nothing better to do," and especially if he is hungry and is accustomed to be fed by you. But the well-trained dog will come at your call, no matter how little this response comports with his pursuit of other goals.

I have dwelt at some length on this elementary principle, because the same problem arises in the training of children, namely: Is it necessary to appeal to fear; and, if so, to what extent? There was a time when fear was the master principle in the training of children, from fear of the whip to fear of hell-fire. I believe there may be instances of perverted natures in which the appeal to fear may be necessary for the establishment of ascendancy and the beginning of discipline. But I am sure that with normal children the duty of parents and teachers is to shield them in every way from all occasions of fear. Fear was very necessary for the survival of primitive man; the instinct needed to be very sensitive and its impulse to be very strong, if it was to preserve him from the many dangers that threatened him. But, under civilized conditions, its operation is hardly needed; and the great strength of this instinct is an anachronistic survival which is the bane of our lives and the source of infinite evil.

In the instances cited above to illustrate the attachment of an instinctive impulse to a new object, the impulse of the instinct of escape was chosen. But all other instinctive impulses are subject to similar adjustments or new attachments. Just as the dog learns to react with fear at the sight or sound of those persons or objects which have evoked his fear in the past by inflicting pain, so he will learn to react with anger to the sight or sound of those who have teased him by trying to take away his bone, or by otherwise obstructing and thwarting his impulses to action. In a similar way he learns to seek foods to which he is by nature indifferent; and to avoid others that at first attracted his food-seeking impulse, but have been found on nearer acquaintance to be disgusting.[1] Or, again, many animal-mothers may learn to pour out their parental care, to direct their protective impulse, upon young creatures of a species other than their own.

The formation of mental habits of this kind is, then, achieved by many animals and is the principal type of learning or profiting by experience that they display. It involves no new sources of energy, the formation of no new springs of action, but merely a redirection of the instinctive impulses; so that the animal responds with an instinctive impulse to some object toward which he was previously indifferent, and achieves a nicer discrimination between objects and between classes of objects.

Perceptual Habits

All that very special development of intelligence which is involved in the return to the nest, or to any other familiar spot, may be regarded as the formation and exercise of habits of a

[1] Compare the experiment with the quinine-soaked sugar, p. 147. At the risk of tedious repetition, I must again insist that the instinctive impulse, thus attached by experience to some previously indifferent object, does not necessarily find expression through any one motor mechanism, but may express itself through a variety of such mechanisms, according to the particular circumstances of the moment. Throughout the discussion of this topic, I have used the expression "attachment of the impulse to an object," in order to avoid tedious repetition of a cumbrous phrase. The more accurate phraseology would run—"the formation of an association between the affective-conative disposition of an instinct and the cognitive disposition concerned in the recognition of the object."

third class. It also involves improvement of discrimination between objects which guide the operations of instinctive impulses.

Animals comparatively low in the scale of intelligence, animals which exhibit no trace of acquisition of skill (in the proper sense of improvement of motor mechanisms), nevertheless exhibit such guidance of present actions through past experience. Let us consider a very simple instance. A crayfish, placed at one end of a long trough of water, which contains at the other end some food, *Z*, attractive by its odor, will swim or crawl toward the food. If the middle part of the trough contains a longitudinal

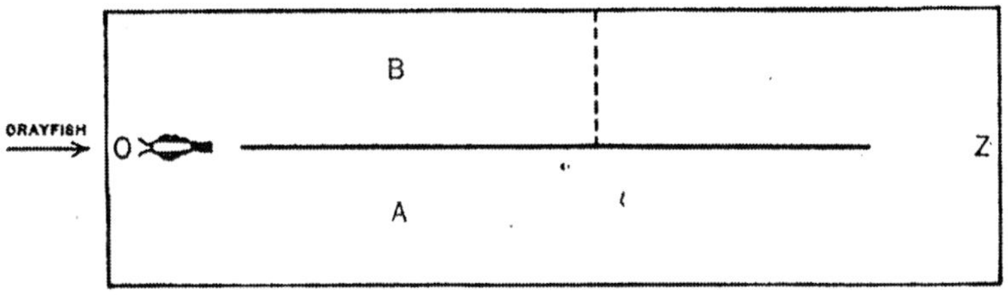

FIG. 4

wall dividing it into two passages, *A* and *B*, as in the figure; and if one of these passages, *B*, is closed by a sheet of glass, the animal will at first show no preference for *A* or *B*. It will sometimes enter *B*, and, continuing its efforts, will wander, until it escapes from *B* and finds the food by way of *A*. On many repetitions of this behavior, it gradually learns to avoid *B* and to seek the food directly and on all occasions by way of *A*. And, if the glass be transferred from *B* to *A*, it will gradually learn to pass directly through *B* rather than to enter *A*.[1] Here we have the simple rudiment of that capacity to "learn the way home" which is so greatly developed in some insects and in many birds and mammals. Here is intelligence at its lowest and simplest level. How shall we interpret the facts? We can hope to do so only very incompletely. For we do not know by what sense-impressions the animal is chiefly guided; and its experience is very remote from our own. The animal may be

[1] This very interesting experiment is one of many of similar type that we owe to the ingenuity of Professor R. M. Yerkes.

said to form the habit of going to the right or left. But how is the habit formed? If the animal were repeatedly guided or led directly through the one passage only, we could imagine that its motor mechanism acquired a "set" which resulted in its working always in that way; as a piece of paper or cloth, folded repeatedly along the same lines, tends to fall into those folds; or water, led through certain channels, wears them, so that it tends of itself to find those channels. But all such simple mechanical analogies fail us before this simplest manifestation of intelligence. For, before the "habit" is acquired in some degree, the animal goes as often to *B* as to *A*; yet begins to acquire a "preference" for *A*. Almost all writers who have dealt with this problem, as presented by numberless instances of animal behavior, invoke the influence of pleasure and pain, of satisfaction and dissatisfaction; appealing to the analogy of our own experience under similar conditions. Pleasure or satisfaction, they say, attends upon and follows from success; pain or displeasure or dissatisfaction attends and follows upon failure and thwarting of efforts. And somehow the pleasure confirms or "stamps in" the tendency to repetition of the movements which it attends and follows; and pain inhibits, checks, and "stamps out" the tendency to movements which it attends upon and follows. Even the mechanists and the reflexists generally admit these correlations of pleasure with success and a tendency to repetition, and of displeasure or pain with failure and a tendency to vary the movements, to seek other ways, other means. But, of course, their principles commit them to the supposition that this all-important role is played not by pleasure and pain as modes of experience, but by two unlike types of physical or chemical process which they assume to be the physical concomitants of pleasure and of pain. And there have been many attempts to suggest the nature of these alleged concomitants of pleasure and of pain. I will not delay to state or criticise these suggestions. I will only say that no one of them has secured, or deserves to secure, general acceptance, and will refer the student to an argument which I have published elsewhere and which has not received the attention it deserves.[1]

[1] "Primer of Physiological Psychology," p. 158.

One attempt to explain mechanistically this fundamental type of profiting by experience has been widely accepted, and therefore, though it seems to me obviously fallacious, requires a few words of criticism. It is said that, each time the animal enters *B*, he must return to and pass through *A* before he can attain his goal; hence, since it may be assumed that he at first will enter *A* and *B* equally often, he must pass through *A* twice as often as he passes into

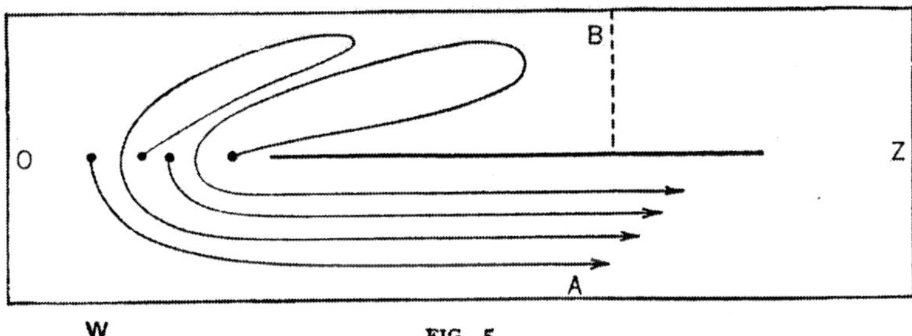

FIG. 5

B; for, when he enters *A*, he does not enter *B*; but each time he enters *B* he must subsequently pass through *A*. Hence he acquires a stronger tendency to enter *A* than to enter *B*, in accordance with the fundamental principle that repetition of any series of reactions strengthens the tendency in proportion to the number of repetitions. The argument may be presented schematically in the form of the diagram (Fig. 5), in which the curved lines represent

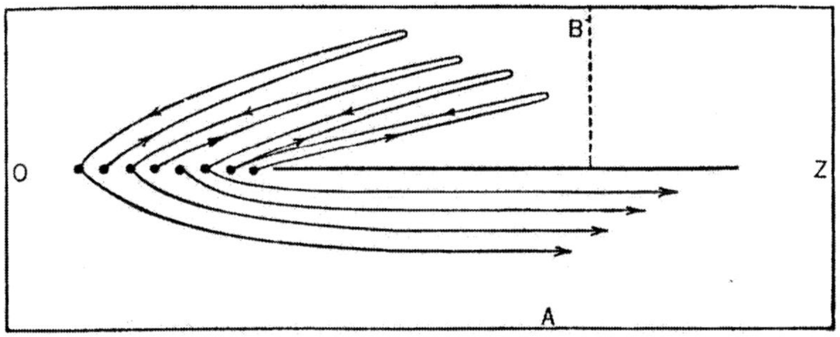

FIG. 6

the hypothetical paths followed by the animal in four successive experiments. But this argument and this diagram are wofully misleading. According to the agreed assumptions, the animal, when situated at or about the starting-point *O*, is as likely to go toward *B* as toward *A*, no matter by what process he reaches, or is placed at, *O*. When, then, he returns to *O*, after entering *B*, he will as often return again to *B* as to *A*, so long as he has not acquired a stronger tendency toward *A* than toward *B*. Hence the diagram which truly schematizes his movements, in accordance with the mechanistic assumptions, is Fig. 6. From this it is clear that, in accordance with the mechanistic assumption, he will strengthen both tendencies, that toward *A* and that toward *B* equally, because he repeats the movements in the two directions equally often.[1]

A less obviously fallacious mechanistic explanation of the facts is the following: It is said that the completion of the act followi ıg upon the entering of *A*, or the near approach to the stimulating object *Z* on passing through *A*, determines a higher level of activity in passing through *A* than in wandering in *B*. Hence the acquirement of a "preference" for *A*. In face of the facts as described above, this explanation is plausible. But consider now a variation of the experiment which rules out both of the above mechanistic explanations. I constructed a tank (Fig. 7) containing a compartment *O* and at

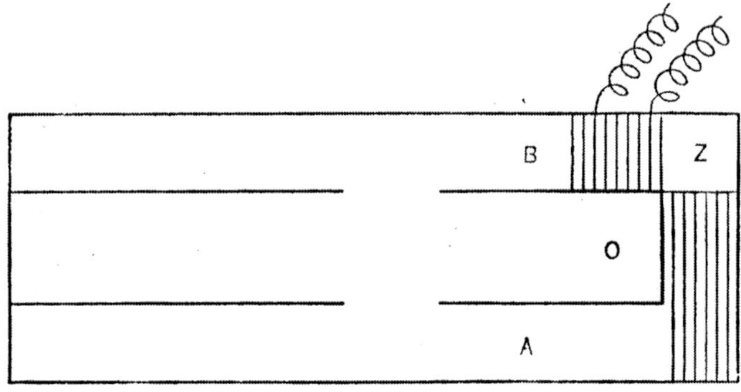

FIG. 7

one end a platform *Z*. From *O* two channels lead to *Z*, a longer one *A* and a shorter one *B*. The tank is half filled with water, leaving the platform *Z* projecting a little above the water. From each of the passages, *A* and *B*, a sloping board leads from the surface of the water to the platform. A white rat is placed in *O*. He swims about and soon finds his way to the platform. At first his tendency is to go by *B* rather than *A*, because *B* is shorter. When this habit has been established, an interrupted electric current is passed through a grating on the sloping way from *B*; so that every time the rat ascends from *B* to *Z* he receives an electric shock. The rat exhibits signs of fear on and after receiving the shock. But nevertheless he persists for some time

[1] This fallacious and widely accepted explanation was, I believe, first suggested by Dr. J. B. Watson in his volume "Behavior." He seems to have been obscurely aware of its fallacy; for he sought to give it plausibility by saying that when the animal, returning from *B*, reaches *O*, the kinæsthetic stimuli will force it to go on via *A*. But if we accept the assumption that the kinæsthetic stimuli will drive it directly forward, it follows that they will drive it from *O* to the wall *W*, on reaching which it will be equally likely to turn to the right or the left, *i. e.*, to enter *A* or return to *B*.

in passing up the slope from *B* to *Z*. He hesitates, approaches, and draws back; and generally he makes a violent dash at the slope *B*, often leaping across it so rapidly that he gets only a momentary shock. This alteration of his manner of approaching and ascending *B* is the first stage of learning. After a certain number of repetitions of the ascent of *B* and of the shock, he refuses to attempt *B* and always goes by *A*; and he refuses to attempt *B* even if his access to *A* is barred by a sliding door. I have repeated this with 11 rats, and the result was in general terms the same with each one, though some learned to avoid *B* more quickly (after fewer repetitions of the shock) than others. Here, then, neither of the foregoing mechanistic explanations is applicable. The rat has gone oftener by *B* than by *A*; and his movements toward his goal have been more vigorous, in going by *B* than in going by *A*; and in both cases he has attained his goal. Yet in the end he refuses to attempt *B*. We can only explain the facts by saying that, on facing the *B* route, the rat anticipates more or less intelligently the consequence of taking that route, namely, the electric shock. Or perhaps we might say that, as he faces the *B* route, the perception of that passage evokes fear, or the impulse to retreat, which inhibits the impulse to go forward. But this last account would not be wholly adequate to the facts; for most of the rats showed unmistakably a strong aversion not only from the *B* slope, but also from the doorway which opens from *O* to *B*. For example, if both doors be kept closed for half a minute after the rat is put into *O*, he will, after learning to avoid *B*, usually cling to or hover before the door to *A*, avoiding all approach to the door to *B*.

The correlation of pleasure with success or with progress toward the end of action, and of displeasure with failure and thwarting of action, must be accepted as fundamental, an ultimate fact of mind.[1] And it is more than a correlation; we find that in ourselves pleasure sustains, prolongs, and confirms the modes of striving which bring pleasure, that is, the successful modes. It is for this reason that we truly say "nothing succeeds like success." Pain or displeasure, on the other hand, checks us, discourages and turns us aside from the line of effort we are pursuing now or have pursued unsuccessfully in the past. To this fundamental feature of its nature the mind owes its directive power, its power to guide and improve our modes of striving toward our goals. We have seen that mental activity is essentially forward-looking and anticipatory. When we encounter a second time circumstances under which we have striven successfully, the satisfaction we have attained on the former occasion revives and colors our anticipation, reinforcing and sustaining our efforts. When we find ourselves striving in a way and

[1] As ultimate as Newton's laws of motion or the gravitation of matter.

under circumstances which formerly brought the dissatisfaction of failure, this dissatisfaction colors our anticipation and turns us aside to other lines of striving. It is in this way that the pleasures and pains of the past guide our actions in the present. We may assume that it is not otherwise with our fellow-men and with the animals. If we try to imagine any creature constituted in the opposite manner, namely, so that it was stimulated by failure to persevere in the same line and discouraged by success, we realize more fully the fundamental nature of this harmony. And, if we imagine a creature so constituted as to know neither pleasure nor pain and to remain indifferent to success and failure, we see that it would not improve its modes of striving; for under the same circumstances it would strive in the same way on successive occasions; it would learn neither to discriminate more nicely than it is fitted to do by its innate constitution, nor to adapt its behavior to the varying features of the objects to which it reacts.

These, then, are the functions of pleasure and of pain. We live in a world in which we meet again and again objects and situations similar to those we have encountered in the past. If each recurrent object and situation were quite unchanged on these successive occasions, if they were modelled exactly upon the eternal "Ideas" of Plato, our instincts would suffice to guide us in all situations, and we should have no need of the guidance of pleasure and displeasure. But the world we live in with the animals is not of that nature; every object in it is unique, and we never find ourselves a second time in the presence of the same circumstances. Hence it affords indefinite scope for discrimination and the discriminative guidance of action by pleasure and pain. It is just because animals and plants run so nearly true to the type of the species, because all members of each species are so nearly alike, and because Instinct is so largely concerned with reactions to animals and plants, that Instinct in the lower animals can achieve so much with little help from Intelligence.

There is a strong tradition in psychology which sees in pleasure and pain the source, spring, or motive of all action. This view, known as "psychological hedonism," readily gains acceptance among the vulgar, because it seems so obvious that we do shrink and turn aside from pain and do pursue pleasure. It is incapable of exact formulation and has been very variously stated, just because it is false. Its falsity is easily seen, when it is attempted to apply it, in any one of its various forms, to animal behavior. Yesterday I drove down the village street, and a large collie dog raced along the road beside the car. His course, which was perfectly straight, led him within a few feet of a hen which was anxiously gathering her chicks at the roadside. As he passed the hen, she flew at him with all her feathers ruffled. How can the pleasure-pain theory deal with that behavior of the hen? Was she moved by the "idea" of the pain she would experience if he hurt one of her chicks; or by the "idea" of the pleasure of giving him a good sharp peck? Or was it some pain or pleasure that she actually experienced on the dog's approach that impelled her to the assault?

I do not know whether this hen had ever before found herself in a similar situation. But there can be no doubt that she would have behaved in the same way, even though this were the first occasion on which she led forth her brood from the shelter of the hen-coop. In other words, her action was purely instinctive, owed little or nothing to previous experience, and was impelled neither by pleasure nor by pain, and was not an effort to secure pleasure or to avoid pain. The behavior of the animal mother who fights to the death in defense of her young is only the most striking illustration of the ineptitude of the hedonist theory of action. Almost all instances of animal behavior illustrate it only a little less clearly. To apply the hedonist theory to human conduct, as so many philosophers and amateur moralists have done, is to deny the continuity of human with animal evolution and the community of human and animal nature. I shall not trouble my reader with any elaborate refutation of psychological hedonism. Those who have a hankering after the theory may find it discussed *ad nauseam* in ethical treatises.[1]

The Method of Trial and Error

The instance of the crayfish learning to seek his food through the open, rather than the closed, passage is a typical example of what is generally called the "method of trial and error." Much human, as well as animal, learning proceeds in this way, and many experimental studies of such animal learning have been made. Let us consider another instance of such behavior under experimental conditions. We may take the justly famous experiments of Professor E. L. Thorndike, which have served as the model for many other laboratory workers in this field. Thorndike confined young cats in cages of which the front wall consisted of vertical bars and a door; the door was fastened on its inner surface by a catch or button which could easily be turned by the animal. In each instance the animal was placed

[1] Cf. also pp. 219, 268.

in the cage in a condition of "utter hunger"; and food was placed outside the bars of the cage, beyond reach of the cat's paw. The result in general terms was that each animal scratched and clawed about the front of his cage for some time, until, in the course of these "random" movements, he turned the button, escaped, and secured food. Each animal was put through the process again and again; and in the main the result was that he gradually shortened the period of "random" movement, until after many repetitions he learned to go straightway to the button, turn it, and so escape. Such learning by dogs and cats has been widely represented as illustrating the nature and limits of animal intelligence. And the mechanists have seized upon it eagerly; for it seems to them to bear out their contention that Intelligence is only mechanism working in the obscurity imposed by the thickness of our skulls. They interpret the facts in some such way as follows: The animal in the cage is stimulated, by sense-stimuli received from various parts of the cage, to a series of random reflex movements. These are continued, until by happy chance some movement turns the button and releases the prisoner. The pleasure of escape or of the taste of the food then "somehow stamps in" the particular reflex reaction which turns the button; so that, when the same situation recurs, this reflex is more readily fired off than all others; and with each repetition the "stamping in" goes further, until this reflex becomes so preponderatingly sensitive that it is fired off as soon as the animal is placed in the cage. Of course the "behaviorist" of the pure blood knows nothing of pleasure and pain, and therefore nothing of their nervous correlates; and, in face of this relatively simple problem, he can only maintain the lofty attitude that his business as a scientist is to describe facts and not to dabble with explanations and hypotheses. But the less rigidly "scientific" mechanists of the more common kind are confronted with this problem: How does the nervous correlate of the pleasure resulting from escape from the cage, or from the taste of the food, how does this "stamp in" the reflex *which preceded it in time* and led to the opening of the door? It seems to be a clear case of the effect preceding the cause, a sequence entirely inadmissible in a world of pure mechanism.

If we are not committed to the identification of mental activity with mechanical process, we shall see, even in this display of the stupidity of the animal, a revelation of the essentially teleological or purposive nature of mental activity, an instance of that power of Mind to foresee the future in accordance with past experience and to govern action in the light of that foresight which is its fundamental nature. The essential nature of Mind is to govern present action by anticipation of the future in the light of past experience; to make, in short, effects precede and determine their causes. The cats' movements are in the main not merely reflex responses to stimuli. Rather they are throughout governed by the purpose of reaching the food. This involves some anticipation, however vague, of the goal. We may fairly suppose that, as the process is repeated, this anticipation becomes more definite, as also anticipation of the various steps of action by which the goal is reached. Without rejecting the facts, we may criticise the experiments as failing to give fair play to the intelligence of the animals. Let us imagine twenty college professors shut in as many cages in a condition of "utter hunger," while a table is temptingly spread before the line of cages. And let us suppose that each one can secure his release only by scratching a hole in the ground with his finger-nails and rummaging with his nose at the bottom of this hole. The conditions would be comparable to those imposed on his cats by Professor Thorndike. Is it not possible that a Martian observer, knowing little of human nature, might infer from the behavior of the professors that they were creatures of small intelligence, much given to random movements and meaningless vociferations?

Thorndike's experiments were a valuable contribution to methods of study. But those who accept the results of experiments of this kind as illustrating the limits of intelligence of the animals concerned are seriously misled. I suggest that what we now need is not experiments which show how little intelligence the animal may display under highly unfavorable conditions; but rather experiments which will show how much an animal may achieve in the way of intelligent adaptation of behavior, under the most favorable conditions and after continued and varied training upon tasks of the same general nature.[1]

[1] Professor L. T. Hobhouse, in his "Mind in Evolution," has worked along this line with striking success. This book, together with Professor S. J. Holmes's "Evolution of Animal Intelligence," may be warmly recommended to the student who wishes to read further in this field.

As a small contribution to this step in method, I describe the following experiment. I had a lively sociable Airedale terrier who, up to middle age, had never been trained to tackle mechanical problems; though he had learned with assistance to open a heavy wicket-gate, by pulling down the handle of the latch and then pulling the gate toward him, when he sought exit from the garden. I constructed a cubical wooden box, ten inches in diameter, and screwed it to a square board about twenty inches across (Fig. 8). The box had a lid, hinged at one side and provided with a broad handle, *A*, projecting from the hinged side. Pressure on this handle would open the lid. I proceeded to feed the dog by breaking his biscuit into pieces and placing a piece in the box. The dog, watching my procedure with an air of lively interest, showed a tendency to seek the pieces of biscuit which I held in reserve. A

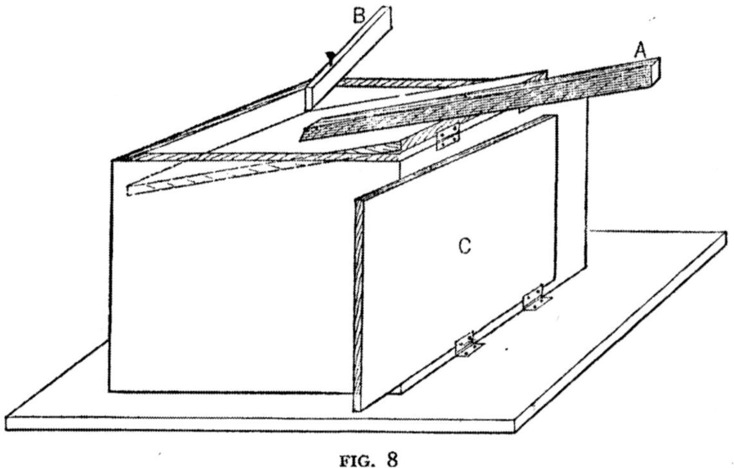

FIG. 8

few stern words sufficed to check this tendency, though not to destroy it; he was always ready to take advantage of any remissness on my part to secure a reserved piece. Forbidden the reserved pieces, and allowed to see the piece in the box before the lid was closed, he turned to the box and quickly secured the biscuit by shoving up the front edge of the lid with his nose. He repeated this promptly several times. I therefore shaved down the margins of the lid, until its front edge could sink below the rim of the box and rest there upon a ledge. The dog's first method was now of no avail; but he pushed his nose so vigorously against the front rim of the box as to overturn it; and then, the lid falling open, he secured his biscuit. Thereafter I usually kept my foot on the ground-plate, to prevent the use of this second method; but, when occasionally I neglected this precaution, he seldom failed to revert to this simple and natural procedure. Finding now the second method futile, he scratched and bit and scrabbled all round the box, often spending some time in persistently licking the lid; until after some few minutes he depressed the handle, *A*, with his forepaw, and so lifted the lid. Immediately he released the handle and rushed to the front of the box; but the lid fell back into place. With admirable good temper and energy he renewed his scrabbling and soon depressed the handle again. This time he quickly inserted his nose under the raised lid before releasing the handle, and so secured his biscuit. On repetition he quickly became more expert and quicker in this simple train of action. I then added a simple latch, consisting in a slat of wood, *B*, about 8 inches in length, loosely pivoted at its middle on the front corner of the box. This prevented the opening of the lid, until it was turned through an angle of 45°. At first he was held up by this latch, but soon learned in random fashion to push *B* aside. He would then usually begin by trying *A*. If the lid refused to rise, he would at once run round to *B* and push it with nose or paw, and then return to press on *A*. Sometimes he had not pushed *B* far enough, and *A* would still resist his pressure. Then he would quickly return to *B* and give it another push. When he had learned to deal with *B*, I added a third obstacle, namely, a board, *C*, hinged to the foot-piece so that, when set vertically, it prevented the depression of *A*, and had to be pushed down before the lid could be opened. He soon learned to deal also with *C*, and would throw down *C* and turn *B*, either with his nose or paw, indifferently, and not always in the same order.

How shall we interpret this process of learning? Certainly there was much of more or less random effort, and only a gradual acquisition of the art of opening the box. But the whole process was in several respects essentially different from the establishment of a chain of reflexes by simple repetition of completely random movements and the "stamping in" of the accidentally successful movements. From the first it was obvious that the dog was *trying* to open the lid *in order* to obtain the biscuit which he had seen put into the box. His action was purposive. It is true that throughout he did not understand the mechanism of the box any better than the average driver of an automobile understands the mechanism which he learns "by rule of thumb" intelligently to control. But, when he had watched me put a piece of biscuit in the box, he knew it was there, just as I knew it. It is true he did not formulate this knowledge in words, and he did not achieve it by the aid of a formal syllogism; but no more did I. And his knowledge or his implicit judgment of the presence of the biscuit was liable to error. And so was mine. Occasionally he did struggle with the empty box, but only very rarely; though he had many opportunities. And when he had seen the biscuit put into the box, I never knew him to give up the struggle; though in some cases it was prolonged for twenty minutes before he attained success. Even his first method, simple as it was, was entirely different from a reflex. And the intelligent nature of his second almost equally simple method (that of overturning the box) was shown by the fact that, though he had used it successfully only a few times, he was quick to seize any opportunity of reverting to it.

When he had learned the whole trick and could in a few seconds work all three bits of mechanism, the movements by which he achieved success were anything but a fixed habitual series; not only did the movements not occur in the same order upon successive occasions, but the nature of the movements themselves continued to vary widely. Often he would begin by pressing the handle with his paw; and this was done sometimes with the right, sometimes and more often with the left, forefoot. On finding it resist his pressure, he would usually run round at once to the latch *B*; and this he would turn, sometimes with his nose, sometimes with his paw. Often he failed at first to move it far enough, and he never seemed to discover this by vision, but only by trying the handle *A* again; when, if it still resisted, he would usually return to *B* and give it another shove. The throwing down of *C* was done generally by a single definite stroke of the paw, either before or after turning *B*, and either before or after trying *A*. I cannot see any ground for denying that in a vague and imperfect manner he understood the nature of his task, and that, in fact, his manipulation of the mechanism was strictly comparable to the manipulation of an automobile by one who does not understand the machinery; differing chiefly in that he learned how to work it by his own repeated trial and error, whereas the automobilist is taught when and how to move his levers and turn his keys. These movements may be said to have been more or less random; but they were far from being completely so. In the first place, they were all directed to the box; and this direction was neither by a reflex nor by a tropism. The odor of the biscuit, if it had any for him, was all around and about the scene of his operations. Secondly, his efforts were directed almost exclusively to the lid and its handle, and very seldom to other parts of the box. His first throwing down of *C* was no doubt in the course of random pawings; but his success quickly led him to direct his movements to it, either pawing or pushing with his nose. Very striking was his quick appreciation of the uselessness of pressing on the handle so long as it did not yield; often he fumbled the handle badly, and let it slip after raising the lid and before getting his nose under it. But this was largely due to the defects of his paw as an instrument of manipulation. This course of events implies that, while the dog's behavior was from the first purposive, a striving toward the goal of obtaining the biscuit, the goal, and especially the steps toward the goal, became more defined in the dog's mind as he became more expert in his task. He never thought out any complete plan of procedure; and even at the end he probably never imagined, even in outline as a complete series, all the steps he had to take to attain his goal.

But, while his anticipation of each step of action was at first vague in the extreme, we must suppose that it became more clearly defined; until in the end each step of action was thought of more or less definitely, as the occasion for it arose out of his preceding action.

I will describe one more of this dog's achievements; for, though it was not observed under laboratory conditions, it was none the less highly significant. He would seek and find a piece of biscuit hidden in the room. After he had played this game many times, it was varied by taking the biscuit to other rooms; with very little experience of this more difficult task, he learned to sit listening intently in a room down-stairs, while the biscuit was hidden in any one of a number of rooms up-stairs. Then, when the hider returned and gave the signal, he would dash up-stairs, and generally would quickly enter the right room and find the biscuit. The mechanist, of course, will say that he was guided by the scented trail; but the whole house, inhabited as it was by a large family, must have been saturated with a multitude of odors for him. What exactly his mental process was it is impossible to say; but it would, I think, be pedantic to deny that it involved an intelligent appreciation of the whole situation, to which an acquired knowledge of the house and of its various parts was essential—an appreciation and a knowledge analogous to our own.

Laboratory experiments are valuable; but they must not lightly pretend to determine the limits of the animal's intelligence. For in the laboratory the conditions are inevitably so remote from the natural as to be highly unfavorable to the animal's exercise of his highest powers. How many centuries of laboratory experiment with wasps might have elapsed without revealing any action comparable to the use by *Ammophila* of a pebble for pounding down the earth over her nest!

In this connection I will refer to the Elberfeld horses and other parallel instances of animal behavior, only to indicate them as a warning to those who would minimize the intelligence of animals.[1] For the interpretation of these instances remains too enigmatic and disputable. But at the very least they proved, on the part of the horse, a delicacy of perceptual discrimination far surpassing anything that his best friends had previously claimed for him in that line.

It is probable that only the higher animals learn to discriminate or distinguish and recognize individual objects as such. Instinctive perception is essentially the discrimination of objects only as representatives of their class or species. But it is clear that all animals that form enduring partnerships with their mates, and those that return to their nests or homes under the guidance of acquired familiarity with the neighborhood, learn to discriminate and recognize particular objects as such. And it is clear that an intelligent dog achieves the discrimination and recognition of a large number of persons and other objects. Such recognition implies elementary judgment, which becomes more explicit when the animal hesitates before acting. For example, I enter at my garden-gate, while my dog lies before the house-door some sixty yards away. He barks at me, as he would bark at a stranger, and comes toward me in a threatening man-

[1] One horse, *der kluge Hans*, was alleged to perform arithmetical operations of some complexity, tapping out with his forefoot his answers to the problems set him. It was shown by Professor Stumpf and his pupils that this achievement seemed to depend upon the appreciation by the horse of slight movements made unintentionally by spectators. Herr Krall, of Elberfeld, undertook to teach a number of horses to perform even more complicated calculations. He had great success, apparently, and several scientific critics were unable to explain away their achievements by aid of the principle which had seemed adequate in the case of *der kluge Hans*.

ner; and, if I refrain from speaking or making any familiar gesture, his attitude changes to one of friendly welcome only when we are separated by no more than some twenty yards; for a dog's visual discrimination is less delicate than man's. As he approaches, his behavior is apt to show clearly a blending and alternation of the two attitudes, the hostile and the friendly submissive attitudes; until suddenly the hesitation is resolved and gives place to unrestrained welcoming. If I make the experiment in a dim light and speak in a disguised voice, his hesitation may be more prolonged, and resolved only when his nose comes very near to me. I do not see how we can deny that this behavior is strictly analogous to our own, when we are in doubt about the recognition of an approaching friend. Our attitude is one of hesitation and questioning, and passes into definite recognition and greeting by way of an act of judgment, which may or may not be expressed in the words "It is he." Sometimes this judgment is preceded by the verbal formulation of the question, "Is it he?" But in other cases there is no verbal formulation, but a mere puzzled questioning examination of the approaching figure; until suddenly the judgment of recognition is achieved. In the latter case the mental process would seem to be strictly comparable to the dog's, when he recognizes me after hesitation.

Judgment is the beginning of reasoning; and though reasoning in the full sense implies freely working imagination and the use of language, yet even on the perceptual plane elementary reasoning takes place. The essential feature of reasoning is reaction to some aspect or quality of an object which marks it as appropriate for the purpose of the moment. Of any animals lower in the mental scale than the apes it is difficult to point to behavior that clearly implies reasoning. But when an ape uses various objects, such as sticks, ropes, sacks, in order to draw within his reach some such thing as a nut, we have evidence of perceptual reasoning. For the animal recognizes and reacts to that common quality of such diverse objects which, in spite of their widely unlike properties, renders them all alike serviceable for his purpose, namely, the quality of being more or less heavy, loose, and manageable. The higher apes have frequently been observed to display such evidence of rudimentary reasoning.

Imagination in Animals

Most of the behavior of animals is initiated and guided by perception, that is to say, by appreciation of impressions made on the sense-organs. It is not easy to answer the question: How far can animals think of, or adjust their behavior to, objects not present to their senses? But that the higher animals have this capacity in considerable degree we can hardly doubt. Imagination is the most general term for this capacity or function of thinking of absent or remote objects. When an animal travels steadily toward its home; or a dog gets up from sleep and goes directly to a spot at a distance and digs up a bone which he has buried on the previous day; or a dog waits a long time before the door where his master has entered, refusing to be enticed away, it is difficult to interpret the behavior without the assumption that the animal in some way thinks of or imagines his home, his bone, or his master. The behavior of a sleeping dog sometimes strongly suggests that he is dreaming of the chase.

Professor W. S. Hunter has made ingenious and exact investigation of the capacity of animals and young children to be guided by sense-perceptions that lie in the past.[1] The subject of the experiment learned by many repetitions to find food in one of three chambers, which was distinguished from the other two by a bright patch of light. The subject was then prevented from approaching the chamber until an interval had elapsed (its duration varying in successive experiments) after the exposure of the signal-light. In this way it was found that each species of subject failed to be guided aright, if the interval was prolonged beyond a certain maximum period. This period was for rats ten seconds, for dogs five minutes, and for children much longer periods, according to their age. Köhler (*op. cit.*) reports the following observations. He buried a pear in the sand before a cage in which sat a chimpanzee keenly watching his operations. The sand was smoothed over with a rake. After intervals ranging up to an hour, a stick was put into the cage; the animal took the stick and, thrusting it between the bars, began to dig at the spot where the pear had been buried, and quickly secured the fruit. In other experiments the animals were allowed into the arena where sixteen hours earlier they had watched the burying of fruit in the sand. In many cases they went directly to the spot and dug up the fruit. The necessary controls were observed; and the experiment seems to establish beyond doubt that these animals were guided by memory of the observed place and procedure. It would be pedantic to deny that, as they proceeded to dig in the

[1] "The Delayed Reaction in Animals and Children," "Behavior Monographs," 2, 1, 1913.

sand at the right spot, they in some sense thought of the fruit as buried at that spot.

Most of such instances of imagining by animals seem to depend upon familiarity acquired by the individual creature. But in some few instances we seem compelled to suppose that the power of thinking of, or imagining, an object not present to the senses is provided in the form of innate mental structure. Such an instance is the building of a complex structure according to a plan common to the species and without previous acquaintance with such structures, as in the case of some spiders and insects. The construction of the complex nests of some birds, especially those of the weaver-birds, seems to fall under this head; for, although the birds have in most such cases been hatched and fledged in a nest such as they will later construct, it is very difficult to suppose that the peculiar structure of the nest is traditional only and that the young birds study the structure in preparation for building which they will undertake some months later. Yet these are the alternatives. There is no question here of a mere chain of reflexes. The animal, while achieving the general form and pattern proper to the species, adapts his work in a multitude of ways to special circumstances; he knows how to repair accidental injuries to the structure, and how to make use of unusual materials and positions that may offer themselves.

In these pages I cannot attempt to discuss the evolution of mental functions in the animal kingdom. I will only emphasize in passing the view that Instinct and Intelligence represent neither two divergent lines of evolution nor two stages of evolution, but rather are always only two aspects of all mental life which we distinguish by an effort of abstraction. A common view represents instinctive behavior as "unconscious" and intelligent behavior as "conscious," and raises the question—At what stage of evolution did Intelligence or "Consciousness" begin to supplant or modify unconscious Instinct. Thus Professor S. J. Holmes writes in his admirable book, "The Evolution of Animal Intelligence," as follows: "It is scarcely possible at present to fix, even with the rudest approximation, the point where intelligence makes its first appearance in the course of evolution. There is little doubt that the step from instinct to intelligence has been made, not once merely, but several times. The intelligence of the higher mollusca had, in all probability, an origin independent from that of the arthropods, and the intelligence of the vertebrates was probably developed independently of that of other groups. Among the arthropods themselves it is not likely that the intelligence manifested by the arachnids had a common origin with that of the insects, and within both of these large groups intelligence may have been independently developed out of behavior of the purely instinctive type." This is a half-hearted evolutionism which smacks too much of the Spencerian doctrine that "consciousness" somehow arose out of the compounding and recompounding of mechanical reflexes, when the structures concerned had attained an unspecified degree of complexity. We shall never achieve understanding of the evolution of Mind by following this false lead. I have tried to show my readers that the rudiments of Mind are implied by the behavior of the most lowly animals, and that we cannot hope to trace the genesis of purposive behavior out of mechanical processes; because the two conceptions are radically different. Eventually it may be shown that all processes are of one type; but it seems more likely that the processes of inorganic nature may ultimately be shown to be purposive than that the behavior of animals will be shown to be purely mechanical. Hitherto all attempts to resolve the one type of process into the other have proved fruitless. Both conceptions, mechanical process and purposive action, are at present useful and, in fact, indispensable, and therefore valid; and they seem to be equally fundamental, each in its own sphere.

CHAPTER VII

BEHAVIOR OF THE NATURAL MAN

We commonly contrast the natural and the artificial; and, if we inquire more nearly into the nature of this contrast, we find that the artificial, that which is produced by art, results from the application of the accumulated traditions of thinking, feeling, and doing, which constitute human culture in its various degrees. The normal development of every human being is influenced profoundly by these traditions; the constitution that each of us inherits from his ancestors is molded by a multitude of contacts with his fellows, especially with his elders, who in turn have been molded in a similar way. The immense extent of the influence of tradition upon us may be most readily brought to mind by reflecting that our command of language is almost wholly the result of our absorption of tradition, and that on the use of language thus absorbed depends the development of all our higher capacities.

It is useful to try to imagine the life of a small community of men grown up together in detacnment from all tradition. Such a community has probably never existed; but it is not in principle impossible and might be experimentally produced with immense advantages to psychology, if there were no moral objections to such an experiment. But, though we cannot make the experiment actually, we may profitably attempt it in imagination. We may hope, by doing so, to realize more vividly the essential similarities between human and animal behavior, bridging in imagination the immense gap made, between the lowest known men and the highest animals, by the accumulated mass of traditional knowledge, belief, and sentiment which the most primitive human societies have acquired. The members of such a community might properly be called natural men and women and natural children. What sort of a creature would be such a natural man? How would he differ from the higher animals, on the one hand, and from the rudest savages known to us on the other? Mowgli[1] would enjoy all the sensory capacities that we enjoy and, in respect of the natural objects with which he was led by his instincts to concern himself, his powers of perceptual discrimination would probably be very highly developed, as we find among many savages. He would be endowed with the instincts which we have seen reason to suppose are common to the higher gregarious mammals. He would be moved, on the perception of various objects and situations, to strive impulsively toward the natural goals of his instincts. He would experience the appetites or cravings of his several instincts and the emotional excitements proper to them. He would feel pleasure or satisfaction on success, pain or displeasure on failure or thwarting of his impulsive efforts. He would have no command of language, beyond a few emotional cries and interjections, aided by expressive gestures.

If we made friends with such a man and studied his behavior, we should have no other means of interpreting it than those we apply to animal behavior; and we should be able to interpret it only a little more fully and confidently than we interpret the behavior of an intelligent dog. The chief difference between his behavior and that of the higher animals would be that it would be guided more largely by, would imply more reference to, things previously perceived, but no longer present to the senses, and situations previously experienced and likely to be experienced again. We should probably find that he possessed and jealously secreted and guarded some little store of food and a few material possessions, such as a few skins and a few very rude utensils or tools. These would be fashioned to his uses hardly at all, but merely chosen in virtue of their lending themselves to his purposes. He would probably have a home or lair in some cave, which he would share with other men and women; and he would probably show some attachment to some one female, who would be the mother of his children; though whether he would show any special interest in his own children, would defend them,

[1] Kipling has depicted such a natural man in Mowgli, the hero of his "Jungle Tales." I venture to borrow the name.

feed them, or claim possession of and obedience from them, in a way that would mark them off from the children of his fellows, we cannot confidently say. From the extent to which his behavior referred to remote objects, we should infer that his power of thinking of such objects, his Imagination, was much more developed and active than that of any animal. For his behavior would imply more foresight of the future in accordance with past experiences; a certain more far-reaching planning of action to forestall and prepare for future events. And, in the execution of such plans, he and his fellows would probably achieve a more effective and varied co-operation than any of the other mammals attain to; showing thereby that they achieved a better mutual understanding, by means of gestures and their very limited vocabulary.

Desire

Mowgli's greater power of imagination would reveal itself also in a higher degree of spontaneity and initiative, and in a greater continuity of effort. Most, though not all, of the trains of behavior of an animal are initiated by sense-impressions; and, if the object which evokes its instinctive response is withdrawn from the range of its senses, the impulse in most cases soon dies away, or is supplanted by a new impulse evoked by some other object.[1] An animal, if it is diverted from a train of activity started by one sense-impression, and if the interruption is not of very brief duration only, seldom resumes that activity; unless it finds itself again in the presence of the object which initiated it. But a dog digs up a bone he has buried on the previous day; a beaver returns again and again to work at felling the same tree; beasts of prey will return to the carcass they have left partly devoured; the wasp returns to the hole she has prepared; and the bee returns to the syrup in the bee-hunter's box, after transporting a load to the hive. In all such cases we observe a continuity of effort or behavior which seems to imply that the animal thinks of or imagines the object, while remote from it; and thinks of it not simply as such, but also as located in a known position.

[1] If the appetite is strong, it may continue to manifest itself in the vague undirected restlessness characteristic of appetite.

Such action directed toward a remote[1] object implies the state which in ourselves we call *desire.* Desire in the widest sense may be defined as an impulse directed toward a remote object. So defined it includes aversive desires, which more commonly are called aversions. If I am reminded of an impending danger, a threatening object, such as a wild beast, which I cannot perceive, I nevertheless experience the impulse to escape and hide myself. This is an aversive desire. In the narrowest and strictest sense, desire denotes our state when imagination of an object evokes in us an impulse to action, yet action is suspended or prevented by some physical or moral or intellectual difficulty; as when I desire to obtain food, but am securely confined in a prison cell, or fear to venture forth, or know that there is no food within the reach of my utmost efforts. It is probable that the animals never experience desire in this fullest sense, but only that lower form of desire which is a striving toward, or in relation to, a remote object. That is to say, the animal in which any instinctive impulse is excited does not suspend action, even though the object be remote; the impulse probably always expresses itself in action. In this respect our natural man would show his superiority to the animals. He would be capable of the higher form of desire, namely, impulse toward or away from a remote object, with suspension of action. This suspension of action results from his more developed imagination. The higher animal, we may reasonably infer, is capable of imagining the remote food or the remote danger; and, as it thinks of the one or the other, the corresponding impulse expresses itself in action. But the natural man could imagine the remote food and the remote danger as co-existing in the same place; and so he might experience a desire for the food, while the action to which it prompted was suspended or inhibited by the impulse of fear or, as we loosely say, by the desire for safety. Such suspension of action, while the impulse to action continues to work in the form of desire kept alive by imagination of its object, is the

[1] I use the word "remote" here and hereafter to imply that the object so characterized is beyond the range of the senses; by this specialization of the word we may fill an inconvenient gap in our terminology. I shall also use the adjective "present" in the opposite sense, *i. e.*, to denote objects present to, or affecting, the senses.

essential condition of all higher intellectual activity, of all thinking in the fuller and more usual sense of the word.

Desire and Imagination

Our natural man, desiring the remote food, yet kept within the shelter of his cave by the fear of a remote object, would continue to think about the food and about the dangerous object; he would imagine himself approaching the food cautiously in various ways. It might be that the desired food is game, such as deer, obtainable only by night, at a drinking pool frequented by lions as well as by the deer. As he lies in his cave, imagining both the deer and the lions, impelled by hunger and restrained by fear, our natural man, Mowgli, may imagine himself taking refuge in a tree beside the pool, as he may have done when threatened by lions in the past. Then he imagines himself going in safety to the tree in daylight and remaining there till nightfall, and thence descending upon his game at a moment when there is no sign of lions at hand. He would then, having imagined this line of behavior, which promises to satisfy his hunger without incurring great risk, proceed to work it out in action. He would have formed a plan, And, if he had imagined and successfully executed such plans several times, he would, when confronted with a new problem, probably set himself more or less deliberately to imagine a plan. In this way Mowgli would achieve real planning, the thinking out of a line of action before beginning to act. It is very doubtful whether any animal achieves this level of thinking. Animals, if they are confronted by a problem, solve it, if at all, *ambulando*, in the course of action; they do not sit down and think out a plan; still less do they sit down in order to think out a plan. Such planning, such purposive deliberation, would be the principal condition of the natural man's superiority to the animals. When confronted by difficulties, he would imagine various alternative lines of action; and, when he had imagined a line of action which avoided or circumvented the difficulty or danger, he would proceed to action on that plan. Having no language, beyond rude gestures and exclamations, his planning would be almost purely the imagining of concrete objects and situations; but even so it might aid him greatly in his struggle for existence.[1]

Rudimentary Sentiments

In another way Mowgli would attain to greater continuity and consistency of behavior than the animals do. We have seen how such an animal as the dog may acquire the tendency to react with a particular instinctive impulse to an object toward which he was naturally indifferent; as when he learns to shrink in fear from a whip, or to be habitually submissive to some one man or to another dog. Mowgli, aided by his greater power of imagining, would more readily acquire through experience such enduring attitudes toward various objects. Let us imagine him discovering the entrance to a deep cave. Impelled by curiosity, he enters and penetrates cautiously, until the light is very dim. Suddenly a loud rumbling resounds through the cave, and he flees in terror. On reaching his own abode, he lives again in imagination through this event. His imagination depicts the terrifying noise as coming from some great agency capable of seizing and destroying him. He cannot think of this vague agency without fear; and yet it strongly evokes his curiosity. After a few days, during which he suffers no harm, he finds himself again, in the course of his roaming, in the neighborhood of the cave. He approaches it, his curiosity more strongly excited than before; but also he is more strongly restrained by fear, which arrests him after every few steps and prompts him to peer and listen, ready to flee at the slightest unfamiliar sound or movement. But nothing happens; and, perhaps, his curiosity is increased and his fear diminished by the presence of companions. Slowly he penetrates further than before and finds, to his delight, a spring of cool clear water, at which he slakes his thirst. When, after this discovery, he dwells in imagination on this place, he feels not only fear and curiosity, but also he feels that this mysterious and terrible agent has given him what he greatly needs and values, a constant supply of pure water.

[1] I insist upon and illustrate the value of such concrete imaginative thinking, because it has so often been asserted that we cannot think without making use of words.

Mowgli and his companions now frequent this spot, making their home near to it. He feels submissive or humble before this mysterious power, but does not cease to feel both curiosity and fear on contemplating it. He feels also that here is something that he and his group possess and would possess exclusively. Perhaps they make a barrier of rough stones across the entrance. And when, in a time of drought, the spring does not fail them, they feel gratitude, such as they feel when a fellow-hunter shares his game with them; and they begin to bring and place within the cave small objects of value, such as they would give in return for gifts from their fellows. In this way our natural man may be supposed to build up an enduring complex attitude of the kind that is properly called a *sentiment.*[1] And in the case we have imagined, it would be a rudimentary religious sentiment, a sentiment of awe, developing, by the addition of gratitude, into one of reverence. His imagination would have provided him with an object on which the various impulses of this sentiment are centred; and, whenever he may approach this spot or think of it in any way, these various impulses will be stirred within him, one or other more strongly than the rest, according to the circumstances of the moment.[2]

Suppose again that, in the small community within which our natural man grows up, there is another young male who is stronger than he and who makes ruthless use of his superior strength, snatching away from Mowgli the choice tit-bit on its way to his mouth, and taking away the game that he has secured with much risk and effort. Mowgli fiercely resents these acts; but on several occasions when his anger has blazed out in active resentment, the bully has overcome him and by brutal exercise of his superior strength has inflicted excruciating pain. After some repetition of such experiences, Mowgli will be unable to think of the bully without both fear and anger; the mere sound of his voice in the distance, the mention of his name by others (if names had been invented and were in use among these natural men), the mere thought of him, as he wakens in the morn-

[1] Cf. Chapter XVII.

[2] In just such a cave in the hills of Central India I have seen the wild black hillmen depositing their little gifts beside a bubbling spring.

ing or roams alone in the forest, always brings these two emotions and the corresponding instinctive impulses into play. When the bully is far away, the angry impulse predominates and Mowgli imagines himself attacking the bully, overcoming him, and tearing him in pieces. But, when he hears his rough voice, sees his huge limbs and fierce eyes, fear predominates and checks the impulse to attack. Mowgli has learned to hate the bully; and his hatred consists in this readiness to experience both fear and anger, whenever he perceives the bully or in any way thinks of him. An enduring sentiment of hatred has been built up in the structure of his mind; the growth of the sentiment is the linkage of the affective dispositions of the instincts of fear and anger with the disposition which is concerned in and alone renders possible the discriminating, the recognizing, and the imagining of this individual, the bully.

Consider another phase of the life of the natural man. As Mowgli becomes adolescent, he feels a new impulse of attraction toward the young women whom he encounters. One such dwells in a neighboring cave; but her parents keep him at a distance, and she is shy. When spring puts an end to the hardships of the long winter, the sexual appetite waxes strong in Mowgli; and his imagination dwells upon the girl, sustained by a strong desire. He lies in wait for her and intercepts her returning from the spring with a gourd full of water. She repels his nearer approach with fierce cries and gestures, and flees to the shelter of her cave. On the following day, Mowgli approaches her again, but this time more cautiously. Aware that her cries may bring her fierce old father to the spot, his attitude is submissive; and he humbly lays at her feet a plump hare which he has caught for this purpose. On repetition of such meetings the girl learns to suffer his approach without fear, and even welcomes him. One day their meeting is disturbed by an encounter with a wild beast. The girl turns to him with a cry of fear and distress. His protective impulse is aroused and, putting out all his strength and skill, he slays the beast Another day, when Mowgli meets her, she is fleeing before a rival suitor. With a sudden fury Mowgli falls upon him and drives him in headlong flight. Or perhaps he is worsted in the combat; his rival is too strong for him and leaves him on the field, stunned and wounded and weak. He drags himself back to his cave, nursing his wounds, and thinking constantly of the girl and of his rival. He is torn by conflicting desires—his desire to destroy his rival, as a step to his undisputed possession of the girl, and his fear of him (his desire to avoid him). Thus brooding and imagining, he thinks out a plan; and, when his strength is renewed, he executes it; he lies in wait for his rival at the old meeting-place and stretches him dead by a stealthy blow from behind. Then Mowgli resumes his courting, and soon he leads the girl to a cave he has newly discovered; there they set up housekeeping and found a new family.

Such, we may suppose, was the life of the natural man, before language and tools and firm social traditions had raised him far above the level of animal behavior. It was not a life of reason, principle, conscience, and duty; nor was it the pursuit of pleasure for its own sake, modified by avoidance of pains; nor yet a series of chain reflexes. It was a life of instinctive impulse and desire, impulse often expressing itself immediately in action, but often checked by difficulties encountered or foreseen, and then working on, as desire, to sustain imaginative thinking, which sometimes issued in plans of action more or less well suited to overcome the difficulties.

We do not know whether, at the stage we have tried to imagine, man lived chiefly in the trees or on the ground; we know nothing of the details of his mode of life; but we may feel sure that, whatever its details and general habit, arboreal or other, it was a life of the kind we have imagined, a life governed by instinctive impulses similar to those of the other higher mammals, and differing from their mode of life chiefly in the greater foresight and restraint which result from greater power of imagining the remote in time and place, and in the greater continuity of effort rendered possible by more enduring sentiments for a greater variety of objects. The life of social man is sustained by impulses and desires springing from the same instincts. It differs from that of the natural man in two ways: (1) In that he learns to make use of a vast store of traditional knowledge; and (2) in that, under the influence of example and precept, he builds up many sentiments which are traditional in his society, enduring attitudes toward a multitude of objects, both the concrete objects which the natural man knows, and the abstract objects which only the use of language enables the social man to think of or conceive.

The Hormic Theory of Human Action Contrasted with Other Theories

We have examined and found wanting some of the alternative views or theories of human action, the reflex theory and the pleasure-pain theory. We have rejected by implication another widely held theory of human action, namely, the ideo-motor theory, which proclaims that all acts are the expression of "ideas," and that every "idea" is by its very nature a tendency to movement; for I have rejected "idea" as a confused and confusing term. But something more in criticism of this ideo-motor theory must be said on a later page. For the sake of completeness of review of theories of action, let me very briefly state and examine yet other alternatives.

Some authors, while recognizing that animals are moved wholly or chiefly by instinctive impulses, are yet unwilling to admit that the same is true of man. Or, while recognizing in man some very simple instincts, such as instincts to crawl, to walk, to climb, to suck, to run, to vociferate, they ascribe his more complex modes of behavior to what they are pleased to call "innate propensities." These authors seldom take the trouble to attempt to define these "propensities." If they did so, they would, I think, find them to be identical with what we have called the instinctive tendencies. The word "propensities" is a good one. There is no reason why we should not speak of instinctive tendencies as "innate propensities," and of the individually acquired tendencies that we have called sentiments as "acquired propensities." But the use of the word merely to obscure the fact of the essential similarity of human to animal behavior is to be deprecated. I think that those who recognize as instincts in man his various motor capacities, while ascribing his more complex behavior to "propensities," are misled by the false doctrine which identifies an instinct with a mere motor mechanism. We may fairly ask such persons where they will class the behavior of the higher mammals. Is it the expression of instincts or of "propensities"? And if the latter, what is the relation of "propensities" to instincts? Does the startled rabbit bolting to his hole exhibit instinct, and the dog shrinking or fleeing from his enemy exhibit a "propensity"? Is the return of the solitary wasp to her nest due to an instinct or a "propensity"? Are the strutting and sexual self-display of the male pigeon and all his varied behavior of courtship due to the pairing instinct, while the strictly analogous behavior of the youth is to be ascribed to a pairing propensity? Clearly, this distinction is one of no value and cannot be observed. If we give the name "innate propensity" to the relatively unspecialized instincts of the human species, and the name instinct to the more highly specialized propensities of the insects, we shall be in difficulties with the mammals and birds, whose instincts are in the main intermediate in the scale of specialization between those of the insects and those of man. The differences between the less and the more specialized instincts are perfectly gradual.

There is another great theory of human action beloved of some moralists. They tell us that our higher forms of conduct are due to Reason, while they ascribe our simpler and more impulsive actions to what they call our passions, propensities, or instincts, usually prefixing the adjective "baser" or "lower" to these words. They are not much interested in these simpler modes of action and do not much care how they are described or explained, so long as Reason is admitted to be a supreme principle of action. Some of them identify Reason with Conscience and with Will. I propose to discuss Reason, Conscience, and Will in later chapters. Here I will only point out that, if only certain of our most complex modes of behavior, those we call moral efforts, are to be attributed to these abstract principles, the problem of interpreting all our simpler modes of behavior remains unaffected, except in so far as a new problem is created, namely, that of defining the relations of the lower modes of behavior to those higher modes which are attributed to some utterly unlike principle. Further, I would point out that reasoning (as distinct from Reason) plays its part in the lower forms of behavior of man. Even our natural man must be supposed to reason in a simple manner, when he thinks out a plan of action. That is not to say that his actions in such cases are not due to his instinctive impulses; it is merely to recognize that reasoning plays its part in the discovery of better means for attaining the ends prescribed by his instincts. And it is the same with ourselves—reasoning, like all other forms of intellectual process, is but the servant of the instinctive impulses; it does not prompt or impel us to action. By reasoning we discover new means for the attainment of our goals; and by its aid we envisage more clearly the nature and the further consequences of the goals we seek. But, unless we seek or desire some goal because it is our nature so to do, no reasoning can make us seek or desire it; it can at most reveal to us some probable consequence of action as of the kind which is a natural goal for us, that is to say, of a kind in the attainment of which some instinctive impulse of our nature will find satisfaction.

Qualities of Conduct and Character

There is a popular method of explaining human behavior which we must very briefly examine; for it is capable of giving rise to some confusion. We see a man carry through some resolute action in the face of obvious danger; and we say that it was a brave or courageous act and that it was due to the man's bravery or courage. We see another shrink and run away from danger; and we say this behavior was due to his timidity. We see a man give away his worldly goods, or his reputation, for the sake of the welfare of another; and we say he is generous, and ascribe his action to his generosity. Or we see him refuse all assistance to a deserving suppliant; and we say that he is mean, and ascribe the action to his meanness. We see a boy bullying another or teasing a caged animal; and we say he is cruel, and ascribe his action to his cruelty. And often in popular speech these abstract qualities of conduct—courage, timidity, generosity, meanness, cruelty and many others—are referred to as instincts. The bullying or teasing boy is said to be moved by an instinct of cruelty, or the generous man by an instinct of generosity. Or, again, these qualities are spoken of as emotions—the emotion of courage, of cruelty, of generosity. There are, I suppose, some hundreds of adjectives which we use in describing conduct and character. And each one of these adjectives, with few exceptions, has its substantival form, the name of the abstract quality which, we say, is displayed in the concrete action. And, when any man displays such a quality frequently or constantly under the appropriate circumstances, we say that his character possesses this quality. From this it is but a small step to ascribe all actions displaying this quality to the quality itself as a factor in the man's constitution. This usage of language is not confined to the popular tradition, but figures largely in the literary tradition also. And even some of the prominent schools of psychology continue to confuse these abstract qualities of conduct and character with the instincts and the emotions. *It is of the first importance that the beginner should understand the difference between the instincts and these abstract qualities.*

To ascribe an action to a quality is to indulge our inveterate tendency to reïfy, to make things and agents of whatever we think of by aid of a substantive. To explain a man's giving away his coat by saying that he was prompted or impelled to do so by his generosity, his goodness, his kindness, or his benevolence, is strictly comparable to explaining his falling asleep by ascribing it to his sleepiness. In each such case, if the man has frequently displayed in his conduct the quality named, the ascription of the act to the quality does provide an explanation of a sort; for it asserts that the particular act is in conformity with his character, and is the sort of action which previous experience would lead us to expect from him. But such ascription of an action to some abstract quality of character does not carry the explanation of it beyond this very limited range. Whereas, when we can confidently ascribe it to an instinct, to the working of an instinctive impulse or some conjunction of instinctive impulses, then we have explained the action as fully as we can hope to do; except in so far as we can give some account of the genesis of instincts in the race and of the growth of the individual's character by the redirection of instinctive impulses to form acquired propensities or sentiments.

Consider an action which would generally be called courageous or brave. A boy, entering a barn on his father's farm, finds a group of strange rough boys of his own age torturing some animal. He intervenes and, though they tell him with oaths and threatening gestures to go away, he stands up to them and insists on their departure. His action is courageous. But do we satisfactorily explain it by ascribing it to his courage? We explain his action only when we correctly assign or name its motive. Can we say that his courage was his motive? Clearly—no. If he showed anger and furiously attacked the other boys, we should say his immediate motive was anger. But what was the ground of his anger? What other impulse was it that turned to anger? Perhaps it was pity for the tortured animal; or perhaps his sense of ownership was stirred by the trespassing gang and their refusal to go away. Perhaps their insulting replies stung him. In the last case, this anger, as is so frequently the case, sprang from the obstruction to his self-assertive impulse. If he is strong and confident and skilful in combat, he may drive off the gang in perfect coolness, without any symptom or feeling of anger, perhaps planting a few blows with cool and scientific skill. Perhaps, on the other hand, he is filled with fear and only screws himself up to intervene by a great effort, calling himself a coward for shrinking. In all these cases, his intervention would be courageous, perhaps most truly so in the last case. But courage would not be his motive. Even if his motive were wholly or chiefly the desire to prove or display his courage, still courage would not be his motive. In this case his principal motive would be his self-assertive impulse; and in any case this motive would probably co-operate with his pity for the animal, that is to say, his protective tender impulse. Thus, in order to evaluate conduct and apply the correct adjectives to it, we need to know the motive at work; and we cannot explain conduct by finding a more or less suitable adjective and then turning the adjective into a substantive, reifying the quality so named and making of it the active agent, impulsive power, or motive. No matter how courageous the boy, he would not have interfered without some motive; his quality of courage is displayed only when he is moved to action by some impulse springing from some instinct. If he felt no pity for the animal, no sense of ownership in the place, no desire to assert his authority, he might look on curiously, or contemptuously, or sympathetically joining in the laughter of the gang, in spite of all his courage.

It is an excellent exercise in psychology to take actual or imaginary instances of behavior, one's own or others', and to attempt to assign the possible or actual motives. The main thesis of this book is that in every case the motive, when truly assigned, will be found to be some instinctive impulse or some conjunction of two or more such impulses. Hence, as I have written elsewhere, "the instincts are the prime movers of all human activity; by the conative or impulsive force of some instinct, every train of thought, however cold and passionless it may seem, is borne along toward its end, and every bodily activity is initiated and sustained. The instinctive impulses determine the ends of all activities and supply the driving power by which all mental activities are sustained; and all the complex intellectual apparatus of the most highly developed mind is but the instrument by which these impulses seek their satisfactions, while pleasure and pain do but serve to guide them in their choice of the means. Take away these instinctive dispositions, with their powerful impulses, and the organism would become incapable of activity of any kind; it would lie inert and motionless, like a wonderful clockwork whose mainspring had been removed or a steam-engine whose fires had been drawn. These impulses are the mental forces that maintain and shape all the life of individuals and societies, and in them we are confronted with the central mystery of life and mind and will." [1]

I cite this passage as a concise statement of the theory of action which is maintained in these pages; the one we have called "*the hormic theory of action.*" It is not a new theory, but a very old one; and it is radically opposed to all the theories enumerated on page 126.[2]

I have modified the foregoing passage by leaving out a reference to habits as springs of action derived from the instincts, because I seem now to see clearly that, as I have argued on pages 114 and 180, motor habits are not in

[1] "Introduction to Social Psychology," p. 44.

[2] Cf. Chap. II, p. 71, for fuller statement of the hormic theory.

themselves springs of energy or "drives." I feel that a further qualification of this earlier statement is, perhaps, necessary. It is possible that the statement does not adequately cover the case of the Epicure, the highly sophisticated individual who deliberately aims at and pursues pleasure, and perhaps certain instances in which the normal man acts after the fashion of the Epicure. In Chapter IX I shall examine this type of action and the hedonist theory to which it seems to give plausibility. Here it may suffice to recognize that we do learn to desire and to seek opportunities for the successful and therefore pleasurable exercise of our instinctive impulses. This is indeed a consequence of the fundamental influence of pleasure, which inevitably develops with the development of our power of foreseeing the future. Having attained the satisfaction of some instinctive impulse by a certain line of action, the influence of pleasure determines us to act again in the same way under similar circumstances; and, as a further stage of influence, it determines us to seek the circumstances which will evoke the impulse and give scope to the same kind of successful activity and so bring us the same kind of satisfaction; as when we go hunting or fishing, without needing the game for the pot; or as when we merely "go out to get an appetite for dinner."

To recognize the reality of such desire for pleasurable exercise of our natural tendencies is by no means to accept the theory of psychological hedonism. For that theory asserts that pleasure or the desire for pleasure (or pain or the aversion from pain) is the primary spring or motive of all action. Whereas we realize that the so-called desire for pleasure is always secondary to instinctive impulse; that both the pleasure that we have experienced in the past and the pleasure that we desire to attain in the future are dependent upon and secondary to the working in us of instinctive tendencies, without which we should neither act nor experience pleasure.

We may suppose that the natural man would be moved to some slight extent by the desire for pleasurable activity such as he has experienced in the past. Most of his activities would be directly prompted by instinctive impulses and desire in the way we have imagined. But we may suppose that, in a time of unusual ease and plenty, he might be moved to go out hunting, not by any desire for food, but merely because his imagination depicts with delight the seizing of his quarry, and because he desires to renew this activity. If he was moved in this way, his hunting would be *sport*. Undoubtedly sport is largely of this nature; it is the putting ourselves under such circumstances as will evoke our instinctive impulses, in order that we may enjoy the satisfactions that attend their successful exercise. Sports are closely allied to games; and what was said of games in an earlier chapter must be supplemented in the light of the present discussion of the secondary desires for pleasure, by recognizing that games are renewed largely for the sake of the satisfactions which we have learned to find in them, the satisfaction of successful striving, of display of our skill and strength, of association with others, or (in such games as the solving of puzzles) the satisfaction of our curiosity by successful effort to solve the puzzle.

We have now reviewed the behavior of animals and of man regarded externally as an animal; and we have carried our explanation of his behavior in general terms as far as is possible without such more exact description of the course of experience as is rendered possible only by systematic introspective study. We must now turn to such introspective study, the study of behavior from within.

We have not only described types of behavior in general terms, but also we have made from the observed facts of behavior certain inferences as to the nature and structure of mind in general and of the minds of various species of animals, including the human species. In a similar way, in making our introspective study, we have to aim not merely at describing the course of experience in general terms, but also at extending and supplementing our inferential account of the nature and structure of the normal human mind.

CHAPTER VIII

PERCEPTUAL THINKING

In any attempt to describe the course of experience, the choice of an appropriate terminology is all important, as I have pointed out in the introductory chapter. If we begin by talking of "sensations" and "ideas" as things, or as fragments or mosaics of stuff called "consciousness," that terminology will infect the whole of our description with incurable confusion. We must hold fast to the fact that to experience is to be mentally active; that *experiencing is an activity of some being or subject who experiences something, or somewhat.* The word "object," like the word "thing," is apt to mean for us in common speech a material thing, continuously existing and separable as a coherent whole from its environment of any particular moment. But we may use it in a wider sense as the most general name for whatever we can think of, or whatever any subject can think of.

The simplest, most elementary kind of thinking, almost all the thinking of animals and of young children, is thinking of objects present to and affecting the senses, what we may call "present objects" in distinction from "remote objects." The "present object" may, of course, be very remote from us in space; but we speak of it as present, so long as energy coming from it affects our sense-organs appreciably. The fire across the room is a "present object," if its radiant heat effectively stimulates my skin. My dog is a "present object," when I hear him barking in the distance or scratching at the door. The moon is a "present object," when the sunlight reflected from it falls into my eye and stimulates the retina. But if, while I gaze at the moon through the window, a thick cloud swims across it or you close the shutter, it becomes for me a "remote object." Our life is passed among many and ever-changing "present objects," and during waking life, at least, we often think of present objects; but, if we think of remote objects, we are apt to ignore present objects. When we think of a present object we are said to perceive it. That is the technical usage of the word "perceive." In common speech it is used more widely and loosely; as when we say "I perceive your intention."

It is commonly said that we can think of only one thing at once. How far that statement requires qualification we must consider later. At present we may accept it as approximately true, if we interpret the words widely. Of all the "present objects" about us, we commonly are concerned with and perceive some one only; but this one may be highly complex; it may comprise many physical things, all of which are "present objects" and each of which I may perceive separately and individually, if I wish to do so; as when I look down on a village from a mountain-top or look at a trayful of china. How much of the total field of present objects I shall perceive, shall think of, at any moment, is determined by my purpose at the moment. If my purpose is to recognize the distant village, I perceive the whole of it as one object set in a certain environment of meadow or forest. If my purpose is to recognize a particular house in it, I perceive the individual houses in turn, each in its peculiar setting of spatial relations to other things. The perception of any thing is only possible so long as that thing, or energy radiating from it, affects some sense-organ and initiates in it a nervous current which transmits itself to the brain.

Thus all our perception of the beauty and wonder of the material world about us is only possible in virtue of these streams of energy poured upon us from material things. And our appreciation of the moral world is equally dependent upon such streams of energy affecting our sense-organs. For it is only through the medium of our sense-organs that we become aware of one another, that we perceive one another and communicate our experience, our knowing, our feeling, and our striving.[1] Each kind of sense-organ is specially adapted to receive some one

[1] Some considerable evidence exists in favor of the view that this is not strictly true and that communication in some more direct mode sometimes occurs. But if such "telepathic" communications occur, they would seem to be rare exceptions to the general truth of the statement.

kind of energy and to concentrate it effectively upon the tips of the sensory nerves within it, while shielding them from the incidence of other forms of energy. In this way ***our sense-organs are instruments of selection among the streams of energy playing upon us***, a passive selection, like that of a sieve which, in virtue of its structure, lets pass the smaller particles and keeps out the larger. The eye is specially adapted to concentrate light upon the tips of the optic nerves (spread out in a single layer over the inner surface of the eyeball) while shielding them from heat, mechanical pressure or tension, and chemical influences. The ear is adapted to bring to bear, as effective stimuli upon the auditory nerve, the most delicate vibrations of the air, while shielding it from all other influences. The nose and tongue contain sense-organs that respond to the chemical stimulus of substances floating in the air or dissolved in water, respectively. The skin contains organs delicately affected by all mechanical pressure and tension, and others which are effectively stimulated by changes of temperature. And the muscles, tendons, ligaments, joint-surfaces, and various membranous surfaces within the body, contain other organs readily stimulated by pressure or tension of the parts. This, in brief, is our array of sensory-organs through which all perception is achieved.

There are forms of energy in the world about us to which no sense-organ of our own is specially attuned and which, therefore, play little or no part in our perceiving. The physiology of the sense-organs is in itself a very large field of study, with an immense literature and a multitude of recorded facts. But unfortunately the difficulties of the study are so great that we cannot yet give any satisfactory account of the way in which the energies stimulate the sensory nerves, nor of the way in which the nerves respond to these stimulations. There are many rival hypothetical accounts, but none which is entirely satisfactory. Our ignorance may be illustrated by reference to our vision.

Visual Perception

The normal man, on looking at the rainbow or other spectrum of sunlight, sees an array of colors—red, orange, yellow, green, green-blue, blue, and purple, and between these many distinguishable transition qualities. We know that each distinguishable part of this array of color-qualities corresponds to ethereal vibrations of a certain frequency, constituting the light of that part of the spectrum. And we infer, with considerable confidence, that our perception of each distinguishable quality of color implies and depends upon some physico-chemical process going on in the brain which is peculiar to, or specific to, that quality. Further, if our color-perception is to serve us faithfully in the discrimination and recognition of material objects, there must be some specific and constant correspondence between these brain-processes and the vibration-frequency of each ray of light that falls into the eye. But how this correspondence is secured we do not know. There are hypotheses of two principal types. Those of one type assume that each sensory nerve is capable of many kinds of excitation or vibration, and that each nerve-fibre somehow takes up and transmits to the brain a vibration corresponding in frequency to the ethereal vibration that falls upon it. Those of the other type (known as the "theory of specific nervous energies") assume that the kinds of nervous process in the visual parts of the brain are very limited in number, some three, four, five, or six only. Thus, one famous theory, that of Thomas Young, which has the merit of an elegant simplicity, assumes only three such kinds of nervous process in the brain resulting from stimulation of the eye; that these three determine our perception of red, green, and blue color respectively, when they occur singly; and that all other color-qualities are experienced upon conjunctions of these three fundamental brain-processes in various proportions or intensities. As originally propounded, this theory assumed three kinds of fibre in the retina and optic nerve and brain, each kind capable of one of the three fundamental modes of change, and each most sensitive to light of one part of the spectrum only. Various modifications of the theory have been proposed.[1] But there are very great difficulties in the way of all varieties of either type of theory, so that no one of them holds the field.

[1] I have attempted to render this famous theory adequate to the facts by adding a number of supplementary hypotheses. "Thomas Young's Theory of Light and Colour Vision," *Mind*, N. S., Vol. X.

Sensory Qualities Are Signs of Objects

We are in no better case with the other senses. Hence, although the study of the senses is a most fascinating one and should be a part of the discipline of every professed psychologist, and though it bristles with problems of the greatest theoretical interest, it has not yet advanced so far as to put any sure detailed knowledge at the disposal of the psychologist. One great fact of fundamental importance we may regard as established, namely, that somehow, in some way that we do not understand, the various qualities of our sensory experience are correlated in fairly constant fashion with the specific modes of stimulation of our sense-organs that come to them from the things around us; so that these qualities of experience serve us as signs of the presence of the things from which such stimulations come.

It is these qualities of experience, resulting from stimulations of our sense-organs, that are called "sensations." And there is no harm in the word, so long as we do not make entities or things of these "sensations," and do not yield to the temptation to describe experience, or the mind itself, as a mosaic constructed by the juxtaposition of these so-called elements.

Philosophers, who for the most part are very ignorant of the facts of sensory experience and of the physiology of the senses, have raised an immense amount of dust over these so-called "sensations." And it must be admitted that the exact statement of the part played by sensory experience in our mental life is extremely difficult. The difficulty and confusion arise largely from the fact that, though the sensory qualities normally and primitively serve merely as signs of objects, guiding us in our discriminations and recognitions, nevertheless, when we become introspective, we readily make any one of these qualities the object of our thinking; just as, though even more readily than, we make other modes of experience, such as our desires, our satisfactions, and our emotional excitements, objects of our thinking. One consequence of this is that the sensory quality, which is a mere sign of the object, is readily confused with the object of which it is a sign, and is sometimes said to be identical with it; or the physical object is said to be a complex or conjunction of such sensory experiences or "sensations." Thus it is said that, when I look at the moon, I perceive a yellow patch in the sky, and that this yellow patch is what I perceive; and so the moon is identified with the experience of yellow, with this "extensive sensation of yellow quality"; and all the physical world is said similarly to consist of patches of "sensation." Then, of course, arises a hubbub over the question whether the "sensations," which are said to be the physical objects, are in my mind or out there in space; and some say one thing and some the other. All this confusion is largely due to the fact that it is, unfortunately, the customary practice of philosophers to choose visual experiences and objects visually perceived, as illustrations in their discussions of perception.[1]

If we consider any other type of sensory experience, we have no difficulty in avoiding this mass of confusion. For, when we hear the stroke of a bell or the humming of an engine, no one would be so foolish as to maintain deliberately that the sensory experience is the bell or the engine; or that the odor of a skunk is a skunk; or that the warmth we feel on approaching the fire (or on going out into the sunshine) is the fire (or is the sun). In all these cases *the sensory quality of experience resulting from the sense-stimulation is clearly not the physical object itself, but only a sign of it, an occasion for our thinking of the object; it is a sign of the presence of the object, a sign which may suggest it to the mind, or may set us thinking of it.*[2] It is seldom that a simple sensory quality suffices to determine us to perceive, or to enable us to recognize, a physical object.

[1] Much confusion would be avoided if all philosophers were born blind or were forbidden to refer to visual perception.

[2] Perhaps the most troublesome case of perception to deal with in a satisfactory way is the case of the double images we see on looking at anything (such as the moon or a candle-flame) without accurate convergence of the two eyes upon it. Shall we say that we see two moons, or two images of one moon? Or that the abnormal functioning of the sense-organ disturbs the correlation which normally obtains between sensory experience and the stimulating thing?

A Simplified World

We may imagine a physical world consisting of distinct physical things of a limited number of classes or species, the members of each species being exactly alike, and each species capable of affecting our sense-organs in a way peculiar to itself and in that one way alone. We should then enjoy as many qualities of sensory experience as there were species of things; and each quality would correspond to one species and serve as the invariable sign of its presence (or, rather, of the presence of some member of the species). And we may imagine a creature, living in that simple world, to be endowed with as many instinctive tendencies as sensory qualities, one tendency corresponding to each quality and to each species of thing, a tendency which would be released or set in action by the sense-impression peculiar to each species. The life of such a creature would be a series of impulsive actions, each provoked in turn by the appropriate simple sense-impression. The life of the simpler animals approximates to this type; not because they live in a simpler world; but because they ignore a vast number of objects, and react to objects not as distinct individual objects but only as generic objects, as objects representative of their genus, class, or species.

Recognition is Based on Sensory Patterns of Three Kinds

But the physical world is infinitely diversified; no two physical things are exactly alike. Even the proverbial two peas are found to be unlike, when they are closely examined. Hence there is infinite scope for discrimination between kinds of things, and between individual things of the same kind; and the creature which discriminates most nicely between things will in the main be the most successful. The development of the power of perceptual discrimination between things and between classes of things is the basis of all the higher forms of mental life. Such discrimination is only possible in virtue of the infinite complexity and variety of the impressions, the stimulations, which physical things are capable of making upon our sense-organs.

The complexity and variety of these impressions are of three kinds; physical things present *patterns* of three kinds—qualitative, temporal, and spatial.

Qualitative Patterns

First, the thing may transmit to us a physically complex impression, each of the elements or constituents of which is capable of exciting in us a correspondingly simple sensory experience; it presents a *qualitative pattern.* When a sense-organ is affected by such a complex impression, the resulting sensory experience is of a quality unlike the simple quality which results from stimulation by any one of the constituents of the complex stimulus; and often, though not in all cases, we can, upon introspection, become aware of a complexity of quality corresponding to the complexity of the physical stimulus. This is best illustrated by musical tones. A good tuning-fork, reinforced by an appropriate resonator, will send to the ear a sound-wave which is physically simple. And, on listening to the fork, our sensory experience is of simple quality. No amount of practice and effort of discrimination, it seems, will enable us to discover any complexity in it. Consequently we cannot, by hearing, discriminate one such fork from any other which emits a similar wave. But, when a bell is struck, or a stretched wire or string is plucked, it communicates to the air a complex vibration, consisting of several simple vibrations of different frequencies superimposed on one another. If the slowest of these vibrations is of the same frequency as that of the pure tuning-fork, we recognize the note as similar to that of the fork; but we are at the same time aware of a difference of quality; and, if we are practised in observation of this kind, we can detect in the sensory experience a complexity corresponding to the complexity of the stimulating air-wave; we can detect within the complex quality elements corresponding to each of the vibration rates within the complex air-wave. The facts are commonly described by saying that the tuning-fork excites a simple "sensation" of tone; and that the vibrating string excites a complex or compound "sensation" formed by the fusion of several simple "sensations."

This way of describing the facts is perhaps justified by its brevity and convenience; but it is apt to be very misleading;

for it seems to imply that the several "sensations" come into existence as separate things (or perhaps that they are separately hauled out of the "unconscious" into the light of "consciousness"), which then proceed to fuse together; as molten drops of two metals may fuse to form an alloy that has some of the properties of both constituents.

It is important to notice that we become aware of this complexity of the sensory quality only when we adopt the introspective attitude and make the quality of experience the object of our thinking. So long as we remain in the natural attitude (when our sensory experiences serve merely as signs of the presence of physical objects) the complexity of the impression merely serves as the basis of our discrimination and recognition. When we hear the pure tone, we say "There is a tuning-fork"; and when we hear the complex note of the bell, we say "There is the bell ringing." In a similar way, if a bell and a stretched wire emit in turn air-waves the lowest or fundamental vibrations of which are of the same frequency, we recognize the two notes as alike (of the same fundamental pitch, as we say); but, at the same time, the two qualities of experience differ in a way which enables us to distinguish the notes and to recognize the bell and the string. For the complex waves emitted by the two instruments, though alike in the frequency of the fundamental partial wave, are unlike in the frequency of their upper partial waves. If we are practised in such discrimination, we can detect, in each of the complex impressions, the qualities corresponding to each of these partial waves. But such analytic discrimination is not a necessary condition of our recognition of the bell and of the wire, or of our judgment that the two sounds are different. The more nearly alike are the distinguishable qualities within the complex quality of any sensory experience, the more difficult is it to distinguish them; or, as is commonly said, the more intimately do they fuse together; in other words, the more difficult is it to analyze the complex experience when we introspectively examine it.

In the main the various qualities resulting from stimulation of any one sense-organ are more alike than those excited through two different sense-organs; all auditory qualities are more like one another than they are like visual qualities, or taste or touch qualities. Hence the complex qualities excited by simultaneous stimulation of different senses may, in nearly all cases, be easily analyzed in the sense defined above. Yet our recognition of an object sometimes depends upon such a conjunction of stimulations of several senses. Thus, if you take a sip of lemonade, normally you merely recognize it as lemonade; the complex sensory experience is for you the sign of lemonade. But, if your purpose leads you to adopt the introspective attitude, you easily detect the acidity and the sweetness (two qualities due to stimulation of distinct sense-organs in the tongue) as well as the flavor characteristic of lemons (a quality excited through sense-organs in the nose) and the cool contact qualities that depend on stimulation of sense-organs distributed over the mucous membrane of the mouth. And, in the light of previous experience, you may accept each of these distinguished qualities as the sign of one of the constituents of the complex physical thing, the lemonade. The sweetness is the sign of sugar; the acidity and the flavor are the sign of lemon; the coolness and contact experiences are the sign of the water. In a similar way the musician, analyzing his complex auditory experience in the presence of an orchestra, may accept the various qualities which by analysis he discovers within the whole as signs of the various instruments; or the naturalist in the tropical forest may hear in the sudden chorus which breaks out at sundown, and which to the stranger is a mere chaos of sound, the voices of a hundred different species of bird and beast and insect.

Such successive discrimination of qualities within a qualitative pattern, or such recognition of the various objects which they suggest or signify, requires time. Nevertheless, though the complex sense-impression endure but a single moment, we are able to effect some such discrimination; because the sensory experience outlives the stimulation.

Temporal Patterns

A second great aid to recognition is the succession of sense-impressions giving rise to a changing course of sensory experience, a temporal pattern. Thus, if I hear the cry "Cuck-coo," it suggests to my mind the bird of that name; whereas the cry "cuck" or "coo" alone would probably not do so. The repeated experience of the succession of the two qualities has rendered them a significant whole for me; so that, when I again have the experience, I am apt to think of the bird, and may rightly say that I hear or perceive him. Auditory impressions are especially apt to occur in characteristic sequences, as in the cries and songs of most animals; and in such cases our recognition depends, not only on the quality and intensity of the sensory experience, but also upon the succession and the rate of succession of qualities. When we are familiar with the order of succession and with the relations of quality and intensity between the phases that make up such a course of experience, recognition may be determined by the temporal succession, even though the actual qualities are very different upon successive occasions. This fact is best illustrated by our recognition of a melody, though it be given on successive occasions in very different keys and by instruments of very different tones.

The apprehension of successive phases of sensory experience, making a *temporal pattern* which serves as a sign of an object, is sometimes called temporal colligation of sensations. If we use this phrase, we must beware again of implying the putting together of separately existing entities called "sensations." Temporal pattern is of chief importance in auditory perception. It plays some part in tactual perception, but very little in other modes of perception. The facts may also be described by naming the pattern (the rhythm or the melody) "an object of a higher order," an object, that is to say, which is recognizable as such, even though it be presented on successive occasions through the medium of very different sensory qualities.[1]

Spatial Patterns

The third great aid to perception derives from the fact that two or more sense-impressions, affecting different parts of our sensory surfaces, can in many cases be distinguished as locally

[1] Here again is a case which clearly illustrates the absurdity of identifying the sensory qualities with the object; for the object, the melody, remains "the same," though all the sensory qualities be different.

separate or distinct, even though the qualities of the resulting experience be indistinguishable as such. Thus, if I look up and see the two stars, Castor and Pollux, in the clear night sky, the quality of my sensory experience is not appreciably different if I turn from Castor to Pollux; and, if I regard them as two parts of one whole, I am aware of a difference between them which is wholly and only of that peculiar nature we call "a difference of locality or position." If I turn my gaze to the constellation we call "The Plough," I recognize it immediately in virtue of the relative positions of the several points of light. For, in virtue of previous experience, these points in these relative positions are for me a whole; the pattern is the distinctive feature and suggests to me the constellation.

This combining of locally distinct parts of a total sensory experience is sometimes called spatial colligation. The spatial distinction of parts of a complex sensory impression and their colligation play an immense role in visual perception. Just as temporal pattern, the temporal relations of parts, may suffice to determine recognition of an object, though its qualities be changed; so also, in visual perception, recognition may be based wholly on *spatial pattern*. Every spatial pattern recognizable by me, such as an equilateral triangle, a square, a pentagon, is for me, like a familiar melody, "an object of higher order."

The importance of spatial relations in vision goes further than that of temporal relations in hearing. If, in sequences of auditory impressions, all differences of quality are abolished, so that the same quality is repeated in various temporal patterns or rhythms, the variety of such patterns that we can learn to recognize is very limited. But in vision, in the absence of all differences of quality, we can still recognize an immense variety of spatial patterns, as, for example, all the constellations of the heavens. And my recognition of the pattern is not dependent upon its extension or the apparent distances between the parts, nor upon their locations relative to myself or the parts of my body. We recognize "The Plough" in the sky, no matter what position in its path about the Pole-star it may occupy; though, in describing that path, its long axis turns through 360°. And, if the same pattern be reproduced on paper in any combination of colors and in any size, we recognize it equally readily. In this last respect spatial pattern is far more elastic than temporal pattern. If the time-intervals of a temporal pattern are varied beyond very narrow limits, we do not recognize the pattern. But, in visual perception, the spatial intervals may be varied within extreme limits, without seriously disturbing our recognition of the pattern. The importance of pattern in visual perception is well illustrated by black-and-white drawings and by the art of the silhouette. There we see how visual pattern alone, unaided by differences of quality and intensity of sensory experience, can suggest to us, or be the ground of our recognition of, an almost infinite variety of objects. In fact, differences of quality, of color, are of relatively small practical importance in visual perception; pattern predominates vastly.

The Varieties of Sensory Qualities

To the practical man the complexities of quality of sensory experience serve as signs of things; he seldom or never makes these qualities the objects of his thinking. It is only artists, psychologists, and certain specialists, such as wine and tea tasters, who become interested in qualities as such and learn to think of them in abstraction from the objects they signify. Accordingly, the variety of words used in common speech to denote these qualities is very inadequate. The musicians have devised a technical notation which supplements the inadequacy of common speech to the qualities of auditory experience; but in the sphere of visual qualities little has been done by the artists in this direction.

There can be little doubt that the range of sensory qualities of our experience is much wider (richer in varieties) than that of the lower animals; and, if we accept the continuity of human and animal evolution from primitive forms of life, it seems necessary to suppose that the various qualities have become gradually differentiated from some primordial sensory experience. But this is a very speculative topic of which little can be said with any confidence. At present we have to accept the human capacities for sensory experience as a bare fact. We do not even know how far we are alike or different in respect of these capacities. Instances of well-marked color-blindness are not rare; and these, together with other anomalies of sensory capacity, warn us against the assumption that we are uniformly endowed. Yet it seems in the highest degree probable that, apart from a small percentage of individuals who suffer from pathological or developmental defects, and apart from some slight racial differences, the whole human species enjoys a range of sensory capacities which is nearly the same for all individuals.[1]

Individual differences of capacity for sensory discrimination seem to be mainly, though not wholly, due to different degrees of practice in discrimination. I say "mainly, though not wholly"; because apart from gross defects, such as color-blindness, individuals do differ in respect of sensory discrimination in a way which cannot be attributed to degrees of practice or of general intelligence. There are highly intelligent persons who seem incapable of achieving the finer discriminations of one sense, while surpassing the average man in the discrimination of another sense. And there are others who, with comparatively little effort and practice, carry their fineness of discrimination in some one sense-province far beyond the level of the average man.

Temporal Perception

Our capacities for temporal discrimination and colligation seem to follow from the nature of experience as a succession of phases, each giving place more or less gradually to its successor. This is not due merely to the fact that we live in a physical world that is constantly changing and raining new stimuli upon our sense-organs. It is due also to the fact that the very nature of mental activity is to progress from the present toward the future, to reach out toward the future, anticipating the coming changes. In this respect, as in so many others, our minds are adapted to the world we live in, a constantly changing world.

[1] Cf. "Reports of the Cambridge Anthropological Expedition to Torres Straits." Members of this party attempted for the first time a complete survey of the sensory capacities of a people of primitive culture. We found evidence of only slight differences from Europeans.

But if, as now constituted, we could suddenly be transplanted to a changeless environment, our experience would still be a constant succession of phases; because we should turn from one object to another and perceive them successively. Nevertheless the continuity of changes in the physical world, especially of changes of position and of changes of the sounds uttered by our fellow-creatures, is an important condition of our temporal perception. We learn to accept a continuously changing sound as significant of one object, and a continuously changing visual experience as similarly the sign of one object. Yet our capacity for temporal colligation is narrowly limited. We can recognize a series of sounds of uniform quality, only if it is very short; and, even if the sounds follow upon one another in a regular rhythm marked by differences of intensity or of time interval, we can colligate them in one recognizable whole only if the series does not endure for more than a few seconds. And even when we get further help from differences of tone, as in a bar of music, our range of colligation is not greatly extended. It is for this reason, one may suppose, that the songs of birds and the cries of animals, which serve as recognition-marks, are never more than the repetition of a short series of tones, a temporal pattern of brief duration.

Spatial Perception

Spatial discrimination seems to be the fundamental and most primitive form of spatial experience—to hear two successive sounds as coming from different directions, to see successively two points of light as in different positions, to feel two touches as in different positions on the skin. Though we cannot imagine a creature lacking all appreciation of temporal succession, we can imagine one devoid of all capacity for this most primitive mode of spatial experience. The perceptual discriminations of such a creature would be based wholly on differences of sensory quality and on temporal pattern. It is obvious that it would be but very poorly adapted to live in our spatial world of moving things. It would lack the most fundamental function of mind, which seems to be the guidance of bodily movement so as to effect changes in our relations to the objects about us—

changes of a kind that will promote our own welfare and that of the race.

Our spatial experience has been studied and discussed at great length by thousands of philosophers and psychologists; the whole topic bristles with fascinating problems and an immense amount of fine experimental work has been done with the aim of throwing light upon it. And yet we are very far from having attained to an intelligible and generally acceptable way of describing and explaining it.

It is not easy to classify in groups the rival views or theories, or to state concisely the type theory of each group. The discussion has raged largely round the alternatives of nativistic and genetic theories. These are perhaps the two most comprehensive headings. By a "genetic theory" is meant one which assumes that all the capacity for spatial experience enjoyed by any individual is acquired or built up by him in the course of his life; that he brings with him at birth no ready-made, though perhaps latent, capacity for spatial discrimination or spatial colligation. By a "nativistic theory" is meant one which does assume some such capacity as hereditarily given or innate in our constitution, even though it may develop in the individual only gradually under the influence of experience.

The principal theories of spatial perception fall into three fairly distinct groups: (1) Associationist theories; these are in general frankly sensationist. The more recent exponents of theories of this type supplement or replace the principle that sensations cohere or cluster together in virtue of "association" by the principle that they fuse or become synthesized into compounds unlike themselves (namely, in spatial perception, the spatially extended qualities); this is the principle of mental chemistry. (2) The extensity theory which, when combined, as by James, with sensationism, asserts that every sensation, every atom of mind-stuff, possesses the attribute of extensity, and must always exhibit extensity in some degree, just as it must always have some degree of intensity. (3) The psychic-stimulus theory, which asserts that the immediate sensory effects of a spatial pattern serve merely to provoke the mind to think the perceived object as having spatial attributes; the capacity for spatial thinking being inherent in the mind, over and above its capacity for responding to the sense-stimuli with divers sensory qualities.

The most extreme form of genetic theory is that of the English Associationist School, the tradition of which descends from Locke and Hume through Hartley, James Mill, John Stuart Mill, and Alexander Bain. Accepting John Locke's dictum that the mind at birth is a *tabula rasa*, a clean sheet, upon which the sense-impressions of the physical world record themselves as "sensations," psychologists of this school recognize only one principle of mental activity, namely, "association." They set out to describe the genesis of spatial "ideas" according to this principle as follows: Perception of position and distance is, it is clear, connected with bodily movement. In order to reach a spot seen in any direction and at a given distance, with my finger, my eye, or by bodily locomotion, I must make some train of movements. Such movements excite "sensations" through the sense-organs embedded in the muscles, tendons, and joints of the moving parts. Through repetition of such movements directed to a spot in the same position relative to myself, the "sensation" of light or color becomes indissolubly associated with the "sensation of movement"; and such association of the "sensations of movement" with a "visual sensation" (or with any "sensation" of the other senses) renders the latter spatial, gives it locality. Further, a group of such seen spots excites a group of sensations of color, each of which, being thus localized by association with a "sensation of movement," coheres with its fellows to form the "compound sensation" of a colored surface. Some of the Associationists, recognizing that this account involves the transformation of "sensations of movement" into something quite different, namely, extension or other spatial qualities, followed John Mill in supplementing the principle of association with that of "mental chemistry"; the sensations of movement, in fusing or combining with sensations of color or touch, are transformed, they said, as a chemical element is transformed on combining with another.

The late Professor Wundt, seeing that this simple theory would not work, attempted to improve it (1) by giving more explicit recognition and greater scope to the principle of mental chemistry, renaming it more appropriately as "the principle of creative synthesis," and (2) by postulating a greater variety of the adjuvant sensations which were supposed to enter into the synthesis. Adopting a term first used by Hermann Lotze, the Associationists had called "the sensations of movement" the "local signs of the sensations of color or of touch." Wundt saw that the Associationist theory encounters this difficulty—How, in the perception of several or many points of light, does each local sign find its own visual sensation, in order to fuse with it? Reducing the problem to its simplest terms, it may be stated as follows: Two stars, one on my right and a second on my left, throw their images on my retina, each exciting a "sensation" of color, *R* and *L* respectively. Each excites also a "sensation" of movement which is peculiar or proper to the spot of the retina stimulated; call these *r* and *l*. According to the theory, *r* must fuse with *R*, and *l* with *L*, to give it local quality or position. But how is *r* to come together with *R*, and *l* with *L*? May not *r* just as well rush into the arms of *L*? Is it a matter of habits? The theory of neural habit will not help here at all; for the habits must be attributed to the sensations themselves; which is going a long way toward not only reifying, but also personifying, the "sensations." But, even granting that a "sensation" of a given quality may form a habit, a difficulty remains. The "sensation" from *R* (or rather every "sensation" excited from this one retinal spot) may have on successive occasions any one of the whole range of visual qualities; and so may that from *L*. We cannot therefore identify the "sensation" *R* on successive occasions, personify it, and attribute to it the habit of fusing with *r*. Some authors, seeing this difficulty, have assumed that the various "sensations" excited on successive occasions from any one point of the retina have not only their color-qualities, but also some further quality which is peculiar to all color-qualities excited from this point; and they have proposed to call this hypothetical-quality element the local sign of the "sensation" from that point. Of course this peculiar quality must be assumed to be, like the alleged "movement sensations," subconscious. Wundt's "theory of complex local signs" combines these two theories of local signs and aims, by so doing, to overcome their obvious inadequacies. For, on the assumption of the reality of both kinds of local sign, the "sensation" from each point of the retina, no matter what its color-quality, is labelled by this adjuvant subconscious quality; the "motor sensation" excited from that point may therefore recognize it; *r* may recognize *R*, and *l* recognize *L*, and each proceed to fuse with its appropriate fellow to give it a locality or position distinct from all others. This theory of Wundt's is the high-water mark of the genetic theories. What shall we say of it? First, that it involves in an extreme degree the illegitimate process of making abstract entities, the so-called "sensations," into concrete things, and endowing them with quasi-personal powers. For they are credited not only with the power of seeking out their appropriate fellows and of fusing with them, but also with the power of creating out of a complex mass of sensation-qualities something of an entirely different order, namely, experience of spatial extension and pattern, including extension in the third dimension; for the theory professes to explain that also on similar lines.

The chapter on "Space-perception" in James's "Principles" is perhaps the best discussion of the problem ever written. He rejects the Associationist theory root and branch, agreeing with those who assert that spatial qualities cannot be generated by, or out of, "sensations" which are entirely devoid of spatiality. "The truth is," he wrote, "that the English Associationist School, in trying to show how much their principle can accomplish, have altogether overshot the mark and espoused a kind of theory in respect to space-perception which the general tenor of their philosophy should lead them to abhor. Really there are but three possible kinds of theory concerning space. Either (1) there is no spatial *quality* of sensation at all, and space is a mere symbol of succession; or (2) there is an *extensive quality given* immediately in certain particular sensations; or, finally, (3) there is a quality produced out of the inward resources of the mind, to envelop sensations which, as given originally, are not spatial, but which, on being cast into the spatial form become united and orderly. This last is the Kantian view. Stumpf admirably designates it as the "psychic stimulus" theory, the crude sensations being considered as "goads to the mind to put forth its slumbering power." [1] James rejects the

[1] Vol. II, p. 271.

first and the third theories, in the main because he has set himself to construct his psychology on a sensationist basis. He accepts the second theory, namely, that "there is an *extensive quality given* immediately in certain particular sensations." Others who adopt this theory speak of this "extensive quality" of sensations as "extensity" or "voluminosity" and allege that it is a quality or attribute common to all "sensations." It is said that experience, while it cannot lead to the creation of spatiality, does, especially through repeated movements of our sense-organs over extended surfaces, lead to the orderly discrimination of positions within this natively given "extensity" which is common to all "sensations."

This second theory is thus nativistic and sensationist. Is it acceptable and satisfactory so far as it goes? I think not. First, it involves all the radical errors of "sensationism," especially the error of regarding "the sensation," an abstract object which we learn to think of only by the exercise and development of the highly intellectual function of abstraction, as a concrete entity after the pattern of a physical thing, an entity possessing a number of attributes and powers. This is shown by the language which James inevitably uses in expounding the theory. "All our sensations," he says, "are positively and inexplicably extensive wholes."[1] But "a whole" is just what any sensory quality of experience never is. The "wholes," the "entities," we think of, we constitute by our thinking. As James has so well shown in another connection, they are purely relative to our interests and purposes. It is wholly impossible to point to any "sensation" which is a natural "whole," which we can think of as such. A whole must have limits or boundaries that mark it off from other "wholes." A sensory quality is no more a whole than Space, or Time, or Strength, or Speed, or Courage, or Virtue, or Beauty, or any other abstraction; and what is called "a sensation" is only some sensory quality of experience that we choose to make the object of our thinking, instead of accepting it as a sign of the presence of some physical object. Hence, to say that sensations are "extensive wholes" is to answer in the affirmative a meaningless question that should never be asked, the question: Are "sensations" spatial, extended, extensive? And the affirmative answer is a long step on the way toward that pseudo-Realism which asserts that the physical world is made up of "sensations." James's sensationist account is not even consistent with itself. For, while on one page we are told that "all our sensations are . . . extensive wholes," on another (page 216) we are told that distance, height, and breadth are in strictness themselves sensations. And this is only one of many illustrations of the fact that the Sensationist who, like James, takes his program seriously and attempts to carry it through, finds himself compelled (as James himself did) to invent "sensations" of many strange kinds, in order to have an adequate variety of material with which to build up or compose "the stream of consciousness," "sensations" of relations of many kinds besides spatial and temporal relations, for example, sensations of likeness and of difference and of all the relations expressed by "if" and "or" and "of," and by all other conjunctions and prepositions and adverbs.

Let us hold fast to the truth that what is called "a sensation" is a quality of experience arising, as a reaction of the mind (or, if you prefer, of the organism) to a physical stimulus: such experience is not given us by the brain-process as a ready-made article, like a cake or a lollipop, as James's account

[1] *Op. cit.*, p. 268.

seems to imply. It is a psychic reaction to a stimulus. We shall, then, not shrink from the epithet "psychical stimulist," and may turn to the "psychic stimulus" theory of spatial perception, to see if it can be intelligibly stated.[1] James's statement of the theory runs as follows: "There is a *quality produced* out of the inward resources of the mind, to envelop sensations which, as given originally, are not spatial, but which, on being cast into the spatial form, become united and orderly."[2] I am not prepared to say whether this is, as James says, the Kantian view; like some others, I find it difficult to know what that view exactly is. But I am sure that it is not a good statement of the psychic-stimulus theory. It queers the pitch for that theory from the outset by attempting to combine it with the sensationist-theory, for whose errors it is not responsible. The "sensations" are assumed to be "given" as non-spatial wholes, which have to be subsequently converted into spatial wholes, and then placed side by side in orderly fashion, exactly like so many bricks. James is so dominated by the mosaic-theory of consciousness that he imports it even into his statement of rival theories.

Hermann Lotze has given the best statement of the "psychic stimulus" theory. His term "local-signs" has been borrowed by many authors, most of whom have used it in a sense quite other than Lotze's, many of them, like Wundt, assuming that the local sign is necessarily a "sensation" of some sort. Lotze's great contribution was essentially this: he pointed out that, when the images of two spots of light of similar physical quality, like two stars, are projected onto two separate spots of the retina and are seen as two spots, *R* and *L*, of similar quality and brightness but of different position, we must assume that the two nervous processes initiated in the retina are alike in respect of those factors which determine quality and brightness; but that we must postulate in each process, in addition to these factors which are alike in both, some factor or element which is peculiar to each and which is the same for every process initiated at each of the spots, no matter what the quality of the sensory experience it gives rise to. This factor or element in the total nervous process initiated by stimulation of any spot of the retina, a factor which remains constant for that spot, no matter what the physical nature of the stimulus or the quality of the resulting sensory experience, is

[1] I am glad to find evidence that leading German psychologists are now revolting against the "mosaic" theory of consciousness which has so long been dominant. In illustration of the fact I cite a single untranslatable passage from an article by Professor M. Wertheimer, the whole of which is an expansion of the view implied: "Bei der wissenschaftlichen Behandlung der Wahrnehmung ist hiernach nicht fundierend auszugehen von der 'Summe' der Einzelreize einerseits und der 'Summe' der Empfindungen andererseits in Einzelentsprechung unter sekundärer summativer Hinzufügung weiterer Factoren, sondern—und das ist schlicht tatsachennäher—von der Reizkonstellation einerseits und dem psychisch tatsächlich Gegebenen in seinem Gestalthaften andererseits. Neben den Faktoren der Reizkonstellation (deren Ganzfaktoren schon zu berücksichtigen sind) sind gesetzliche subjektive Faktoren bestimmend, welche in wesentlicher Hinsicht charakteristische Ganzbedingtheiten darstellen." "Untersuchungen zur Lehre von der Gestalt," *Psychologische Forschung*, Vol. 1, 1921. The position taken is essentially similar to that maintained in these pages and briefly set out in the chapter on "Meaning" in my "Body and Mind," 1911.

[2] *Op. cit.*, p. 272.

what Lotze proposed to call the "local sign." Without some such factor it would be impossible for the subject to distinguish the two stars as two locally distinct spots of light. Since so much confusion and misrepresentation have been current, it seems worth while to restate the reasoning in another way. If any one spot of the retina is stimulated successively by light of many different vibration-rates and amplitudes, the subject sees a spot of light of varying color and brightness, but sees it occupying constantly the same position. From this we may confidently infer that the nervous process initiated in the retina is a complex of factors; there are at least three factors, which determine, or are the ground of, the subject's knowledge or awareness of the color, of the brightness, and of the position of the spot of light, respectively. Of these three factors, the third, that which is the ground of the subject's appreciation of the position of the spot of light, is the local sign. It is constant (under normal conditions) and specific for each spot of the retina stimulation of which may result in the subject's seeing a locally distinct spot of light.

Lotze's local sign is, then, not a "sensation" and not any mode or quality of experience.[1] It is a purely nervous process, initiated by the stimulus to the retina; and its specific nature depends upon the locality of the retinal spot stimulated. So far, it seems to me, Lotze's theory of local signs must be accepted by every one. His reasoning is as conclusive and convincing as any reasoning can be. Lotze went on to inquire, What sort of nervous process (or factor in the total nervous process initiated by the stimulus) this may be? He pointed out that the eyeball is moved by a complex system of motor mechanisms, such that the stimulation of any eccentric point of the retina results, if not counteracted, in a reflex rotational movement of the eyeball which brings the *fovea*, the central spot of the retina, into the position of the stimulated spot, so that the *fovea* then receives the optical image of the star (or other source of the stimulating light). The movement of the eyeball, required to effect by the shortest route this translation of the *fovea* to the position of the optical image, is specific for each point of the retina; it requires therefore a specific conjunction of the nervous processes which determine the movements or the contractions of the muscles of the eye. Lotze suggested that this specific conjunction of innervation processes is the factor in the total nervous process initiated by the stimulus which is the local sign in visual perception. He did not say that the innervation process gives rise to a "sensation of movement" which becomes fused or "creatively synthesized" with the "sensation" of color. The activity, call it creative or not, as you please, which constitutes the knowing of the position of the star, the recognition of its direction and distance, and the capacity for such knowing, such recognition, he attributed not to "sensations," but to the mind, soul, or subject of experience. Lotze's doctrine thus brings us back to fundamentals. The essence of the sensationist position is that knowing and thinking of every kind consist in "having sensations," in "sensations" coming into existence or being hauled out of "the unconscious," in various complex conjunctions. The anti-sensationist doctrine is that thinking or knowing cannot be adequately described in that way; it asserts that all thinking, all experience, involves a knowing of something (technically called "cognition") and a striving in relation to it (technically called "conation"), and

[1] This is true of his original statement. Later statements were modified by him.

that the qualities of sensory experience are merely occasions or provocatives of this cognitive-conative activity which is thinking.

What were the grounds of James's rejection of the psychic-stimulus theory, apart from his resolute adhesion to his sensationist program? He wrote: "The essence of the Kantian contention is that there are not *spaces*, but *Space*—one infinite continuous Unit—and that our knowledge of *this* cannot be a piecemeal sensational affair, produced by summation and abstraction, to which the obvious reply is that, if any known thing bears on its front the appearance of piecemeal construction and abstraction, it is this very notion of the infinite unitary space of the world."[1] I imagine that this is not an accurate statement of the Kantian view; it seems to me to be an instance of the neglect of a rule, the nice observance of which is essential to all clear psychological and philosophical thinking, a rule seldom carefully observed, the rule, namely, that we should always distinguish with the utmost care between, on the one hand, the object we think of and, on the other hand, our thinking of it.[2] Of course, if "Solipsism" is true, if I am alone in the world, or, rather, if I am the world, then the objects I think of, other than the modes of my own experience, have no existence, and my thinking alone is real. But, when I think of them, I think of them as existing, and, whether I am right or wrong in so thinking, I must distinguish between the object as so thought of and my thinking of it. Space, then, is an object which I think of, in various ways at various times. The question at issue between nativists and geneticists is not: Do I bring this object ready-made with me into the world? Nor is it: Do I bring with me, or hereditarily possess, a "category," or a "concept," or an "idea" of Space? But rather the question is: Does my innate constitution comprise a capacity, or a disposition to develop a capacity, for perceiving spatial relations and for thinking spatially in the many ways I do come to think spatially? Or does each of us acquire and build up this capacity *de novo* in the course of his individual life?

If we reflect on the extreme complexity of the processes involved in spatial thinking, and on the fact that some animals seem, as we have seen, to exercise a similar power of spatial thinking with very little prior individual experience, we must decide in favor of the nativistic view. But we cannot be content, like James, to say that "sensations" are natively endowed with "extensity." This statement is really an illusory subterfuge. It is an attempt to put into the "sensations" something out of which we may suppose our spatial thinking to be constructed, namely, by juxtaposition of bits of "extensity." We may agree with James in holding that, if the world of extended things (or our thinking of it) is to be made up of "sensations," it is necessary to assume that the "sensations" are themselves extended or extensive. But, if we are of the opinion that this way of describing either the physical world, or our thinking of it, is wrong, misleading, not conducive to success in our practical activities, then we may relegate the extensity of sensations to the limbo to which "sensations," "ideas," "percepts," "concepts," and all such phantasmagoria properly belong.

Another objection raised by James to the "psychic stimulus" theory is the following: After citing a long passage from Schopenhauer, which leads up to

[1] *Op. cit.*, p. 275.

[2] What is called "idealism" in philosophy has generally taken the form of an elaborate effort to abolish this distinction without falling into Solipsism.

the conclusion that "the perception of the external world is essentially an intellectual process, a work of the understanding, to *which sensation furnishes merely the occasion* and the data to be interpreted in each particular case," James writes: "I call this view mythological, because I am conscious of no such Kantian machine-shop in my mind, and feel no call to disparage the powers of poor sensation in this merciless way. I have no introspective experience of mentally producing or creating space. My space-intuitions occur not in two times, but in one. There is not one moment of passive inextensive sensation, succeeded by another of active extensive perception, but the form I see is as immediately felt as the color which fills it out."[1] This argument has weight if directed against the assumption that "local signs" are "sensations" of movement, or of some other kind, which first come into existence and then proceed to fuse or "creatively synthesize" themselves with other sensations. But it can have little weight against the psychic-stimulus theory. We frequently have experiences in which, while the sensory impressions and sensory qualities remain unchanged, we radically change our interpretation of the object from which these impressions come. The field of visual perception bristles with examples, many of which James has cited in his chapter. Consider a single instance. The figure 9 is an arrangement of straight lines drawn on the flat surface. At first glance one is apt to see it as such, perhaps as a mere confusion of lines. And it is safe to say that, at a certain age, I was incapable of seeing it otherwise than as such a confusion of lines. But, if I continue to examine this figure, trying what I can make of it, I am apt to see it as a cube of which the nearest point is the angle *a*, and the remotest the angle *b*. And, if I still continue to examine it, I may perceive it as a cube of which *b* is the nearest and *a* the remotest point, the spatial significance of every part of the figure undergoing a corresponding change. In such instances the perceiving of the spatial properties of the object is, as a matter of experience, a two-stage, or even a three-stage, affair. The extensive properties of the figure are not contained in the "sensations" it excites; nor are they generated by the juxtaposition of "extensive sensations." And, though we cannot be mentally active about the figure, cannot make it the object of our thinking, without thinking it as extensive; yet, by analogy with the difference between seeing it as cubical and seeing it as flat, we may imagine our awareness of its spatial properties still further reduced and simplified, while the sensory qualities remain unchanged. If this reduction could be carried to the point of total unawareness of spatial properties, leaving merely the sensory qualities, that would be a form of anoëtic or passive experience. All that we discover in the object, beyond such sensory qualities, is discovered by an activity, a constructive

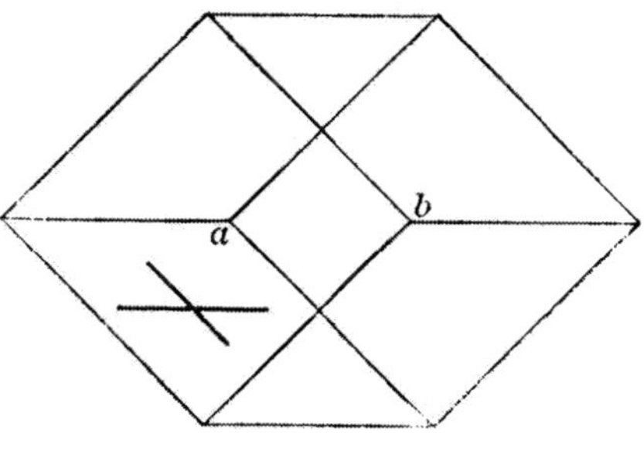

FIG. 9

[1] *Op. cit.*, p. 275.

activity, which may work in various ways and with various degrees of success upon the same sensory data, producing, as we see in this case, various results.[1]

In the interests of Sensationism and of various impossible theories of spatial perception of the type of Wundt's, a number of psychologists, of whom perhaps Münsterberg did most to promote the fashion, have assumed and even asserted that, in all such cases of varied perception on the basis of constant sensory stimulation, the muscular or motor or kinæsthetic sensations are changed at each change of perception, and that this is the essence of the change; the changed motor sensations fusing with the constant color or brightness sensations to give or constitute the changed "percept." And they apply this assumption to the explanation of a large variety of illusions of sense. This is one instance of a mythology of kinæsthetic "sensations" and their doings which we shall come across again. It has been worked to death by the behaviorists; though it should have received its quietus years ago, when Professor Stratton[2] showed, by an ingenious photographic method, that the eye-movements made during perception of simple geometrical figures bear little relation to the shapes of the figures, and, in the case of illusions, no constant or regular relation to the nature of the illusion. I have shown the same fact by the study of illusions of reversible perspective, such as that produced by Fig. 9.[3]

Let me try to summarize this very difficult section. Theories of spatial perception are of three main types: (1) Associationist theories; these are usually sensationist, that is to say, they assume that our spatial thinking is a mosaic formed by the juxtaposition or cohering of atoms of mind-stuff (called "sensations") which in themselves are utterly devoid of spatiality; and, further, they are usually "genetic," that is to say, they assume that each of us builds up all his capacity for spatial thinking, *de novo*, in the course of his individual life. Wundt has modified this by substituting for the principle of simple clustering of associated "sensations" the principle of "creative synthesis," endowing the non-spatial "sensations" with the capacity to engender spatial awareness when they fuse together. (2) Extensity theories; these are necessarily nativistic, and they may be sensationist, as in the hands

[1] The determination of the meaning of the parts by the meaning read into the whole in such instances as the perception of Fig. 9 illustrates a principle which has been well named "relative suggestion." Let the reader isolate the small cross drawn below *a* in Fig. 9 by covering the rest of the figure with a sheet of paper in which is a small hole. He will see the cross as oblique, the horizontal line being cut by the other at an angle of 45°. Removing the paper screen, the cross will appear as, will be given the meaning of, a right-angled cross, because it now appears as drawn upon one side of the cube. This process of "relative suggestion" may be well studied by the aid of after-images. Let the reader cut a right-angled cross out of a white card, place it in a strong light on a dark ground, and fixate its centre for thirty seconds. Then let him project the after-image on the walls of his chamber. When he projects it on a surface which is at right angles to his line of vision, the after-image will appear as a right-angled cross. But on all other surfaces the cross will suffer distortion of its angles; the meaning of its angles will be adapted to the fixed meanings of the rectangular but obliquely seen walls of the chamber.

[2] "Experimental Psychology and Culture," Chap. XII.

[3] "Physiological Factors of the Attention-Process," *Mind*, N. S., Vol. XII.

of James, or non-sensationist, as in the hands of Professor James Ward or Professor Stout. (In the latter form the distinction between this and the third type of theory is hardly discernible.) (3) The psychic-stimulus theory; this may be held in a Kantian form which postulates the conception of tridimensional space as given once for all in our constitution, a category or form of thought or intuition which we impose upon the "manifold data of sense"; or it may be held in an evolutionary sense, the capacity for spatial thinking being regarded as one which has been slowly built up in the course of organic evolution, in a way which each of us recapitulates more or less fully in the course of his individual development; the capacity for such recapitulation must then be regarded as an inborn tendency to the spontaneous development of the complex mental structure that is presupposed by all developed spatial perception.[1]

The outcome of an unprejudiced review of theories of spatial perception is that the acceptable theory must be nativistic and of the psychic-stimulus type; that is to say (1) it must recognize that spatial perception, as enjoyed by ourselves and the higher animals, is an extremely complex function, the capacity for which is not built up by each of us *de novo*, but is laid down in our innate constitution, its spontaneous development during the life of the individual being promoted and furthered and refined by exercise: (2) it must admit that our recognition of spatial qualities of things, their position, distance, size, shape, and pattern, is achieved only by a mental activity, to which the sense-stimulations and the qualities of sensory experience that immediately follow upon them are but the provocations. As all the world knows, since Plato and Herbart, each subject perceives only what he is capable of perceiving, only what he is prepared by nature and by experience to perceive.[2] We may fairly assume that, in any two normally constituted persons, the sensory effects of similar sense-stimulations, the sensory qualities experi-

[1] The student may ask—What is "an inborn tendency to development"? He may ask the same question in regard to all our innate endowments, bodily and mental; and in all cases the answer is—"We do not know." The same is true also of the specific structure and functions of the simplest plant.

[2] Coleridge has perfectly expressed this truth in the ode "Dejection":

"O Lady! we receive but what we give
And in ourselves alone does Nature live.
Ours is her wedding garment, ours her shroud!
And would we aught behold of higher worth
Than that inanimate cold world allowed
To the poor loveless, ever-anxious crowd,

enced, are alike; yet, as we know, they may perceive, in response to similar sensory stimulations, very different objects, or perceive the object with very different degrees of adequacy. In every field the expert perceives far more than the inexpert; because he reacts upon similar sense-impressions with a more adequately prepared mind. In some sense the stored traces of his many experiences in his special field of observation rise up to meet the sense-impressions and to mould them in conformity with those past experiences.

This fact, that the mind is active in perception, supplying from its own resources something very essential, over and above the sensory qualities with which it responds to sense-stimulations, this fact is occasionally brought home to us very vividly by some such experience as the following: As I walk quietly through the forest, something, probably some slight movement or sound, provokes me to gaze curiously in a certain direction. There before me is a confused patchwork of light and shade and color, which, perhaps, I perceive as a rock partially concealed by foliage; until suddenly, without any change in the sense-stimulations I am receiving, I perceive an animal standing motionless gazing at me; the patchwork of light and shade and color has resolved itself into the animal; or rather, my mind, working under the impulse of curiosity, has suddenly found a richer "meaning" in the confused visual impression. We have a similar experience in examining one of those puzzle-pictures in which the outlines of some familiar object, such as a man or an animal, are so combined with other lines as to form part of a landscape. We may be told to find the man, or the elephant, or what not. And this helps one greatly; but, even with such a cue, one may search the drawing for some time and fail to see the elephant. Then suddenly it seems to leap out from its background, and is perceived so clearly, is so obtrusive, that we cannot glance at the picture in any position without perceiving it; and we are puz-

Ah! from the soul itself must issue forth
A light, a glory, a fair luminous cloud
Enveloping the earth—
And from the soul itself must there be sent
A sweet and potent voice, of its own birth,
Of all sweet sounds the life and element!"

zled to understand how we could have failed to see it at first glance.

It is the same in the simplest spatial perception. When my retina receives the optical images of four stars disposed at the corners of a square, I do not necessarily see a square. The visual impression does not necessarily or always evoke that meaning or, as we say, convey that meaning. I can perceive a square only in so far as I have learned to think of a square (or possibly am prepared by heredity to do so). Every visual pattern is seen by me as such, or as an object of definite shape, only in so far as I have, by heredity or by training, a mental disposition corresponding to that object, and in so far as the retinal stimulus brings this disposition into play. The figure 9 is an instance in which the same retinal stimulation is equally capable of bringing any one of several pre-formed dispositions into play; hence the facility with which it suggests, or signifies to me, any one of several objects; or, in other words, the facility with which I find different spatial meanings in it, see it as first this object, then that. In general terms, we may say that shapes, positions, and all spatial attributes are objects which the mind, or the subject, thinks in response to solicitations of the senses; they are "meanings" which we find in the object or read into it. For every object which the subject can think of, he must possess a corresponding cognitive disposition, innate or acquired; and no amount of "extensity," postulated as inhering in "sensations," will enable the "sensations" to do the thinking, or to find a "meaning" for themselves. As we said in dealing with instincts, *the cognitive disposition is a lock which can be turned by a key of appropriate pattern, and the key which is operative in perception is the qualitative, the temporal, or the spatial pattern of the complex sense-impression.*

Just as there are rhythms or temporal patterns which are too complex to be perceived as such by me (because I have not built up the required cognitive dispositions), so there are spatial patterns too complex for me, and which I can resolve into significant objects of my thinking, only by neglecting some part of the total field of sense-impression; as when I single out "The Plough" in the heavens, neglecting all the rest of the visual field.

The fact that "I am conscious of no machine-shop in my mind," that I do not become aware by direct introspection of the complexity of the processes involved in spatial perception, is no guarantee of their simplicity. In this respect spatial perception is not peculiar, but merely conforms to the general rule that our experience is very far from adequately expressing the complexity of the mental processes which issue in acts of knowing and in behavior. The processes that go on in our heads never can be revealed in all their vast complexity to the introspective glance of any psychologist—not even of a William James. Recent developments of mental pathology are forcing the recognition of this fact more strongly upon psychologists every day; so that few remain who have not some acquaintance with it.

Perception of a Solid Object

Having glanced at the three great types of complexity upon which our perception, our perceptual recognition of objects, depends, namely, qualitative, temporal, and spatial patterns, let us, in order to realize more fully the complexity of perception, consider the process of perception of some material thing; and let us take the traditional orange. The sensationist account runs in some such way as follows: "I see the orange on the table" means that rays reflected from the orange enter my eye and form an optical image on my retina. The optical image, by stimulating the fibres of the optic nerve, excites the "visual sensation" of orange quality and also a complex of "motor sensations," which, fusing with the "visual sensation," give it shape and position. In addition to this, in virtue of previous experience of oranges, the *images* of sensations of taste, smell, contact, and weight, previously experienced on handling and tasting oranges, are revived, reproduced, or brought back into consciousness; because, according to the law of association by temporal contiguity, all these images are associated with the visual "sensation" of orange quality.[1] The "sensations," visual and motor,

[1] At this point the account may or may not be complicated, according to taste, by the statement that of course the links of association do not obtain between "sensations" and "images" as such, but between corresponding elements of the cortex of the brain, each link of association being a brain-fact, a path of low resistance in the cortex.

together with all these "images" or revived "sensations" of various senses, form a coherent cluster which is the "percept" of the orange. This "percept," once constituted, is capable of being revived, reproduced in "consciousness," by the mere hearing of the word "orange," or in many other ways, in the absence of any sense-stimulation coming directly from the orange. The "percept" has become an "idea" of an orange, which "idea" may become variously associated with other similarly constituted "ideas," such as an "idea" of an apple.

What shall we say of this account of perception? We cannot say that it is altogether false. But we can say that it is very inadequate and, in certain respects, misleading. It is true that in perception the sensory qualities are often complicated by imagery.

Imagery

Let us grapple at once with imagery. Most adult persons understand what it is "to have an image in the mind," to depict "in the mind's eye" the face of some friend or some familiar scene or object. Such depiction is thinking of a remote object by aid of imagery; just as perceiving the object is thinking of it by the aid of sensory qualities. Most persons also can in some measure depict familiar sounds, such as the voice of a friend or the striking of the hall clock, "in the mind's ear." And some can think of odorous and tasting things, of hard and soft and smooth and hot or cold things, in the same sort of way. Though in these respects individuals seem to differ widely. In all such cases we seem to experience in a faint, thin, ghostlike fashion the sensory qualities on which we rely in perception. These faint experiences of the sensory qualities are what are commonly called "images"; and "images" are treated by the sensationists in much the same way as "sensations" and are assigned much the same role as "sensations." The objections that we have raised against "sensations" lie equally against this usage of the term "images." The "image," like the "sensation," is an abstraction, not a concrete entity. Recognizing the similarity of imagery to sensory experience, we may best speak of it as imaginal experience or the experiencing of imaginal qualities. The difference between the two kinds of experience cannot be adequately described, though it is familiar to us. Perhaps it is best described by saying that imaginal qualities lack sensory vividness. Sensory vividness seems normally to attach only to qualities evoked by stimulation of the sense organs. What are the neural conditions of the difference is a fair topic of speculation and inquiry. It is commonly assumed that imagery depends upon neural processes going on in those parts of the brain-cortex on excitement of which the corresponding sensory qualities are experienced. This, however, is a deep question, by no means decided yet, though capable of being decided by empirical evidence.[1]

Can "Meaning" be Analyzed into "Images"?

The more important question for psychology is that of the role or function of imagery in thinking in general, and in perceptual thinking in particular. The Sensationists will have it that the "images," clustering round the "sensations" excited by sense-stimulation, give "meaning" to them and convert the "sensations" into a "percept" of the object. Thus, when I see an orange, "images" of its flavor, its contact, its weight cluster round the "color-sensation" of orange quality and constitute the "meaning" of the "percept."

"Meaning" is a topic of lively contemporary discussion. It is commonly raised under the form: How are we to describe "the meaning" of an "idea"? Is it the imagery comprised in the "idea"? Or is it something of a different nature? But the problem is best raised in connection with perception. Behaviorists at one extreme assert that "meaning" is wholly and solely a bodily attitude, an innervation of certain muscles. Others, as we have seen, assert that "imagery" is the "meaning" of the "percept"; that a "percept" is sensations and images combined somehow in one whole. Thus, they say, the spatial "meaning" of a point of light is the "images" of the movements I should have to make in order to touch that spot with my finger. For the spatial qualities of things are undoubtedly "meanings."

[1] Professor Bergson is the most thorough critic of the common view. He rejects it utterly and brings forward an imposing array of evidence. Cf. his "Matter and Memory." In my opinion the question is still open.

James introduced a more subtle variety of the sensationist account of "meaning" in his famous doctrine of "the fringe of thought." Every substantive part of the "stream of consciousness" is, he said, surrounded by and bathed in a vague mass of waxing and waning elements, "sensations" or "images," and these it is which give "meaning" to the "sensations" or "images" occupying the "focus of consciousness." According to this doctrine, that which is vague and obscure in the experience of any moment constitutes the "meaning" of that which is clear and prominent to introspection. A strange theory, indeed! For my "meaning" is the all-important fact in my thinking. To perceive an object, or otherwise think of it, is essentially to mean that object and no other. So long as I mean the object, it matters little what sensory or imaginal qualities enter into my experience. When I use the word "orange," or when I set about to do something to or with an orange, to eat it or throw it at your head, the all-important thing for the success of my undertaking is that I should "mean" the physical thing, the orange; or, if I want to call attention to, or to reason about, only the color-quality, orange, it is essential that I should mean the color-quality and not the physical thing. In both cases I may use the word "orange," or may experience the imaginal color-quality; and in both cases the imagery may include other sensory properties of the orange; but in the two cases my "meaning" is very different. And we know that there are some persons who may use the word "orange" in both of these distinct senses or meanings and who, though they are incapable of visual imagery, nevertheless are perfectly well aware in which sense they use the word, what they mean by it as they speak it.

To mean an object is, then, the very essence of thinking of it, and is something quite different from having any cluster of "sensations" or "images," whether clear and vivid, or waning or otherwise obscure, marginal, or fringy. If we must describe thinking as made up of entities put together, we might say that perception, or a "percept," is "sensations" plus "images" plus "meaning," and that an "idea" is "images" plus "meaning." And we might say that the "sensations" and "images," in some qualitative, temporal, or spatial complex, are the psychic stimuli which evoke the meaning. What, then, is the "meaning"? How is it to be introspectively described, if it consists of neither sensory nor imaginal qualities?

This question is very puzzling; and it is, perhaps, no cause for wonder that many psychologists, without subscribing to the extravagances of the behaviorists or those of the neo-realists, deny that "meanings," over and above the sensory qualities or "contents of consciousness," are facts of experience in any sense whatever. We have thus at the present time this remarkable state of affairs among psychologists. One party affirms that "meaning" is a fact of experience not to be identified with sensory or imaginal qualities, and is the all-important fact in all experience. A second party identifies "meaning" with the "sensations" and "images" at the focus of consciousness. A third, admitting the all-importance of "meaning," identifies it with a mass of vague marginal sensations and images, largely motor or kinæsthetic.[1] A fourth admits the reality and all-importance of "meaning" in mental life, and agrees with the first party that it is not to be identified with "sensations" and "images": but maintains that psychology must restrict itself to describing these latter, and must leave "meaning" to be dealt with by logic. This is one way of rendering psychology a strictly useless science and preserving it from all contaminating contact with problems of human life and human nature.[2] A fifth party (the behaviorist) says that "meaning" is, like all experience, an illusion, a fiction, an error, if conceived as other than physical vibrations in the brain.

This divergence of opinion is due to the fact that the experience of "meaning" cannot itself be made an object of introspective observation, as sensory qualities and other modes of experience can, and for this sufficient reason: when we perceive

[1] In order to show the reader that this view is by no means extinct but is seriously held in an extreme form, I cite the concluding sentence of a recent article on the "Development of Meaning" by Doctor R. H. Wheeler (*Am. Jour. of Psych.*, 1922): "It is quite probable that pure meanings, so-called, are in reality masses of diffuse muscular sensations which the reagent has not succeeded in recognizing and in describing."

[2] This seems to be, *e. g.*, Professor Titchener's doctrine, as set forth most clearly in his "Beginner's Psychology."

a physical object, we mean it; but, if we become introspective in the presence of the physical object, if we introspectively examine our perceptual activity, we find the sensory and imaginal qualities; and at that very moment the "meaning" is changed; we no longer mean the physical object, we no longer think of it; rather, we mean, or think of, the thinking of the object; and, when we do that and analyze the thinking, we discover the sensory qualities, but the "meaning" necessarily eludes our introspective observation; it always runs ahead of our introspective glance. The attempt is like driving in a buggy and trying to catch up with the horse by whipping him up or turning him this way and that; however we hasten the pace and however quickly we turn, he is always ahead of us. And yet, though we were blind and deaf, we should know he was there, by inference from the fact that we are borne along and from the control we can exercise over him.

Here, perhaps, we have the explanation of another remarkable divergence of opinion, namely, between those who tell us that the essential and complete program of psychology is to give a systematic account of the findings of introspection, and those who say that introspection is essentially impossible. For the former party are content to describe the sensory qualities, to display "consciousness" as a flowing mosaic of "sensations" and "images"; while the others rightly see that such a description fails to include the essence of "consciousness," of experience, of thinking, namely, the activity of knowing or meaning an object.

The fact is, we cannot describe "meaning" otherwise than in terms of the object that we mean; we can only say "I mean this or that object." And it is misleading to use the word "meaning" as a substantive; just as it is misleading to describe any fact of experience in substantival terms.

Let us notice that some of the authors who, in discussing perception, neglect "meaning" or identify it with imagery, reintroduce it in a chapter devoted to *conception*. It is common form among psychologists to discuss perception and conception as though they were entirely different functions, conception being a loftier kind of thinking which only the cultivated adult attains to.

Yet to think of an object is to conceive it; to know, to recognize, to be aware of, or conscious of, any object is to conceive it, even when our knowing is a perceptual knowing. To mean an object is to conceive it. The usual discussion of conception identifies it with, or restricts it to, the conceiving of abstract objects. But this restriction of the word is indefensible.[1] The difference between thinking of a concrete thing and of an abstraction is not properly described by saying that, in the former case, I have "a concrete idea" and, in the latter, "an abstract idea" or a "concept" in consciousness. We should rather say that I think of or conceive, in the former case, a concrete object, and, in the second case, an abstract object. When I look at this fly on my page, I may say that I conceive it to be a fly, no less truly than I may say that I conceive its vitality, its beauty, its noxiousness, its size, its shape, its color, its powers of flight, its genus, or its species. Perceiving is one mode of conceiving.[2]

Let us return to our orange. In perceiving it, I know it, cognize or recognize it as an orange. The word "recognize" is sometimes used in the stricter sense of recognizing some particu-

[1] Thus Professor Stout writes: "Evidently conception and perception stand in antithesis to each other. This antithesis is often represented as identical with that between the universal and the particular. Now if this is taken to imply that perception involves no universal element, it is entirely false and misleading. All thought implies a universal, and a perception is a thought. At the least, it implies distinction and recognition, and so carries with it a reference to an object which remains the same in its varying appearances. The transition from the percept to the concept is not a transition from the merely particular to the universal. The difference is rather this: in perception, universal and particular are indistinguishably blended; the universal element lies entirely in the bare fact that the particular is recognized. Now the essential character of conception is that in it the universal is thought of as such, in contradistinction to the particular; implicit in the percept, it is explicit in the concept." ("Analytic Psychology," Vol. 2, p. 173.) This seems to me sound doctrine. I take exception only to the terminology. It seems to me better practice to follow James in using "conception" as the most general name for the function of apprehending or thinking "the universal," whether in perception or in thinking of abstract objects by the aid of names. The process which Stout defines as conception I would then call "thinking of abstract objects." In perception we may exercise this function; as when we pay attention to the color of a thing in abstraction from the thing as such, or when we perceive, on looking at a man's face, moral qualities such as kindliness, cruelty, or honesty.

[2] The nature of "meaning" has been much investigated in laboratories of late years. While some of the investigators continue stoutly to deny "meaning" as

lar object previously perceived; but, considered as a mental function, the recognition of an object as a representative of its class is not essentially different from the recognition of an individual as such; therefore it is better to use the word in the wider sense. Almost all our perceiving is recognition in the wider sense; it is a knowing, a cognizing of the object as of a kind previously known. If the cry of an animal, unlike any I have heard before, suddenly breaks upon my ear, claiming my attention by its loudness, I do not recognize the animal; but I may recognize some animal; the sound signifies to me some animal. Or, even if it fails to do that, I recognize at least a sound of a certain character; which is to say that the sensory experience suggests or signifies some object, the source of the sound.

Perhaps the only instances of pure cognition, as distinct from recognition, are those in which a creature is confronted for the first time with an object of the kind that evokes an instinctive reaction. When the solitary wasp encounters for the first time a creature of the kind which is the natural and sole prey of its species; when the hen nightingale hears for the first time the song of the male; when the gregarious animal, brought up in lonely captivity, encounters for the first time another member of his own species; then, we may suppose, an act of pure cognition is achieved.

Now note that, when I perceive the orange, there is somehow

a fact of experience over and above all sensory and imaginal qualities, the balance of such testimony seems to be inclining steadily in favor of the other view. Those who adhere consistently to the sensationist program find themselves driven to escape the task of dealing with "meaning" by relegating it to the logicians, as they relegate motives to the moralists. They thus preserve the purity of the sensationist psychology, at the cost of rendering it perfectly useless. As good examples of such laboratory work on "meaning," I refer the student to two articles in *The Psychological Review*. In one of these (Vol. 22) Doctor T. V. Moore reports evidence against the identification of "meaning" with imagery of the following nature. Subjects were instructed to react to printed words, in one series as soon as they took the meaning of each word, in the second series as soon as the word evoked an image. In nearly all cases, the reactions of the former series were more rapid than those of the second series. From which the author infers that the "meaning" precedes the image in time. Further, all his subjects found it possible to distinguish introspectively between "meaning" and image. In the other article (Vol. 24) Doctor E. C. Tolman, using a similar method and a larger array of subjects, reports similar results, namely, discrepancy in time between "meaning" and image, though in some cases the image preceded the meaning.

operative in the act of perception not only my previous experience of oranges, constituting the act one of recognition, but also a vast amount of other experience, experience of material objects of many kinds—experiences of seeing, of handling, of tasting, of hearing, and so forth. And all this mass of past experience contributes to determine the "meaning" of the object, or, more strictly, my "meaning" as I perceive the orange. I know it not merely as something that may yield me sensory experiences of taste and odor and touch, but also as a solid object out there in space, with all the properties that I have learned to expect of solid objects. If I put out my hand to raise it to my lips, the strength of my innervation of my muscles is nicely adjusted to its weight, without my reflecting on, or being explicitly aware of, its weight; as I realize, if the object proves to be a mere hollow shell, of less weight than a normal orange; for it flies up in the air in a way which surprises me. Similarly, if you push it off the edge of the table and it remains suspended in the air instead of falling to the ground, I realize that its gravitational property was implicit in my perception. Or if I take a knife to cut it, and the knife meets with no resistance; or if I throw it forcibly against the wall, and it is not shattered. In a multitude of such ways I may be brought to realize the extreme complexity of my act of perception, to understand how much is implicit in my recognition of the orange, and how much previous experience has gone to the formation of this mass of knowledge of material things which is implicitly operative in my act of perception, guiding my behavior in relation to the object.

All this mass of knowledge contributes to the "meaning" which I find in the object, the "meaning" which is evoked by the pattern of the sensory stimulation. And this "meaning" is far richer than any imagery which I may introspectively discover as playing a part in the act of perception or recognition.

Of the total "meaning," the total knowledge which is operative in the mind as I perceive the orange, one part or another is apt to be more prominent and to play a larger part than others in the guidance of my behavior, according to my purpose at the moment my glance falls on it. If I am thirsty and seeking to allay my thirst, I seize the orange or, at least, perceive it as an object that will satisfy that desire; I perceive it as a succulent cool fruit; that part of its total "meaning" is most prominent. If I am looking for a missile to throw at an intruding burglar, I probably pass it by. But, if I am looking for one to throw playfully at a friend, I may seize it for that purpose; then its weight, softness, its property of going "squash" on impact, are the prominent part of the "meaning" I find in the visual impression.

Take another example. I enter my study in the dusk and see an irregular brown mass on the hearth-rug. I cannot at first recognize it more exactly. Continuing to gaze, I recognize it as a dog lying curled up. My "meaning" has become very much richer. The brown patch is now not merely a solid material object of a given shape and size and position; but all my acquired knowledge of animals and of dogs in general becomes operative and determines my behavior. I may retreat; or I may go forward and kick at the object.[1] In the latter case, if my foot meets with no resistance, I am puzzled and disturbed, perhaps even frightened. I feel that my recognition has been profoundly at fault; the object is not a dog and not even a material mass. If my foot meets with the normal soft resistance, implicitly expected by me, but the mass makes no movement, again I feel I am at fault. I have perceived a live dog, implicitly recognizing the object as having the normal reaction tendencies which I have learned to expect in all live dogs; and I have been at fault: the dog is a dead dog.

Or, again, my perception may advance to a third stage of explicitness and adequacy; I recognize the brown mass, not only as a dog, but as my dog, Jack. Then the "meaning" I read into the sensory experience, the "meaning" evoked in my mind by the sense-impression, is far richer than before. I know the object as having not only all the properties common to solid masses and those common to dogs in general, but also as having all the moral peculiarities of my dog Jack. And my behavior

[1] It is important to notice that my reaction to the sense-impression is determined only indirectly by the nature of the sensory pattern. The "meaning" I read into the sensory pattern is the immediate determinant of my reaction, my impulse to retreat or advance. How absurd, then, for psychologists to ignore the "meaning" and content themselves with an analytic description of the sensory pattern, as some would have us do.

is determined by this mass of implicit knowledge of a kind which is utterly incapable of being represented in any sensory terms less complicated than a page of print or a long disquisition on his virtues and vices. I may step over him, or pat him, or speak a word, or stir him with my foot; and he may respond merely by cocking an eye or an ear at me. Both actions, mine and his, are then enormously significant; each implies an act of recognition rich in "meaning"; all our past relations of mutual confidence and service have gone to build up in each of us a knowledge of the other which is implicit in the act of recognition.[1]

Perception, then, cannot be adequately described as the rise to "consciousness" of certain "sensations" surrounded by a cluster of "images," whether these images be described as focal or as constituting a "fringe of thought." What rises to "consciousness" is the object perceived or thought of.

The Herbartian psychologists made a considerable advance on sheer associationism. They made much of facts of the order we have considered in the last few pages. That rising up in the mind of a rich mass of effects of former experience to greet the sense-impression of the moment was called by them *apperception*. They conceived the mind as constituted of a mass of "ideas," arranged in more or less orderly fashion in the subconscious chamber of the mind, like books in a well-classified library. The "apperception" of a sense-impression consisted in the "ideas" of similar objects rising above the "threshold of consciousness" to greet and welcome it, and to lead it to its appropriate dwelling-place in the subconscious chamber of "ideas" among its nearest relatives.

[1] I have sometimes let myself into my house in the small hours of the morning, while the dog mentioned on page 196 lay in his usual sleeping-place in the hall. On these occasions he made no other movement than to cock his eye or ear, and sometimes only a hardly perceptible movement of his tail. Yet, if a stranger came down the garden during the night, he would make a furious noise. This was no result of training by me; there was no question of the "stamping in" of one reflex by pleasure and the "stamping out" of another by pain. The same dog, if my absence from home lasted several days and nights, would always spontaneously choose for his sleeping-place the mat outside my wife's door, instead of his usual place down-stairs in the hall. Such behavior is difficult to interpret, but it is certainly not a matter of substituting one reflex for another. In both cases the dog showed a more or less intelligent appreciation of the total situation.

We have rejected the use of the word "idea" because (among other reasons) it confuses the act of thinking of an object with the enduring conditions which render possible the thinking of that object. And we prefer to call that which endures in the mind, as the condition of our thinking of any object, not "an idea," but a *cognitive disposition.*[1]

The complexity of the perceptual process in the developed mind and the working of a highly complex cognitive disposition may be illustrated by the process of examining such an object as a strange flower, with the purpose of classifying it. A person having no botanical knowledge may merely recognize it as a flower, and perhaps enjoy its beauty. But in the mind of the botanist the disposition which is brought into play by the sight of the flower is highly complex, a system of definitely related parts. If, moved by curiosity, he proceeds to examine the flower, his attention turns from one feature to another, petals, stamens, pistil, ovules, etc., until he has explicitly perceived all these parts and their relations to one another. In this train of activity, the successive acts of perception imply the successive coming into predominant activity of the parts of the total mental system built up by much previous perception of flowers. The whole system is excited from the first; and the systematic relation of the parts governs the order of the perceptual activity. The parts may be said to be implicitly apprehended throughout the process, while each part in turn becomes explicitly apprehended. Such *schematic implicit apprehension* is characteristic of all our more intelligent and purposeful perception.

We see now that the cognitive disposition concerned in any act of developed perception is no simple element of the mental structure; it must rather be conceived as very complex and as related in very complex fashion with other parts of the structure of the mind. The facts of perception of the order of those we have considered show that the cognitive structure of the mind must be conceived somewhat after the pattern of a tree. Perhaps a banyan-tree would be a less inadequate simile than an ordinary tree.

Perception is primarily and fundamentally the cognition, the conception, of a material object in space. As James said: "The function by which we thus identify a numerically distinct and

[1] If the word "idea" is to be retained in the scientific vocabulary, it would be best used as the most general name for enduring cognitive dispositions and systems of dispositions, rather than to denote acts of thinking. Its double use, to perform both of these services, is the main ground of its convenience and of the confusion to which it has given rise.

permanent subject of discourse [*i. e.*, an object] is called conception." [1] He went on to say that an object may be conceived with a very minimum of connotation or meaning. "The essential point is that it should be reidentified by us as that which the talk is about. . . . In this sense creatures extremely low in the intellectual scale may have conception. All that is required is that they should recognize the same experience again. A polyp would be a conceptual thinker if a feeling of 'Hollo! thingumbob, again!' ever flitted through its mind."[2] This seems to me true doctrine; but it is quite inconsistent with James's sensationism. It implies the truth that the most rudimentary mind is capable of thinking of an object, no matter how inadequately it may think of it. Unless we postulate this function of cognition or conception as of the essence of mental life and present wherever mind is active, at the very bottom of the evolutionary scale as well as at its higher levels, we shall never evolve it by compounding "sensations" together, not even if we endow them with "extensity" or describe them as "extensive wholes." [3]

The simplest mind we can legitimately conceive is, then, one which would respond to a sense-impression, not by merely "having a sensation," but by an act of knowing; this act we could only describe as becoming aware of *something there*, an object in space, no matter how completely undefined the nature of the object as thought of and the nature of its spatial relations. Such a mind, of simplest possible structure, must be conceived as consisting of one cognitive disposition linked with a single conative disposition. Such a mind would respond to every sense-impression that affected it at all (no matter what its nature) with simple awareness of *something there* and a vague undirected impulse of appetition, of striving toward the object. Or perhaps, as a matter of speculative probability, we ought to

[1] "Principles," Vol. I., p. 461. [2] *Op. cit.*, p. 463.

[3] Knowing, cognizing, recognizing, or conceiving is then a fundamental function or faculty of mind. We cannot hope to describe or explain the genesis of this out of any process of a different type, whether physical process or some hypothetical simpler mode of experience, such as "having sensations." All we can hope to do is to understand the relation of the more complex modes of exercise of this function to simpler modes, and the evolution of minds capable of the higher modes from minds of more lowly constitution and capacity.

postulate in the simplest possible mind two unlike cognitive dispositions, linked respectively with two conative dispositions, one of appetition, one of aversion. A creature so endowed would respond to all impressions in one of two ways; the one response would be the cognizing of something there to be pursued; the other would be the cognizing of something there to be avoided. It would, that is to say, have two instincts of the most highly generalized type. A creature so endowed might get on in the world; and from such a rudimentary mental structure the evolution of minds of more complex structure may be imagined.

This seems to be the explanation of the fact that, whatever we may think of, we tend to think of it as a thing somewhere in space; for to think in that way is the primordial thinking, and we only emancipate ourselves from this primordial mode of all thinking by much discipline, if at all. Of course I do not mean to imply that the most primitive mind possesses a "concept" of Euclidean tri-dimensional Space with which it envelops its "sensations," or within which it locates them; rather, knowledge of space, the capacity for spatial perception and conception, must be supposed to have been evolved, to have been differentiated out of this primordial "there," with the increasing complexity of mental structure.

All the wealth of things that we learn to perceive and recognize has been differentiated out of this primordial something—this object of widest possible denotation and so nearly lacking in all connotation—by successive discriminations between classes of objects previously indistinguishable. Each new discrimination has involved a further differentiation of the cognitive structure of the mind, the whole structure growing, like a tree that puts out new twigs from the stem, forming new growing points, which in turn divide; until in the developed human mind the structure is like a vast tree. The common stem, which supports all the branches, twigs, and leaves, is the primordial undifferentiated cognitive disposition. The main branches correspond to the great classes of things; the smaller branches to the more special classes; the twigs to still smaller classes; and the leaves to individual objects.

Consider this simile in relation to a single department of knowledge, the knowledge of the animal kingdom in the orderly mind of a naturalist. This knowledge consists not in a mere mass of "ideas" lying latent and unconscious, but in the cognitive mental structure which he has built up by a multitude of acts of discriminative perception. He recognizes all living things as material objects occupying and moving in space; but he recognizes them also as living. That is to say, he has differentiated in his mind a branch of the tree of knowledge, a cognitive disposition, corresponding to living things; and this branch has branched again into two branches, one corresponding to animals, the other to plants. The animal branch in turn has grown out into smaller branches, each one of which corresponds to one of the great divisions of the animal kingdom. Each of these has put forth twigs corresponding to the various genera and species of each kingdom.

When such a man, one who has acquired all this systematic knowledge, who has built up all this orderly mental structure, perceives an animal and recognizes it as a member of a particular species, he thinks of it, conceives it, not merely as an object presenting a particular color-pattern to the eye or sound-pattern to the ear. His meaning is far richer than that. He conceives it, in that moment of perception, as having not only its specific qualities, but also the qualities or properties of its genus, family, and phylum, and also the properties common to all animals and those common to all living things, and also those common to all material things. All this knowledge is implicit and operative in his act of recognition; for, if on further observation, the animal failed to conform to any one of these categories, the observer would be utterly puzzled and the impulse of curiosity which led him to examine the creature, instead of attaining satisfaction in the act of recognition and correct classification, would be strongly provoked to further activity.

Just as any leaf or twig of a tree cannot perform its function without the co-operation of the branches and stem which support it and from which it was derived by an evolutionary differentiation, so also the highly special cognitive disposition concerned in the recognition of the individual or of the species cannot function without the co-operation of the whole of the more fundamental dispositions from which it has been differentiated. The normal functioning of the leaf or twig implies the functioning of the branches and stem which support it; and in a similar way the functioning of the special cognitive disposition implies and involves the functioning of its parent dispositions.

The mental structure may then be compared not only to a tree but also to a family tree, of which the successive generations remain alive and active, becoming a nation of many coexistent co-operating generations. In successive generations specialization of labor is carried further; and the work of the youngest most highly specialized generation implies, and is only possible in virtue of, the co-operation of the less specialized and older generations.

If we apply this way of thinking to the whole of the cognitive structure of a well-developed and well-organized mind, we see that it approximates to a *microcosm* which mirrors the *macrocosm*, the world in which it lives and about which it thinks. The perfectly developed and organized mind would have a cognitive disposition for every individual object and for every species, genus, and class of objects; and these would not be a mere unorganized crowd of dispositions, but would be related in a perfectly definite treelike system; the relations between the parts of the system would correspond to the actual relations between all the objects and classes of objects which the subject was capable of recognizing or in any way thinking of.

In a later chapter we must consider the processes of growth of mental structure. But first we must inquire into the facts implied by the word "attention."

On an earlier page I wrote that perception is essentially a synthetic activity. We have now seen something of the complexity and variety of this synthetic activity, which responds to the stimulus of sensory patterns (qualitative, temporal, and spatial) with awareness or cognition of objects. The complex object is thought of as a whole or unity comprising many parts; but the act of knowing or thinking the complex whole is a single act, though it may prolong itself through successive phases. In the total process the various sense-impressions composing the sensory pattern play their parts, contributing to the total unitary resultant. But the synthetic activity does not consist merely in holding or binding together a number of discrete sensory elements. The thinking of the object is a unitary act, a psychic response to a multiplicity of stimuli. If we could follow and describe the process in all its details, we should have to describe a hierarchy of processes, each step of which involves the synthetic function, the unity of the act of cognition being the final product of the converging hierarchic series. New evidence of this vast complexity underlying and constituting the synthetic activity of perception has been discovered by the researches of Dr. Henry Head in the domain of mental disorders resulting from injuries to the brain. ("Studies in Neurology," 1920.)

CHAPTER IX

ATTENTION AND INTEREST

All thinking, all experience is a process, an activity rather than a state or a thing. That is one reason why it cannot be adequately described in static terms such as "sensations" and "ideas," "percepts" and "concepts," but only in dynamic terms, by the use of verbs; and, because the activity is always concerned with some object, the verbs chosen should as far as possible be transitive rather than intransitive, and in the active rather than the passive voice.

The word "attention" is often used in psychology as a substantive; and then the question is asked—What is attention? And attention is said to do this, that, and the other, to make sensations or ideas more intense, or clearer, or more prominent in "Consciousness," or to single out this object or that. This is a survival of the way of speaking proper to the faculty psychology. Such language is confusing. Let us hold fast to the fact that there is only one agent in all forms of mental activity, you or I, he, she, or it, an agent who can properly be denoted only by a proper name or a pronoun, or generally as "the subject." It is true that the agent is also a patient, in so far as he suffers the consequences of his actions, the satisfactions of success, the dissatisfactions of failure.

The Cycle of Mental Activity

Mental activity is a cyclic process, a series of cycles of activity. Each cycle begins with some cognition; the subject recognizes or thinks of some object. This evokes in him an impulse to effect some change, if only fuller cognition, more definite recognition. The striving thus brings about further cognition, which either satisfies the impulse (when the process terminates) or fails to do so, when the subject continues to strive, varying the direction and nature of his efforts. This cyclic character is perhaps most obvious in such an activity as thinking out the moves of a game of chess. It is almost equally clear in the case of taking in the hand some complex object, as a flower or an insect, and examining it with a view to a fuller knowledge of it. In such cases the successive cycles are clearly so many steps in a larger process which has a certain unity, a unity of aim or purpose. If we use the convenient Latin word "conation" to denote the striving aspect of mental process, we may conveniently speak of this as the "conative unity" of the process. We might use the word "conate" as a verb, in order to complete our technical vocabulary. We should then have the parallel terms, "cognize, cognition, cognitive," and "conate, conation, and conative," for the description of mental activity in its double aspect of knowing and striving.

The passive aspect of experience, the suffering of pain or dissatisfaction, the enjoying of pleasure or satisfaction, is conveniently called "affective"; and, if a corresponding substantive is needed, as the most general term, we may speak of "feeling" or "affection." The word "feel" is commonly used as a transitive verb, equivalent to "perceive," as when we say "I feel the roughness of this surface." This usage is apt to create confusion. We do not need an active verb to denote facts of this order; for that reason the words "affective" and "affection" are better than "feeling." As a verb "feel" should be used only in the intransitive sense, as when we say, "I feel tired or lazy or hungry"; and even there we do better to say "I am tired," etc. We often speak of an intellectual or cognitive activity; or of an act of willing or of resolving, choosing, striving, purposing; or again of a state of feeling. But it is generally admitted that all mental activity has these three aspects, cognitive, conative, and affective; and when we apply one of these three adjectives to any phase of mental process, we mean merely that the aspect named is the most prominent of the three at that moment. Each cycle of activity has this triple aspect; though each tends to pass through three phases in which cognition, conation, and affection are in turn most prominent; as when the naturalist, catching sight of a specimen, recognizes it, captures it, and gloats over his capture.

Is Striving Initiated by Feeling? Or Is Feeling Secondary to Striving?

It is perhaps a fair question for discussion, whether the three phases of dominance of the cycle by cognition, conation, and affection, always succeed one another in this order. Many authors, including all the psychological hedonists (if there still be any) hold that conation naturally succeeds affection and is determined by it; that all striving is prompted by feeling, by pleasure or pain. This is a very speculative question, though of great theoretic interest; it can hardly be answered positively by any introspective skill. Theoretically it would seem that the natural order of predominance of the three aspects of the cycle is cognition, conation, changed cognition, affection.

The type of experience which gives most color to the hedonist position is that in which we suffer some bodily injury and make efforts to escape or withdraw. For here, it is said, the pain initiates the striving. But in strictness this statement involves, as is now generally recognized, a confusion of two senses of the word "pain," namely, what is called "pain-sensation" or bodily pain and disagreeable feeling or dissatisfaction or mental pain. The German language distinguishes these two kinds of experience better than the English; it uses the words *Schmerz* or *Stichempfindung* for bodily pain, *Unlust* for mental pain; though the distinction is carefully observed only by psychologists.[1]

Bodily pain is a variety of sensory experience; it may be regarded as the primordial undifferentiated sensory quality pushed to a high intensity. It serves as the sign of something to be escaped and avoided; that is to say it is a specific provocative of fear. If one's effort to withdraw or escape is impeded, prevented or in any way unsuccessful, and if the strong stimulus continues to work, mental pain supervenes immediately and grows stronger in proportion to the strength of our unsuccessful efforts to escape. If, on the other hand, one can subdue or prevent the

[1] The word "displeasure" would be the best term for "mental pain" but for the fact that it is so commonly used to denote a mild degree of anger. It seems to me best to continue to use the word "pain" for "mental pain" and to use some other term to denote pain-sensation.

fear, with its strong impulse, and welcome the sensory experience as a sign of some beneficial object, the experience is robbed of all mental pain, all pain in the true sense; though the quality of the sensory experience remains unchanged. We may fairly suppose that this is what those martyrs accomplished who, we are told, submitted themselves to torture with a calm smile on their faces; such martyrs as Cranmer, who is said to have calmly held his hand in the consuming flames. Few men can accept bodily injuries in this spirit, without any impulse to shrink or desire to escape. But most of us can achieve it in respect of minor bodily hurts. This afternoon the surgeon has put a row of stitches through my scalp. He told me, as kindly surgeons do, that it would be a little painful. But he was mistaken, if the term painful be taken in its strict sense. After being kept waiting some little time, I was glad to feel the needle go through my scalp; although of course my sensory experience was of a stinging burning quality, from which I should have shrunk if I had not known its source and full significance.[1] Our suffering in the dentist's chair and in similar situations is in the main the suffering that comes from ineffectual conflict of impulses, in which fear plays a prominent part.

The doctrine that affection or feeling, in the form of pleasure or pain, determines attention and all forms of mental and bodily activity (except merely reflex actions) has a long history and has had a great influence, not only in psychological speculation, but also in other fields of theory and practice. This doctrine (psychological hedonism) was adopted by the founders of the utilitarian philosophy, and it is generally regarded as an intrinsic part of utilitarian ethics; although the two principles, hedonism and utilitarianism, are distinct and neither necessarily implies the other. It has been accepted also by many philosophers and psychologists who do not adhere to the utilitarian principle in ethics. The doctrine is peculiarly plausible and is easily accepted as obviously true by many men who have made no study of philosophy or psychology. It was stated in the most uncompromising way by Jeremy Bentham, the father of modern utilitarianism. He opened his "Principles of Morals and Legislation" with these words: "Nature has placed mankind under the governance of two sovereign masters, pain and pleasure. It is for them alone to point out what we ought to do, as well as to determine

[1] Such a stimulus as an unexpected needle-prick gives rise to that kind of sensory experience which most seems to justify the term "a sensation"; for the sharp stinging quality breaks suddenly across one's train of thinking without other connection with it; and its "meaning" is very vague and general, namely, *something to be avoided;* that is to say, it approximates to anoëtic experience.

what we shall do. On the one hand the standard of right and wrong, on the other the chain of causes and effects, are fastened to their throne. They govern us in all we do, in all we say, in all we think: every effort we can make to throw off our subjection will serve but to demonstrate and confirm it. In words a man may pretend to abjure their empire, but in reality he will remain subject to it all the while. The *principle of utility* recognizes this subjection, and assumes it for the foundation of that system the object of which is to rear the fabric of felicity by the hand of reason and of law. Systems which attempt to question it deal in sounds instead of sense, in caprice instead of reason, in darkness instead of light." With this fine piece of dogmatic rhetoric Bentham laid the foundation of utilitarian morals and legislation and, without more ado, proceeded to build upon it a vast structure, accepting this foundation as an axiom, a truth which needs only to be stated in order to secure universal acceptance. Few of his disciples have maintained it quite consistently. Alexander Bain, who may be said to have given it its most complete expression, combined it (as also did Bentham and the two Mills) with the principle of the association of ideas, making of these two principles the keys to all psychological problems, the master principles of all thought and action. Yet Bain wavered in his assertion of the doctrine in the most astonishing and amusing manner; and in this respect very many modern philosophers and psychologists resemble Bain.

The rival doctrine, the hormic theory,[1] which is maintained in these pages, asserts that conation (action, attention, striving, desire, volition, activity of every kind) is immediately determined by cognition, and that pleasure and pain result from the conation, are determined by the striving; pleasure, when the striving attains its natural goal or progresses toward it; pain, when striving is thwarted or obstructed and fails to achieve, or progress toward, its goal. This doctrine comes down to us from Aristotle. It has had few consistent exponents in the modern period; of these Edward von Hartmann (author of "The Philosophy of the Unconscious") is the most notable and uncompromising.[2] Schopenhauer came near to maintaining it consistently, but in the end compromised with the hedonist theory.

Most of the psychologists of the Scottish School rejected the hedonist doctrine and taught the hormic theory more or less explicitly. They sought the prime movers of human activity in what they called "the implanted propensities." Dugald Stewart, in whose voluminous works the Scottish psychology reached its most mature expression, distinguished five distinct classes of such propensities, falling into two natural groups, namely, "instinctive propensities" (comprising appetites, desires, and affections) and rational principles of action (comprising Self-love and the Moral Faculty). The chaotic condition of psychological theory on this fundamental question is well illustrated by the writings of Wundt and of William James, and at the present time by those of Professor Freud and the other psychoanalysts. Of contemporary authors Professor G. F. Stout is the most able and consistent advocate of the dependence of feeling on conation (in his "Analytic Psychology"); but even he wobbles a little in his later writings.

The student will naturally ask: "If, accepting the hormic theory, you

[1] Cf. pp. 71, 213, 218.

[2] The senior student should consult von Hartmann's "Die moderne Psychologie," which contains an excellent sketch of modern views on this problem.

identify pleasure with the satisfaction of success, and pain with the dissatisfaction that comes from thwarting and failure of our strivings, would you have us believe that pleasure and pain are merely consequences or expressions in consciousness of degrees of success and failure, and that they have no influence on the course of mental process?" The answer is—by no means. Pleasure and pain influence the further course of mental process very powerfully; each influences it in two ways which, although closely allied, may be usefully distinguished. First, pleasure, arising in the course of mental activity, supports that activity, sustains our striving in the direction, or of the kind, which brings pleasure; it strengthens and prolongs the impulse or conative tendency at work in us. Secondly, on recurrence of a situation of the kind in which we have striven successfully, our tendency to strive again in the same way is stronger; the tendency seems to be confirmed by the previous experience of success; and this confirmation of the tendency may fairly be regarded as a consequence or result of the pleasure experienced on the former occasion. Conversely pain, arising during striving, tends to divert the striving to other directions; and on renewal of the situation in which we have striven unsuccessfully and (in consequence) painfully, our tendency to strive again in the same way is weakened or abolished or diverted to some new direction; these weakenings and diversions of the impulse seem to be the effects or consequences of the pain experienced on the former occasion.[1]

But, it may be objected, does this formulation of the role of feeling cover the facts? Is it not a fact that sometimes we act simply in order to secure pleasure or in order to avoid pain, as the hedonists assert of all our activities? It must be admitted that this is a very difficult question. Can the hormic theory deal with the facts of the order referred to, without admitting the hedonist principle to be equally fundamental with the hormic? The most difficult type of behavior for the hormic theory is that of the habitual pleasure-seeker.

Let us consider the problem as it is presented in relatively simple and crude form by the glutton. The glutton is the man who seems to be governed largely, to be sustained in much of his bodily and mental activity, by the desire of the pleasure of eating. I well remember falling into conversation with a worthy citizen of Glasgow on the deck of a steamer in the Firth of Clyde. It was a perfect day and the hills and sea most beautiful. Presently my acquaintance, rubbing his hands together and smacking his lips, said: "I like these steamer trips. They give me a splendid appetite, and the food supplied is very good." He gave the impression that he had taken the trip chiefly and primarily for the sake of the pleasure which his meals would bring him under the favorable conditions of the voyage. The case is typical of the behavior of the libertine and of pleasure-seekers of more refined types. Here desire of pleasure seems to be the primary and fundamental motive; pleasure seems to be the goal of action. But the glutton's own words and actions showed the dependence of pleasure upon impulse. He knew well that, if he went to the table without appetite, he would attain

[1] Some authors who in other respects are pure mechanists (or nearly so) nevertheless recognize the second kind of influence of feeling; they inadequately express the facts by saying that pleasure "stamps in" the associations formed during pleasurable activity, while pain "stamps out," or tends to prevent the formation of, associations in the course of the activities which it accompanies. Cf. p. 194.

no pleasure; the pleasure he sought was the pleasure of satisfying the food-seeking impulse, sustained by the appetite we call hunger.

The case, then, illustrates the primacy of conation, the dependence of feeling on conation, rather than of conation on feeling. But, it may be objected, the man desired the appetite, and strove to induce the impulse to eat, for the sake of the pleasure which would accompany and follow upon the eating. In a similar way the worn-out *roué* is said to desire to recover the strong sexual desire or impulse which, he has learned, is the essential condition of attainment of his favorite form of pleasure. Therefore, it may be said, it is true to say that the motive of such actions as our glutton's is the desire of pleasure. The answer of the hormic theory is that such instances only arise as the result of a long process of sophistication; that primarily what the glutton desired was to eat food; that gradually, by exercise of the power of abstraction, he learned to distinguish the pleasure that accompanies eating from the eating itself, and to emphasize this aspect of the total experience of eating.[1] And, in psychologizing on such instances, we are apt to carry still further the separation between eating and the pleasure that goes with it. In reality the goal of the desire, which is the moving force or motive, is pleasurable eating. The pleasure of eating, or rather pleasurable eating, many times experienced, has strengthened the desire to eat and confirmed the tendency to seek those conditions under which eating will be most pleasurable.

The case of the glutton is typical of all instances in which we are said to act for the sake of securing pleasure, or to be moved by the desire of pleasure. Without exception they fall under the general law that pleasure or satisfaction, accompanying and following upon any particular mode of activity, strengthens or confirms the tendency to repeat the activity. On the perceptual plane of mental life the facts are simple and obvious. It is in regard to action guided by imagination that the hedonist error arises. We recollect or depict in imagination some mode of activity which was pleasurable, including the circumstances which evoked that activity and the goal attained by it. The imagined situation evokes the same impulse as the formerly perceived situation. The impulse works toward the same goal by some train of imaginary action, and, in doing so, attains again in an imperfect degree the satisfaction of success. This working of an impulse on the plane of imaginative representation of the goal is what we call "desire"; and, since an impulse working on the plane of imagination follows in the main the lines of action through which in the past it has attained satisfaction, it becomes plausible to say that in desiring we desire pleasure. The glutton (or the libertine) who takes measures to promote his appetite cannot properly be said to be prompted to such measures by desire of the pleasure of eating; rather, he is seeking to escape from the tedium of a round of actions in which he finds no satisfaction, either because he is sustained in such actions by no strong impulse, or because, through lack of knowledge, strength, or skill, impulses directed to these other goals attain no success.

Affection, then, does not, as is sometimes said, initiate "attention." For "*attention*" *is merely conation or striving considered*

[1] Pleasure and pain, it should be noted, are abstractions; what is desired is the total experience in which pleasure predominates; and what is avoided (or averted) is the total experience in which pain predominates.

from the point of view of its effects on cognitive process. The more strongly we strive to see, to hear, to understand, or in any way to achieve better or fuller cognition, the more attentive are we. And conversely, we are less attentive the less strongly we strive to know or cognize the object in hand, the more we are relaxed, the more nearly we sink into mere passivity.

We have already seen what is the fundamental condition of striving, namely, that thinking of some object shall stir up some conative disposition, shall evoke the hormic energy within us in the form of the impulse of some instinct; that, accordingly, is the fundamental condition of "attention" or attending. The higher form of attention which is achieved by an effort of will we must consider under the head of volition in a later chapter. At present we are concerned only with what is generally distinguished as non-voluntary or spontaneous attention; and this offers a number of points for discussion.

The Sensationists, who are content to describe mental life as the mere flow of "sensations" and "images," tell us that, for introspection, "attention" is essentially clearness of "sensations." But this "clearness" is itself very unclear. The truth seems to be that the experience they describe as clearness of "sensations" is clearness of cognition of the object. Thus, if the image of a falling meteorite, or of an animal moving quickly from cover to cover, is projected on the peripheral part of my retina, the Sensationist would describe my experience by saying that my visual sensations lack clearness; whereas the fact is that my apprehension of the object, of its position, shape, and nature, lacks clearness.

Intensity and Suddenness of Sense-Impression Not in Themselves Determinants of Attention

It is commonly said that intensity of sense-impression determines attention; or that the more intense a "sensation" the more strongly it tends to attract attention. A sudden flash of light, like the flash of lightning, a sudden loud noise, like the banging of a door, a sudden strong sense-impression in any part of the body—all these may strongly divert our attention from any task in hand, and may set us wondering what is the source of the impression, or shrinking and striving to escape. That is to say, such sense-impressions attract our attention, not merely because they excite sensations of high intensity, but because they excite in us the impulse of curiosity, or of fear, or both impulses together; they are specific excitants of these instincts. That the mere intensity of such a sense-impression is not the essential condition of its power to determine attention is shown by the fact that a continued bright light, such as the blaze of the sunny sky at my window, or a continued loud noise, such as the roar of the railroad train in which I sit, has no such effect, so long as I understand its source.

Suddenness of a sense-impression also does not suffice to enable it to draw attention. As I finished writing the foregoing sentence, I became retrospectively aware that, while I wrote, a railroad train had thundered past not a quarter of a mile away; yet it had failed to divert my attention. On the other hand, a loud sound or a blaze of light may strongly attract my attention, even though it swells gradually from zero, on condition that I do not understand its nature and origin. And it may continue strongly to distract my attention from my book or my writing, so long as I do not understand its significance. Instead of accommodating myself to the strong impression, I grow more and more uneasy, I find it more and more difficult to attend to the task in hand; until at last I spring up, saying "I must go and find out what that is." And the impulse that moves me is either fear or curiosity, or both.

A faint sound or light, whether sudden and short or gradual and long continued, may produce similar effects. We are apt to respond to the strong and sudden impression with fear; to the faint and gradual with curiosity.

What Is Interest?

Again, you are driving your automobile, and the continued roar it makes does not hold or divert or attract your attention. But presently a new element, perhaps of relatively low intensity, enters into the complex stimulation, and your attention is at once attracted; you notice the new sound and begin to wonder what it means; while your friend by your side, who perhaps is as familiar with the roar as yourself, fails to notice the new element, even when you ask him to direct his attention to it. The difference between you (manifested in the fact that your attention is drawn to the sound, while his is not), is that you are "*interested*" in the sounds made by the automobile and he is not. Such instances are numerous and familiar. It is commonly said that "interest" determines "attention." What, then, is "interest"? Is it an agent, an entity, or a faculty, that we have hitherto overlooked? "Interest" is a vague word; but the facts implied by it are very important.

A man is said to be interested in a certain object or topic, even though he may be thinking of other things. But we know that, if he is interested in it, his attention can readily be drawn to it and, when so drawn, will usually be sustained and keen, or, as we say, concentrated. That, in fact, is what we mean by saying that he is interested in the object. Being interested is, then, an enduring condition of the subject. What is the nature of this condition of mind that we call "being interested" or "having an interest" in anything? Animal behavior gives us the clue to the answer.

Interest Is Conative

Clearly, an animal is interested in all those things that are capable of evoking any of its instinctive impulses. It is not always equally interested in all those things; because appetite, as we have seen, waxes and wanes with changes in the bodily condition. When an animal is replete from a good meal, it is not at all, or but little, interested in its natural food-objects or its prey. The mice may play with the tail of the overfed cat. But, when hungry, every animal is keenly interested in all its natural food-objects. With this necessary qualification, allowing for the variation of appetites, we may lay down the generalization that *animals are "interested" in objects in so far as the objects are of kinds that evoke their instinctive impulses, and in proportion to the strength of those impulses.*

In man the matter is more complex (as also in animals so remote from the natural condition as the domesticated dog). Let us go back to the automobile which begins during a journey to emit a new sound. You, the owner and driver, quickly detect this sound; it readily draws your attention. Of your two companions in the car, A is accustomed to drive a similar car, B is quite inexperienced in the driving or care of cars, though he has ridden in them as much as A or yourself. A hears the sound that troubles you, as soon as you draw his attention to it, and, like yourself, he continues to show "interest" in it or, rather, in the problem of its source. B, on the other hand, has the greatest difficulty in hearing it; and, if you succeed in getting him to hear it, by describing its peculiar quality and perhaps pointing out its variations of intensity, he very soon ceases to pay any attention to it; his attention was not spontaneous, but rather the expression of a voluntary effort. What are the differences between yourself, A, and B, which determine these differences of "attention"? You and A have learned, by previous efforts, to discriminate the various elements in the complex of noises emitted by the car and to attribute to each its significance; that is to say, you have differentiated corresponding cognitive dispositions in the structure of your minds. B has not previously made such efforts of discrimination; he has been content to accept the noise of the car as an unanalyzed complex impression. Further, he feels no responsibility for the car, and is quite incurious as to all its operations. You and A are equally well equipped with the sort of mental structure required for the discrimination of the sounds and the appreciation of their significance. And both of you are interested in automobiles. But your interest in this particular machine is greater than his, because it is your machine and you are responsible for operating it.

This example shows us that our "interest" is essentially conative, as it is in the animals. It is sometimes alleged that "interest" in any object or topic depends upon, or consists in, the possession of appropriate knowledge or (in terms of the "idea" theory) of a mass or system of "ideas" related to the object or topic.[1] That is, I believe, false doctrine. Like the animals,

[1] "An apperceptive mass," as the Herbartians say. This intellectualist doctrine of "interest" was the great contribution of Herbart's psychology to educational theory. Professor R. Woodworth's "Dynamic Psychology" contains the most modern and forcible defense of this view. I refer the senior student to his statement of it, and to my criticism of it, "Motives in the Light of Recent Discussion," in *Mind*, N. S., Vol. 29, 1920.

we are interested only in those things that evoke in us one or other (or several) of the instinctive impulses. The difference between ourselves and the animals is that, while their "interests" are in the main such as Nature provides in the form of instincts, we acquire a great variety of new interests through the building up of *sentiments* for a great variety of objects. We have seen that a dog may and normally does extend the field of his "interests" through acquiring some simple sentiments, a sentiment of dread of one person, of devotion to another, and so on. The human being goes much further along this line of development, acquiring sentiments for many more objects; and so extends more widely his field of acquired interests.

The fuller discussion of this topic must be reserved for a later page.[1] Here I only insist on the view that "interest," being essentially conative, is a matter of the enduring settings of our conative tendencies or impulses, and is therefore determined by our instincts and our sentiments. Knowledge about an object is not in itself a condition of "interest"; though such knowledge favors the sustaining of attention: without such knowledge our attention to any object, determined by conative interest, soon wanes; because we quickly exhaust upon it our limited powers of discriminative perception. Thus a naturalist and a layman may discover some strange plant or animal; it excites the curiosity of both, and both are interested in it; but the attention of the naturalist is more sustained, as well as more effective; for he has the knowledge, or cognitive mental structure, that enables him to examine it systematically and in detail, noticing a hundred features which entirely escape his companion.

That "interest" is conative rather than cognitive; that it depends upon the strength of the conative tendencies excited, rather than upon the extent and variety and systematic organization of the cognitive systems of the mind (knowledge), is clearly shown by those cases in which a man develops a mass of systematic knowledge in the service of some great natural purpose, such as the support of his family; and, after years of practice, when that goal has been secured by the saving of a competency or perhaps by its inheritance, he gladly escapes from the posi-

[1] Chapter XVII.

tion he has occupied, and asks nothing better than to be allowed to forget all he has learned. He may have devoted half his life to acquiring an intimate knowledge of hardware and the hardware trade, because this has been the means of building up his fortune: but, the fortune once acquired, this derived interest, secondary wholly to his purpose of acquiring a fortune, lapses entirely; though his knowledge remains; and he devotes himself perhaps to art or golf or gardening or philanthropy, displaying not the least interest in hardware. Nevertheless, if circumstances arise which evoke some effective motive for busying himself again with the hardware trade; if he finds it necessary to earn more money, or wishes to advise some less fortunate friend still in the trade, he is quite capable of bringing his store of knowledge effectively to bear once more, and of displaying a sustained attention; for the new motive gives him a new interest in the topic. To have an "interest" in any object is, then, to be ready to pay attention to it. Interest is latent attention; and attention is interest in action. The essential condition of both interest in and attention to any object is that the mind shall be so organized, either natively or through experience, that it can think of the object, and that such thinking shall evoke some impulse or desire which maintains a train of activity in relation to the object.

Conative Unity

There is a further peculiarity of mental activity which is commonly discussed under the head of attention, namely, the fact that a train of mental activity has, not only conative continuity, but also conative unity. The fact is sometimes expressed by saying that we can think of only one thing at one time, or can do only one thing at a time; or, again, it is said that "consciousness" has a narrow focus, so that only one "idea" can be at the focus of "consciousness" at any moment. If we accept the second formulation of the facts, and say that we can think of, or do, only one thing at a time, we must use the word "thing" in a very wide sense. For, obviously, many physical things may be comprised in the object to which you pay attention; as when you look down on a village from a mountain-top and perceive and recognize it as a whole. In such a whole, you may proceed to single out in turn the various parts, such as the several houses within the village, and, within each house again, parts such as doors and windows. To single out a part within a whole in this way is to narrow the field of one's attention. The degree to which we narrow or restrict our attention is determined by our purpose at the moment.

The term "concentration" is sometimes applied to this restriction of attention. But, if we use "concentration of attention" in this sense, we must not confuse it with the degree or intensity of attention; the latter depends upon the strength of the impulse at work within us. If we look down on a village in the course of a ramble over the hills, and if our attitude and interest in it are merely such as may be expressed by the words "What village is that?"—our attention is likely to be of low degree; it is determined and sustained by a mild impulse of curiosity. But, if we are scouts, carrying our lives in our hands, and, if the village is one that may have been occupied by the enemy, the attention we give it will be of high degree or intensity and may be properly said to be concentrated, whether we pay attention to the village as a whole or to some detailed part of it.[1]

The measures of the degree of attention are (1) the efficiency with which the subject works toward his goal; (2) the resistance displayed to all diverting influences. When the impulse which sustains our attention is feeble, our mental process is relatively ineffective; we do not bring all our knowledge effectively to bear upon the task in hand; we are half, or more than half, asleep.[2] The stronger the impulse, the more completely awake we are. The highest degree of mental activity, of attention, is achieved when some strong impulse sustains our attention to some topic of which we have a rich and systematically organized knowledge, gained through much and varied experience. When the object or topic does not directly evoke some strong impulse, our interest

[1] Physiologically, concentration of attention seems to involve concentration of the disposable free energy of the brain in one system of channels. The student interested in physiological speculation should consult my series of papers, "The Physiological Factors of the Attention Process," in *Mind*, N. S., Vol. XII.

[2] Sleep will be discussed in Part II.

in it being secondary or derived from its connection with some other purpose, our attention may be intense and well sustained, if we clearly see that the object is a necessary means to some strongly desired goal. But often, in such cases, we have to sustain our attention as best we can, by effort of the will; a task which few, if any, of us achieve with any high degree of success, and which is possible only in proportion as we have disciplined and practised ourselves in such efforts.[1]

The most effective effort of the will never achieves the high degree of concentration of attention which the awakening of any strong impulse immediately produces. Let any object or situation appeal directly and strongly to any instinct or to any strong sentiment, and we cannot, though we try our best, divert our attention from it. We may resolutely turn away our eyes, or otherwise shut it away from our senses; yet we continue to think of it, intermittently at least, in spite of our best efforts to occupy ourselves with other things. When we lie down to sleep and try to bring our minds to rest, the topic becomes, as we say, insistent; and, even when we have fallen asleep, it crops up in our dreams, perhaps in some distorted and more or less disguised fashion.[2]

When our attention is most concentrated, as in the midst of some exciting game, in the heat of battle, in the presence of

[1] It is probable that the principal effect of the old-fashioned education, which aimed at "training the faculties" by drilling in Latin grammar and similar subjects, was the development of this power of voluntary concentration of attention on things in which we have only a derived interest, an interest which depends upon our belief that the things or processes in question are means toward some goal desired for its own sake.

[2] Major R. E. Priestly ("The Psychology of Exploration," *Psyche*, Vol. II, No. I, 1921) describes the hunger experiences of a "man-hauling" sledge-party in the Antarctic as follows: The diet, he says, "leaves the man-hauling party with a craving which nothing can allay but the next meal, and that but for all too short a time. The effect of this hunger upon the waking mind is to concentrate the thoughts upon every variety of savory food that the individual has known. Its effect in sleep is to lead to a succession of food dreams which carry the dreamer from one paradise of the gourmand to another, until he awakes to find the craving for food almost unbearable. The normally constituted party talk food, think food, dream food. Jealous eyes watch every crumb of the ration which falls to the floor. The most unsavory morsel . . . is watched with the eager solicitude of a dog for a bone." This statement illuminates the fundamental conditions of attention infinitely better than hundreds of philosophical disquisitions on this question.

some awful object, when food is before us and we are very hungry, at all such times (that is, whenever any strong impulse is at work in us), things unconnected with the purpose in hand may rain strong stimuli upon our senses without diverting our attention, and therefore without our perceiving them; so that even a bullet or sabre wound may pass unnoticed until, when attention is relaxed, blood is seen to be flowing, or the continued strong sense-impressions from the wound draw our attention to it.

If we try to interpret these facts in physiological terms, we can only infer that the activity of one system of neurones in the brain inhibits the activity of all other systems; and we may suppose that, the higher the degree of activity in one system, the more strongly does that system inhibit all others.

Unfortunately, we still are ignorant of the nature of nervous inhibition, even in its simplest instances, such as the reciprocal inhibitions of the antagonistic reflexes which extend and flex the limbs. The hypothesis of inhibition by drainage seems to be the only one that can interpret these facts of reciprocal inhibition in the higher brain-levels.[1] Without identifying a system of mental dispositions with a system of nervous arcs in the brain, we may yet assume that to every system of mental dispositions there corresponds a neural system in the brain, and that each of these constitutes a main channel for discharge of nervous energy into the muscles and other executive organs. The drainage hypothesis assumes that the activity of any one such system inhibits all other systems, because they all draw upon a common stock or reservoir of free nervous energy. The student who is interested in physiological speculations should combine this view with the hypothetical account of the neural basis of instincts suggested on page 109, and also with the discussion of the "law of the attraction of the impulse" in my "Physiological Psychology" (pp. 126–134).

Conative Persistence and Reversion of Attention

Degree of resistance to diversion of attention is a measure of the energy with which the subject devotes himself to the purpose in hand, with which he strives toward his goal. We are familiar with the fact that, when we are interrupted in any task which we keenly pursue, we naturally revert to it as soon as the distracting influence ceases to work upon us. Our interest in the task bridges the gap and gives to the whole process a conative continuity, in spite of the interruption. The interruption may be momentary only; or it may endure for years, and yet, if

[1] Cf. my "Physiological Psychology," pp. 36 and 103, and "The Nature of Inhibitory Processes Within the Nervous System," *Brain*, Vol. 26.

our purpose be strong and unsatisfied (that is, if our interest is keen) we may, after the long interval, take up our task afresh at the point where we reluctantly laid it down. This forms a third rough measure of the intensity of our attention and of the keenness of our interest.[1] Our interest in a trivial task, such as a game of checkers, will hardly survive an interruption of a few minutes; our interest in some larger purpose, such as the writing of a book, may survive an interruption of years. Such continuity of interest of high degree implies not only that some impulse is strongly evoked, but also that the impulse comes from some enduring organization of interests of the kind we have to consider later under the head of "sentiments" and "character."

This tendency of attention to revert to the unfinished task, and to bridge the gap in the series of activities by which we pursue our goal, is the manifestation on the intellectual plane of that fundamental persistency of all mental impulse, striving, or conation, which we noticed on an earlier page (44). We cannot hope to explain it; we can only accept it as one of the fundamental attributes of mental or purposive activity, one which is conspicuous by its absence in all purely physical processes.

Distribution of Attention

We all have in various degrees the power of distributing our attention and of carrying on two or more tasks concurrently. If I am writing an easy straightforward letter, I can, without interrupting my writing, overhear and understand conversation going on in the same room, and may even intervene in it. Some men seem to be able to write one letter and to dictate another at the same time. In most of us this power is very limited; as we easily discover by attempting to recite some familiar verse while we write another. Most of us find that the one task interferes with the other, words of the one verse appearing incongruously in the other. Such power as we have of this sort is in part an expression of the tendency of attention to revert readily to the

[1] The other two measures being (1) the effectiveness with which we apply ourselves or bring our knowledge to bear, (2) resistance to distracting influences.

interrupted task. But in part it is another mode of manifestation of the persistency of conation toward its goal. Namely, an impulse, once set to work toward a goal, continues in some degree to operate after we cease to think of the goal or the means toward it. That is to say, *conation outlasts the cognition which initiates it.* This principle is of the greatest importance in connection with all the higher forms of conation, all that we call volition, will, determination, resolution, purpose in the fuller sense. Here we are only concerned to notice its simpler manifestations. In writing, one's pen flows on, producing the appropriate words, while one thinks perhaps of the sentence or phrase that must come next. And sometimes the fact is brought vividly home to one by an error or slip, which consists in writing some word thought of but rejected, or belonging to a phrase next in order to that which the hand is writing. Or at table one thinks momentarily of taking salt and continues the conversation, while one's hand carries out the purpose thus momentarily formed; and again an error, such as seizing the pepper-pot instead of the salt-cellar, may make one realize how we commonly rely upon this subconscious execution of purposes consciously formed. The routine details of practical life are largely executed in this way. Sometimes one is made still more acutely aware that conation outlasts cognition; we find ourselves walking toward some spot, opening a drawer or desk or standing before a table, and aware that we have come with some purpose; and yet we cannot recover, cannot rethink, the goal we had in view. Or, more vaguely still, we perhaps pass through a familiar village or street with an uneasy sense that there is something we ought to do there, something we have intended to do; and yet for the life of us we cannot remember what the task is.[1]

[1] I have learned to trust this uneasy feeling as a sure indication of a forgotten task or goal; and it seldom, if ever, is at fault. Another illustration of the subconscious working of the conative impulse, after it has been set toward a particular goal, is waking at a particular hour in the morning. Closely allied is the following experimental observation: I fall asleep holding in my fist something of appropriate size and shape. If I resolve to hold it fast, I usually find it firmly grasped when I awake. If I make no such resolve, I find on waking that the article has fallen from my grasp. Hypnotic experiment affords many more striking illustrations of the same principle.

It is this persistence of conation in spite of deflection of our cognition from the task in hand that enables us not only to revert easily to the interrupted task, but actually to carry on continuously two unconnected tasks. Our attention oscillates between the two tasks, and, in the intervals in which it is directed to the one, our executive organs continue to carry out the movements appropriate to the other.

Individuals differ widely in respect of their capacity for distributing their attention in this way. And the difference seems to be one of native constitution. Extreme instances of such division of the attention, or duplication of the stream of mental activity, fall in the province of morbid psychology.

CHAPTER X

IMAGINING—ANTICIPATING—RECOLLECTING

Imagination is sometimes defined as the capacity for imagery or for having "images" in consciousness. This is an unduly narrow definition. We properly speak of the imagination of the mathematician or of the creative artist or of the philosopher; and in these cases "imagery," though it may play some part, is often of minor importance. We may properly define imagination or imagining as thinking of remote objects.[1]

The simplest form of imagining is pictorial thinking; we depict to ourselves the object as we have perceived it, as we have seen, heard, touched, or otherwise sensed it. In such imagining, "imagery" seems to take the place and perform the functions of sensory experience. Such pictorial thinking is sometimes called "the rise of representations to consciousness," or "the having of free ideas," or "the passing of a train of ideas through consciousness," in order to distinguish it from thinking of present objects, in which, as we have seen, "imagery" may complicate the sensory qualities directly due to sense-impressions.

The Use of Names

The simple use of names constitutes a form of thinking intermediate[2] between perceiving and imagining. For a name is a quality of a thing which is assigned to it by human convention; and the hearing of the name suggests the object, or signifies it, to the person familiar with it; just as does the sensory pattern presented by the physical thing. The name of an object is one of the keys which may set in action the appropriate cognitive disposition or "idea,"[3] and so set us thinking of the object. If you

[1] "Remote" being used in the special sense defined on p. 207, *i. e.*, a "remote object" is any object not affecting the senses at the moment of thinking of it.

[2] Not necessarily intermediate in the evolutionary or developmental sense, for, as we have seen, there is reason to believe that some animals are capable of imagining in some degree.

[3] I remind the reader that I use the word "idea" here and hereafter as a convenient synonym for "cognitive disposition."

meet a friend face to face in the daylight, you perceive him through the medium of the pattern made on your retina by the light reflected from his face. If you meet him in the dusk, you may perceive him through the medium of the auditory pattern of his voice. But your hearing may be imperfect, or his voice may be disguised, so that you do not recognize it as his, but merely as a voice, somebody's voice; then, if he utters his name, you perceive him as such, you recognize him, and the vague sense-impressions made on eye and ear then become definitely significant of him. The name as a sensory pattern has brought into play the appropriate mental disposition, or system of dispositions; and your thinking of your friend, thus initiated, *assimilates* the vague confused sensory patterns made by his face and voice. That is to say, although these patterns are in themselves inadequate to arouse the appropriate cognitive system, after the system (the "idea") has been brought into play by the sound of the name, they contribute to determine the further course of your perception of your friend. The case is not essentially different, if your friend's name is spoken by a third person. The sound of the name is a sensory pattern which makes you think of him and so prepares you to perceive him.

Pre-perception the Most Primitive Kind of Imagining

Thinking of an object before perceiving it greatly facilitates perception or perceptual recognition; such thinking is appropriately called *pre-perception.* Pre-perception plays a great part in determining the course of perception, the selection of this or that object or feature out of the wealth of "present objects."[1] It constitutes a third great selective factor in perception. We have seen how the constitution of the sense-organs determines a selection of the first stage, by rendering us much more sensitive to some physical stimuli than to others. The structure of the mind, hereditary and acquired, is the selective factor of the second stage; determining that, of all the sensory patterns received by the senses, we are influenced most effectively by those which

[1] It is sometimes represented to be a principal determinant of attention. With our discussion of attention (Chap. IX) in mind, the reader will see that this is not strictly correct.

fit some cognitive disposition, as a key fits the lock, and so bring one or another impulse into play. And now we see that selection of a third stage is due to the fact that a disposition, if it is already active, is stirred by sense-impression to further activity more readily than if it be quiescent. Since some thinking goes on during all waking life, it follows that this kind of selection is frequently operative in perception, determining both which of the things impressing the senses we shall attend to and the manner in which we shall interpret the sense-impressions, the significance or "meaning" we shall attach to them.

It is important to notice that perception may be influenced in this way, not only by present thinking of a remote object, but also by recent thinking of it. When you come face to face with a friend in the dusk, you will, if you have recently thought of him, recognize him more readily than if you have not thought of him for some considerable time. The fact that you were thinking of him five minutes ago facilitates your recognition of him. It is as though the mental system, after being stirred to activity in any way, sinks only slowly back to a condition of complete quiescence.[1] It is not clear that such residual activity may be attributed to the cognitive disposition or "idea" as such. It seems more probable that, in all such cases, it is the conative disposition involved in the recently active system which continues subconsciously active. If that is true, the facts of pre-perception we are now considering would be but another evidence of that conative continuity and persistence which we discussed in the foregoing chapter and formulated as the law that conation outlasts the cognition which initiates it. This interpretation is borne out by the fact that the more keenly attentive we are to the imagined object, the more potently does such imagining govern the course of perception, both at the moment of imagining and for a subsequent period of indefinite duration. Thus, if you are thinking of a friend and strongly desire to see him, or if you have recently thought of him with this strong desire, you will perceive him, will recognize him in the dusk, or single him out of a crowd of strangers, more readily than if you think of him,

[1] This we may correlate with the evidence of residual excitement in nervous "centres" after they have ceased to function actively.

or have recently thought of him, without strong desire. The same is true of the hated enemy of whom you think with strong aversion, keenly fearing to meet him.

In extreme instances such strong desire (or aversion) determines errors of perception of the kind we call illusions, or even hallucinations. We falsely recognize, as the desired friend or the feared enemy, some stranger, or even some stump or bush, seen in the moonlight; or we falsely single out his voice or footstep among the confused mass of sounds that fall on the ear. Such instances of false recognition or illusory perception bring vividly home to us the fact that perception is not a passive reception of a sense-impression, but is rather a reaction of the mind upon a cue supplied by the sense-impression; they illustrate the fact that the sensory qualities, the so-called "sensations," no matter how specific their pattern, merely signify the object which the subject thinks of as there; the fact that the mind supplies from its inner resources the "meaning" which the sense-impression suggests; in short, *the fact that the "psychic-stimulus theory" is essentially correct,*[1] that objects are not "given" us ready made in the form of complexes of "sensations," but are thought of by the subject according to his capacity for thinking them, his interest in them, and his purpose at the moment of thinking.

Language as Stimulus to Imagination

Pre-perception, or the influence of imagination on perception, is greatest when we not only think of the object before perceiving it, but also expect to perceive it; that is to say, when our anticipation of it is definite and explicit.[2] The primary and es-

[1] I remind the reader that in our discussion of spatial perception in Chap. VIII we arrived at the conclusion that the psychic-stimulus theory is the true one, that spatial meanings are evoked as reactions of the mind to sensory patterns, rather than given with the sensory qualities as attributes of those qualities or as properties of "sensations."

[2] The seeing of faces or other definite forms in the fire, in the clouds, in rocks or other features of the landscape is a familiar illustration of the influence of imagination upon perception; and, when we see such a form because our companion points it out and names the object which it suggests, we have a clear instance of pre-perception determining the course of perception. The name sets the appropriate mental system to work and so facilitates the assimilation of the vague form by the system in question.

sential function of language is to determine pre-perception by creating expectation. Words are primarily indicative of objects and of their actions or movements. The first words were presumably merely specializations of the instinctive cries of animals. The dog uses a primitive language when he utters his bark of anger or of welcome, or his hunting yelp. In each case the bark of peculiar quality may be called merely an emotional expression; but it is also a rudimentary word which suggests to his fellows the meaning "an enemy," "a friend," or "prey"; and it determines in them pre-perception of a vague highly general kind and the corresponding movements of appropriate general type.

The primitive danger cry of man, we may suppose, became differentiated into several unlike cries, signifying bear, tiger, or wolf; and each of these would determine in his fellows the appropriate pre-perception and the corresponding form of behavior, differentiated out of the instinctive fear reaction through experiences of dangerous animals of one of these different kinds.

But, though the primitive function of words was to determine pre-perception and expectation, and though words continued to be used for this purpose, they quickly, we may suppose, came to be used in order to make one's fellows think of remote objects as well as of present objects. It may be that the boy who cried "wolf," when there was no wolf present, was the first to achieve this higher use of language, and that our intellectual life was initiated by a practical joke.

However that may have been, it is clear that the use of words must have greatly stimulated imagination, and that, once men had begun to use words to make their fellows think of remote objects, they would quickly come to use them to facilitate their own thinking. For the name of an object, once learned, becomes the most convenient key to the disposition concerned in thinking of that object. It is a key which we control much more effectually than any other keys to our mental systems; for by uttering the word we can give a quasi-perceptual reality or "presentness" to the object we think of. Hence we find that young children and primitive men tend to think aloud. Silent thinking of remote objects is only secondarily acquired by the suppression of the actual movements of speech; and the words continue to be "uttered" silently in most of our imagining, especially in thinking that is not wholly concerned with particular concrete objects in definite positions, such as the chessmen on the board.

In animals, and primitively in man, every cycle of mental activity expresses itself in the bodily behavior which is the natural outcome of all conation. The utterance of a word is a form of bodily behavior which, as language and the power of imagining developed hand in hand, became the terminus of an increasing proportion of cycles of mental activity. And, when words are "uttered" silently, the case is not in principle altered. Silent thinking by the aid of words is a series of cycles of activity, each of which terminates in the suppressed bodily behavior of speech.

Exaggeration of the Role of Movement in Thinking

To recognize that every cycle of mental activity naturally expresses itself in bodily movement and that, in imagining, this bodily expression may take the form of suppressed words, to recognize these facts is not to accept the extravagant behaviorist doctrine that all thinking *is merely* the innervation of the organs of speech or of other muscles. The truth here stated gives to this doctrine a certain plausibility which enables it to be swallowed by some of those who are prejudiced in favor of mechanistic theories. That actual movement or innervation of the muscles of the speech-organs is not necessary to verbal thinking may be proved by the simple experiment of inwardly repeating a familiar verse or other train of verbal thought, while rapidly counting aloud or repeating the alphabet. This is a task which most readers will, I think, find quite possible. There is some interference of the two processes, but no more than (and, I think, distinctly less than) in the case of attempting to recite one verse while writing another. This shows that such interference is not due to the fact that the organs of speech cannot be innervated for the continued utterance of two different series of words, and that the interference is mental, or at least central; an illustration of the strict limitation of our capacity to duplicate the stream of mental activity. If the interference were due to incompatibility of the muscular innervations appropriate to the two processes, it should be very much more serious, when both processes involve a continued stream of words, than when they naturally express themselves in movements of quite separate bodily organs. Yet such interference is very formidable, if we merely try to beat one rhythm with the foot and another with the hand (as every student of "Eurhythmics" knows), or to make simultaneously any two prescribed but unpractised movements. For example, let the reader stretch out the fingers of his left hand and touch the tip of each rapidly in turn with his right forefinger. Then let him, sitting on the edge of his chair, describe a figure of eight on the floor with the toe of his right foot. Nothing is easier than to repeat either series of movements smoothly, rapidly, and continuously. Then let him try to repeat them simultaneously. He will find, I venture to say, more difficulty and interference than in inwardly reciting verse while rapidly counting.

The behaviorist dogma that thinking *is* the innervation of speech organs (or other organs of expression) is even less plausible when applied to that kind of thinking which consists in pictorially imagining a series of scenes or complex musical sounds. Any one who is a good visualizer may sit down with closed eyes and imagine in turn a succession of scenes, recent or more remote, for example, the scenes of yesterday's drive in the country. In such an exercise one does not rethink the whole train of scenes and objects perceived, but, on setting oneself to the general task, the principal scenes, those in which one was most vividly interested, come to mind, often in no regular order; though they tend to conform roughly to the original time-order. In what innervation does such a train of pictorial thinking consist? It is difficult even to sustain in such a case the thesis, propounded above, that every cycle of thinking tends to express itself in bodily movement. The only movements involved in the original perceptual activity were those of the eyes, head, and body which facilitated the processes of perception; and, no doubt, the imagining of the same scenes involves some tendency to similar innervations. But it must be admitted that any motor expressions of this sort are extremely inadequate at the best, and in other cases are entirely suppressed as movements; for, as we have seen,[1] even in the visual perception of simple geometrical figures, the movements of the eyes are quite inadequate to the complexity of the figures and bear no constant relation to them; and it is easy to satisfy oneself that, while imagining a scene, the eyes may be moved in any irrelevant manner (oscillated from right to left or continuously rotated) without appreciably interfering with the visualizing process.

The same truth is even more indisputable in the case of a musician reading the score of an orchestral symphony by the aid of auditory imagery. I am told by some musicians that they perfer to enjoy such a composition in this way, because they are then not troubled by the imperfections which they cannot ignore in any actual performance. Now such a musician may be utterly incapable of singing or whistling more than the merest fragments of the melodies involved in the complex whole; he has only the most inadequate means of partially expressing the music in movements; and yet he imagines it in all its rich complexity.

An older and less extravagant dogma than the behaviorist's is the doctrine of "ideo-motor action," which, like it, is an exaggeration and distortion of the truth that every cycle of mental activity tends naturally and primitively to express itself in bodily movement.[2] The "ideo-motor theory" has been widely accepted and may be found dogmatically stated in many recent books. It asserts that every "idea" is not only a state or act of knowing but also a tendency to movement; and this is made the basis of a widely accepted general theory of action, the "ideo-motor theory." This ideo-motor theory is most plausible in the case of "ideas" of bodily movement. It has frequently been alleged that, if we think of a movement, that movement inevitably

[1] Page 244.

[2] This is in a sense the converse of the doctrine that we control our "ideas" by making movements; for it asserts that we control our movements by calling up "ideas" of them.

occurs, unless we somehow inhibit it. And one theory of volition asserts that volition is essentially the inhibition of "ideas" which inhibit the "idea" of movement. I cannot discover any substantial foundation for such assertions. It is clearly possible to think of such a movement as raising the hand, either as a movement to be made or as a movement not to be made. And I can find no truth in the assertion that, when I think of such a movement, my limb fairly tingles with the tendency to move, and that it is necessary to exert some inhibitory power in order to prevent its movement. To merely think of a movement and to intend or to will a movement are entirely distinct ways of thinking. The relation of our impulses, intentions, and volitions to the actual movements of our limbs remains entirely obscure, a part of the larger mystery of the relation between experience and bodily processes. The ideo-motor theory is a mistaken attempt to resolve this mystery.

I insist that all these allied doctrines, which so greatly overestimate the role of movement in thinking, have their very partial justification in the truth that all mental activity involves conation, and conation does primitively tend to express itself in bodily movement. But we must recognize that, with the development of our capacity for imagining, the suppression of the bodily factor has become more and more complete; until the bodily attitude appropriate to intense thought has become one of complete immobility (as so well expressed in Rodin's sculpture "Le Penseur") rather than a state of abundant and varied movement, as these "motor" theories would imply.

We may suppose that the development of language and the use of words stimulated greatly the exercise of imagination, although not essential to it. However that may be, the normal adult enjoys considerable power of imagination. We may usefully distinguish three levels of imagination. The lowest is what is commonly called *reproductive* or representative imagination. The second is *constructive* imagination. The third is *creative* imagination. But though in principle we may distinguish these forms or levels of imagination, in actual living they are commonly mingled inextricably.

Anticipatory and Reproductive Imagination

Persons differ widely in respect of the faithfulness with which they can depict objects, and in respect of the kind of imagery that they habitually use. One person, a visualizer, tends to think of things predominantly by the aid of visual imagery, another by the aid of auditory imagery, and some seem to use largely motor imagery; while others seem to imagine very well with the aid of very little imagery. It is usually assumed that persons of this last class use verbal imagery, visual, auditory, or motor; and this is probably true of many of them.

Most of us can depict objects most faithfully and vividly immediately after perceiving them. If, when the sense-impression dies away or is suddenly cut short, we continue to think of the object, many of us do, and probably all of us can, if we try, depict it, imagery taking the place of the sensory experience. Even under these most favorable conditions, "the primary memory image," as it is called, differs from the sensory experience not only in lacking the indefinable quality of sensory vividness, but also in lacking some of the detailed variety of the sensory experience and also its steadiness. As we think in turn of the various parts and aspects of the thing perceived a moment ago, the imagery tends to come and go. After the lapse of one or two minutes "the primary memory image" is apt to fall still lower in the scale of detailed faithfulness and steadiness.

The imagining of concrete physical things is inferior to perceptual thinking, in that it is more liable to error; but, on the other hand, it is immensely superior, in that it reaches out into the future and foresees much that is beyond the range of the senses. We have seen that all thinking, even the primitive perceptual thinking of animals and young children, involves some degree of anticipation of that which is to come, of the next steps to be achieved by bodily and mental activity. And in this respect the transition, from the most purely perceptual to the most purely imaginative thinking, is perfectly gradual. *The more developed the perceptual thinking, the more it involves an admixture of imagining.* When the young child plays chess, his thinking is almost purely perceptual; with more practice and advancing age, he learns to foresee several moves ahead, depicting the pieces as they will be after being moved; and the expert can carry this process much further, until, as in playing blindfold, the perceptual element becomes relatively insignificant.

The essential and primary function of imagination is to carry out the process of trial and error on the imaginary plane, to depict each situation and the consequences of each step of action, before the action is accomplished or even begun. *It is thus a development of the primary anticipatory function of mind.* In so far as it works truly, it effects an immense economy of action, by rendering actual trial and error unnecessary. And it does or may work truly, just because the world we live in is one in which similar antecedents are followed very often by similar consequences. This is only roughly true; often the apparently similar is essentially dissimilar, and the apparently unlike situation is essentially like and capable of yielding the like consequences. Hence merely reproductive imagination avails little, and imagination requires for its higher and more productive flights the co-operation of *reasoning*—the function which selects in any object or situation the features essential to the purpose in hand and constructs the picture of the future, not in the exact semblance of the past, but as it is likely to flow from the particular conditions of the present. When our purpose is purely reminiscent, when we wish for any reason merely to imagine past events and scenes as we experienced them, then imagination approximates the purely reproductive. It would be an error to suppose that faithful reproduction of past scenes is the most primitive mode of imagination. For, as was said above, *the primary function of imagination is to depict the future, to anticipate the course of events.*

All imagining, like every other form of thinking, is purposive in the wider sense of the word; that is to say, it is conative. But in this respect imagining varies widely, ranging from mere reverie or day-dreaming, in which the conative factor, the motive, is most obscure, the purpose least explicit, to such imagining as is involved in the working out of a definite plan for the attainment of some clearly purposed or willed end. I shall say something of day-dreaming and its motives in discussing dreams and the abnormal mental processes with which it is allied.[1]

Experiments on "Memory"

Reproductive imagination has been intensively studied in the laboratory; such work is usually described as experimental in-

[1] In Part II. It must suffice to say here that modern research has clearly proved that even the most fanciful day-dreaming and the most chaotic dream of the sleeper can usually be shown to be the expression of some impulse, some conative trend, which is unable to attain full satisfaction in that intercourse with men and things which we naturally and properly call "real life."

vestigation of memory and association. The aim has usually been to make the conditions as simple as possible, in order to arrive at the most elementary laws of reproductive imagination.[1]

This type of experimental investigation was first made by Ebbinghaus[2] and has been carried to a higher point of technical exactitude by Professor G. E. Müller[3] and many others. Ebbinghaus began by committing verses to heart by a number of readings of each verse, and, after various intervals of time, determining how many re-readings were required in order to enable him to repeat the verses once more by heart. He was able in this way to measure, in terms of the number of re-readings required, the amounts of "forgetting" that had resulted after various intervals, and to establish a curve of obliviscence.

But it was clear that some verses were remembered more easily than others, because they were more interesting or of an easier rhythm or richer in rhymes. Ebbinghaus therefore refined his procedure by committing to heart rows of meaningless syllables in place of verses, and by presenting these to the eye by a simple mechanical method. He used a rotating drum carrying the list of syllables, each of which appears in turn at a window in a screen. This secured a constant optimum rate of reading and prevented the eye from wandering back and forth over the list. Most of the more recent experimental investiga-

[1] The reader should notice, in order to avoid it, a confusion liable to arise from the ambiguous usage of the word "reproduce." To speak of reproducing in imagination or memory the scenes of the past is a natural and convenient expression. But, clearly, in imagining the mountain, or the person I saw yesterday, I do not literally reproduce the object any more than, on seeing it, I produced or created it. But since the word "reproduction" implies that something which remains identical with itself has been produced on two occasions, as I may produce and reproduce an apple from a basket, many psychologists have fallen into the way of saying that "percepts" or "ideas" or "sensations" or "images" are reproduced; and often it is said that a "percept" is reproduced in the form of an "idea," and a "sensation" in the form of an "image." This is yet another instance of the laxity and ambiguity of language which have caused so much trouble in philosophy and psychology. To guard against it, let me say explicitly that, when the expression "reproductive imagination" is used in these pages, it implies merely the thinking again of an object previously thought of; and faithful reproduction of an object means merely thinking it again as it was perceived or thought of on the previous occasion.

[2] "Grundzüge der Psychologie."

[3] "Experimentelle Beiträge zur Theorie des Gedächtnisses."

tions of memory and association have been made by methods which are essentially refinements or variations of this simple procedure. Many interesting results have been obtained; they cannot be stated here even in the most summary manner.

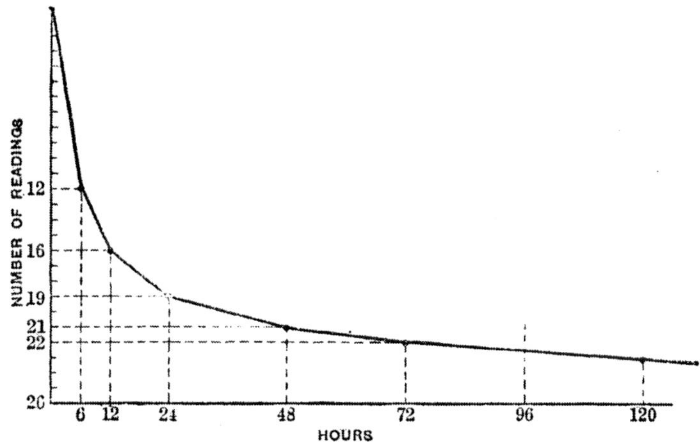

FIG. 10.—CURVE OF OBLIVISCENCE

A curve of this kind is obtained by learning at intervals rows of syllables of equal length and relearning them after the intervals indicated (in hours) along the base line. The units of the vertical scale are the readings of the row. Thus the curve reports that for the learning of a row this subject required twenty-six readings; that to relearn it after six hours he required twelve readings; after twelve hours, sixteen readings; after twenty-four hours, nineteen readings; and so on. The curve approaches the base line (the level of complete obliviscence) asymptotically.

The establishment of the curve of obliviscence by the method of "learning and relearning" is one of the results of most general interest. It is found that while individuals differ in this respect as in all others, it is generally true that the rate of forgetting is most rapid at first and gradually declines, becoming after a time exceedingly slow; so that, long (even years) after the subject has ceased to be able "to reproduce" any part of a series of syllables "learned by heart," some trace is retained which facilitates the relearning of the series.

Another question of great general interest on which these methods seem capable of throwing light is—How far and in what sense can "memory" be improved by practice? The popular belief, which is the basis of much educational practice, is that "memory" can be indefinitely improved by practice or cultivation. The financial success and the abundance of testimonials displayed by the numerous commercial agencies which undertake to improve the "memories" of their clients testify to the wide diffusion of this belief, and afford a certain presumption in its favor. But the term "memory" is used in popular speech to denote a "faculty" in the sense of the old faculty psychology. We must distinguish clearly three factors which are commonly lumped together under the head of "memory." There are (1) the power of "committing to memory"; (2) the retaining of the traces which facilitate "reproduction"; (3) the capacity for "reproducing" by the aid of these traces. There can be no doubt that the first of these functions is susceptible of much improvement by judicious practice. Every one who experiments with rows of nonsense syllables finds that he quickly improves in the art of committing them to memory. Take such a row as mon—tek—nab—luz—dal—bik—noor—peef—loug—wut. You may find that you require to read such a row some twenty or more times, before becoming able to repeat it smoothly; but, after some practice with similar rows, you will find that you can repeat one by heart after, perhaps, only ten or five readings. Professor Meumann and his pupils have shown in an elaborate study[1] how great such improvement may be; and they have shown that practice in the task of "memorizing" nonsense syllables effects improvement of one's power to "memorize" other matter. But it may be that this improvement affects only the first, or the first and third of the three factors mentioned above. Undoubtedly we do learn by practice to set ourselves to such a task more effectively, to "concentrate and distribute our attention" more suitably, to use rhythm skilfully; and we are apt to acquire a more vivid interest in the task as, day after day, we note our improvement and are encouraged to strive for more. Professor Meumann's results leave untouched the question—Is the second factor, retention, or retentiveness, susceptible of improvement by practice? Most psychologists have answered this question in the negative, somewhat dogmatically, deducing their answer from general principles. William James, for example, wrote: "No amount of culture would seem capable of modifying a man's general retentiveness. This is a physiological quality, given once for all with his organization, and which he can never hope to change. It differs no doubt in disease and health, and it is a fact of observation that it is better in fresh and vigorous hours than when we are fagged and ill. We may say, then, that a man's native tenacity will fluctuate somewhat with his hygiene, and that whatever is good for his tone of health will also be good for his memory. We may even say that whatever amount of intellectual exercise is bracing to the general tone and nutrition of the brain will also be profitable to the general retentiveness. But more than this we cannot say, and this, it is obvious, is far less than most people believe."[2]

This passage illustrates very forcibly the difficulty of clear thinking in psychology. For here even James has grossly confused two things that should be carefully distinguished, namely, our second and third factors, retention or retentiveness and capacity to reproduce. All that he says of variations of capacity with general conditions, such as fatigue and state of health, applies not to retentiveness, as he says, but to our power of reproduction. During fatigue or ill-health you may be unable to recollect many things which at normal times you can easily recollect at will. You may even be unable to recall your own name or that of a familiar friend. But, on recovery of your normal condition, all this inability disappears; which shows that, not your retentiveness, but your power of reproduction was impaired.

James's statement that a man's general retentiveness or tenacity of mem-

[1] "The Psychology of Learning," N. Y., 1913.

[2] "Principles," Vol. II, p. 664.

ory cannot be improved by cultivation is a deduction from the view that all retention is a matter of the persistence of traces in the brain. In assuming the truth of this view, James was at one with many other psychologists; but he was begging a question of the profoundest interest which is still entirely open to dispute.[1] There are philosophers and psychologists, such as Professor Bergson, who maintain that memory is not conditioned by the persistence of traces in the brain, but is a purely spiritual or mental function; who assert that all our experience leaves an indelible trace in the mind and is never forgotten, and who maintain that, when we are unable to recollect, it is the third of our three factors that is at fault, not the second. The psychology of Professor Freud and his disciples, the psychoanalysts, seems to imply this doctrine; although Freud has not, so far as I know, explicitly affirmed it. It is mainly based on the fact that in hypnosis and certain other abnormal states (especially the state of approaching death through drowning or other violence) the subject seems sometimes to remember many things which in his normal state he is quite incapable of recollecting.

Is Retentiveness Improved by Practice?

Either view of the nature of "retention" leaves open the question of the improvability of retentiveness by practice; and this question can only be answered by empirical observation. It is a straightforward question of fact which may be answered by experimental observation, though we remain ignorant of the nature of retentiveness. So far as I am aware, only one experimental investigation of this question has been made, namely, one conducted by Miss M. Smith and myself.[2]

It is clear that the simple application of the method of learning and relearning cannot solve this problem. For any improvement of "learning" due to practice may equally affect the process of "relearning." What we have to do, in order to discover any improvement of "retention," is to compare the improvement effected by a period of practice in "learning" and in "relearning" respectively. If they show an equal improvement, there is no evidence of improvement of retention. If, however, "relearning" shows a greater improvement than "learning," this excess of improvement may fairly be regarded as implying an improvement of "retention" through practice. That was the plan of our prolonged experiment, in the course of which each of six subjects "learned" a new row of syllables each day and "relearned" it after twenty-four hours, day after day, during many months. The result showed a large improvement both of "learning" and of "relearning"; and in three subjects the improvement of "relearning" was decidedly greater than the improvement of "learning"—a result which seems to imply improvement of "retention" through practice. The definite establishment of so important a conclusion would, of course, require the repetition of experiments of this kind on many subjects. And, even if all of them yielded the same result, the interpretation of it might remain disputable. It may be that practice improves the third more than the first of the three functions indicated above as con-

[1] And which James himself in later writings treated as an open question.

[2] "Some Experiments in Learning and Retention," *British Journal of Psychology*, Vol. X, 1920.

stituting together what is commonly treated as a single function, under the head of "memory," namely, the function of voluntary recall or reproduction. I have mentioned this research only to show the reader that experimental work of this kind is capable of throwing light on problems of the greatest practical importance and of the highest theoretical interest.

Are Habit and Memory Identical Functions?

Of more general interest than the detailed conclusions established by these experimental investigations of "memory" is the question (seldom raised by those who conduct such experiments): What exactly is the function investigated? Almost all the practical workers in this field have assumed the truth of the physiological theory of memory and association. This theory asserts that all that we call memory and association is a matter of the formation and persistence of paths of low resistance in the brain: a theory which combines very readily with the theory of "ideas" and of "ideas" as made up of "sensations" and "images" associated with one another in groups or clusters, and also with the mechanistic theory of behavior. For just as "ideas" are said to be clusters of associated "images," so complex forms of behavior are said to be clusters of associated reflexes; and the several "sensations" or "images" are supposed to be attached in some way to the several reflexes; the "association" being a path of low resistance which combines two reflex arcs into one more complex arc.

These theories combine so well to make a comprehensible compound theory (the theory that memory and bodily habit are identical functions) that, with minor variations, the latter has been very widely accepted, often very uncritically and without any attempt to think out its difficulties. Only an unusually independent and original mind will challenge such a theory, when it is familiar with the wide range of facts on which the theory is based and which it claims to resume. Professor Bergson is such a mind; and he has boldly challenged these far-reaching assumptions, which are of the essence of the mechanistic interpretation of Life and Mind. Without closely following Bergson's argument, I will indicate the kind of criticism he suggests.

We must distinguish, says Bergson, between habit and true

memory; habit is of the body, memory of the mind.[1] The physiological theory of paths of low resistance in the nervous system, formed and deepened by each passage of the nervous current, is probably a true account of the nature of habit; but it is wholly inadequate to throw light on pure memory. The so-called investigations of memory, by such methods as the learning of rows of nonsense syllables, really deal with habit rather than with memory; the conclusions they reach are in the main laws of habit rather than laws of memory. But, in almost all instances of reproductive imagination, we have to do with a complex of habit and memory functions. In the nonsense syllable experiments, all the precautions taken to simplify and standardize the procedure tend to throw the emphasis on habit and to diminish the share of memory. Nonsense syllables are chosen in order, it is said, to have material free from preformed associations, such as cling to every familiar word. In reality this is to reduce the factor of "meaning" or significance to a minimum. At the same time the factor of purpose is rendered as constant as possible, but also minimized; one learns the syllables under the driving power of a general volition to carry through the process in the interests of science. Yet, with all this simplification, which makes for the predominance of habit and tends to reduce reproduction of the syllables to the mere unrolling of a motor habit, a motor mechanism we have formed by practice, the influence of true mental activity and of true memory is unmistakable. Many of the experimental results show clearly that, both in the learning and in the reproducing of a row of syllables, the several syllables do not merely hang together like the links of a chain. Rather, the row is a unity for the mind, because of the subject's purpose to regard it as a unity, a coherent object. That is to say, the row as thought of has conative continuity; or, more strictly, the thinking of the row is not a series or succession of "ideas" or of movements, but is the thinking of one whole

[1] "The past survives under two distinct forms: first in motor mechanisms; secondly, in independent recollections. . . . The memory of a lesson remembered in the sense of learned by heart has all the marks of a habit . . .; the memory of each successive reading has none of the marks of a habit . . .; of these two memories one is pure memory, the other is habit interpreted by memory."—"Matière et Mémoire," Chap. II.

object whose parts are named successively. It is for this reason that the learning of a long row is disproportionately difficult; for example, if you require for the learning of a row of eight syllables only six readings, you may require for the learning of a row of sixteen syllables not six, nor yet twelve readings, but perhaps forty or fifty or more.

When you have re-read the row many times, it rolls itself off your tongue, without deliberation on your part, and without your being aware of each syllable before you speak it. It is as though you heard the syllables projected by a gramophone. And any effort to control the process is apt to interfere with the smooth repetition of the syllables. That is the mark of a well-formed motor habit, a "secondarily automatic process," as it is commonly called. The exercise of such a motor habit involves no remembering of the experiences through which it was acquired. It is as nearly as possible a mechanical process, the reeling off of a mechanism, such as the mechanists allege all our behavior to be. But, as Bergson points out, you can generally exert true memory, while the habit action proceeds; you can remember any one of the readings through the repetition of which you have learned the row. Each of these readings was a unique event; and the remembering of any one of them is an equally unique event, distinct from every other mental event and related in a unique manner to the event remembered. The motor habit, on the other hand, is a cumulative effect of all the successive readings, and bears no such unique relation to any one of them.

Again, we know that, in order to create a habit of movement, it is necessary to repeat the series or chain of movements many times, under conditions as nearly as possible alike on each occasion; whereas perception on a single occasion of some intensely interesting scene or of some fascinating melody may leave us with the power to remember the scene or the melody, to "reproduce" faithfully the sensory pattern in all its wealth of detail. Yet, if "memory" and "habit" are identical functions, the reproduction of the sensory pattern must be regarded as dependent upon a multitude of neural links of the same order as those few involved in the motor habit. How, then, are we to account, in terms of the hypothesis, for the immense superiority of sensory to motor memory? Facts of this order seem to me to constitute in themselves an insuperable objection to the hypothesis of the identity of memory with motor habit.

The common assumption that "habit" and "memory" are fundamentally identical functions and both alike explicable by the principle of "association" (understood in terms of paths of low resistance in the brain) is then highly disputable on the face of it.

The assumption can be experimentally tested by the use of the *correlation method*, a method which in recent years has been developed and applied in psychology with most interesting results.[1] Its application to our present problem depends on the following reasoning: If all habit and memory and association are dependent upon a common function, namely, the plasticity of the brain structure, or the facility with which new paths are formed and retained in the brain, and if, as James asserts, "This is a physiological quality, given once for all" in a man's native constitution, it follows that all the wide differences between men in respect of retentiveness are expressions of native differences of this one "physiological quality"; and the man who has a good memory will also form readily and retain faithfully motor habits and "associations" of all kinds. If, on the other hand, this assumption is false, if memory and habit are radically distinct functions (as Bergson maintains), then it may well be that individuals who have good memories may have poor facility for habit formation, and conversely. That is to say, if James's assumption is true, there should be high positive correlation between excellence in memory-tasks and excellence in habit-tasks. Whereas, if the assumption is false, there *may be* no such correlation, but possibly even an inverse or negative correlation. More popularly expressed, if James's assumption is true, excellence in tasks of the two kinds should "go together" in the same individuals; whereas, if it is false, they may not "go together." Further (and this is the essential argument), if we find, on empirical observation of a large number of individuals, that the two forms of excellence do not "go together," but that many persons who are strong in memory are weak in habit-formation (if degrees of excellence in memory and in habit are not positively correlated), then we have strong evidence that the assumption is false, and that habit and memory are radically distinct functions. Such observations have been made by Miss M. Smith and myself. Recognizing that, if memory and habit are distinct functions, they nevertheless are conjoined in almost all operations in which degrees of excellence can be exactly determined, we tested a considerable number of subjects (forty-one) in four tasks of two types. Two of one type were devised in such a way as to involve predominantly habit-formation; two of the other type were devised to involve as far as possible true memory

[1] The development and application of this method in psychology are largely due to the labors of Professor C. Spearman, reported in many articles in *The British Journal of Psychology* and elsewhere. An excellent discussion of the method may be found in "Essentials of Mental Measurement," by William Brown and Godfrey Thomson, London, 1921.

and as little as possible of habit-formation. When our subjects had been tested and a figure assigned to each denoting his degree of excellence in each of the four tasks, we determined the coefficients of correlation between degrees of excellence of all the subjects in each task and their excellence in each other of the four tasks.[1] The result was to show a high positive correlation between the two habit-tasks and also between the two memory-tasks; but a low or negative correlation between the habit-tasks and the memory-tasks. This evidence, then, indicates that the common assumption is false, and that Bergson is right in insisting upon the essentially different natures of habit and memory.

The Role of "Meaning" in Remembering

The distinction between motor habit and memory is further borne out, when we consider the immense influence of "meaning" in facilitating reproduction. When we learn rows of nonsense syllables, we are setting ourselves to a task in which the part of true memory is small, and the formation of motor habit is the principal factor. But, when we learn verses by heart, the task is one in which memory predominates and motor habit is of minor importance. Accordingly we find that the learning of verses is immensely easier. Many of us can learn a four-line verse by a single reading (or if not, then by two or three readings); though it may contain as many as fifty syllables. Whereas, in order to learn a row of fifty nonsense syllables, the same persons would require to read the row some hundreds of times. How are we to account for this immense difference? The mechanists, who deny the distinction between habit and memory, can only say that the words are rich in pre-formed associations, while the nonsense syllables are not. But a multiplicity of pre-formed associations clustering about each word must in itself tend (as experiment has clearly shown) to complicate and make more difficult the task of forming new associations between the words. And this explanation is therefore no explanation at all. The truth is that, in learning the row of nonsense syllables, we are in the main setting up a speech habit or motor mechanism. Whereas, in learning the verse, we appreciate the mean-

[1] By applying the formulæ which the mathematicians have worked out. See "Essentials of Mental Measurement," by Wm. Brown and G. Thomson. The research briefly summarized is reported in *The British Journal of Psychology*, Vol. X, 1920.

ing, not only of the words, but of the conjunctions of words which make the sentences, and we remember the meaning of the whole sequence of words and of the component phrases. And sometimes we can remember the meaning, without being able to reproduce the words. But the memory of their meaning immensely facilitates the reproduction of the words; because these meanings tend to express themselves in just such words.

Just as we have distinguished between bodily and mental habits, so now we must distinguish between neural and mental association. Motor habit is formed by neural association; true memory involves mental association, a principle which seems to be of a very different order. The difference is well illustrated by the following simple experiment: Make a list of twenty words each of which denotes an object; and let each object be related to the object named next in order in the list in some obvious and familiar manner (as, for example, tree—mast—ship—sail—purchase—market—stall—stable—horse—wagon—sledge—snow—hail—thunder—Jove—Venus—Cupid—cupidity—stupidity—genius). You will find that most educated persons can repeat this list of words after once hearing it *slowly* read aloud—on two conditions, (1) that they set themselves to the task of remembering the words in order; (2) that they seize the meaning of the words and notice the relations between the objects named. Yet, as we have seen, to learn to repeat a list of twenty or thirty nonsense syllables (there are twenty words and more than thirty syllables in our list) is a very difficult task for most of us, requiring a hundred or more repetitions of the list, with concentrated attention.[1] What, then, is the ground of this immense difference? Clearly, it is that in the one case we are dealing with association by habit, and in the other with association by "mean-

[1] Even in setting up the motor habit which facilitates the repetition of the list, effort, *i. e.*, conation, plays a very large role. If a list be merely read over and over again in an attitude of slack indifference, the number of readings required before it can be repeated "by heart" will be very much larger than if a deliberate effort is made to learn the list. (Cf. Smith and McDougall, *loc. cit.*) One subject, when by practice he had acquired the art of maintaining an attitude as nearly as possible passive while reading again and again a row of twelve syllables, required more than two hundred such passive repetitions in order to learn the row; whereas, when he read a similar row with concentrated attention, only nine repetitions were necessary.

ing." The nonsense syllables are mere sounds, significant of nothing beyond their appearance as written or printed. The words are significant of objects; each brings into play some great mental system which already has its place in the organized structure of the mind; and, on noticing the relations of any two objects successively named, each system interacts with the other. The words as mere sounds, or as mere movements of the speech-organs, are as nothing; their meanings are all-important. If you are equally familiar with two languages, half the words might have been of one language and half of the other, and, so long as their meanings were the same, the process in your mind would not have been essentially different, or the task appreciably more difficult. It is true that such words as "hail" and "thunder," or "Venus" and "Cupid" may have been heard or spoken by you on several occasions in immediate succession; but the association in your mind between the objects of each pair is not due to that; it is due to the fact that the objects named belong to the same "universe of discourse." And when, after saying "sail," the word "purchase" comes to mind, that is not due to any merely verbal association, but depends upon your having noticed, on hearing the words, the double meaning of the sound "sail." If, on hearing the word "purchase," you did not become aware of the second meaning of the sound "sail," you will be at a loss when you come to that point in the process of recall. And the word "cupidity" follows easily upon "Cupid," not because the two sounds as such are associated in your mind, or because the same motor mechanisms are involved in the utterance of both words; but because the juxtaposition of the two words leads you to recognize a relation between the two objects named, a relation which very possibly you have never before noticed.

Reproductive imagining is, then, very different from the exercise of a motor habit; to attempt to identify them, as the mechanists do, is to give a spurious and very misleading simplicity to the account of mental process. We must further consider the processes of association under the general heading of mental growth.[1] Let us now consider certain distinctions in the operations of the developed mind.

[1] Chap. XV.

Memory or Remembering in the Strict Sense

It is usual to treat of imagination and of memory in separate chapters, as though they were radically distinct functions or faculties; but I do not see how they can be profitably separated.

Imagination, or thinking of remote objects, takes three forms —mere imagination, anticipation, and remembering. The anticipatory form of imagination would seem to be the most primitive and fundamental; for, as we have seen, it is an aid to, and an extension into the future of, the anticipation involved in all perceptual thinking. The retrospective attitude, which makes of imagining a thinking of the past or a remembering, seems to be a relatively late development, implying as it does a reversal of the primitive forward-looking attitude. It seems probable that no animal achieves this retrospective attitude and imagines the past as past. Simple imagining, without definite reference forward or backward in time, forms perhaps a transition stage in the development of remembering from anticipation. In a higher degree than imaginative anticipation, it implies suspension of action. The child remembers little explicitly; his remembering is in the main for the sake of action in the near future. Only the old or middle-aged learn "to muse and brood and live again in memory." The child has difficulty in distinguishing between his past perceiving and his past imagining. Savage man also draws this distinction with difficulty; he is apt to confuse his day-dreams and the imaginings of sleep with his perceptual experiences. The distinction is a difficult one; we learn to make it clearly and accurately only by much discipline.

The word "memory" is sometimes used, in the widest possible sense, to cover all influence of our past upon our present experience; and past experience plays its part, in determining the course of present experience, through the medium of the modifications of mental structure induced by that past experience. Enduring modifications or developments of mental structure are the links between past and present experiences. In the wide sense, all or most imagining, and indeed most perceiving, involves memory: for the structure of the mind is built up from its innate basis through experience; and in the adult human being the acquired structure preponderates greatly in richness and complexity over the innate basis of structure. In the strictest or narrowest sense, on the other hand, memory or remembering implies imagining of events as experienced in the past; that is to say, the subject, in the act of imagining the event, knows it or recognizes it as belonging to his own past experience. Between these extremes lie many degrees of explicitness of memory.

The simplest form of true remembering is perceptual recognition. All perception based on past experience involves recognition in the looser sense, namely, an implicit classing of the present object with its fellows of the same class. In the strictest sense, recognition implies the distinguishing of the individual object as such and reference to the time and the place at which it was formerly perceived; as when we say: "This is the man I saw yesterday as I turned the corner of S—— Street on my way to lunch." It has been commonly assumed in practical life that such remembering is a feat easily and accurately accomplished by all normal human beings. But psychological research has begun to make it clear that this assumption is not valid; and elaborate researches into testimony and its trustworthiness have revealed many sources of error and the extent to which the normal man is liable to such errors.[1] In reality, remembering, in the full sense of the word, is a very complex introspective activity which implies a well-developed capacity of self-reflection or self-awareness, or, as it is commonly expressed, well-developed self-consciousness. Our knowledge of the time-order of the events we remember is for the most part vague and uncertain, except in so far as we make use of a conventional system of dates.

How Do We "Place" Our Memories in the Past?

Apart from our use of some such system of dates (which among primitive peoples is apt to be extremely crude and simple) our knowledge of the time-order of past events seems to be based on two factors only. First, after the lapse of time, *the past object or event is remembered with a certain vagueness, a loss of detail and accuracy and vividness, which, being in the main more*

[1] Cf. W. Stern, "Psychologie der Aussage."

marked the greater the interval of time, serves as a rough mark of remoteness in time. This in itself is very apt to mislead us; for past events are remembered clearly and vividly in proportion to the keenness of our interest in them at the time of their happening. Hence we say of the highly interesting event: "It seems as though it happened only yesterday." This loss of vividness and detail, which becomes more marked with the lapse of time, is no doubt due to the development of our mental structure which has taken place in the interval. If, like "Sleeping Beauty," we could absolutely arrest our life for a hundred years, we should presumably remember the events of a century ago as vividly and faithfully as we remember those of yesterday. We find accordingly that the fuller and richer our activities during any period of time, the more do the events preceding that period bear in memory the mark of remoteness. Especially is this so, if in the interval we have been actively concerned with events of a similar type; for then that part of the structure of our minds which is concerned in all thinking of such things has undergone much change and development; hence even a short period, filled with intense activity about objects of a certain class, may result in our feeling that the experiences of the same class preceding that period are very remote. Whereas, if the intervening period is filled with activity of a different type and concerning objects of a different class from those familiar activities and objects to which you return after an interval (even of years), you are astonished to find how it all seems the same, how the interval has made no difference; the same old postman knocks on the same old door, the same old servant lays the table for dinner in the same old way, and all comes back to you as though you had been away but a few days.

The second time-mark for memory (apart from conventional dates) depends upon the fact that in remembering our *thinking tends to run forward in time.* We think of a certain past event and then, so far as we continue in the reminiscent attitude, we tend to think of succeeding rather than of preceding events. To reverse this natural sequence in remembering requires a deliberate effort and is not easy; in fact, we accomplish it only imperfectly by taking short sequences of the past in inverted order.

It is commonly said that this tendency is the expression of a "law of forward association." In reality it goes deeper than this; it seems to be the expression of the fundamental tendency of Mind to look forward, to work toward the future, to anticipate the event which is about to happen.

The Essence of Recognition

But a more fundamental question remains: What is the essence of recognition? What is its essential condition? When you see a man and say to yourself "I have seen that man before," you achieve an act of recognition of a simple kind in which is involved the essential function of all memory, as distinct from mere imagination. Here we must distinguish between *implicit* recognition and *explicit* recognition. The former is primitive; the latter develops out of it. The dog that runs away at sight of the man who kicked him yesterday recognizes him implicitly. It is probably true to say that the perceiving of the same man merely evokes again the fear-impulse which yesterday was evoked by his brutal act. The dog does not think "That is the man who kicked me yesterday; I will get out of his way lest he kick me again." All sense-impressions which evoke the same reaction are signs of the same object. In ourselves the utterance of the proper name of the object is an important part of recognition. But, even apart from this, the similarity of the effect upon us is the essential ground of recognition.

We may attempt further to explain the act of recognition by speaking of a "sense of familiarity" or "a feeling or sensation of familiarity" accompanying the act of perception. But we do not really advance our understanding of the process by so doing. The capacity for recognition, and so of all remembering, is at bottom that fundamental function which James calls "conception" and which perhaps is better called simply "knowing." Even in its simplest forms it involves a rudimentary act of judgment, the judgment of sameness—"Hello! Thingumbob, again!" This we have to accept as one of the fundamental faculties of Mind; we can give no further account or explanation of it, because we cannot explain the generation of Mind out of something that is not Mind, whether physical movements or mere "sensations" or logical entities, such as "universals" or "essences" or "concepts" or "ideas."

We have rather to recognize that all those specialized highly developed forms of mental activity which are usually treated in text-books in separate chapters on imagination, memory, conation, affection, association, conception, judgment, comparing, reasoning, and so forth, that all these functions are involved in the simplest mental acts; and that the process of mental evolution in the individual, as in the race, does not consist in the adding or creation or development of new faculties. Mental development consists rather in the becoming more explicit of these distinguishable, but not distinct, modes of activity, by the accentuation in various acts of this or that aspect of mental activity. So *remembering is an act in which that reference to the past which is implicit in all mental activity is more explicit and more prominent than in other acts.*[1]

The biological function of Mind is to bring the past to bear upon present action, guiding it in anticipation of the future. This it is able to do, because it (the "mind" of the individual) has an enduring structure which constantly grows and is developed by every mental activity. "Memory" is our most general term for connoting this bearing of the past upon our present action through the medium of our developing mental structure. *To have a good memory is to have a well-organized mind.* Yet we are bound to recognize individual peculiarities of memory that are not wholly explicable in terms of differences of organized structure. Two men may have equally well and systematically organized minds; yet one seems to work predominantly in the form of explicit remembering of the past; while in the other man the stores of systematic knowledge remain implicit; his mind is occupied constantly with the future, and his knowledge oper-

[1] The beginner should be specially warned against a certain naïve way of explaining acts of recognition and comparison, which consists in saying that, when I recognize an object, I bring out of the storehouse of the mind an "idea" of the object as previously perceived, and place it alongside my present "idea" or "percept," and then, seeing that the two "ideas" are alike, deduce the sameness of the object. Such "explanation" is purely fictitious, one of the many excrescences of the "idea" theory.

ates implicitly in the devising of schemes of action. Such difference of type may be largely due to difference of acquired interests; yet it seems probable that it has also a basis in some obscure difference of native constitution.

Memory and Conation

Like all other thinking, remembering is a conative activity. We remember and recollect effectively in proportion as we have strong motives for doing so. This truth is too often ignored; we are apt to regard our "memory" fatalistically, as a mysterious automatic machine over which we have no control; either it works or it does not, and that is all there is to say of it. The physiological theory of memory, which identifies it with neural habit, has done much to accentuate this fatalistic attitude toward our "memories"; while at the same time the professional memory-trainers have been claiming the most striking successes and making their fortunes.

It is true that, in the sphere of recollection, our volition often seems to be peculiarly ineffective. But in no kind of task is our volition uniformly successful. And it is notorious that we remember emotionally exciting events better than others; which means that the strength of our conation, our interest, during any experience is a main condition of our remembering. There can be no doubt that an explicit volition, purpose, or intention to remember greatly favors remembering and recollecting. For example, in the experiment with the list of words (p. 303) our success largely depends on our intention to remember.[1] On striving to recollect, our volition often fails; we cannot recover the name or the anecdote, though we know what it is we want to recall, we know that it is the name of that place or person, or a story about it. But, though our purpose to recollect may fail at the moment to achieve its goal, it often becomes effective after an interval. We think of something else; and then our unsatisfied conation or purpose to recollect works subconsciously (another striking illustration of the law that conation outlasts cognition) and we suddenly become aware of the name, fact, or

[1] Cf. also the foot-note on p. 303.

anecdote. Often we may notice that this "popping up into consciousness" of the fact we could not immediately recollect occurs when the mind is occupied with some allied topic; for example, I cannot recollect the name of one of the battle-fields of Flanders, though I could put my finger on the spot on the map; then after an interval I am led to think of the war again in some other aspect, and suddenly the name recurs to me. Recollection of this kind is too often treated as though it were merely an accidental result of the working of cerebral machinery. But there can be no doubt that, in such cases, our desire or purpose to recollect is the determining factor of our subsequent recollection.

The influence of conation on "memory" is very forcibly illustrated in mental pathology, especially by instances of functional amnesia or forgetting. For conation can determine not only remembering, but also forgetting; or, more correctly, just as desire for an object leads us frequently to remember that object, so aversion from an object (rooted in fear, disgust, or painful experiences connected with it) may prevent the remembering of it, and may even make it impossible to recollect it by the most genuine voluntary effort. Amnesia of this kind occurred in thousands of instances among the soldiers who suffered the horrors of "the front" during the Great War. Here it must suffice to say that, in very many such cases (and in principle probably in all) it is possible to discover the motive which prevents recollection; and possible also to overcome it by evoking sufficiently strong motives of the opposite tendency. Hypnotic suggestion also affords ample evidence of the same truth. The essence of hypnotic suggestion is that the operator largely controls and directs the conative energies of the subject; and one of the most striking effects of such suggestion is to prevent by a few words of instruction the recollection of certain events; or, equally simply, to enable the patient to recollect some amnesic period, some event, or even a large tract of his past, which he could not voluntarily recall.[1]

[1] For discussion of these topics see Part II.

The influence of conation on imagination of the future is more generally and adequately recognized under the head of *Desire.* Desire is conative impulse working on the plane of imagination. Just as we cannot draw a sharp line between perception and imagination, because imagination co-operates with and is a further development of the anticipatory function of perception, so we cannot draw any sharp line between impulse and desire. In the fullest sense of the word, desire implies that we imagine the goal, the change of circumstance toward which we feel impelled to strive, while nevertheless we suspend all bodily behavior directed toward that goal, because we recognize either the physical or the moral impossibility of successful action in the present. Thus, when I am hungry and no food is within reach, to imagine food is at the same time to desire it. And (as so well described by Major Priestly, p. 279) the food-impulse, when it is very strong, may dominate our thinking in the form of desire. Everything that can make us think of food starts up our desire afresh; and the desire tends to keep us thinking of its object, determining anticipation and recollection as well as simple imagining of meals and of various forms of food, and makes us sensitive to every suggestion of food. Desire is thus essentially a self-sustaining circular or reciprocal process between two mental dispositions or systems; in this instance, between the cognitive system concerned in all thinking of food and the conative disposition from which springs the impulse to seek food. By reason of the impossibility of present action toward the natural end of securing food, the impulse operates to keep us imagining the various possibilities of action in the future. Desire is thus the great sustainer of productive imagination, the imagination which runs before action and devises remote means to remote ends.

More loosely we speak of "desire" under circumstances of two other types. First, if we pursue a train of action as means to a remote end, we may say in accordance with common usage that desire for the end sustains our action. Secondly, the desired object may be in view, may be present, and yet (like Major

Priestly and his hungry men watching each morsel eaten by their companions) we restrain our impulse to act. Impulse, thus suspended in the presence of the object, is the simplest form of desire; one of which we may suppose most of the higher animals to be capable, as when the hungry dog sits looking eagerly at his biscuit, restrained from action by his master's prohibition. A still lower form of desire than the last (in which the impulse is suspended by a stronger conflicting impulse) is that of the hungry animal separated by bars from the food he strives to reach. A dog or cat in such a situation may, after striving in vain for a time, sit down and lick his lips, with his eyes fixed upon the food. That is suspension of action while the impulse still works. Such presumably are the moments when productive imagination achieves its first triumphs.

By older writers (*e. g.*, Descartes and some of the philosophers of the Scottish school) desire was classed as one of the emotions. This was a very confusing treatment. For desire (using the term in the wider sense to cover aversion as well as appetition) may spring from any one of the instinctive dispositions, and its relation to emotional excitement is essentially the same as that of impulse; for desire is impulse working on the more intellectual plane on which the goal of endeavor is explicitly thought of as distinct from the present circumstances.

CHAPTER XI

EMOTION

We all know what it is to be emotionally excited. And we know that the experience of being emotionally excited is not always of the same quality; we experience emotional excitements of many distinguishable qualities. We confidently use a large number of words to describe these experiences. Most of these words are used in both adjectival and substantival forms, and some are used also as verbs, transitive or intransitive. We say "I was angry or afraid," or we say "I felt anger or fear"; or again we say "I raged" or "I feared him" or "I admired him." And the substantival form may be used as the name of an agent; as when we say "I was moved by anger or impelled by fear," or "Curiosity carried me away," or "Anger overwhelmed me, or gave me strength," or "Fear lent wings to my feet." The last usage is the most forcible; it is appropriate to poetical and romantic description. The poets legitimately personify these emotional experiences and speak of them as personal powers or agents. Plato set this fashion long ago, when he described Reason as striving to control the Passions, which drag us along like a team of spirited horses. It results from this usage that psychologists commonly speak of "the emotions" or of "an emotion," just as they speak of "sensations" or "an idea." And, as in these cases, the usage is misleading and confusing; though perhaps not so seriously misleading. Some psychologists, indulging our natural tendency to reïfy whatever we name, seem to assume that we have to recognize "an emotion" of distinctive quality corresponding to every name used in popular and literary description of emotional experience. Let us begin our study of emotional experience by putting aside this popular and literary usage; let us hold to the obvious fact that there are no such things as "emotions," any more than there are such things as "sensations" or "ideas" or "concepts." And, if we find it difficult or impossible to avoid altogether the use of the substantival forms, such as "anger" and "fright" and "curiosity" and "wonder" and "admiration," let us at least be clear that the adjectival form is preferable wherever possible, and that the use of a substantive does not imply a thing or agent, but always a mode or quality of experience.

Qualitative Varieties of Emotional Experience

We shall, then, not begin by asking, What is an emotion? Rather, we shall ask, What are the varieties of emotional experience? And what are the conditions, internal and external, under which we experience these varieties or qualities? And we may further inquire, What part do these qualities play in our mental life? What is their function? How do they contribute toward the attainment of our natural goals?

The emotional qualities are more difficult to describe than the sensory qualities. In both cases we can only indicate the quality we experience by pointing to an object or situation and saying: "It is what I experience when I perceive or think of that." But our sensory reactions are more true to type, more constant in relation to the objects and impressions that excite them, than are our emotional reactions. In the presence of the same object, the emotional experiences of different persons may be very different, and even those of the same person on successive occasions may vary widely with changes in his general condition. Though similar differences and variations of our sensory experiences occur, they are far less extreme. Hence, while the sensory qualities are commonly said to be "objective," or significant of the nature of the object, the emotional qualities are said to be subjective, or significant of the nature of the subject. As we have seen, some eccentric philosophers have endeavored in various ingenious ways to identify sensory experiences with physical objects; but few go so far as to seek to identify our emotional experiences with the objects that evoke them. Yet in a general way the quality of our emotional reaction to an object does signify the nature of the object. Common speech and literary usage recognize this fact; as when they describe as "fearful" an object that frightens us; as "provoking" one that angers us; as "strange" or "marvellous" or "wondrous" or "curious" one that evokes our curiosity; or describe a landscape as sublime or awful, a work of art as admirable or tender, a person as disgusting or reverend or hateful or awe-inspiring. Common speech goes even further and invents substantives to denote those qualities of things in virtue of which they excite in us the various emotional qualities; such substantives as awfulness, hatefulness, sublimity, frightfulness, mysteriousness.

These facts seem to suggest that, as regards their place and function in our mental activity, emotional qualities are not essentially different from the sensory qualities; that, like them, they are essentially cognitive, though their significance or signifying function is more ambiguous and variable. This is the view implied in the famous Lange-James theory of the emotions, which we must examine on a later page.

Two Senses of the Word "Emotion"

One source of confusion in discussions of emotional experience is that the expression "an emotion" is used in two very different senses. Sometimes it is used to mean only some emotional quality of experience. This is something we can readily conceive to be lacking in an experience otherwise similar; for it is variable in quality and intensity, while other distinguishable features persist or recur. For example, on catching sight of some strange object out in the forest or on the prairie, your experience may be tinged with that emotional quality we call fear. You continue to gaze at it and, as you do so, this quality fades out, leaving in its place, as it were, the quality we call curiosity. You continue to gaze, and presently, having recognized the object more fully, this quality also subsides and you turn away satisfied. Here the change is wholly internal. The object remains the same object, and the sense-impressions you receive from it remain unchanged; while your emotional reaction changes in quality and then fades away, as your cognition becomes more adequate. It is their relative independence of the object which leads us to call the emotional qualities subjective; while we call the sensory qualities objective. And it is this which leads us to speak of the emotional quality as "an emotion."

But sometimes "an emotion" is used to imply the whole mental and bodily process of the moment; and in this sense "an emotion" means much more than the emotional quality of our experience at that moment. Either usage seems legitimate, if we make clear in which sense we use the words. The second usage arises from the facts (1) that each kind of emotional experience is normally accompanied by bodily changes which are called "the expressions of the emotion"; (2) that every emotional excitement of the organism involves, beside the emotional quality and its bodily expressions, a third distinguishable factor which is very often ignored in discussions of the emotions, namely, the conative factor in the total experience. This we must now consider, with the utmost effort to think clearly.

Conation as a Mode of Experience

Hitherto I have discussed conation or striving, under the heads of impulse and desire, as a factor in, or aspect of, all mental activity. We have noted how conation expresses itself, in behavior and in all mental activity, as a persistent striving toward a goal with variation of means. We have regarded such behavior as indicative of an energy that works teleologically, and which is therefore radically different from the energies which physical science conceives as working always mechanistically. I have now to insist that we conceive this energy, not only on the basis of our observation of all those peculiarities which are the marks of behavior, which distinguish behavior from all mechanical processes, but also on the basis of *our immediate experience of striving.*

When we strive, we are immediately aware of striving; and this conative experience, which is always present in some degree as an element or quality in our experience, varies in strength or intensity with the intensity of our striving. *It is distinguishable or introspectively recognizable just because it so varies in intensity.* If it were a constant factor of all experience, varying neither in quality nor intensity, we should never become explicitly aware of it. Whether it varies qualitatively is a very difficult question; but its variations of intensity are very marked. It is at a minimum when we are relaxed, indifferent, and sluggish; at a maximum when we are on the alert, keenly pursuing any goal, whether by the aid of bodily activity or by purely mental activity. We experience it in the most distinct manner, when we are moved by some uncontrollable craving or desire which we cannot satisfy and which will allow us neither to rest, nor to turn our attention to other things.

This factor in experience is so subtle and elusive to introspection that many psychologists ignore it altogether; while others, admitting its reality, regard it as merely a quality of sensory experience. James, for example, in the interests of the sensationist psychology which he had espoused, endeavored to show that all our conative experience is merely a special kind of sensory experience, namely, kinæsthetic or motor sensations. He pointed out that, when we strive intensely with bodily effort, the strong action of our muscles excites strongly the sensory nerves of the muscles, joints, and tendons; and he held that the sensory qualities so excited are the essence of such experience of effort, being more intense the stronger our efforts. He asserted that, when we make what we call a purely mental effort, such activity is invariably accompanied by contractions of certain muscles which produce no large movements, but which nevertheless excite kinæsthetic "sensations" of an intensity proportional to the strength of our effort. And he inclined to the view that these "sensations" of strain from such muscles as those of the scalp, the forehead, the throat, and the other parts of the breathing mechanism *are* "the feeling of effort" in such purely mental activities.[1] In this matter James has been followed by very many psychologists.

The question at issue is very theoretical. Psychology can make much progress without having solved the problem. James claimed to base his view on his own introspection; and it is obvious that, if so skilled a psychologist could find in introspection a warrant for the sensationist answer to this question, those who take the opposite view cannot hope to establish it by simple appeal to the verdict of introspection. They can only testify, as I do, that their "sense of effort" seems to vary independently of muscular strains and tensions; that they are sometimes aware of intense mental effort, when there is no discoverable strain or tension of any muscles of corresponding degree. Those who take this view, maintaining that the "sense of effort" is radically distinct from all sensory experience, have to admit that in bodily effort the straining of the muscles does yield sensory qualities whose intensity runs parallel with the intensity of our striving, and that, in making any strong efforts of an intellectual kind, we are apt to wrinkle our brows or modify the breathing processes. But we can support our view with strong evidence of two kinds. First, our muscles sometimes contract very strongly, exciting

[1] I say "inclined to this view," because James, although he could find no place for conative experience in his sensationist psychology, nevertheless believed on moral grounds in the reality of spiritual force or effort, and therefore left the question open in psychology.

intense kinæsthetic qualities, without our making any effort or having any "sense of effort"; as, for example, in muscular cramp, or when the muscles of a limb are caused to contract violently by an electric current passed through the limb. On such occasions we remain as nearly as possible passive spectators of the contortions of our limbs, with little or no "sense of effort"; or we may make an effort to straighten out the cramped limb, or to stand the pain of the electric current without shrinking, or to escape from it, or to analyze introspectively its effects upon us. And in all these cases our "sense of effort" runs parallel, not with the strength of the contractions of our muscles, but with the intensity of the mental effort that we make.

Evidence of the second kind, pointing strongly in the same direction, is afforded by certain pathological cases. A patient suffering from some severe shock may lie as though in a trance, showing hardly any sign of life, beyond faint pulse and breathing.[1] Yet on recovery of his normal state, such a patient may relate how during that period he was intensely active mentally, suffering an acute conflict, or overwhelmed with intense fear, which effectively inhibited all movement, or making intense efforts to recollect.[2]

Some authors have confused this question of the nature of conative experience with another, namely, the question of the reality of the alleged "feelings of innervation." These "feelings of innervation" were supposed by Wundt and others to be qualities of experience strictly analogous to "sensations," differing from them only in that, while "sensations" were excited by nervous currents arriving in the brain-cortex from sensory nerves and sense-organs, "feelings of innervation" were, it was said, excited by nervous currents going out from the cortex along the motor nerves. It must be admitted that James argued very forcibly and effectively against "feelings of innervation" so conceived. But to reject "feelings of innervation" is not to accept the sensationist view of our "sense of effort." If we reject the "feelings of innervation" and accept the sensationist view of the "sense of effort," we shall be driven to the conclusion that we never know what degree of effort we are putting forth, or to put forth, until our muscles contract. But this is obviously absurd. It is clearly true that we often intend to make a movement with a certain force or enegry, before we begin to make it; and, in so far as our motor apparatus faithfully executes our intention, we may truly be said to know the strength of our muscular effort before we initiate bodily action. The rejection of "feelings of innervation" thus only renders stronger the argument against the sensationist's view of the "sense of effort."

One subterfuge remains for the sensationist, and he has usually seized upon it. He may say that, when we intend a strong or a weak muscular effort, the essence of such intention is imagery corresponding in quality to the strong or

[1] In such cases among "shell-shocked" soldiers I have observed a complete absence of all deep reflexes, with complete flaccidity of all limbs, a condition which seems to imply a complete absence, or at least a minimal intensity, of all sensory qualities of the kinæsthetic class. And some of them who have described to me retrospectively their mental activity during the trancelike state have been able to give some account of events in their vicinity during this state. This constitutes evidence of the truth of their statements, and I can see no reason for doubting their substantial accuracy.

[2] Cf. the account given of his experience during such a state by the very intelligent Mr. Hanna, the hero of Doctors Sidis's and Goodhart's "Multiple Personality."

the weak "sensations" of muscular strain that will result when the muscles begin to work. It is a sufficient answer to this last refinement of the sensationist's theory to point out that, if in such instances the essence of our conative experience, of our sense of effort, is merely the imagining of the kinæsthetic sensory experience that will result from our muscular action, then to imagine a feeble movement must be identical with weakly intending, willing, or resolving it; and to imagine a strong movement must be identical with strongly intending it; which is not the case. *We may strongly intend or resolve to produce a feeble muscular contraction; and we may also weakly resolve, may intend with little sense of effort, to produce strong muscular contractions; and these two experiences of effort of different degrees of intensity are quite distinct.* The strength of our effort (and of our "sense of effort") bears no constant relation to the strength of the muscular contractions we are producing or intending to produce. We see this most clearly, perhaps, when we make a great effort to keep the body perfectly passive under conditions which naturally stimulate us to bodily activity. We see it also if we compare the intensities of our "sense of effort," when we execute some gymnastic feat which involves considerable muscular strain, and when we attempt to beat one rhythm with the right hand and another with the left. If our bodily condition is good and we are well practised, we may achieve the former feat with little "sense of effort," but rather with a sense of ease and mastery; whereas, in attempting the feeble muscular movements involved in the second task, we may experience a very acute "sense of effort," and may, moreover, find the second task much more fatiguing than the other. Consider also the intense sense of effort that we may experience in trying to keep awake when, after a bad night, we listen to a dull lecture; or when we are called upon to rise from bed on a cold morning before we are fully awake.

Mental effort or conation, then, cannot be identified with bodily effort; and our experience of effort cannot be analyzed into any sensational or imaginal elements or qualities.

Conative Experience in Emotional Excitement

Conative experience is the felt impulse to action; and it is felt, or is prominent in experience, in proportion to the strength of the working of the impulse. It takes the forms of mere craving for some undefined goal, of definitely directed desire, of conflict of desires, of resolving, choosing, willing; and, when we are actively occupied in working toward our goal, either by thinking or by bodily activity, this conative experience is complicated and obscured for introspection by the kinæsthetic sensory qualities set up by muscular strains. *Now such felt impulse is present in all emotional experience.* When we are afraid, we feel the impulse to retreat or escape from the object that frightens us;

when we are angry, we feel the impulse to attack the object that angers us; when we are curious, we feel the impulse to draw nearer and examine the object that excites our curiosity. It is true that we become introspectively aware of the impulse, only when we do not give ourselves up to it, but, arresting or suspending it, turn our attention from the object to ourselves; but that is the peculiarity of all introspective awareness.

If the conative factor could be subtracted from an emotional experience, without other change, that experience would seem to be radically altered. We might still think of the object, and our thinking would still be colored by the emotional quality: but the whole experience would be profoundly different; it would seem to lack its very essence, to be empty and unreal. It would be like the simulation of emotion. We cannot, then, properly abstract from this conative factor, in describing or discussing emotional experience. That impulse to action is an essential feature of emotion is recognized by common speech and literary usage; as when it is said that anger or fear or disgust makes us do this or that, or impels us to act.

Emotion, Impulse, and Bodily Adjustments

There is only one way in which this impulsive power of "the emotions" can be intelligibly accounted for and brought into line with any systematic description of our mental life and structure. That is the way pointed out by Charles Darwin [1] and developed in my "Social Psychology." That way is to recognize that all the bodily changes of any species of animal which we call "expressions of the emotions" are adaptations of the body to the modes of instinctive activity proper to the species. Each mode of instinctive activity requires, for its most efficient execution, the co-operation of all the parts and organs of the body; for, as we have seen, an instinctive action is essentially a "total" reaction, and the processes of every part of the body are subordinated to, and adapted to aid or supplement, the actual

[1] In his "Expression of the Emotions in Men and Animals." Of course, if in the interests of the mechanistic theory, we ignore or deny the fact that emotion and impulse to action are closely correlated, the problem of the relation between them does not arise.

movements of limbs, or other parts, which immediately contribute toward the attainment of the natural goal. Thus, when the instinct of escape is excited, the impulse vents itself, and attains its goal, primarily and chiefly by swift locomotion. But, in order that these locomotory movements (of running, flying, swimming, or what not) shall attain the highest possible effectiveness, it is necessary that all the visceral organs shall be regulated in appropriate fashion. The heart and lungs must work more rapidly; and the blood must be driven away from the digestive and secretory organs and from the skin, by the contraction of their arterioles; it must be concentrated in the lungs, muscles, and brain; the bladder and intestine must be emptied; and the pupil of the eye must be dilated, so that the greatest amount of light may be admitted from every part of the field of vision. All these adjustments are actually made, as parts or features of the total reaction which is the instinctive behavior of escape.

The adjustment of the working of each of these organs is effected by an executive nervous mechanism which is a part of the total native mechanism through which the instinctive impulse most readily finds expression; and, whenever the instinct is excited, these several physiological mechanisms are brought into play with an intensity proportional to the intensity of the instinctive impulse. *It is the sum of these effects which we call the expression of the emotion of fear*—the dilated pupil, the staring eye, the dry mouth, the arrested digestion, the pallor of the skin, the rapid pulse and breathing, the voiding of urine, all these are symptoms of fear—together they constitute the unmistakable expression of fear. Such a complex of symptoms enables us confidently to recognize fear, either in another man or in ourselves; even though the subject suppresses, by an effort, the major movements of locomotion and the cry of fear which we naturally emit when the instinct is suddenly excited.

In recent years the physiologists, especially Professor W. B. Cannon,[1] have shown that the total instinctive reaction involves a further subtle and admirable adjustment which supports and supplements these primary bodily adjustments. This secondary adjustment is effected by chemical means. Thus, the excitement of the instinct of escape sends a nervous current to the suprarenal glands (small glandular masses lying close to the kidneys), which

[1] "Bodily Changes in Pain, Hunger, Fear, and Rage," New York, 1915.

then secrete into the blood a complex substance (adrenalin); this, by direct action upon various tissues, stimulates them to sustain the same kind of activity to which they are primarily stimulated through their own nerves. It causes, among other effects, a conversion of the glycogen stored in the liver into sugar, which at once is taken into the blood and so conveyed to the muscles; the muscles involved in flight, being thus fed with a copious supply of their chief fuel, are enabled to sustain their activity at a high pitch of effectiveness.

These secondary adjustments of the bodily organs are what Darwin called "serviceable associated actions." They are characteristic or specific for each instinct; and are most abundant and intense in the case of those instincts, especially of escape and combat, which require an instant and maximal bodily activity, if the instinctive impulse is to attain its goal with the greatest possible efficiency. Hence we find that the emotions of anger and fear have the most violent, sudden, and uncontrollable expressions; while those instincts whose goals may be attained by actions of a more leisurely kind, involving less prompt and intense bodily activity, are accompanied by emotional excitements whose expressions are less complex, less violent, and less distinctive. The instinct of curiosity, for example, is one that may and must work in a more or less leisurely and quiet fashion, requiring no violent muscular action. Hence its bodily expressions are relatively simple and few and, therefore, less characteristic than those of escape and combat. Again, the gregarious or social instinct does not require, for the attainment of its end, any highly specific mode of action; nor does it require action of extreme promptness and vigor; hence the instinct has not at its service any complicated system of nervous mechanisms for the adjustment of the various bodily organs.

If now we review the instincts of the human species (as enumerated and shortly defined in Chapter V) and the emotional excitements that accompany the operation of the several instincts, we notice a close correspondence between the complexity and specificity of the bodily adjustments which constitute the whole of each instinctive reaction and the distinctness or specificity of quality of these emotional excitements. We may arrange the instincts in a scale, in the descending order of complexity of bodily adjustments; and we find that the corresponding qualities of emotional excitement then form a scale of diminishing degrees of specificity. Accordingly, common speech has definite names, and indeed a variety of synonyms, for the qualities of the upper end of the scale, and no special names for the qualities of the lower end. For the emotional qualities that accompany the play of the instincts of the upper part of the scale are as easily recognizable as are the symptoms or bodily expressions of these instinctive excitements; while the qualities of the lower end of the scale are as little specific as are the bodily expressions: and, if we wish for psychological purposes to refer to the latter, we have to invent names for them; or, where there is no well-recognized emotional quality, we may use the expression "feeling of . . ." The two lists would run in my opinion as follows, but others might arrange the lists in a slightly different order:

Names of Instincts (Synonyms in Parentheses)	*Names of Emotional Qualities Accompanying the Instinctive Activities*
1. Instinct of escape (of self-preservation, of avoidance, danger instinct)	Fear (terror, fright, alarm, trepidation)
2. Instinct of combat (aggression, pugnacity)	Anger (rage, fury, annoyance, irritation, displeasure).
3. Repulsion (repugnance)	Disgust (nausea, loathing, repugnance).
4. Parental (protective)	Tender emotion (love, tenderness, tender feeling).
5. Appeal	Distress (feeling of helplessness).
6. Pairing (mating, reproduction, sexual)	Lust (sexual emotion or excitement, sometimes called love—an unfortunate and confusing usage).
7. Curiosity (inquiry, discovery, investigation)	Curiosity (feeling of mystery, of strangeness, of the unknown, wonder).
8. Submission (self-abasement)	Feeling of subjection (of inferiority, of devotion, of humility, of attachment, of submission, negative self-feeling).
9. Assertion (self-display)	Elation (feeling of superiority, of masterfulness, of pride, of domination, positive self-feeling).
10. Social or gregarious instinct	Feeling of loneliness, of isolation, nostalgia.
11. Food-seeking (hunting)	Appetite or craving in narrower sense (gusto).
12. Acquisition (hoarding instinct)	Feeling of ownership, of possession (protective feeling).
13. Construction	Feeling of creativeness, of making, of productivity.
14. Laughter	Amusement (jollity, carelessness, relaxation).

The minor instincts of scratching, sneezing, coughing, urination, and defecation, are so simple in their bodily expressions that we cannot recognize as specific qualities the excitements which accompany their exercise; though the impulse of each may on occasion be excited in great strength.

The Primary Emotions

It is obvious that this list of emotional qualities does not include all the well-recognized specific qualities of emotion. We must discuss presently those other emotional qualities and the conditions under which they are experienced. We may conveniently speak of the qualities in the foregoing list as the *primary emotional qualities*, or, if we permit ourselves to speak of "emotions" as entities, we may say that they are the primary emotions.

Since the relation between these primary qualities of emotion and the several instinctive impulses was first clearly formulated in my "Social Psychology," many psychologists have raised objections to this view that the primary "emotions" are essentially indicators of the working of instinctive impulses. But no one of these objections has seemed to me to carry weight; and the formulation is so obviously true to any unprejudiced mind that it has been very widely accepted.[1]

The primary "emotion" is then an indicator of the instinctive impulse at work; its bodily expressions serve to indicate the nature of the impulse to our fellows and to evoke in them the same instinctive impulse, attitude, and emotional excitement; and the

[1] As in so many other cases of the definite enunciation of some psychological principle, this formula may be said to have divided psychologists into two parties, one consisting of those who entirely repudiate it, and the other of those to whom it seems so familiar and obvious that they regard it as a platitude or truism. When writers of the former class attempt to formulate the grounds of their objection to this view of the relation of emotion to instinct, they insist mainly on the obvious truth that we cannot adequately imagine the qualities of emotional excitement that accompany the instinctive activities of animals. But our inability to imagine, or appropriately name, such emotional excitements is no ground for doubting or denying that they are experienced by the animals. The demand, that we should be able to do this, is intrinsically absurd; and the absurdity reaches its climax when the demand is made in relation to the instinctive actions of insects, creatures which are so remote from us in constitution, mode of life, and racial history.

emotional quality serves also to indicate, to the subject himself, the nature of his excitement and the kind of action to which he is impelled. This last we may fairly suppose to be the essential function of the emotional qualities in our mental life. They enable us to recognize our own state, and to regulate, direct, and in some degree control the impulses by which we are moved. And the expressions of similar emotions in our fellows enable us to infer, or to foresee, their probable course of action; so that we may prepare to meet their action with appropriate co-operation or opposition. If the emotional excitements accompanying all instinctive reactions were alike in quality, we should make little progress in self-control. A man so constituted might see another approaching him in a threatening manner, and he might feel a strong impulse and violent excitement; but he would not know to what kind of action he was impelled, until he found himself rushing to attack, or fleeing headlong from the field: he would therefore be incapable of the foresighted control and adjustment of action which are the essence of all the higher forms of behavior, properly called "conduct." On the other hand, if all the primary emotional qualities were more distinctive, more widely differentiated, and more prominent as modes of experience, if all were as distinctive as the qualities of fear and anger, we should seldom be in doubt or error as to the motives of our actions.

The emotional qualities have, then, a cognitive function; they signify to us primarily not the nature of things, but rather the nature of our impulsive reactions to things; they are the cognitive basis of self-knowledge and self-control. In this sense they are subjective rather than objective; the function they primarily subserve is cognition not of the object, but of the subject, of the state or activity of the organism.

The Lange-James Theory of Emotion

We are now prepared to consider the famous Lange-James theory of the emotions, and to understand in what sense it is true, and in what respects erroneous. The essence of the theory is the assertion that the "emotions" are essentially of the same nature as "sensations"; that "an emotion," as felt or as an emotional quality, is a mass or complex of confused sensory experience arising from the sensory impressions made by the processes going on in the various organs of the body, and that each distinguishable quality of emotion owes whatever is specific or peculiar in its quality to the specific conjunction of sensory impressions made by a specific conjunction of bodily activities, the visceral organs playing a predominant part in this sensory stimulation. If this statement is modified or supplemented by recognizing that, just as the sensory qualities of the special senses are duplicated in imagery, the sensory qualities of the visceral or bodily senses are also duplicated in imagery, we must, I think, accept it as substantially true.

But James, in stating his theory, went further than this and overstated it in a manner that gave it a needlessly paradoxical air; this, while it attracts many minds, repels others. Taking the confused popular and literary mode of speech, which asserts that our emotions cause, determine, or impel our actions, he simply inverted the popular statement and asserted that our bodily actions cause or determine our emotions. He wrote: "Emotion is a consequence, not the cause, of the bodily expression," and "Common sense says, we lose our fortune, are sorry and weep; we meet a bear, are frightened and run; we are insulted by a rival, are angry and strike. The hypothesis here to be defended says that this order of sequence is incorrect, that the one mental state is not immediately induced by the other, *that the bodily manifestations must first be interposed between*, and that the more rational statement is that we feel sorry because we cry, angry because we strike, afraid because we tremble, and not that we cry, strike, or tremble, because we are sorry, angry, or fearful, as the case may be. *Without the bodily states following on the perception, the latter would be purely cognitive in form*, pale, colorless, destitute of emotional warmth."[1] . . . "Emotion dissociated from all bodily feeling is inconceivable. The more closely I scrutinize my states, the more persuaded I become that whatever moods, affections, and passions I have are in very truth constituted by and made up of those bodily changes which we ordinarily call their expression or consequence; and the more it seems to me that if I were to become corporeally anæsthetic I should be excluded from the life of the affections, harsh and tender alike, and drag out an existence of merely cognitive or intellectual form."[2] "*Each emotion is the resultant of a sum of elements*, and each element is caused by a physiological process of a sort already well known. The elements are all organic changes, and each of them is the reflex effect of the exciting object."[3]

In these extracts we may see three respects in which James overstated his theory and fell into error; they are indicated in the three passages I have italicized. Consider the last of these first. The passage seems to imply not only James's sensationism, but sensationism of the crudest form combined with the crudest form of the reflex theory. The first of the italicized passages implies that the various bodily changes which are "the expression of the emotion" must actually occur on each particular occasion before the emotional quality can be experienced; that is to say, the statement makes no recognition of what we may call imagery of the bodily senses. It is as though James should assert that every time we think of the color of an orange or of the sound of a bell, such thinking must be preceded by the appropriate stimulation of the retina or of the ear. He ignores the fact that sensational qualities may be centrally excited in the form of imagery, independently of stimulation of the sense-organs.

Thirdly, and this is the most serious error, James, having reduced all cona-

[1] "Principles," Vol. II, p. 450. [2] *Op. cit.*, p. 452. [3] *Op. cit.*, p. 453.

tive experience, all "sense of effort," all feeling of impulse, all experience of striving, to motor "sensations," includes these motor "sensations" with the mass of organic "sensations" that are supposed to constitute the emotional experience. I have already argued that conative experience cannot be reduced to or identified with sensory experience. And I have pointed out that the felt impulse is an essential part of all instinctive reactions. If, then, as James suggests in the second italicized passage, all the sensational qualities were cut out of an emotional experience through anæsthesia of the whole body, the remaining experience would not be, as he says, purely cognitive in form; and this for two reasons: first, it might retain the specific emotional quality, because this might be centrally excited; secondly, the experience would remain strongly conative as well as cognitive; that is to say, the subject would continue to be aware of a strong impulse to action of some kind. This conative factor in emotional experience is perhaps its most essential mark. If this could be subtracted, leaving the specific emotional quality, we should perhaps recognize the emotion, but it would seem as though all the life and strength and all that constitutes its urgency and vital significance were gone out of it.[1]

Putting these criticisms together, I would say that, while James's theory is fundamentally correct, his statement of it errs in implying a more intimate dependence of our mental process upon bodily changes than is actually the case. Further, he ignores the conative factor, the part of impulse in emotion, considered either as a phase of experience or as a phase of behavior. He ignores the fact that an impulsive striving toward a goal is the essence of every emotional reaction. When we say "I feel angry," or explain our striking at an offender by saying "I struck because I was angry," we do not mean that the emotional quality of our experience was the active agent that caused the striking; rather, we mean quite properly that the being angry does, as a matter of empirical fact and experience, involve an impulsive tendency to strike; and our explanation is true and valid; we implicitly use the emotional quality that we recognize as the indicator of the instinctive tendency that has been aroused in us. Hence the ordinary statement, "I struck because I was angry," is essentially truer, gives a truer explanation of my action, than James's inverted statement, "I am angry because I struck." For the former statement means that the person whom I struck had so behaved as to provoke in me the impulse of the combative instinct; and to assign an action to the impulse of which it is the outcome and expression is the only valid proximate explanation of any of our actions.

I do not propose to attempt any description of the emotional qualities nor of the bodily expressions of "the emotions." If the reader does not know what it is to be afraid, or angry, or disgusted, if he does not recognize a quite peculiar quality of experience when he hastens to comfort a little child sobbing in distress, no amount of description, however eloquent, will enlighten

[1] It is probable that an approximation to this state of affairs does actually occur in those morbid conditions in which the patient complains of the unreality of all things.

him. I will only remark that the confusions and misunderstandings in our discussions of "emotions" are due, no doubt, in some degree to differences of natural endowment. We are endowed with, or inherit, the various instincts in different degrees of strength; and it seems probable that, in the innate constitution of some individuals, one or other of the normal human instincts may be completely lacking, or so feeble and so little strengthened by exercise that the corresponding primary quality of emotion is unknown to them.

There is a curious dogma which crops up from time to time in the discussions of emotion and which requires a remark in passing. It asserts that emotions are experienced only when our natural tendencies to action are obstructed or in some way suspended.[1] I have recognized that this is true of angry emotion; that such obstruction is the specific condition of excitement of the combative instinct; and that the impulse of this instinct serves to re-enforce all other impulses, when they are obstructed. But as regards other emotions, I can see no jot of valid evidence that supports this doctrine. It would seem to be a distortion of the simple truth that we do not become explicitly aware of our emotions, so long as we give ourselves wholly to action. We become self-consciously aware of the quality of our emotion only when we are not wholly absorbed in action, in the pursuit of our goal, and in the choice of means toward it. But that is not to say that the emotional quality is not there, qualifying all our experience while we strive. It would be equally false to assert that the sensory qualities of experience are not experienced in perception of an object, until we cease to think of the object and become introspectively interested in the qualities as such.

Hitherto we have discussed only the emotional experiences that accompany our instinctive strivings. These perhaps may, without serious risk of misunderstanding, be spoken of as "emotions," that is to say, as recognizable modes of experience, and they may be appropriately called "the primary emotions." Beside these we have to recognize two other principal classes of emotions, namely, the blended or secondary emotions and the derived emotions.

The Blended or Secondary Emotions

We have already noted the fact that two instinctive impulses may be excited simultaneously; as when an animal's behavior is clearly the expression of a conflict and alternation between

[1] The latest exponent of this view is Doctor James Drever in his "Instinct in Man," a book with which I am happy to find myself in general agreement.

the aversion of fear and the attraction of curiosity. Horses in a meadow often exhibit such behavior unmistakably. In ourselves the greater development of imagination and of the sentiments renders us more liable than the animals to be moved simultaneously by more than one impulse; and the behavior of a cultivated adult expresses at almost all times more or less complex conjunctions of impulses. Some of the instinctive impulses are so directly opposed in tendency that they cannot harmoniously co-operate in the determination of behavior; if simultaneously excited, they inevitably conflict; and the dominance of one necessarily inhibits the other. This is, perhaps, most clearly and invariably true of the impulse of disgust or repugnance and that of the food-instinct. The two instincts are directed toward two opposite goals; and the actions in which they naturally find expression are wholly incompatible with one another and cannot be combined. Hence the one impulse inevitably inhibits the other. When we are seasick, we cannot even remotely imagine ourselves desirous of food. When we are replete, the sight of a beefsteak, the odor of the kitchen, or the least trace of dirt upon food, is apt to excite disgust; but, when we are hungry, we cannot imagine how we could be so squeamish.

No other two of the instinctive impulses are so utterly opposed as these; and some of them are quite capable of co-operating harmoniously to determine behavior which is a blend of the actions proper to the several impulses at work. When two or more impulses cooperate in this way, we experience an emotional excitement whose quality is, in a sense, a blending of the primary qualities proper to the several instincts concerned. The case is parallel to the case of the complex sensory qualities. It is a convenient, though not a correct, way of stating the facts to say that purple is a blending or fusion of the sensations of red and blue qualities; or that a musical clang or chord is a blending or fusion of the partial tones which we can discover in the complex by introspective analysis. It is more correct to say that the complex quality is the reaction of the mind to a complex of sensory impressions. In a similar way it is convenient, though not strictly correct, to say that, when we find our purpose obstructed by a mean dirty action, we experience an emotion which is a blending of the primary emotions of anger and disgust. For, under these conditions, the impulses of the instincts of combat and of repugnance are simultaneously excited, our actions tend to express both tendencies, and the emotional expressions proper to both tendencies are blended on our faces and in all our bodily reactions; at the same time we experience an emotional quality which is allied to both anger and disgust and which may vary from moment to moment, anger predominating at one moment, disgust at the next; according as we have more prominently in mind the obstruction of our purpose or the meanness and "dirtiness" of the behavior of our opponent. At one moment we feel we would strike him down or tear him to pieces; at the next we shrink from contact with such a disgusting object.

Such a complex emotional experience is not literally formed by the separate excitement, the coming together, and the subsequent blending of the two emotions, anger and disgust; rather it is the immediate response to the complex situation. But, with this understanding, it seems legitimate, in order to avoid a cumbrous phraseology, to speak of such complex emotional reactions as blended emotions, or as emotional compounds formed by the blending of two or more of the primary qualities of emotion.[1]

It is obvious that, if the primary emotional qualities may be blended (in the sense defined above) to form binary, tertiary, and even more complex qualities, the variety of emotional experiences which we may learn to recognize and to name must be very large. It is obvious also that, since the various qualities may be blended in various proportions, these complex emotional qualities cannot be enumerated as an array of distinct qualities; but rather that, like the color qualities of the solar spectrum, they form a continuous quality series in which the transition from one part to another is gradual. It is natural therefore that, as with the color series, our nomenclature is confused, shifting, and uncertain. Yet for some of these qualities we have names which serve to suggest them with some degree of accuracy. The quality in which we detect affinity to both anger and disgust is well sug-

[1] I have dwelt tediously on this point because some of the critics of my "Social Psychology" have complained that my treatment of the secondary emotions is guilty of the errors of Mills' "Mental Chemistry."

gested to most of us by the name "scorn." Other emotional qualities of similar complex nature are denoted by such names as contempt, loathing, horror, awe, admiration, reverence, gratitude, reproach, envy, resentment, vengeful emotion, embarrassment, shame, jealousy, and many others. It would be an instructive exercise to attempt to analyze each of these complex qualities, supplementing our introspection by observation of the bodily expressions and actions proper to each of the emotions so named. But I must be content to cite a few examples of such analysis from an earlier work.[1]

"Scorn is very apt to be complicated by positive self-feeling (or elation); we feel ourselves magnified by the presence of the moral weakness or littleness of the other, just as on a lower plane the physical weakness or smallness of those about one excites this positive self-feeling, with its tendency to expand the chest, throw up the head, and strut in easy confidence. The name 'scorn' is often applied to an affective state of which this emotion is an element; but if this element is dominant, we are said to despise the object, and the name commonly given to the emotion is 'contempt,' the substantive corresponding to the verb 'despise'; scorn, then, is a binary compound of anger and disgust, or a tertiary compound, if positive self-feeling is added to these; while contempt is a binary compound of disgust and positive self-feeling, differing from scorn in the absence of the element of anger.

"Fear and disgust are very apt to be combined, as on the near view of a snake or an alligator; and in some persons this binary emotion is provoked by a large number of animals, rats, moths, worms, spiders, and so on, and also by the mere appearance of some men, though more often by their characters. It is the emotion we call 'loathing,' and, in its most intense form, 'horror.'

"Admiration is certainly a true emotion, and is as certainly not primary. It is distinctly a complex affective state and implies a considerable degree of mental development. We can hardly suppose any of the animals to be capable of admiration in the proper sense of the word, nor is it displayed by very young children. It is not merely a pleasurable perception or contemplation. One may get a certain pleasure from the perception or contemplation of an object without feeling any admiration for it; *e. g.*, a popular ditty played on a barrel-organ may give one pleasure, though one admires neither the ditty nor the mode of its production, and though one may a little despise oneself on account of the pleasure one feels. Nor is it merely intellectual and pleasurable appreciation of the greatness or excellence of the object. There seem to be two primary emotions essentially involved in the complex state provoked by the contemplation of the admired object, namely, wonder and negative self-feeling or the emotion of submission. Wonder is revealed by the impulse to approach and to continue to contemplate the admired object; for, as we saw, this is the characteristic impulse of the instinct of curiosity, and wonder

[1] The reader may find others in my "Social Psychology," Chap. V, from which these passages are taken.

is clearly expressed on the face in intense admiration. In children one may observe the element of wonder very clearly expressed and dominant. 'Oh, how wonderful!' or 'Oh, how clever!' or 'How did you do it?' are phrases in which a child naturally expresses its admiration and by which the element of wonder and the impulse of curiosity are clearly revealed. And as soon as we feel that we completely understand the object we have admired and can wholly account for it, our wonder ceases and the emotion evoked by it is no longer admiration.

"But admiration is more than wonder. We do not simply proceed to examine the admired object, as we should one that provokes merely our curiosity or wonder. We approach it slowly, with a certain hesitation; we are humbled by its presence, and, in the case of a person whom we intensely admire we become shy, like a child in the presence of an adult stranger; we have the impulse to shrink together, to be still, and to avoid attracting his attention; that is to say, the instinct of submission, of self-abasement, is excited, with its corresponding emotion of negative self-feeling, by the perception that we are in the presence of a superior power, something greater than ourselves. Now, this instinct and this emotion are primarily and essentially social. The primary condition of their excitement is the presence of a person bigger and more powerful than oneself; and when we admire such an object as a picture or a machine, or other work of art, the emotion still has this social character and personal reference; the creator of the work of art is more or less clearly present to our minds as the object of our emotion, and often we say, 'What a wonderful man he is!'

"Is, then, the emotion of admiration capable of being evoked in us only by other persons and their works? It is obviously true that we admire natural objects, a beautiful flower or landscape, or a shell, or the perfect structure of an animal and its nice adaptation to its mode of life. In these cases no known person is called to mind as the object of our admiration; but, just because admiration implies and refers to another person, is essentially, in so far as it involves negative self-feeling, an attitude toward a person, it leads us to postulate a person or personal power as the creator of the object that calls it forth. Hence, in all ages the admiration of men for natural objects has led them to personify the power, or powers, that have brought those objects into being, either as superhuman beings who have created, and who preside over, particular classes of objects, or as a supreme Creator of all things; and, if the intellect rejects all such conceptions as anthropomorphic survivals from a ruder age, the admiration of natural objects still leads men to personify, under the name of Nature, the power that has produced them. It is, I think, true that, if this sense of a personal power is not suggested by any object that we contemplate, the emotion we experience is merely wonder, or at least is not admiration. It is because negative self-feeling is an essential element in admiration that the extremely confident, self-satisfied, and thoroughly conceited person is incapable of admiration, and that genuine admiration implies a certain humility and generosity. It may be added that much admiration—all æsthetic admiration, in fact—includes also an element of pleasure, the conditions of which may be very complex.

"As an example of the further complication of an emotion, let us consider the nature of our emotion if the object that excites our admiration is also of a threatening or mysterious nature and, therefore, capable of exciting fear—a tremendous force in action, such as the Victoria Falls, or a display of the *aurora borealis*, or a magnificent thunderstorm. The impulse of admiration to draw near humbly and to contemplate the object is more or less neutralized by an impulse to withdraw, to run away—the impulse of fear. We are kept suspended in the middle distance, neither approaching very near nor going quite away; admiration is blended with fear, and we experience the emotion we call AWE.

"Awe is of many shades, ranging from that in which admiration is but slightly tinged with fear to that in which fear is but slightly tinged with admiration. Admiration is, then, a binary compound, awe a tertiary compound. And awe may be further blended to form a still more complex emotion. Suppose that the power that excites awe is also one that we have reason to regard as beneficent, one that, while capable of annihilating us in a moment, yet works for our good, sustains and protects us, one that evokes our gratitude. Awe then becomes compounded with gratitude and we experience the highly compound emotion of REVERENCE. Reverence is the religious emotion *par excellence;* few merely human powers are capable of exciting reverence, this blend of wonder, fear, gratitude, and negative self feeling. Those human beings who inspire reverence, or who are by custom and convention considered to be entitled to inspire it, usually owe their reverend character to their being regarded as the ministers and dispensers of Divine power.

"What, then, is GRATITUDE, which enters into the emotion of reverence for the Divine power? Gratitude is itself complex. It is a binary compound of tender emotion and negative self-feeling. To this view it may be objected—If tender emotion is the emotion of the parental instinct whose impulse is to protect, how can this emotion be evoked by the Divine power? The answer to this question is—In the same way as the child's tender emotion toward the parent is evoked, namely, by sympathy. Tender emotion occupies a peculiar position among the primary emotions, in that, being directed toward some other person and its impulse directly making for the good of that other, it is peculiarly apt to evoke by sympathetic reaction, of the kind we studied in Chapter IV, the same emotion in its object; and this sympathetically evoked tender emotion then finds its object most readily in the person to whom it owes its rise. But gratitude is not simply tender emotion sympathetically excited; a child or even an animal may excite our tender emotion in this way; *e. g.*, it may give us something that is utterly useless or embarrassing to us, and by doing so may touch our hearts, as we say; but I do not think that we then feel gratitude, even if the gift involves self-sacrifice on the part of the giver. Mr. Shand maintains that into gratitude there enters some sympathetic sorrow for the person who excites it, on account of the loss or sacrifice sustained by him in giving us that for which we are grateful. It is in this way he would account for the tender element in gratitude; for, according to his view, all tenderness is a blending of joy and sorrow, which are for him primary emotions But surely we may experience gratitude for a kindness done to us that involves no loss or sacrifice for the giver, but is for him an act of purely pleasurable beneficence. I submit, then, that the other element in gratitude, the element that renders it different from, and more complex than, simple tenderness, is that negative self-feeling which is evoked by the sense of the superior power of another. The act that is to inspire gratitude must make us aware not only of the kindly feeling, the tender emotion, of the other toward us; it must also make us aware of his power, we must see that he is able to do for us something that we cannot do for ourselves. This element of negative self-feeling, then, is blended with tenderness in true gratitude, and its impulse, the impulse to withdraw from the attention of, or to humble oneself in the presence of, its object, more or less neutralizes the impulse of the tender emotion to approach its object; the attitude typical and symbolical of gratitude is that of kneeling to kiss the hand that gives. This element of negative self-feeling renders gratitude an emotion that is not purely pleasurable to many natures, makes it one that a proud man does not easily experience, and one that does less to develop a sentiment of affection than the giver of good things is apt to expect. And if the seemingly beneficent act is done, not from pure kindliness or tenderness, but with condescension, if positive self-feeling and a gratified sense of power accompany or enter into the motive of the act, it is apt to evoke negative self-feeling without tenderness, a negative self-feeling painful in quality that may lead to the growth of a sentiment of dislike rather than of love.

"Into reverence of the kind we have considered negative self-feeling enters from two sources, as an element of admiration and again as an element of gratitude. But there is a different kind of reverence into which tenderness enters directly, and not merely as an element of gratitude. Let us imagine ourselves standing before a great Gothic cathedral whose delicate and beautiful stonework is crumbling to dust. We shall probably feel admiration for it; and the spectacle of its decay, or of its delicate and perishable nature, awakens directly our tender emotion and protective impulse; *i. e.*, we experience a tender admiration, a complex emotion for which we have no special name. Now let us imagine ourselves entering the cathedral, passing between vast columns of stone where the dim mysterious light is lost in dark recesses and where reign a stillness and a gloom like that of a great forest; an element of fear is added to our emotion of tender admiration, and this converts it to reverence (or, if our tender emotion does not persist, to awe). This is a reverence that has less of the personal note, because less of negative self-feeling, than that of which gratitude is a component."[1]

An emotion of the first importance which belongs to this group is "pity." We feel pity for those who are in pain or distress; and we feel pity the more readily the more fragile, delicate, and helpless is the object we contemplate. Of all persons the most easily moved to pity are tender-hearted women; and the object which moves them most quickly and strongly to pity is the spectacle of a mother distressed or burdened by the care of her offspring. So ready are they to pity and so subtly does their imagination work that "as a father pitieth his children," so they pity even the happy young mother absorbed in the care of

[1] One is tempted to ask, Was it because the external aspect of the Gothic cathedral is apt to fall short of exciting the fear which is essential to reverence that in so many cases the artists of the Middle Ages covered the exterior with grotesque and horrible figures, like those of Notre Dame of Paris?

her infant. For they know well the pains and anxieties through which she has passed and still must pass, before she shall accomplish that task which ends only with the grave, a task which, though it may bring much joy, is yet a series of self-sacrificing and often painful efforts. Watch such a woman as she sees the mother bird hovering anxiously near the nest, while strangers peep at her brood, or sees the cow whose calf is kept from her. "Poor thing!" is her inevitable cry; and she will take endless pains to prevent or cut short the suffering that she so delicately shares and understands, or will blaze out into fierce anger against him who needlessly prolongs it. But, of all objects, the little child, in pain or fear or distress of any kind, is the surest most universal provocative of pity. These facts give us the clue to the nature of pity. Pity is the tender emotion of the parental or protective instinct, tinged with sympathetic pain or distress. If the object pitied is one we love and whose pain we can promptly relieve, pity is a sweet and joyful emotion, in which our sympathetic pain becomes swallowed up in, and overcome by, the satisfaction of successful ministration. But, if the suffering is severe and of such a nature that we are helpless to relieve it, then pity is a very painful emotion; for our sympathetic pain is augmented by the pain that comes from the thwarting of the protective impulse. And so it happens that the tender heart that pities helplessly may suffer more acutely than the object of its pity.[1]

Some of the secondary emotions can hardly be experienced save in relation to objects for which we have acquired sentiments or enduring affective-conative attitudes. Reproach may serve as the type of such emotions. It seems to be essentially a blend (in the sense defined above) of tender feeling with anger. The impulses of the two instincts concerned are so opposed in tendency that they necessarily conflict; each tends to exclude the other. Hence we hardly feel reproach toward a stranger. If a strange child upsets the ink over our manuscript, or persists

[1] The word "sympathy" is popularly used as almost synonymous with "pity"; but it seems better for psychological purposes to restrict "sympathy" to the primitive passive sympathy and to the active sympathy which I have discussed on other pages.

in making noises that interrupt our work, we are apt to feel merely angry and to act accordingly. But, if the child is one whom we have learned to love, one whom we cannot see or think of, without the stirring of the parental impulse with its tender emotion; then our angry impulse is checked by this very different impulse, its expressions are modified, and the quality of our emotion is that complex one we call reproach; in this the blended qualities of anger and tender feeling are further complicated by the pain that arises from the conflict of their impulses.[1] Jealousy, shame, and vengeful emotion are other members of this class; for their analysis I must again refer the student to the same work.

[1] "A more complex form (of reproach) arises when the sentiment is reciprocated, or supposed to be reciprocated, and its object acts in a way that seems to show indifference to us. In this case the pain of the wound given to our self-regarding sentiment and of the check to our tender emotion is the prominent feature of the affective state and overshadows anger; perhaps the name 'reproach' is most properly given to this more complex state." ("Social Psychology," p. 137.)

CHAPTER XII

THE DERIVED EMOTIONS

Literature and common speech recognize and name as distinct emotions a number of states of mind or modes of experience which can be classed neither with the primary nor with the blended emotions, as defined in the foregoing pages. The chief of these are joy, sorrow, chagrin, disappointment, surprise, regret, remorse, confidence, hope, anxiety, despondency, despair. None of these can be shown by analytic introspection to be a blend of any two or more of the primary emotional qualities. Nor do they conform to the type of the primary emotion. For it is impossible to point out any one instinctive impulse with which any one of these "emotions" is constantly conjoined, as anger with the impulse of aggression, fear with the impulse of escape, curiosity with the impulse to draw near and examine. It is, I think, largely owing to the fact that the emotions of this class cannot be brought under the formula relating the primary emotions with the instincts that so many psychologists hesitate to accept that formulation. It would be useless to suggest that the emotions of this class should not be called "emotions" but rather varieties of *feeling;* the usage is now too firmly established in common speech. The best we can do by way of avoiding the confusion and marking the difference between the two classes, on the one hand the true emotions, the primary and the blended, and on the other hand the varieties of feeling we are now considering, is to speak of the latter as emotions of a third distinct class, that of the *derived emotions.* The word derived is here used to denote the fact that an emotion of this class is not constantly correlated with any one impulse or tendency, but rather may arise in the course of the operation of any strong impulse or tendency; the emotion being dependent upon or derived from the working of the impulse under certain conditions which we have now to specify.

Prospective Emotions of Desire

Let us consider first the following five emotions: *confidence, hope, anxiety, despondency,* and *despair.* All these presuppose the operation of some strong impulse or desire; and, since they presuppose also a certain level of development of intelligence, namely, that level upon which the goal of impulse is more or less clearly imagined and impulse takes the form of desire, we may say that they presuppose desire and arise only in the course of activity prompted and sustained by desire. The desire itself is independent of, and must come into operation before, the rise of these emotions. And during the working of any one strong desire (no matter what may be the nature of the instinctive impulse at work and what the nature of the object or goal to which it is directed) all these five emotions are apt to be experienced. They are, in fact, only so many named points in a scale of feeling or emotion of which confidence and despair are the two extremes. The transition from one point in the scale to another is perfectly gradual; though it may be effected, according to circumstances, either rapidly or slowly.

I have cited in an earlier chapter, as illustrating the working of desire, Major Priestly's description of a party of Polar explorers tormented by desire for a good meal. Let us take this type of crude but strong desire, springing directly from an instinct, and develop imaginatively the emotional experience of such a party; we may suppose it to have used up its supply of food, while returning on foot from the Pole and still separated by fifty miles of snow-covered ice from a store of food, deposited on the outward journey. All members of the party strongly desire to reach this store of food. This strong desire springs primarily from the food-instinct; but it is reinforced by the intellectual understanding that the survival of the party depends upon their reaching this goal; for this understanding brings to the support of the primitive hunger-impulse many remoter desires, the desire to see wife and child again, to report the scientific results of their labors, to announce their success to an admiring world; in fact, all those desires which together constitute what common speech calls "the love of life" or "the fear of death." All members of the party are strong, the weather is good, the snow under foot is hard, the position and distance of the food-store are well known. Impelled by strong desire they tramp on with *confidence.* That is to say, they see no reason to doubt their ability to reach their immediate goal, the store of food, which means not only a good meal but also safety.

When they have travelled but half-way to their goal, an adverse wind springs up, bringing clouds and a threat of snow. Each man knows that, if the wind should blow stronger and the snow fall thickly, they will need all their strength to achieve their goal. Success no longer seems certain. Their confidence is no longer sure and untroubled. But they *hope* for the best. That is to say, the prospect of possible failure converts confidence to hope.

As they march on hopefully, the adverse wind grows stronger, and the snow falls more thickly. Each man secretly becomes a prey to *anxiety.* He still does his best to be and to appear hopeful. But now his desire prompts not only the imagination of a good meal and of a successful issue to all their labors, but also a careful consideration of all the possibilities and chances of failure as well as of success. During the phases of confidence and of hope, their striving was sustained and reinforced by the pleasurable anticipation of success; perhaps they joked about the enormous meal they were presently to enjoy. Now, if they converse at all, it is only to discuss the prospect of the wind and snow abating; and the painful contemplation of possible failure depresses their energies. But the transition from confidence to hope and to anxiety is gradual; hope and anxiety alternate with every veering of the wind and every gust of snow; there is no sharp line to be drawn between the two states. We might recognize finer divisions of the emotional scale by speaking of anxious hope and hopeful anxiety.

The weather grows still worse; the men feel their strength ebbing; every step is a painful effort. At length one blurts out: "We shall never make it!" And all in their hearts know that there is but too good ground for his remark. "Oh! Shut up!" they say, "We must make it." And they trudge on. But now anxiety passes into despondency. Presently they agree to sit on their sledge to rest awhile; and the attitude of despondency is clearly expressed by each relaxed figure, the bent back, the drooping head, the eyes staring vacantly. Their imaginations now are filled with painful depressing anticipations of final failure. They rise and struggle on, with utmost exertions of will-power.

But now they come upon a wide opening in the ice, stretching indefinitely far in either direction across their course. Now they know that they cannot reach their goal. In consequence, despondency passes into despair; and they fall on the snow, content to pass into that last sleep which will end their labors.

The five derived emotions we have depicted above have been well named by Mr. A. F. Shand "the prospective emotions of desire";[1] for all of them imply desire that looks forward to a goal. In the instance we have imagined, these "emotions" would occur in great intensity; for the desire from which they derive was, we assumed, of great strength or urgency. But a similar gamut of "emotions" may be experienced in the course of the working of any sustained desire. Thus, if you set out on foot to catch a train at the railroad station, you may pass through, or up and down, this scale of "emotions," according as your prospect of catching the train appears to you to vary from a certainty of success to a certainty of failure. And the "emotions" will be strong in proportion to the strength of your desire. If your desire to catch the train derives from the desire to keep some trivial appointment or perform some trivial errand, the prospective emotions of desire will be faint and hardly recognizable. But, if you have given your word of honor to keep that appointment or punctually to perform that errand, or if you are to meet a much-loved friend, long unseen, and the catching of that train is the indispensable means to your goal, your desire to catch it will be strong and your prospective emotions of desire correspondingly intense.

Retrospective Emotions of Desire

Although primitively desire looks only toward some goal imagined as lying in the future, yet, in the developed mind, desire may be directed towards the past. Hence we must recognize

ndations of Character," Second Edition, London, 1921.

also *retrospective emotions of desire.* Of this group of derived emotions REGRET, REMORSE, and SORROW are the principal members. Regret naturally follows upon despair, when the attainment of the desired goal is no longer possible, when the possibility of attaining that goal lies wholly in the past. For then desire still prompts the imagination to dwell upon the goal; but the desire is wholly retrospective and, being futile and necessarily thwarted, is painful in proportion to its strength. Such painful retrospective desire is REGRET.

In regret we dwell longingly upon what might have been. In our Polar explorers regret will succeed despair, if they retain sufficient vitality to be mentally active as they lie awaiting death. They will regret that they did not do this or that, did not make their food-stores at shorter intervals, did not push on a little more rapidly while the weather was good; a thousand regrets, as we say, or one painful retrospective desire after another, may occupy their minds. And if the leader, or any member of the party, sees clearly that the disaster was due to some fault of his, some misjudgment, some failure of moral or physical strength on his part, then self-reproach or angry humiliation or shame will complicate his regret and so generate that most painful and very complex state of feeling we call REMORSE.

SORROW is a retrospective emotion of desire, for it is essentially tender regret. By a loose usage the word is sometimes extended to cover that primary emotion which we have called distress (p. 163). But sorrow, in the proper sense of the word, can be experienced only by the subject who is sufficiently developed to have acquired a sentiment of love or devotion. We have to discuss the nature and formation of such sentiments in a later chapter. Here it must suffice to say that the sentiment of love for an object consists essentially in the habitual direction of the parental impulse upon that object; though every sentiment of love tends to become complex, through the inclusion within its system of other impulses.

The purest type of love is the love of the mother for her child; and the very type of sorrow is the emotion of the mother bereft of her much-loved child. Imagine the emotions of a mother who loses her child through a fatal sickness. During the course of the sickness she will pass through all the prospective emotions of desire, the desires of love to protect, to relieve, to preserve its object. At the time of the fatal issue, distress may be the dominant emotion; the mother, having exhausted all her resources in vain, gives herself up to weeping and to crying on God and man for help. This phase soon gives place to pure sorrow or tender regret; the tender emotion and impulse of her love bring its object frequently, almost constantly, to mind; and in imagination she dwells upon all that she would do, if the object still were with her, and on all that she might have done before she lost it. All such retrospective desires are painful, because they are necessarily thwarted; but, with the passage of time, the tender impulse learns to find some degree of satisfaction in recollections of past joys, of tender services given and reciprocated, and by expressing itself in speech and in such acts as tend to keep alive and do honor to the memory of the lost one. Thus the sorrow becomes sweetened by partial satisfaction of the desires of love and by the discovery of new ways of attaining such satisfaction.

It is an undesirably loose usage to extend the name "sorrow" indiscriminately to all painful retrospective desires; for sorrow essentially involves the tender emotion. The painful retrospective desire of hate should therefore not be called sorrow, but is more properly called CHAGRIN; it is that state in which we regret the success of the hated person or the failure of our striving to thwart him. The name GRIEF is properly used to denote an emotion closely allied to sorrow, but differing from it in that, in the sentiment from which it springs, the tender protective impulse is subordinated to the impulses of extended self-regard. (Cf. Chapter XVII.)

Joy a Derived Emotion

JOY also is one of the derived emotions; for, like the others, it implies or presupposes the working within us of some strong desire; and, like sorrow, joy, in the full sense of the word, is derived from the desires of some strong and enduring sentiment. We may sometimes speak of the joy of a hungry man when dinner is announced, or of the joy of a child in a new toy. But this again is a loose usage which degrades the word. For "pleasure" is the appropriate word for such occasions; and joy is more than the pleasure that comes with the satisfaction, or the anticipation of satisfaction, of our unorganized desires and sporadic impulses. The joy that springs from love is the true opposite of sorrow in respect of its conditions; for, as sorrow comes from the baffling of the tender desires of love, joy attends the success of our tender efforts on behalf of the loved person; it is essentially the progressive satisfaction of the desires of love. But joy differs from sorrow not only in that it comes with the success, while sorrow comes with the baffling, of the desires of love, but in two other respects also. Sorrow is essentially an emotion of retrospective desire; but joy derives from both retrospective and prospective desires. Further, while sorrow derives from the desires of love only, joy attends the success (or the recollection or the prospect of success) of the desires of hate, as well as of those of love, especially perhaps the desires of the complex form of hate properly called revenge.

A kind of joy, which in some natures is apt to be peculiarly intense, springs from the desires of the sentiment commonly spoken of as "self-love," but more properly called "self-regard." Joy of this kind is perhaps more properly called "elation." Its main condition is the regard of other persons who admire (or are imagined by us as admiring) our achievements or the excellencies of our persons. Its essence is the gratification of the self-assertive impulse organized within the self-regarding sentiment.

Surprise

Surprise is an emotional experience concerning which I must confess to some perplexity. Like Joy and Sorrow, it has usually been classed with the primary emotions, ever since Descartes distinguished primary and secondary or blended emotions. But it seems clear that surprise presupposes some more or less definite anticipation of the course of events; surprise is experienced only when we suddenly apprehend a state of affairs that contradicts our anticipation. Now the anticipation or expectation implies, as we have seen, the working of some impulse, some desire or aversion, that prompts us to anticipate. Surprise therefore is dependent upon, or derived from, the anticipating desire; it is therefore a derived emotion. In nearly all cases of intense surprise, the derived emotion is complicated by fear or by curiosity, or by both of these; and it is very apt to pass over into one or other of these primary emotions. It is this complication of surprise that tends to obscure the fact that it belongs to the class of derived emotions.[1]

The Distinction Between Primary and Derived Emotions

We have now discussed the principal varieties of derived emotion. The student should clearly grasp the distinction between them and the primary emotions. The principal points of distinction are these: (1) The primary emotion arises as the immediate consequence of thinking of some object or situation; and it does not presuppose, is not conditioned by, any impulse already operative, when that object or situation is apprehended.[2] The derived emotion, on the other hand, in all cases presupposes and is conditioned by some impulse, some desire or aversion, already at work within us, and is the product of the influence of a new cognition concerning the object to which that impulse is directed. (2) Secondly, each primary emotion springs from, and is the indication of the excitement of, a corresponding instinctive disposition; whereas each derived emotion bears no such constant relation to any one instinctive disposition, but, rather, may arise in the developed mind in the course of the operation of any one of the instinctive impulses. (3) The primary emotion may be spoken of (somewhat loosely but without serious error) as a force, since it is constantly accompanied by an impulse toward some specific goal, an impulse which, as we have seen, is an essential feature of what we commonly speak of as the emotion; and common speech and literary tradition, as well as the language of many psychologists, recognize the propriety of regarding the primary emotions as driving forces or energies. The derived

[1] I doubt whether the most skilful artist could depict "surprise" in a way that would be surely distinguishable from both fear and curiosity.

[2] With the exception of anger.

emotions, on the other hand, cannot properly be regarded as forces. They are merely incidents in the working of the instinctive impulses, which are the only true forces that prompt and sustain thought and action.[1]

The force or energy which literary convention and common speech attribute to such emotions as hope or anxiety or joy is in reality the energy of the desire from which the derived emotion springs; this energy is reinforced in hope and joy by the pleasurable anticipation of success; moderated or checked in anxiety and despondency by the anticipation of failure; and rendered painful in sorrow by the baffling of all action.[2]

(4) Fourthly, since each of the primary emotions springs from a disposition which is an enduring feature of the constitution of the organism, it is not gravely misleading to speak of such emotions as becoming organized within the sentiments; although it is more strictly correct to say that the affective-conative disposition of the corresponding instinct becomes thus organized or incorporated. (Cf. Chapter XVII.) On the other hand, it would be a grave error to assume that any derived emotion (or any disposition corresponding to any derived emotion) can become thus organized within the structure of the mind; for no derived emo-

[1] It is true that in common speech and still more in literature the derived emotions are recognized as forces. The poets especially are apt to personify such emotions as hope, despondency, joy, sorrow, and surprise, as agents that govern our thought and action, just as they personify the primary emotions. But, though the psychologist should give heed to the poets, he should not slavishly submit to the poetic conventions. There is probably no quality of character or conduct that has not been personified by some poet, painter, or sculptor. We may admire Shelley's magnificent ode, "Adonais," without accepting as an independent force or element of personality each of the figures so beautifully depicted by him. We may see confirmation of the distinction made in these pages between the primary and the derived emotions in the fact that artists, while they have no difficulty in representing by facial expressions, the principal primary emotions, have to resort to indirect means for the suggestion of the derived emotions. Thus, when so great an artist as G. F. Watts depicted Hope, he painted a maiden whose face was veiled and whose significance was suggested symbolically by her position and attitude and by her broken lyre.

[2] What then of "the energy of despair"? the reader may ask. I reply that this is a misleading phrase, that despair has no energy; that if, in despair, any energy of desire persists, it turns to regret. The so-called "energy of despair" is the energy of the man who, when his situation becomes "desperate," throws aside all precautions, all self-control, all previously conceived plan of action, and abandons himself to the crude instinctive impulse and the primary emotion.

tion springs from any one enduring disposition; rather, as we have seen, each of them is incidental to the operation of any one, or all, of the conative dispositions.[1]

The Use of the Word "Feeling"

Pleasure and pain are, by common consent, the true types of feeling. The word "feeling" has been used by some psychologists in a very wide loose way. Many of the atomists or mosaic psychologists have, like Herbert Spencer, used "feeling" as the most general name for the hypothetical elements of which they assumed "consciousness" to be composed, by processes of juxtaposition, cohesion, association, fusion, synthesis, or what not. Other atomists have described feelings, not as themselves elements or substantial atoms of "consciousness," or of mind stuff, but as attributes of such elements, all the latter being called "sensations." Feelings are then, according to this school, attributes of "sensations," and every "sensation" is said to have the attribute of feeling or feeling-tone, as it is said to have the attribute of intensity. This is a clumsy and unprofitable manner of describing the facts of feeling. As we have seen, it is always a subject, you or I, he, she, or it, who feels, who experiences pleasure or pain, enjoys or suffers; and the notion of an atom of sensation, with a particle of pleasure or of pain adhering to it, or endowed with the attribute of pleasure or of pain, is a radical absurdity; in spite of all the eminence of such psychologists as Wundt and Münsterberg and Titchener, who have countenanced such modes of description. It is in relation to the facts of feeling that the ineffectiveness and insuperable difficulties of the mosaic psychology become most obvious.

Varieties of Feeling

Some authorities recognize only two qualities of feeling, namely, pleasure and pain. Others, while using "feeling" in the strict sense, would recognize a larger variety of qualities of

[1] What, then, of the phrase "hopeful disposition"? Here again we must beware of being misled by the loose and indiscriminating usage of common speech. The quality of a personality commonly implied by this term should more properly be called "hopeful temper." For "temper" see following section.

feeling. Wundt, for example, proposed to distinguish, in addition to pleasure and pain, feelings of strain and relaxation, and of excitement and depression. It seems to me that by these terms he made confused recognition of the reality of conative experience as an irreducible mode.

We have seen that pleasure and pain are conditioned by the interplay of cognition and conation; appreciation of the progress or success of conation determining pleasure, of its thwarting or failure, pain. Now, the derived emotions are conditioned in a similar manner; they are in all cases the consequences of imaginative appreciation of the probabilities of success or failure of the conations, the desires, from which they derive. And, like pleasure and pain, they are not in any sense sensational (*i. e.*, they do not, like the primary emotions, owe their specific qualities to sense-impressions, visceral, kinæsthetic, or other) but are truly subjective; they cannot by any stretch of the imagination be assigned to the objects of our thinking. I may contemplate hopefully a despairing or despondent student, or despondently a hopeful student, or hopefully a hopeful student; and, though common speech uses these words ambiguously, it is clear that, even in this last case, my hope is so clearly mine and the student's so clearly his own, that the most perverse philosopher will hardly succeed in confusing them for us.

The derived emotions are, then, affections or feelings in the strict sense of the word. They may with some plausibility be regarded as resulting from a differentiation of the fundamental forms of feeling, pleasure and pain. This differentiation accompanies the development of the powers of imagination and the increase of capacity for the conjunction of pleasure with pain that goes with mental development.

Blending of Pleasure and Pain

The last remark requires further explanation. It has been widely asserted that pleasure and pain are antagonists which cannot coexist, because each destroys or neutralizes the other, like acid and alkali in solution; or, otherwise stated, that they are quantities of opposite signs which undergo algebraic summation, so that the feeling-tone of the subject is always one of pleasure or of pain, or, if the pleasurable and painful influences are equally balanced, neutral (*i. e.*, non-existent). I have no hesitation in rejecting this doctrine and in following Professor Stout, in recognizing states of feeling in which pleasure and pain are conjoined. The fact is most clearly illustrated perhaps by such emotions as pity and sorrow. In both of these emotions, pleasure and pain would seem to be blended in all proportions, from the very painful pity of the tender-hearted person who can do nothing to relieve the suffering he witnesses and sympathetically shares, to the sweet pity of the ministering angel who finds a supreme satisfaction in relieving the suffering which still, so long as it is not wholly relieved, she shares in some degree. Or, again, the feeling of the mother who kisses away the pain of the little one's bruise. "Parting is such sweet sorrow" said a great master of the secrets of the human heart; for the pain of the lovers at parting was sweetened by the anticipation of reunion.[1]

Feelings and Emotions Disentangled

We are now in a position to understand why there have been so much confusion and uncertainty in respect of the terms "feeling" and "emotion"; and we are able to disentangle this confusion. We have seen that the primary emotions largely owe

[1] By a very elaborate experimental study of feeling ("Pleasure and Unpleasure," *Brit. Jour. of Psychol., Monog. Suppl.*, No. VI) Doctor A. Wohlgemuth has arrived at the conclusion not only that pleasure and pain may coexist as blended states of feeling, but also that pleasures (as also pains) of different origins may coexist without blending, and that pleasure and pain may also coexist without blending. These latter statements are perhaps open to question, but I can see no reason to doubt that pleasure and pain may coexist and blend in some degree. As one quick boy retorted to my question, the fact may be described in three words, "eating a lemon." And another suggested "the pleasure of expecting dessert and the pain of waiting for it." Our emotional reactions to very beautiful scenes illustrate the fact no less well than pity and sorrow. Many of us find a strange pain in very beautiful scenes, at the same time that we delight in them. The poets have expressed the fact again and again; thus Tennyson:

"Tears, idle tears, I know not what they mean,
Tears from the depths of some divine despair
Rise to the heart and gather to the eyes
In gazing on the happy autumn fields,
In thinking of the days that are no more."

their specific qualities to the visceral sense-impressions made by the bodily adjustments that accompany instinctive strivings. So much of truth we have conceded to the James-Lange theory. But, in the developed mind, every excitement of a primary emotion (or of any conjunction of primary emotions) involves conation and also cognition of the degree and the probability of success or failure of conation. Hence, in all our concrete experiences of the primary and blended emotions, these are complicated by the derived emotions or feelings; they are tinged with hope, anxiety, joy, sorrow, surprise, or simple pleasure or pain. That is to say, such experiences are feelings as well as emotions; hence common speech uses the two words almost interchangeably.

CHAPTER XIII

DISPOSITION, TEMPER, TEMPERAMENT, AND MOODS

These four words are in common use and, like all such words, they require some definition and restriction, if they are to be used in scientific discourse. We require the first three words, in order to distinguish three ways in which individuals, in spite of inheriting the same instinctive dispositions and the same degree and type of intelligence, and in spite of closely similar environmental and educational influences, may yet differ widely from one another.

Disposition

A man's "disposition" is the sum total of his instinctive tendencies. It is possible that in some individuals one or more of the instincts may be wholly lacking, as seems to be the case in some domesticated animals.[1] But apart from that possibility, it seems clear that individuals inherit the instinctive impulses in very different degrees of strength. Thus there are men and races of men in which the instinct of curiosity seems to be innately feeble, others in which it is innately strong. The same seems to be true of other instinctive impulses, notably sex, fear, anger, self-assertion, and submission, and the gregarious impulse.[2] When some one of the instinctive tendencies is disproportionately strong, that one characterizes the individual's "disposition." Thus, when a man is by nature extremely pugnacious, we say that he has a pugnacious disposition. We may conveniently illustrate the facts, by drawing up the list of instincts, and writing opposite each one the adjective we

[1] I remind the reader that instincts are very possibly Mendelian units.

[2] In a little book, "Is America Safe for Democracy?" I have put together some evidences of racial differences of this kind.

commonly use to denote the kind of disposition characterized by excessive strength of that tendency, as follows:

Instinctive Impulse	*Disposition*
Impulse of Anger	Irascible or pugnacious.
" Curiosity	Curious, inquisitive, or inquiring.
" Fear	Timid, cautious, or fearful.
" Reproduction	Lustful or amorous.
" Food-seeking	Gluttonous or greedy.
" Self-assertion	Vain, proud, conceited, showy, or ambitious.
" Submission	Humble, meek, submissive, or docile.
" Gregariousness	Sociable.
" Repulsion	Fastidious or dainty.
" Acquisition	Acquisitive, miserly, or thrifty.
" Laughter	Merry, gay.
" Distress	Complaining, tearful, or dependent.

These alternative adjectives are used not as strictly synonymous, but as implying different modes of habitual manifestation of the dominant impulse. Since the instinctive impulses, like all other features of our organization, are subject to the law of increase through use and of atrophy through disuse, it is clear that, in a person endowed by nature with excessive strength of any one of the instinctive tendencies, that tendency will be apt to increase in strength relatively to the rest, if it is not checked and inhibited by discipline and wise self-control, aiming at a due balance of tendencies. This is one of the most frequent sources of inharmonious and unbalanced personalities; in some such instances, the personality may seem to be little more than a mass of gluttony or of lust, of vanity or of irritability. The student should notice that in this usage the word "disposition" has a meaning very different from, though allied to, that with which it has been used in the preceding chapters. The two meanings should lead to no confusion.

Temper

By the temper of a man we mean something allied to, though distinct from, both disposition and temperament. We properly speak of a man as having a fiery or steadfast or fickle or impulsive or hopeful or despondent temper. The peculiarities of the personality denoted by such phrases cannot be explained by reference to the relative strength of the several instinctive tendencies. Fickleness, steadfastness, hopefulness, impulsiveness, and despondency, each of these is a quality which is apt to be manifested by its possessor in situations of all kinds, no matter what motive, what impulse or desire may be operative in him. The temper of a man seems to be the expression of the way in which the conative impulses work within him. There are, I think, three principal ways in which this working of the impulses varies from one man to another, namely, in respect of (1) strength, intensity, or urgency; (2) of persistency; (3) of affectability. By "affectability" I mean the degree to which the impulses are influenced by pleasure and by pain. It seems clear that some men are more liable than others to be checked and diverted from their course of action, and to be prevented from returning to any similar line of action, by the pain of difficulty and thwarting encountered; and to be more strongly sustained in their striving, and stimulated to further and renewed efforts along similar lines, by the pleasure that comes with progress and success; the temper of such men is of high affectability.

That men differ widely in respect of the strength or urgency of their impulses seems clear. The fiery, impatient, energetic man who, when once moved by impulse or desire, cannot rest until he has attained his goal does not differ from the placid or sluggish man merely in having less self-control. Patience is a virtue which may be cultivated; but it is one which is achieved much more easily by some men than by others, just because in them the impulses and desires are less urgent than in other men.

It seems equally clear that men differ widely also in respect of the persistency of their impulses and desires; and that persistency does not vary with, is not closely correlated with, strength or urgency. There are men whose impulses seem to be very urgent and who yet show little perseverance. Such a man sets out energetically to accomplish his desires or impatiently awaits his opportunity; but, if circumstances prevent immediate accomplishment, the impulse does not renew itself, but dies away, leaving him indifferent to, or oblivious of, the goal so strongly desired but a little time ago, while he turns to some new object. On the other hand, there are men whose impulses seem to be not very urgent, who are not easily excited to desire and action, and yet who, once set upon a goal, hold their course tenaciously or return to it again and again after every diversion. Such persistency can be cultivated in some degree; but it seems clear that, like urgency and affectability, it is given in the innate constitution of some men in a much higher degree than to others.

The average man no doubt is endowed with these three factors of temper in an average degree; and such a man has a temper which can only be characterized as equable or average or ordinary. It is when one or two or all three factors are natively present in exceptionally high or low degree that the temper of a man becomes a prominent and noticeable feature of his personality. The reader will easily see how the various combinations of these three factors in different degrees constitute the large variety of tempers that we denote by such adjectives as fiery, placid, sluggish, despondent, hopeful, anxious, dogged, obstinate, steadfast, or fickle.

It is a fair question whether these three factors of temper are quite general; whether, that is to say, all of a man's impulses exhibit corresponding degrees of the three factors; or whether in the same man some impulses may show these factors in high degree, others only in low degree. There can, I think, be little doubt that they are general, that, for example, the man who is naturally steadfast and persistent in respect of some impulses will show the same quality no matter what motives be at work in him. It is probable, however, that we ought to recognize a further ground of differences of temper in that degrees of affectability by pleasure and by pain do not go strictly together, are not closely correlated. Some men seem to be much influenced by pleasure and but little by pain; others much by pain and but little by pleasure. It is only by recognizing this possibility that we can explain the difference between the hopeful and the despondent tempers.

Temperament

The temperament of a man may be provisionally defined as the sum of the effects upon his mental life of the metabolic or chemical changes that are constantly going on in all the tissues of his body. Some of these effects are produced through chemical substances which pass into the blood from the tissues and are then carried to the brain, where they act upon the nervous tissues, modifying their processes. Some of these chemical substances seem to influence all parts of the nervous system; others seem to be highly selective, influencing some special parts or centres exclusively or much more powerfully than others.

That profound effects on mental life may be exerted by very small amounts of chemical substances in the blood is best illustrated by narcotic or anæsthetic drugs, such as alcohol and chloroform. When vapor of chloroform is mixed with the air we breathe, the drug passes very quickly into the blood and thence into the tissue of the brain; and, after a few breaths have been taken, we become aware of a profound disorder of our mental processes, a disorder which becomes more and more clearly a lowering of our mental activity, until complete arrest seems to supervene.[1] If a man possessed an organ whose metabolism generated alcohol he would, whenever this organ was stirred to increased activity, exhibit a change of temperament of the nature of alcoholic intoxication; for drunkenness in its milder degrees is nothing but a temporary modification of temperament through the influence of alcohol on the processses of the brain.

It is probable that every tissue of the body contributes to determine temperament in this chemical fashion. But certain tissues are of vastly greater influence than others. Chief among these are certain ductless glands which were long thought to be relatively inert and of the nature of vestigial remnants. Recent research has, however, revealed that the secretions (known as hormones or endocrines) passed into the blood by some of the ductless glands, exert profound effects upon the growth and metabolism of other tissues, and especially upon the processes of the nervous system.

The facts are most fully ascertained perhaps in the case of the thyroid gland, a mass of soft tissue that clusters about the windpipe at the base of the neck. When the hormone secreted by this gland is excessive in quantity, the processes of the nervous system, and those of many other tissues also, are accelerated; the

[1] For more detailed study of such effects see section on Alcohol in Part II.

patient becomes unduly excitable, and therefore, unless he be shielded as much as possible from impressions and contacts of all kinds, he is constantly restless and agitated, and soon wears himself into a condition of emaciation. On the other hand, if the secretion of the thyroid gland becomes deficient in quantity, the patient becomes sluggish and unduly calm; his mental processes are slowed until, in extreme cases, he is almost torpid. If the defect occurs in a young child, bodily and mental development proceeds unduly slowly; so that in extreme cases the patient becomes a cretinous idiot. That all these profound effects are produced by the excess or defect of the secretion is proved by the fact that they may be completely counteracted; excess by removing a part of the gland; defect by mixing the hormone (obtained from thyroid glands of sheep) with the patient's food.

Other glands which exert influences hardly less profound are the pituitary (at the base of the brain, whose secretion plays a great part in regulating the growth of the whole body) and the suprarenal gland which caps the kidney. The secretion of the latter, even in minute quantities, influences the muscles of the small arteries and thus plays a great part in regulating the circulation of the blood; besides producing other effects, which in the main are such as to prepare the organs of the body for intense and sustained activity.

The sex glands also, the testes of the male, the ovaries of the female, produce hormones whose effects are more specialized. They determine in the young organism the development of the secondary sexual characters, such as the beard, the deep voice, and the bony prominences of the skeleton in the male; and, what is of primary importance from the psychological point of view, the hormone serves, in some way that we do not fully understand, as sensitizer of the reproductive instinct, and thus plays a principal part in determining the degree of sexual appetite of the individual.

To some minds the contemplation of the facts of this order is profoundly disturbing. Others complacently look forward to the time when further knowledge of them may enable us to intervene in the processes of development, to improve upon the work of Nature.[1] But the facts are of profound importance and must be faced and taken fully into account by the psychologist.

Various organs of the body influence our mental life in another way, namely, by contributing almost constantly faint sense-impressions that make themselves only obscurely felt during health as the *cœnesthesis*, a vague background that colors or tones our thinking more or less favorably or unfavorably. Thus, a perfectly working digestive system tends to a cheerful and contented tone of mind; one which works sluggishly and imperfectly may give a peevish, hypochondriacal, or melancholy tone to the temperament of its possessor. In a similar way an active and efficient muscular system tends to a general alertness and efficiency of mental life.

These factors of temperament are in the main determined in the innate constitution of each man. Yet they are capable of being modified in some degree by such influences as diet, climate, and drugs, and, it would seem, by mental attitudes and experiences. Thus, repeated fear may lead to chronic excess of the chemical activity of the thyroid gland. It is here that mental influences play their chief role in affecting health and disease, and here that suggestion and various other forms of mental healing find possibilities of whose limits we are very ignorant.

It seems proper to include under factors of temperament certain general constitutional peculiarities of the nervous system. Of these, degrees of liability to fatigue, and ease and rapidity of recuperation from fatigue, and, probably, facility in generating an antitoxin of fatigue,[2] are important in determining the general efficiency of the personality.

Very important, also, in determining the course of mental development, is a factor which has been recently brought into prominence by Doctor C. G. Jung, namely, the degree of *introversion*. Doctor Jung distinguishes introversion and extrover-

[1] As, for example, Doctor L. Berman, who (in "Glands Regulating Personality") has drawn with great skill a very highly colored picture of the part played by the endocrine secretions, and who would almost seem to suppose that psychology is about to be superseded by endocrinology.

[2] Cf. "The Effect of Alcohol and Other Drugs During Normal and Fatigued Conditions," by May Smith and W. McDougall. H. M. Stationery Office, London, 1920.

sion as the extremes of a continuous scale formed by degrees of introversion. It is uncertain whether introversion or extroversion should be considered a positive quality, and the other extreme as merely the lowest degree of this positive quality. However this may be, the position of a man's temperament in this scale seems to be in the main a matter of native constitution, though, like other factors of temperament, it is susceptible to environmental and disciplinary influences, especially in early youth. The problem must be discussed in more detail in Part II of this work. Here it must suffice to say that the well-marked extrovert is the man whose emotions and impulses readily and freely express themselves in action, in words, gestures, and all the natural channels of emotional expression. The introvert, on the other hand, is the man whose impulses and emotional stirrings are apt to remain bottled up within him, determining brooding and reflection rather than expression and action.

Enough has been said to show that temperament is a complex resultant of many factors, each of which is in the main natively determined, though susceptible in various degrees to modification by environmental influences and mental discipline. The mental development of the individual is constantly biassed in this or that direction by the peculiarities of his temperament; the trend of the selective activity of the mind, in all its processes of assimilation, discrimination, apperception, and habit formation, is largely determined by temperament; so that two individuals, similarly endowed as regards disposition and intellectual capacities, would develop very differently if they were of widely different temperament. Temperament largely influences the growth both of intellect and of character.

Temperaments being resultants of so many diverse factors, it necessarily follows that the varieties of temperament are innumerable, and that the temperament of any man cannot be adequately characterized by one or a few adjectives. And, in fact, our terminology is here most inadequate. We have only a few appropriate terms, which partially characterize certain types of temperament, adjectives such as buoyant, quick, slow, nervous, active, excitable, sluggish, melancholic, stable, and especially introvert and extrovert.

Disposition, temper, and temperament are the raw materials of personality provided by heredity. From them character is built, under the touch of experience and the guidance of increasing knowledge and intelligence.

Throughout mental development and, in fact, throughout life, they reciprocally influence one another. Though they are laid down in the native constitution, they are modifiable by wise guidance and self-discipline. Wise education consists largely in the continued influencing of these three complex constitutional factors; it may do much to correct any native defect or lack of balance among them.

Moods

Before bringing this chapter to an end, a word must be said about moods. Moods clearly are related in some way to emotions. We speak of angry, cautious, sociable, appreciative, helpful, despondent, respectful, contrary, submissive, and many other moods.

That is to say, in speaking of moods we use the names by which we distinguish emotions and impulses. The mood is clearly an affective-conative fact of immediate experience. We not only display moods by our attitude and behavior, but often we are immediately aware of the mood. Yet we recognize that a mood may persist, even when some emotion of an entirely different quality and tendency dominates the scene. Thus, when in an angry mood, I may be provoked to laughter or to pity, without the angry mood being wholly dispelled. As soon as the intercurrent emotion is spent, the mood may reassert itself. A mood is most commonly engendered by the evocation of some strong emotion which is for any reason denied free expression.[1] When we cease to think of the object or situation that has excited emotion, without having freely expressed the emotion and achieved the natural goal of its impulse, the mood remains, a resonating echo, as it were, of the emotion.

Primarily the mood implies a more or less subconscious persistence of the conation and the emotion, a subexcitement of the affective-conative disposition. No doubt this subexcite-

[1] Hence the introvert is more subject to moods than the extrovert.

ment is commonly aided and abetted by some persistence of the organic resonance of the emotion, in some cases probably by a chemical residue. In fact, we can draw no sharp line between the emotion and the corresponding mood; we can only distinguish them by agreeing to call the affective-conative excitement an "emotion," so long as we continue to think of the object that excites it, and to call it a mood, if it still persists when we cease to think of the object. If we do this, then we must recognize that emotion normally subsides into a mood, before the excitement wholly passes away.

The mood renders us peculiarly susceptible to the reexcitement of the corresponding emotion. Thus, if you have recently been startled or frightened, you will be more readily startled again: for the persisting subexcitement of the fear-disposition renders it more susceptible to a new excitement than it is when completely quiescent. Or, if you have recently been angered and have not worked off your anger in free action and expression, you will remain unusually irritable, or in an irritable mood, as we say, for some little time. So long as the mood persists, the impulse is, as it were, seeking an object, and is apt to fasten upon, and receive new stimulus from, objects which at other times would fail to excite the emotion; as when, in an angry mood, your anger bursts forth afresh at the slightest obstruction of any action, a door-handle that sticks, a pen that splutters, a fly that distracts you from your book by tickling your nose or buzzing on the window-pane.

The most persistent moods, which border upon the morbid, are those which are due to some unresolved conflict of emotional tendencies. Thus, if you have been hurt or offended by some one dear to you, you will be apt to suffer a vague discomfort so long as you have not resolved the conflict between your anger and the habitual tendencies which constitute your sentiment of love for that person. Still more, if, through lack of self-control, you unjustly reproach or blame or scold one you love, you will carry with you a disturbing mood that may cloud all your day and clog all your activities, until you take measures to "put yourself right" with that person by frankly apologizing or in some way expressing your contrition.

It is probable that some moods are largely due to organic conditions which, in the chemical and other ways considered under temperament, strongly predispose the subject to this or that kind of emotional excitement. Thus indigestion and gout and diabetes notoriously favor the irascible mood; and excess of thyroid activity favors the fearful or timid mood. In other cases of long-persistent morbid moods, we naturally suspect the presence of an organic factor, as in the mood which is the leading symptom of the melancholic phase of manic-depressive insanity. Such morbid moods, like those which do not pass the limits of the normal, tend to find suitable objects, and, indeed, create such objects in the form of delusions and hallucinations. This is a process allied to "rationalization." [1]

[1] Cf. Part II.

CHAPTER XIV

BELIEF AND DOUBT

We have seen that the complex feelings which, in deference to established usage, we have called "derived emotions," are produced by the interplay of cognition and conation. Belief and doubt are states of feeling which are similarly conditioned. They also are derived "emotions"; but, because of the exceptional importance and difficulty of the psychology of belief and doubt, I treat of them in a separate chapter. In the past, owing to the dominance in psychology of the intellectualist tradition, they have usually been treated as purely intellectual facts or states of mind, produced by purely intellectual or cognitive processes.

The Association Psychology described and explained belief as the persistence of an "inseparable association." It was said that if two "ideas" succeed one another again and again in "consciousness," they become more and more firmly linked together, until at last it is impossible for one of them to come to "consciousness" without being followed immediately by the other. For example, on innumerable occasions I have grasped my left wrist with my right hand, and on every such occasion I have found it to be solid, or resistant to compression; therefore the "idea" of my left wrist is "inseparably associated" with the "idea" of solidity, and no sooner does the "idea" of my wrist come to "consciousness" than the "idea" of solidity follows it; which is to say that I believe my wrist to be solid. The absurdity of any such account is manifest, if we reflect that the theory demands that, whenever the "idea" of solidity comes to "consciousness" it shall at once be followed by the idea of my left wrist; for this obviously does not occur.

Or again, whatever appears colored and opaque to the eye

has invariably been found to offer some degree of resistance to touch; hence, opaque color becomes inseparably associated with solidity, and, whenever I see an opaque colored surface, I believe it to be in some degree solid or massive, to occupy space. Or, every time I have come up against a solid resisting surface, I have found that there is space, or possibility of further movement, beyond it; hence the "idea" of further space is inseparably associated with every experience of a resistant surface, and I inevitably believe in every case that there is more space beyond it, and cannot conceive of any limit to space. Whereas, if I had always lived in a completely closed chamber, I should as inevitably believe (even though its walls were transparent) that space was limited by my prison walls.

James and a few other psychologists, on the other hand, have asserted that belief is an emotion. But James wisely made no attempt to apply to it his famous theory, did not attempt the impossible task of resolving belief into any complex of organic sensations. Since belief and doubt are closely allied to those modes of feeling (confidence, hope, anxiety, etc.) which in a foregoing chapter we have classed as "derived emotions," we must admit the propriety of calling them emotions; but with the reservation implied by our recognition of the distinction and difference of nature between the emotions proper (the primary and secondary emotions) and the derived "emotions."

How, then, are belief and doubt related to the derived "emotions" which we have already considered? We must first notice that the terms "belief" and "doubt" are properly applicable only to experiences of the developed mind. We cannot properly speak of belief in the young child or in animals. The dog who recognizes his master, or the young child who recognizes his father at sight and promptly greets him, cannot properly be said to believe that the approaching figure is his master (or father). He can, however, be said to greet him, or approach him, with confidence. All primitive perception, being recognition, involves confidence; "seeing is believing," says the old adage. In a similar way the dog (or young child) who hesitates on the approach of the familiar person, oscillating uncertainly between attitudes of welcome and of retreat or antagonism, cannot properly be said to doubt; but he may be said to be in a state of anxiety or of hope.[1]

Belief is, then, confidence on the intellectual plane; and doubt is hesitation or anxiety on the same plane of explicitly formulated propositions. Belief grows up gradually out of confidence with intellectual development, and there is no sharp line to be drawn between them. Belief, in the fullest sense of the word, must be preceded by doubt, by the questioning attitude which issues in judgment, returning the answer "Yes" or "No" to the question.

Imagine yourself going out to meet an expected friend. A figure approaches in the distance, but you cannot certainly recognize your friend. Like the dog or the young child, you hesitate, moved by contradictory impulses. But, unlike the dog, you formulate your question—Is it, or is it not, *A*? And you suspend judgment; you are not merely anxious, but you are in doubt. And when, on nearer approach, your recognition becomes definite, your doubt is suddenly resolved into belief, by perceptual judgment. Definite perception is only one of three ways in which doubt may be supplanted by belief. The second way in which judgment may be determined and doubt resolved into belief is by communication from another person. If, at the moment of doubtful recognition, a friend, of better eyesight than your own, or provided with a telescope, stands beside you and says "Yes, it's *A*," or "No, it's not *A*," your suspended judgment may be determined by your friend's communication and your doubt converted to belief.

Thirdly, doubt may be converted to belief by reasoning. It may be that the distant figure suggests to your mind your friend *A*, and you are in doubt. Then you remember that an hour ago you said farewell to *A*, as he stood on a steamship, leaving the dockside for a distant country. At once your doubt is resolved

[1] I have many times been greeted by my dog in this fashion. He would be lying before the door of my house, as I entered the garden gate some seventy yards away. He would bark and approach threateningly. If I made no sign, at a certain distance he would oscillate between threats and signs of welcome; and at the sound of my voice his hesitation would be instantly resolved. Such hesitation, with conflict of opposed impulses, is the state which in the animal or young child corresponds to the doubt of the developed mind.

into negative belief—this is not *A*. And if, on nearer approach, the figure looks exactly like *A*, you conclude that it must be a "double" or a twin brother of *A*. This belief would normally be determined by a process of implicit reasoning. But, if the friend beside you questions your new belief, and says, "It certainly is *A*," you explicate your reasoning in some such way as this: "I believe that *A* is on that ship far out on the sea. I believe a man cannot be in two places at the same time. Therefore I believe this is not *A*.

Conation and Belief

In one or other of these three ways all beliefs are established, all judgments are determined—by perception, by communication, by reasoning from previously established beliefs. All these are eminently cognitive processes; hence the purely intellectualistic accounts of belief that have commonly been accepted. But notice now that, as in all thinking, the conative factor plays an essential part in each of these processes. If you are not interested in *A* and his whereabouts or in the identity of the approaching figure, you neither believe nor doubt nor disbelieve. And the more keenly interested you are in the identity of the approaching figure, the more intense will be your doubt or your belief. Suppose that it is for you a question of life and death; suppose that you are scouting in a hostile country; then your question will be: Is this approaching figure friend or enemy? And your doubt may be agonizingly intense; and your belief correspondingly intense, when your doubt is resolved.

Let us go back in imagination to the party of Arctic explorers. Let us imagine that they are nearly exhausted and their supplies of food used up; but they have reached a spot at which their comrades have promised to meet them with new supplies. The appointed time is already past; hour after hour they scan the snowfield anxiously for some sign of their comrades' approach. At last, in the distance, several dark figures are seen moving slowly over the surface. The man of hopeful temper, *A*, springs up, crying, "Here they are!" The man of despondent temper, *B*, says, "No, those are penguins, you fool!"[1] The third man,

[1] A mistake often made, Major Priestly tells us. (*Loc. cit.*)

of placid temper, *C*, scrutinizes the distant specks anxiously. His judgment is suspended; he remains in doubt; he neither affirms nor denies. Thus the three men react very differently; but none of them remains indifferent, for they all strongly desire that the distant specks may prove to be their comrades; hence they are mentally active. All of them are impelled to exert judgment about the object and to answer the question, "Are those our comrades?" *A* affirms; *B* denies; *C* suspends judgment. The affirmative judgment of *A* initiates belief. *B*'s denial initiates disbelief. *C*'s continued suspension of judgment is the state of doubt. The sensory pattern presented by the distant object is insufficient to determine recognition. But in *A* desire, strengthened by pleasurable anticipation, prompts the imagination to fill out the vague pattern, so that he clearly sees the human forms and even identifies the individuals by name, imagination working upon and supplementing the slightest sensory cues.

A and *B* begin to argue; each stoutly asserts and defends his view; in each the self-assertive impulse begins to work and confirms him in his attitude of belief or disbelief. *C*, on the other hand, remains in doubt. He weighs the arguments of *A* and *B*; but none convinces him. *B* ceases to argue and sits down, despondent or despairing. *A* continues to affirm his belief and says confidently, "Come on, *C*, let's go to meet them!" *A*'s confident masterly bearing influences *C*; it evokes his submissive impulse, which works on the side of affirmation; that is to say, *A* works on *C* by suggestion. *C* half believes, and as *A* strides forward in confidence, *C* goes behind him, alternating between hope and anxiety, his doubt not quite resolved.

Here we have illustration of the three modes in which belief is determined, and also of the fact that belief is the feeling or "emotion" of confidence on the intellectual plane of formulated propositions, while doubt is the emotion of anixety on the same plane. In belief and confidence, desire is reinforced by pleasurable anticipation of the desired goal, and works simply toward its goal in bodily or mental action. In doubt and anxiety, impulse or desire is checked by painful anticipation of failure, and the imagination, instead of depicting only the goal and the means toward it, depicts various alternatives.

Belief is then confidence in respect of a proposition. Doubt is anxiety in respect of a proposition. Neither is determined merely by cognition; they result from the interplay of cognition and conative impulse—both are essential. And the stronger the impulse or desire, the more intense the emotion of belief or of doubt.

Judgment Converts Doubt to Belief

How, then, is doubt resolved? How is it supplanted by belief? By a process of positive or negative judgment, by affirmation or denial.

Suggestion[1] may evoke the submissive impulse on the side of affirmation. In the hypnotic state, when suggestibility is greatly increased, repeated assertion may lead the subject to accept and affirm the most improbable propositions and to make grossly false recognition and even hallucinatory recognition; just as anticipation, determined by strong desire of any kind, may determine false recognition, illusion, and even, in some persons, hallucination.

Secondly, the desire may sustain a process of investigation on the practical plane of action and perception. We continue to examine the object according to the method of trial and error, that is, we look for marks not hitherto perceived, we anticipate these imaginatively and seek to verify them perceptually. Thirdly, we may conduct the process of investigation by the method of trial and error on the plane of imagination; and this is reasoning. In both these cases we form an hypothesis, a tentative plan of action. In the one case, we work it out to success or failure by bodily movement and perception. In the other, we work out the plan to success or failure in imagination alone. In the two cases, the method is essentially similar; and often our procedure is partly perceptual, partly imaginative. "If this is *X*, it will show *Y*," we say; and we proceed to discover whether it shows *Y*. For example, in the case of the Arctic explorers, the process may run: "Men move steadily onward toward their goal; these figures do not; therefore they are not men, but penguins."

[1] Suggestion will be discussed in more detail in Part II. It affords the most striking evidence of the predominance of the conative factor in judgment.

Notice that in all cases belief implies memory in the wider sense of the word. It always implies reference to past experience. This is obvious in the belief that results from perceptual judgment or recognition. When I recognize a man, and say and believe "This is *X*," the term *X* has meaning only by reference to the *X* I have previously seen or thought of. And, even if my belief is determined by suggestion, it still refers to a previously thought of *X*. The same is true, if my judgment and consequent belief are determined by reasoning.

Some beliefs are established by judgments which rest wholly on memory; as when I am asked "When did you last see *X?*" After a moment's reflection, I reply "Yesterday morning." If this belief is challenged, or my assertion contradicted, I may yield to the suggestion, make a new judgment, and believe "No, I did not see him yesterday"; or I may fall into doubt. Then I may seek to resolve my doubt by remembering various attendant circumstances. If these circumstances all hang together consistently, I cease to doubt; my first judgment is repeated and belief established.[1]

Note that, even in these beliefs determined by memory, inseparable association, determined by many repetitions of the conjunction of two impressions or ideas, has nothing to do with the case. The question may be—Did you see X yesterday at noon? And if I clearly remember seeing X at the moment the clock struck twelve at noon of yesterday, I answer confidently "Yes." Yet here my belief is determined by a perceptual experience which in the nature of things could not be repeated.

[1] Further evidence of the great importance of the conative factor in the determination of belief is afforded by the process of "rationalization." This, although in its milder forms it plays a great part in normal life, in its extremer degrees gives rise to grave symptoms of disorder, especially delusions. It will therefore be discussed in Part II. But the principle may be illustrated here by a simple instance. A subject who passes into hypnosis and afterwards remembers nothing of the events of the hypnotic period, may be given some simple "post-hypnotic suggestion," for example, may be told that, at a certain signal after waking, he will perform some simple train of action, such as rising from his chair, opening the window, and looking up and down the street. At the prescribed signal, the subject gets up in the most natural way, performs the actions, and returns to his seat. You then ask him—Why did you look out of the window? In all probability he will give a perfectly "rational" explanation of his action. For example, he may say: "It occurred to me that So-and-So was likely to be calling for me here, and he might be unable to find the house." That is to say, not knowing the nature and source of the impulse by which he was moved (the submissive impulse directed

Belief in Reality of Things

But a deeper question remains. When we make a judgment, express it in a proposition, and believe that proposition to be true, we always imply the reality of the subject of the proposition, in the sense that we conceive this subject as something that has a certain continuity of existence, that remains self-identical in spite of changes.

How do we arrive at this belief in things, in entities which endure even though they may change in certain respects, exhibiting different qualities on different occasions?

If the physical world about us were in perpetual change, so rapid that nothing remained stable and unchanging to our perception (resembling a series of "dissolving views" or the landscape seen from the window of an express-train), should we ever achieve this belief in things as realities that continue to exist?

The answer seems to be that we should still be able to conceive at least qualities and to make judgments of sameness and difference in respect of them. Though we should not achieve belief in *things*.

But this would only be possible in virtue of the continuity of oneself as the subject of experience. Oneself is the type of enduring reality amidst change; and our belief in the continuity and self-identity of other things and persons that we conceive is founded upon our belief in our own continuity and self-identity.

How, then, is this belief founded? The sensationist account of this belief runs roughly as follows: Experience is a perpetual flux of sensations; but, no matter how unstable and fluctuating

to this train of action by the "suggestion" of the hypnotist) he invents an explanation and puts forward a plausible motive in place of the true one, in perfectly good faith. Such instances illustrate vividly the fact that the motives of our actions and of our beliefs are apt to be very obscure to us, so that we easily fall into error when we seek, however honestly, to state our motives or the grounds of our belief. In doing so, we naturally seek a "rational" explanation of our action or belief, *i. e.*, one which may seem reasonable or rationally defensible; we often act or believe from motives of which we have no understanding; but we always seek to explain our action or belief according to the principle of "sufficient reason." The fact that our motives are commonly so obscure to us gives plausibility to that kind of psychology which explains everything by invoking "The Unconscious."

the sensations we get from the outer world, we experience a mass of sensations that remains relatively stable in spite of minor changes. This is the mass of bodily sensations, the cœnesthesis, consisting of sensations from all our bodily organs, but especially our visceral organs. This relatively stable mass of sensations is the core of our personality; it is the foundation of our belief in our personal identity and continuance. And it is argued that, if this mass of sensations, the cœnesthesis, were to undergo radical and rapid change, we should lose our belief in our own identity. In support of this view, cases are cited in which the patient denies his identity, speaks of his former self as dead or distant, and assumes a new name.[1] Now it is true that in some such cases there is evidence of profound alteration of the cœnesthesis; for example, there may be wide-spread anæsthesia of bodily organs. Yet the doctrine is not established thereby. There are many other instances in which great change of the cœnesthesis does not appreciably disturb the belief in one's identity. Thus in sea-sickness and in some organic diseases, and in every violent emotional excitement, the cœnesthesis is profoundly modified. Yet, though we may say "I hardly feel like the same man," this is but a picturesque expression; we believe ourselves to be the same, in spite of the change.

Clearly, memory is here fundamental. We can only relate the present to the past by memory. Without memory we should not be aware of change, no matter how violent and complete or slight and partial it might be. And memory is not merely having the same "sensations" over again.

Add, then, memory to the power of experiencing the flux of "sensations," and grant the cœnesthesis as a relatively stable core that enters into all experience. Will that account for our belief in the identity and reality first of ourselves and secondarily of other persons and things?

This is where the sensationist and the hormic psychologies reach their most fundamental issue. The sensationist psychology replies "Yes." The hormic psychology says "No." It maintains that the core of personal identity, the foundation of our belief in our own reality and continuity, is the experience of purposive

[1] Cf. account of such cases in Part II.

striving, of doing, of putting forth effort or energy, of resolving and acting, of pursuing a goal; which experience is fundamental and unique and not to be resolved into, or identified with, any qualities of sensation. This immediate awareness of the tides of life surging through the organism, together with memory, the memory of our past strivings, is the ground of our belief in our reality as enduring entities.

What is the evidence for this view? First, like the sensationist doctrine, but with more success, we may invoke the evidence of pathology. In cases of dual or alternating personality of the fully developed kind, we always find two changes: first, a discontinuity of memory; secondly, some radical alteration of the conative tendencies. The changed or secondary personality may have knowledge of some of the past experience of the normal personality, but does not remember it as his own experience; he knows of it merely as he may know of yours or mine. And his system of impulses and desires is quite other. He has a distinct system of sentiments or conative trends. He desires and strives to achieve other goals. It is, in fact, the rise of some system of desire, incompatible with the system that constitutes the core and essence of the normal personality, that leads to the conflict which issues in dual personality.[1]

We may realize something of this imaginatively. Suppose that you woke up one morning, with all your conative trends and settings completely transformed or redirected, hating all those you had loved, disliking all things you had liked, caring nothing for money or reputation, turning your other cheek to the smiter, and loving those that despitefully used you, angry and scornful where you had been tender, pitiful, and sympathetic. Then, indeed, you would feel yourself to be another man, *even in spite of continuity of memory*, if such continuity were possible under those conditions. Something like this is what happens in the sudden conversion of sinner to saint; the saint looks back with horror upon all the ways and tendencies that made him a sinner, and regards the sinner as a stranger.

Pathology illustrates our point in another way. There are patients who become afflicted with a "sense of unreality." Such

[1] Cf. Part II.,

a patient feels that nothing is real, not even himself. This seems to be due, not to any change of the cœnesthesis, nor to any lack of sensational vividness, but to lack of desire, of impulse, of conative energy. Through exhaustion (perhaps by reason of internal conflict) the patient's conative energies are sapped; he no longer responds with strong impulses or desires, and all things become unreal.

We may arrive at the same conclusion by a different line of reasoning. Suppose that you were capable of satisfying immediately every desire, every impulse, by mere wishing; every desired change in the world about you at once realizing itself, as soon as your desire was formulated. No doubt you would believe in the reality of yourself; but you would not believe in the reality of the world about you: it would be a world of fantasy, such as children are apt to create and dwell in; or such as some adults also create, when the real world becomes too hard for them. And you would inevitably be a solipsist.[1] It is the resistance offered by things to our desires and our efforts that is the foundation of our belief in their reality.

The sensationist says that the foundation of all belief in the reality of things is the vividness of sensory experience, which is lacking in imagination or imagined things; and that, when we assert our belief in the real existence of the thing we imagine, what we mean is that under suitable conditions we could perceive it with sensory vividness.

But what we really mean, when we assert the reality of a thing, is that the thing has a nature of its own which reveals itself in the resistance it offers when we strive to change it, compelling us to think out a plan and to exert ourselves for the realization of our desire.

Here is the difference between fantasy and dreaming. In fantasy, our objects are moulded by our desires and changed at will. In dreaming, our objects resist our efforts; often we struggle in vain against them; hence we believe in their reality.

The hallucinated patient in an early stage of his trouble may dismiss by an effort the phantom figure or the voice whispering

[1] A metaphysician who asserts that his experience is alone real and therefore constitutes the whole of reality.

of threats and persecution. And, so long as he can do this, he does not believe them real, in spite of their sensory vividness. But, in a more advanced stage of the disorder, he cannot dismiss them; the phantom or the voice is insistent, resists his best efforts to dismiss it; it is then he begins to believe in its reality. And the most complete proof of the reality of any object is the resistance offered by it to our bodily effort to move or change it. Solidity is overwhelming evidence of reality. There is only one evidence still more convincing; and that is the exertion by the object of active pressure against our efforts. Weight or gravitational pressure is the simplest form of this. More convincing still is the active varied resistance to our manipulations offered by other persons and by animals. No one can doubt the reality of the opponent with whom he wrestles in a life-and-death struggle; or of the enemy who lays a heavy hand upon his neck and forces him to his knees. Opposition, physical or purely moral, offered by other persons to the realization of our desire is what gives us the most complete belief in their reality.

Belief in reality of other things is determined by a projection of one's own reality; and that reality is at bottom one's power of striving, of exerting an effort, of persisting toward a goal.

The animal accepts as real whatever object evokes any instinctive impulse. Primitive man does likewise. This is primitive credulity. We all retain in a measure such primitive credulity. We tend to believe in the reality of whatever evokes an instinctive impulse. A sound in the night evokes fear and is interpreted as the movement of a beast of prey; the beast is imagined and accepted as real, in virtue of the strong impulse evoked.

The primitive credulity of savage man leads him to accept as real whatever exerts strong influence on him, influence that he cannot resist; such things he accepts as real in the fullest sense; that is to say, he regards them as real in the same sense as himself, as active agents of purposive striving. Hence he personifies the sun, the wind, the river, storms, floods, the volcano, pestilences, pests, and all powerful beasts. This is the root of "primitive animism."

On a higher plane of imagination, we tend to believe in the

reality of whatever we strongly desire. "The wish is father to the thought"; that is to say, desire tends to make us believe in that which we desire, whether it be in perception, memory, or anticipation. But aversion may have similar effects; we tend to believe in what we strongly dread. Hell fire and the devil and witches were real to the old Puritans, because they feared these creatures of the imagination.

On the plane of reproductive thinking, the same law governs our believing. In reproductive imagination, or remembering, if we are interested in the question of the reality of that which we remember, the truth of our recollection, we believe it in so far as our imagination of the past is stable and offers resistance to our effort to change it. Consider how your belief in the reality of some past action of yours is founded, if, say in a court of law, your testimony to it is required and challenged. The question is raised—Did you, or did you not, lock the door on leaving your apartment? The ground of your belief in the reality of your locking the door is not the vividness with which you can picture yourself doing it; it is rather the fact that, as you depict your exit on that occasion, the imagination of the act hangs obstinately together with the rest of the sequence of behavior which you depict. If you attempt to excise it from the sequence, you remain aware of the gap which you have made. This again is not the result of an inseparable association, a habit set up by many repetitions. It is rather due to the fact that memory works according to its own law, reproducing the past events in the order of their occurrence, a law or tendency which we can only partially control, which offers resistance to our efforts.

On the highest plane of mental life, that of reasoning, the same law of belief holds good. When we reason from believed premises to a conclusion, our belief in the conclusion derives from our belief in the premises; the former belief arises because in reasoning the mind works according to laws of its own, and resists in some degree our efforts to avoid the conclusion.

One's own self is believed in as real, because we desire and strive and achieve, or fail; any other thing is believed to be real in so far as it seems to us to be like ourselves, that is to say, in so far as it seems to have a determinate nature of its own which resists us; and all our beliefs are dependent upon such beliefs in realities. The universal formula of belief is—this is *X*. And the word "is" means real existence, something of determinate nature which is independent of our desire and will, because it resists. Descartes' famous dictum, then, needs revision; not "I think, therefore I am," but "I strive, therefore I exist," is the foundation of all belief. Our conception of force is derived from our experience of exertion of force, of striving against resistance. That which resists us is credited with a similar force or power of striving; and whatever is real has such force. Hence we properly speak of the force of a convincing argument, the force of the sun, the force of gravity, the force of inertia, or of impact, the force of personality. We see, then, the truth of Professor Stout's statement that belief is conditioned by limitation of activity. "Wherever belief or judgment exists, it involves the control of our activity as thinking beings by conditions which are fixed for us and not by us. In so far as we are left free to think otherwise than we do think, belief is absent; in so far as it is present, the range of subjective selection is confined within definite limits. . . . Our inability to attain ends otherwise than through certain means constitutes a restriction of mental activity within definite channels. If wishing were identical with having, our freedom would be absolute, and there would be no such thing as belief."[1]

Simple Apprehension Without Belief

Some authors, notably Brentano, have maintained that simple apprehension and judgment are two equally fundamental and original modes of cognition. We are now in a position to see that this is not correct. Judgment is not cognitive merely. It is the interplay of cognition and conation. Without interest (*i. e.*, without impulse, conation, or desire, for we have seen that all interest is fundamentally conative) we do not doubt or judge and believe. Primitively, implicit judgment and that lowly form of belief which is more properly called "confidence" accompany all cognition. It is only gradually that we learn to

[1] "Analytic Psychology," Vol. II, p. 239.

suspend judgment, to doubt, to inquire; then, when judgment, affirmation, or denial follows, belief becomes explicit.

It is of the essence of the æsthetic attitude that we do not inquire into the reality of that which we contemplate. We are content to contemplate without belief or doubt; we accept and enjoy the appearance, without inquiry into the reality of that which appears, just because the appearance yields an immediate satisfaction and is so presented as to avoid stirring us to desire and action. How this is achieved—whether by balance of conflicting impulses, by restraint, by the preservation of psychical distance, by detachment from reality—this is the artist's secret. In æsthetic perception we are fully occupied in mere apprehension; conation is, relatively at least, in suspense, and therefore, also, judgment and belief.[1] This attitude is not easily attained; nor can it be maintained for long by those who attain it. Simple apprehension is, then, a late acquired attitude which we maintain but rarely and briefly. Affirmation or denial, acceptance or rejection, appetition or aversion, normally results from and accompanies cognition.

Beliefs

In this chapter we have discussed belief and doubt as modes of experience; and we have found that they are feelings of the kind we have agreed to call "derived emotions." But, by a well-established usage, the word "belief" may convey a second very different meaning. We speak of "a belief" or of a system of beliefs; or we say that a man holds contradictory beliefs, or that his life is governed by certain beliefs. In all such cases we clearly do not mean merely the feeling or derived emotion of belief with which we utter or accept a proposition. The man who holds certain beliefs, in this sense of the word, does not cease to hold them, when he thinks of topics quite unconnected with them. I believe that the earth is "an oblate spheroid"; this belief seldom comes to mind, though I have held it more than forty years;

[1] Professor J. A. Stewart has argued in his book on "The Myths of Plato" that in æsthetic contemplation the individual passes into a state of actual dissociation. This view is based on the consideration of the more extreme cases of rapt contemplation. Some such supposition seems to be required to account for the divorce of cognition from conation in æsthetic apprehension.

yet, when occasion arises, it duly plays its part in determining the course of my thinking. Beliefs, in this sense of the word, are enduring features of my mental structure; and the development of my mind through experience largely consists in the acquiring of beliefs and in the more or less logical organization of these beliefs in systems and systems of systems. Beliefs, then, are equivalent to "ideas" in one of the many senses of that most ambiguous of words. True beliefs are knowledge, and false beliefs are false knowledge or delusions; and both alike are features of the enduring structure of the mind, the development of which we have now to consider more nearly.

CHAPTER XV

GROWTH OF MENTAL STRUCTURE—DEVELOPMENT OF COGNITIVE STRUCTURE OR INTELLECT

On earlier pages it was pointed out that we must conceive any developed mind, not as consisting of a bundle or loose heap of "ideas," but as a highly complex organized structure. I said we might use the old word "idea" to denote distinguishable parts of this structure, and that, if "idea" is to be used at all in psychology, this probably is the best usage. But, I said, in view of the many different senses in which the word "idea" has been used, we shall do better to avoid it and to use the neutral noncommittal term "disposition," meaning by "disposition" any enduring part of the structure of the mind which renders possible some particular mode of mental activity.

Further, I have pointed out that we may properly, nay, must distinguish two principal kinds of disposition, the cognitive and the conative. The mind or the subject has three fundamental faculties—the cognitive, the conative, and the affective—the faculties of knowing, of striving, and of feeling. The ways in which the faculties of knowing and striving are exercised are determined by the dispositions; the cognitive dispositions determine the contents of our knowing, the conative dispositions the forms of our striving.

We have to try to build up the best possible account of the structure of the mind and of the way it develops, in terms of dispositions of these two kinds and of their relations or functional connections. This requires a sustained effort of constructive imagination.

Common speech rightly distinguishes two aspects or sides of the structure of the mind by the words "intellect" and "character." And common experience shows that these two sides, the cognitive and the conative, are, though intimately related, yet relatively distinct organizations. We know, for example, how in one man the intellect may be highly developed and well organized; though his character may be poor, ill organized, and unstable. While in another man character may be strongly organized; though his intellect remains comparatively undeveloped.[1] Further, we see how, in old age or disease, intellect and character may become unequally disordered or decayed. In such a man as the poet Coleridge, character seems to decay under the influence of drugs, while intellect remains rich and brilliantly effective; and in some old men the intellect seems to decay, while character remains firm and well knit.

It is then permissible to consider separately the growth of intellect and of character. It was said in Chapter VIII that the intellect, or cognitive structure of the developed human mind, comprises a vast number of dispositions, one for every distinct object and class of objects (concrete, abstract, or general) which that mind is capable of conceiving (*i. e.*, thinking of), either in the way of perceiving it, or recollecting, anticipating, or

[1] The student should notice the distinction between intellect and intelligence. Intelligence is essentially the capacity for making new adaptations; it cannot be described in terms of structure. Intellect includes intelligence and much more besides; for "a good intellect" implies good intelligence that works through and by means of rich and well-organized cognitive structure. A man may have good intelligence, *i. e.*, high capacity for making new adaptations, while yet his intellect is poor, because he has not enriched it by acquiring much knowledge, or has not logically organized his knowledge as systems of beliefs. On the other hand, a man may become very learned, may possess much knowledge and yet remain comparatively unintelligent, because, lacking native intelligence, though having a retentive memory, he remains relatively incapable of making new adaptations, owing, first, to his native lack of intelligence; secondly, to the lack of systematic organization of his knowledge, which organization is the work of intelligence. Thus, high native intelligence is capable, as it were, of multiplying itself or its efficiency; for the more it is exercised, the more it perfects the instruments through which it works, namely, the cognitive structure of the mind. Thus, the cultivation of intelligence is the most profitable of all exercises; for, unlike the using of a machine, it does not wear out the instrument with which it works, but, rather, like the use of our muscles, strengthens them. Further, it not only strengthens its instruments, as we strengthen and increase the bulk of our muscles by use, but, also, it perpetually differentiates, specializes, and reorganizes the whole system of instruments, the cognitive structure, thus rendering its operations more and more effective. This is the explanation of the vast importance of the comparatively small differences of native intelligence displayed by young children. The small superiority of the more intelligent child may, by cultivation and the development of intellect, become the vast superiority of the man of great intellect to the ordinary man.

merely imagining it; further, I said, we must regard these cognitive dispositions as connected to form systems, and these again as connected in larger systems; so that the whole organization is a treelike structure.

We must repudiate as false an old-fashioned way of describing the growth of the mind, which consists in assuming that the mind begins by acquiring "ideas" of distinct particular objects through perceiving them as such, and that it then associates its "ideas" of these particulars to form more complex "ideas." This is the associationist doctrine. It assumes that we begin by getting, through sense-impressions, distinct "ideas" of the various sensory qualities; that these then become linked or associated together in various groupings, to constitute "ideas" of complex objects or "compound ideas." That, for example, the child gets through sense-impressions an "idea" of red color, an "idea" of roundness, an "idea" of weight, an "idea" of solidity, and then puts these together to form the "idea" of an apple; that in a similar way it forms an "idea" of an orange, of a pear, and of a plum; that later all these particular "ideas" become associated together to form a generic "idea" of an edible fruit, the differences becoming vague through neutralization, the common features becoming accentuated in virtue of their similarity and consequent repetition of similar impressions. This is the doctrine of the "generic image" as a stage in the formation of the "general idea."

It is said that by a similar process, carried to a further stage, the "generic image" may fuse or coalesce with "ideas" or "generic images" of edible things of other kinds; until eventually we arrive at the "general idea" of something edible, in which all special qualities are suppressed or vague, and only the common feature of edibility stands out in consciousness. This alleged process has been likened to composite photography. Suppose that you made a composite photograph of a number of horses; the result would show clearly the features common to all horses, and vaguely or not at all the features peculiar to any one horse. This would be comparable to the generic image of the horse which, according to this purely fanciful account, occupies consciousness when we speak or think of horses in general, or make or understand any proposition referring to horses in general; and it constitutes the "meaning" in consciousness of the word "horse," when the word is used to refer to horses in general.[1]

"Generic images" do occur, in the sense that you may picture or visualize an object in a way which combines features perceived on various occasions, or combines in one picture of, say, a horse features perceived in a number of different horses. But that this is not the way in which we arrive at "general ideas"—that the view of mental growth implied by this theory is fallacious, becomes clear, if we try to carry the account further. Thus, the theory would account for the genesis of "the idea of quadruped" by supposing that the generic images of horses and of dogs, cows and cats and camels become superimposed to form a composite in which the only clear features are the four legs; while all the specific features, the cow's horns, the camel's hump, and the dog's tail, become blurred and vanishingly faint. And it is similarly driven to assume that, when we become able to think of animals in general, this process of blurring is carried still further; until we have a highly general "idea" which is a picture in which the generic images of quadrupeds and birds, fishes and reptiles, crabs and insects, and sea-urchins and sponges and worms, are superimposed and blended to a mere blur of variegated color. This is the *reductio ad absurdum* both of the theory which identifies "meaning" with imagery and of the theory of mental growth by the accretion of distinct entities, sensations, impressions, or images, to form "ideas," according to the principle of association.

This theory of mental growth by association and accretion, which is an inevitable corollary of the mosaic or atomistic psychology, really inverts the true order of events. It describes mental development as beginning with the cognition of particulars and advancing to cognition of the more general; whereas, in reality, we begin by cognition of the highly general and progress gradually to the cognition of particulars.

[1] The late Professors T. H. Huxley and Th. Ribot were leading exponents of this doctrine. Ribot expounded it in his "Evolution of General Ideas" in a less crude form than Huxley in his essay on David Hume.

The advance of intellect is from knowledge of a few objects of very highly general type, towards knowledge of the multitude of concrete individual objects and their peculiar qualities and relations.

The animal perceives, knows, or recognizes few, if any, individual objects as such; rather, it perceives and reacts to objects of certain kinds, those which it is prepared by native constitution to perceive; and each such object is, for the animal, merely a representative of its class, and is marked as such by some relatively simple feature or sensory pattern, corresponding to one of the few cognitive dispositions possessed by the animal. On the other hand, the most richly endowed and perfectly organized mind would be a microcosm which faithfully reflected the macrocosm, the world in which it dwelt and which it was concerned to know. It would comprise a multitude of cognitive dispositions, corresponding, one for one, to every object in its world, every quality and every form of relation. And these dispositions would not merely coexist; rather they would form a logically ordered system, reflecting in its organization all the relations of the world of objects. The cognitive dispositions of such a mind would form a coherent system; because in the main they are evolved by differentiation from a few primitive systems, as a tree evolves by growth and differentiation of its stem into branches, twigs, and leaves. That is to say, each cognitive disposition of the developed mind is not an independent new formation deposited by some sense-impression, but is formed by a gradual growth and differentiation from preexisting dispositions.

The processes of growth are of three principal types, namely, discrimination, apperception, and association. Let us consider them in turn.

Discrimination

The child learns at an early age to discriminate between edible and inedible objects. Consider how such discrimination is effected. His native food-seeking instinct reacts to all small objects presented to the eye with an impulse to grasp the object, carry it to the mouth, and bite it. At first, it is safe to say, the child does not discriminate between a red apple and a ripe tomato. When he bites the apple, the sense-impression of taste stimulates him to continue and complete the process of ingestion. When he bites the tomato, the sense-impression of taste excites a new impulse, that of disgust; and he spews out and throws down the tomato. After one or more experiences of this kind, he will reject a tomato at sight, but will seize and devour an apple with increased gusto. The cognitive disposition by means of which he at first perceived both kinds of fruit has become differentiated into two; of these two, the one corresponding to apples continues to be connected with the conative disposition that impels to eating; the other, that which corresponds to tomato, has become connected with the conative disposition of disgust. Thus the child has learned to discriminate through the bad consequences of his failure to discriminate; and in this his progress is typical of all advance of discrimination; we learn by making mistakes, as we say.

Consider again the way in which a child learns to discriminate between living beings. At first he responds to all large moving objects with vague signs of interest, which we cannot confidently interpret. Then he learns to discriminate between human beings and animals; later between individuals, mother, nurse, father, and brother, and between dog and cat and bird. The making of these discriminations is only possible in so far as the several individuals and classes of objects present different sensory patterns; but the differences of sensory pattern will not in themselves suffice; the passive reception of the various complex sense-impressions would lead to no discrimination. It is only in so far as the child strives to achieve certain goals in relation to the objects, that he learns to discriminate between them. As in the case of the apple and tomato, so in the case of dog and cat, or of mother and sister; the objects, while not discriminated, are different, and they yield or respond to the child's efforts differently, according to their natures, provoking in him, upon nearer acquaintance, different reactions; the differences of reaction thus provoked in the child are the ground of his subsequent discrimination. The undeveloped mind may require few or many repetitions, according to the prominence of the differences of sensory pattern presented by the objects and the strength or urgency of the differential reactions evoked by them. Thus the child may be slow to discriminate at sight between hard green apples and ripe sweet ones; but quickly learns to distinguish tomato from apple, because the former provokes a strong disgust impulse.

The isolated individual child, however well endowed, would make comparatively little progress in such discrimination. The normal child is immensely aided by example, instruction, and the use of names. Successive generations of men have made finer and finer discriminations, and have given conventional or traditional permanence to the discriminated classes and objects by labelling or naming them. And the child is led and aided to repeat these discriminations; is led to split up the flux of sense-impressions, which is the world as presented to its senses, along the traditional lines, to discriminate those kinds of objects which the experience of mankind has found to be of greatest practical importance. Thus the child is guided to differentiate in his own mind, by successive acts of discrimination, the few innately given cognitive dispositions into systems of dispositions corresponding to these classes of practically important objects.

At a later stage the child develops special interests which lead him to effect finer discriminations within special classes of objects, still largely under the guidance of language and of other specialists. For example, he may become an epicure or a wine taster, may develop immensely his discrimination in one or more such spheres. Then, where the average man can hardly distinguish one kind of drink from another, does not know whether a particular wine is port or claret, the specialist can distinguish and recognize perhaps fifty varieties of claret and as many of port, accurately naming each one.

In this process the names serve not only to aid and guide discrimination, by accentuating the differences between objects; but also they enable us to continue to think of a class of objects, after we have learned to discriminate and recognize sub-classes and individual objects within the class. In the process of differentiation of dispositions by discrimination, the name serves to preserve as a system the original disposition within which differentiation takes place. For the hearing of the name of an object fulfils the same function as the sense-impressions of peculiar pattern received from it; namely, it brings the corresponding disposition into activity, and thus enables us to continue to conceive as a whole the class within which we have distinguished kinds or individuals; whereas, in the absence of the class-name, so soon as we had learned to react differently to the objects or varieties of objects within the class, we should cease to think of the class. Thus a child, having learned, through contact with various dogs, to think of dog in general, goes on to discriminate collie dogs and terriers; and we may suppose that he adopts very different attitudes toward the two breeds. owing to the friendliness of the collies and the snappishness of the terriers. Such a child, if deprived altogether of the use of language, would sharply distinguish the two classes and would tend to lose the power of thinking of dog in general. But a child who has first learned to give the name "dog" to dogs of both breeds will continue to think of this more general object on hearing the word "dog," after he has learned to discriminate between collies and terriers.

In this connection it is of interest to note that many primitive languages are very deficient in names for more general objects; though they may have a profusion of names for special classes of objects of practical importance. It is said, for example, that one tribe of American Indians had names for the white, the black, the red, and the burr oak, but none for oak in general. Another tribe used thirty different words to denote different kinds of washing—washing one's own face, washing the face of another, washing hands, washing clothing, etc., but no word to express washing in general. The Australian aborigines, it is said, had no names for general or abstract objects; they had a distinct name for each of many species of trees, but no name for tree in general, and no names for such abstract objects as hardness, softness, warmth, cold, shortness, or roundness. Facts of this order have been mistakenly invoked to support the theory of the formation of "general ideas" by accretion of "particular ideas."

This lack of names for general and abstract objects in the languages of various primitive peoples indicates rather a defect of capacity for the second great type of process by which our mental structure grows and becomes logically organized. This capacity, the most important factor in high intelligence, we must now consider.

The function of comparing two things, or making a comparative judgment, is explicit discrimination. It is discrimination preceded by suspense of judgment, doubt, and explicit inquiry. The young child who has learned to discriminate the tomato from the apple, *i. e.*, has learned to react differently on sight of apple and tomato, may later have occasion to discriminate between two such objects by explicit comparison. This is not fully achieved, until he learns to name the two objects, and to formulate his doubt in the form of a question and the result of his judgment in the form of a proposition. Shortly stated, comparison which discovers difference is discrimination on the plane of explicit judgment; and comparison which discovers likeness is explicit recognition.

Apperception or Apperceptive Synthesis

If a human mind were developed by means of a perfect series of discriminations, under the guidance of a perfect language, it would achieve a structure which would be a perfect microcosm or mirror of the world. But this never actually occurs. The course of development by discrimination diverges widely from such a perfect course; because the human mind is not governed solely or predominatingly by the impulse or desire for complete and perfect knowledge, but rather by a variety of instinctive impulses adapted to secure the survival of the organism in a hostile world and to secure satisfaction of its practical needs.

Hence the process of differentiation of mental structure by successive discriminations requires to be rectified by another process, if the mind is to acquire a high level of effective organization; and this other process is apperception.

Apperception involves the discerning of essential similarities between objects and classes of objects which we have learned to discriminate and distinguish from one another. As an example of this process, take the case of a child who has grown up without learning to regard plants as living beings, but nevertheless has learned to think of them as a distinct class of things. Suddenly it is borne in on him that plants also, like the animals, are alive. At that moment two mental systems (systems of cognitive dispositions) become conjoined in his mind, and thereafter form a single larger system; the living-being system, which had been formed by experience of animals only, incorporates the plant-system with itself. In terms of the analogy between the structure of the mind and the growing family-tree, we may say that two differing stocks or branches of the system become blended by intermarriage.[1]

[1] Some authors (*e. g.*, Professor Stout, in his "Analytic Psychology") would say that the one mental system apperceives the other. But that usage seems to me undesirable. It seems better to describe the fact by saying that the subject apperceives the object, and to understand that apperception involves the conjunction of systems.

As an example of a slightly different mode of this process we may take the young student of physics, who, having learned to think of gases and of liquids as very different states of matter, suddenly becomes aware of those points of similarity in virtue of which they are classed together as fluid matter. The two systems, built up by his observations of gases and of liquids respectively, become conjoined in a new system, the possession of which thereafter enables him to think of a fluid as matter having the properties common to liquid and gases, to the neglect of or in abstraction from those properties in which they differ.

Or, again, a child is familiar with the eggs of animals and with the seeds of plants; but has never thought of their similarities, until he is led to do so by hearing the word "egg" applied to the seed of a plant, or the word "germ" applied to both eggs and seeds. From this time on, the word "germ" will be used by him to mean the properties common to both eggs and seeds.

It is clear from these examples that language here, as in discrimination, plays a great part; that it leads the developing mind to effect processes of apperceptive synthesis. Language embodies in a traditional form the mental achievements of our predecessors. The words which lead us to effect such syntheses embody the achievements of original minds of bygone generations, who in each case achieved the synthesis by some act of independent or original apperception. A classical instance of such original apperception is Newton's discovery of the essential similarity between the motion of the moon about the earth and that of a falling body. The application by him of the name "gravitation," to both these superficially unlike types of phenomena, enables us, who come after him, to repeat his original stroke and to effect a similar synthesis in our mental structure.

The process of apperceptive synthesis thus produces a simplification of the structure of the mind and of the language which reflects it, a simplification by which they are rendered more effective instruments of thinking. Instead of having a separate name and a separate disposition for every class of objects which are essentially similar (or the same in so far as they concern our practical needs) we have names and mental systems corresponding to larger classes the members of which resemble one another less obviously or in less immediately and practically important respects. In this way primitive man's rough classification of the animal world has been refined by successive apperceptions, involving the discovery of a multitude of homologies, until the present scientific classification has been evolved.[1]

Apperceptive synthesis is thus a process of the greatest importance for the higher development of the intellect. It may be said to rectify the failures and imperfections of the process of differentiation of mental structure by successive discriminations. Discrimination is the discovery of differences; apperception is the discovery of similarities.

In the traditional association psychology, the process of apperception was recognized, though very inadequately, and named "association by similarity." Professor Stout[2] has clearly pointed out that, under this term, two essentially different processes of very unequal intellectual value have been confused together. He proposes to distinguish them by the terms "reproduction or revival *by* similars" and "reproduction *of* similars." The former is a very commonplace function. The latter is essentially the process of apperceptive synthesis which we are discussing; it is the main instrument of scientific discovery, the essence of all that can properly be called wit and reasoning, and the soul of poetry. By this operation are discovered all remoter resemblances, all analogies, homologies, similes, and metaphors. In fact, it is an essential part of all the higher operations of the mind.[3]

[1] *E. g.*, the discovery of the segmental nature of the skull of vertebrates and its homology with the vertebrate column; of the homology of the auditory meatus or ear-hole with a gill cleft; or that between forelegs, arms, and wings. The apperception of the skull as a segmental structure seems to have been an original stroke of the poet Goethe.

[2] "Groundwork of Psychology," p. 123.

[3] The capacity or facility for the exercise of this function is a native endowment in respect of which individuals differ greatly. Without possessing it in considerable degree, a man cannot achieve intellectual work of an original kind. He may become a paragon of learning, but not a wit, a discoverer, a poet, or a creator in any field. Doctor Maxwell Garnet has produced an ingenious mathematical argument for the view that all such operations depend upon a single factor or peculiarity of our constitution. ("Education and World Citizenship," London, 1920.)

Let us note a very simple instance of its operation, used by Stout to illustrate the propriety of his description of it as "reproduction of similars." You meet a stranger, *A*, and you are at once reminded of a friend, *B*, who resembles him. That is "reproduction of similars." You do not mistake *A* for *B*. That would be "reproduction by similars." The similarity may be of a gross and obvious kind. It may be that both *A* and *B* have lost an eye, or have a prominent white forelock in a dark pate. No high degree of apperceptive delicacy is then required, in order that the sight of *A* may remind you of *B*. But the similarity may be very much more subtle; it may be a mere slight intonation, the play of some facial muscle, a turn of the head, something perhaps that you cannot single out and define; yet it suffices to make you think of *B*.

If, on the other hand, on sight of *A* you mistake him for *B* and address him as *B*, that is merely a failure of discrimination, permitting the sight of *A* to work upon you in the same way as the sight of *B* would do. To some extent all association on perception is a case of reproduction *by* similars; for even when you see the same man (or a thing) on successive occasions and recognize and name him, the sense-impression is never quite the same on the successive occasions. Reproduction by similars merely brings back in succession two things already associated in the mind; reproduction of similars brings together things not previously thought of together.

Now notice that this process of apperception works in two ways: The one way is the reproduction of similars—as when the perception of *A* leads you to think explicitly of *B*, or of a class of men all of whom have some quality, physical or moral, in common with *A*; or when the bearing and appearance of a girl lead you to think of a lily or a rosebud or a peacock; or foam-crested breakers suggest galloping white horses; or when the poet, roaming idly over the countryside, likens himself to a cloud, the perfect image of leisurely loneliness.[1] Thousands of such resemblances have been embodied in forms of speech which have become familiar to us all, and which guide us to detect them. But every such resemblance, embodied in any simile or metaphor or parable, was first detected by some original mind by the process of reproduction of similars—a process which, in respect of its effect on mental structure, is the apperceptive synthesis of systems.

The same process is involved in what is called "forming abstract ideas." Some quality of one thing suggests another very unlike thing that has the same or a similar quality. We then discriminate this quality and give it a name, and thus become

[1] "I wandered lonely as a cloud that floats on high o'er vales and hills."

capable of thinking of the quality in detachment from all particular things; for example, the grace of a birch-tree, of a woman, of a swan, of a deer, of a landscape. The abstracting of the common quality from many different things and its fixation, as an object of thought, by the aid of a name are the completion and perfection of the process of apperceptive synthesis. The total process involves all three processes of growth, namely, discrimination, apperception, and association. When we use such an abstract word as "grace" or "graceful," all our experience of the things in which we have appreciated this quality, which have influenced or affected us in virtue of this quality, is operative determining the meaning of the word. That is to say, the various mental systems, built up by experience of things presenting this quality and united by apperceptive synthesis to form a single functional system, now function as one system.

The use of the word, or the understanding of it when heard or read, brings this system into operation, and this operation, this activity, is the "meaning" of the word as you utter or hear it. No imagery is essential; though the image of any one of the objects (or of several of them in turn) in which this quality has been perceived may break into consciousness, if we dwell for a moment on the word and explicate its meaning. But for the most part in the ordinary use of language, we take the meaning of such words and use them appropriately with awareness of their meaning, without imagery of the concrete objects. That is to say, a vast amount of mental structure becomes active in the thinking of these abstract qualities, without any coming to consciousness of the concrete objects from which the quality has been abstracted. When you read of "the tender grace of a day that is dead," you take the meaning of the poet more or less adequately; although it is impossible to visualize a graceful day or, indeed, any kind of a day; and though you do not, as a matter of fact, visualize a graceful object of any kind as you become aware of the meaning.

Here we get a glimpse of the fact that, in discourse carried on largely in abstract terms, a vast extent of mental structure becomes active and participates in determining the course of our thinking, without throwing up to consciousness the images which would arise, if we dwelt upon the abstract words in order to explicate their meanings.

Such are the nature and results of explicit apperception. But apperception works also in an implicit fashion, on a lower plane of intellectuality. And apperception of this kind also is of great importance and subtlety. Let us go back to the example of meeting a stranger, *A*. He does not bring to mind any known person; yet, on seeing him, you get an impression of a certain indefinable quality. Perhaps you say: "I wouldn't trust that man"; or, without even so much formulation, you react toward him in the way implied by those words. In this case, some quality, some subtle conjunction of sense-impressions, works upon you, leading you to react to him as you have learned, by experience of their actions, to react to other men who presented similar conjunctions of sensory cues. You may be quite unable, even if challenged to do so, to point to the details of feature, bearing, or intonation which produce this effect, or to define in words the quality to which you react. The effect is a synthetic product; you cannot analyze it, nor state its conditions; yet it may be strong and definite and may determine all your dealings with the man in question. The similarity or resemblance to other persons or things is too subtle for your powers of analysis or explicit abstraction; and yet it works upon you to determine your conative emotional reaction.

Such implicit apperception is, I think, properly called "intuition." Some minds, even of persons who have little power of abstract thinking and little command of abstract terms, work in this way with marvellous subtlety; they are properly said to be gifted with intuition. I know of no other mental function to which this term can be as properly applied. And in its ordinary usage the word does, I think, imply this type of mental operation. Some women possess it in very high degree; young children, whose command of language is very slight, may exhibit it; and even in the higher animals, especially the dog, it is not altogether lacking. As it occurs in them, it may be regarded as the germ from which the power of abstract thinking develops.

The student should notice that, in nearly all cases, the similarity that determines intuitive understanding (implicit apperception) or is discovered by explicit apperception (reproduction of similars) is a similarity of form of combination, rather than simple similarity of sensory qualities. In the chapter on perception I pointed out how the form of the whole object perceived may determine the meanings of the several parts, as in all perception of complex spatial relations. This influence of the meaning or form of the whole upon the meaning of the part was called "relative suggestion." The form of the whole object constitutes what has been called "an object of a higher order" or a "form-quality."[1] It is similarities of such forms or "objects of higher order" that in the main determine apperception. Thus a verse or poem may remind you of another poem, all the words and meanings of which are very different, in virtue of similarity of metrical form. The same is true in even higher degree of musical compositions. Again one play (or novel, or biography) may bring to mind another, not in virtue of any similarity between the personalities or situations of the two plays, but because they are alike in general form or plot; the system of relations is alike in the two plays, though all details and actual relations are different. The construction of an original allegory or parable is clearly due to the co-operation of relative suggestion with apperception. Thus, in the construction of John Bunyan's great allegory, apperception revealed to Bunyan the similarity between the Christian life and a journey through a strange country beset with snares and dangers; relative suggestion then filled out the details of the story in accordance with the scheme common to the two wholes.

The two processes of growth we have discussed, namely, discrimination and apperception, produce the logical structure of the mind; that is to say, the structure of the mind, in so far as it mirrors the world of things and qualities, their differences and resemblances. A mind developed by these two processes only would have knowledge of the nature of things and of the likenesses and differences between them; and it would be able to reason logically about their relations. But it would have no knowledge of the relations of time and place between concrete things; that is to say, it would have no knowledge of the historical order of events. Such historical knowledge is built up by association. Association binds together the dispositions of the logical structure by a system of cross-connections which mirror the historical relations as perceived.

Development of Mental Structure by Association

The traditional association psychology tended to reduce all the alleged varieties of association to the form of association by succession in time or "temporal contiguity"; and this is, in fact,

[1] "Gestalt-qualität," by German writers.

the one fundamental form of association. It also represented this as the only mode of all mental development. The universal formula of mental growth was—"ideas" or impressions that immediately succeed one another in consciousness become associated together, and associated the more firmly the more frequently the succession is repeated. And it was attempted to represent all association as identical with the process of formation of bodily habits by repetition of trains of movement. I have pointed out in Chapter X that we must look with suspicion on this attempt, as one that unduly simplifies the problems of association. I illustrated the difference between formation of habit, on the one hand, and association by meaning, on the other, and the immensely superior efficiency of the latter; admitting that, in much of what we call learning by association, as in the learning of a verse, both factors are operative in various degrees, the true thought factor or association by meaning, and the habit factor.

The speaking of a word is the exercise of a habit of the speech organs, a habit acquired by repetition. And the power of speech implies the formation of a great array of such habits. But intelligent speech is not merely the play of these motor mechanisms. The order in which they are brought into play is determined by the play of meanings, as we see in the recital of the verse; and "the play of meanings" means the play of mental dispositions sustained by purpose or conation. Thus, in reciting a familiar verse, associations of two orders come into play, the associations of the verbal motor mechanisms (as when I recite "Ena meena mina mo)" and the associations between the mental dispositions corresponding to the objects referred to by the verse:

"Among the ungathered rice he lay, his sickle in his hand,
His breast was bare, his matted hair was buried in the sand."

In the recital of such a verse by different persons, the two factors may operate in very different proportions. A dull-witted young child, of little more intelligence than an idiot, may learn the verse by many repetitions and gabble it off with a minimum of appreciation of its meaning. That is little more than the exercise of a chain of motor speech-habits.[1] A person who intelligently appreciates the meaning, with or without the aid of visual imagery, may repeat it by heart after a single reading; the meanings of the various words have, by interplay, generated a total meaning which binds them together and which governs the reproduction of the successive partial meanings and of the words which express them.

The former reciter may substitute words of similar sound without becoming aware of the error, as follows:

"Beside the ungathered rice he lay, his sickle in his sand
His crest was care, his hatted hair was buried in the band."

This example will serve to show how in verse, as in a lesser degree in all verbal reproduction, there are operative associations not merely of one level or kind, but of at least three levels. For, beside the simple links of association which bind the words together as motor mechanisms, and beside the association of meanings, there is a mid-level association which connects the parts in a formal whole or scheme, independently of their meanings; and any words which will satisfy or fill out this scheme are liable to be substituted, when the process of reproduction is not guided by the meanings of the words. The production of such a nonsense parody verse is a case of relative suggestion in which the schema of rhyme, metre, and rhythm is the governing factor. Association and associative reproduction are then, even in relatively simple instances, far from simple processes easily understood in terms of lowered synaptic resistances.

It may be that the difference between true mental association and habit formation is only a matter of difference of level in the nervous system, and that both depend upon changes of nervous structure of essentially similar type. That, however, is a very speculative question. Whatever the true answer to that question may be, we must recognize association between mental dispositions and systems as a real and important process of growth of mental structure.

Of course, every one acquires much knowledge of historical sequences indirectly, from the descriptions given by others; but we may neglect that kind of knowledge; it involves merely some complication of the principles concerned in the acquisition of knowledge of the order of one's own past experience. Consider,

[1] Some children of very low intelligence are remarkably capable in the formation of such quasi-mechanical or habit associations.

then, the work of association as revealed by a simple recital of some train of events, as by a witness in a law court. "I saw the prisoner step into the road and hold up his hand to stop an approaching car. The car stopped, the driver got out, the prisoner shot him down, stepped in, and drove away."

The recital depends upon the faithfulness of association of the succession of events as perceived, and on the working of associative reproduction, reviving the events in imagination in the order of their perception; that is to say, it depends on simple redintegration. I can think of, or imagine, the various objects, because I have the necessary cognitive dispositions; but the thinking of them in an order which reproduces the order of the events is due to association by temporal contiguity; but not to this alone. It is due also to conative continuity. I paid attention to the events, because for some reason I was interested; perhaps the unusual behavior of the prisoner had aroused my curiosity, and I watched to see what would happen. That is, I perceived the events as significant parts of one train, having continuity of interest and meaning for me. This conative continuity was an essential condition of the formation of the associations; and the keener was my attention then, the stronger are the associative links now, and the more surely do they work in the reproduction of the series in imagination or retrospect.

The structure of the mind is full of such associative links between cognitive dispositions; and these links reflect the temporal sequences of its past experiences. But such association begins to work at a relatively late stage of development only. Using the language of "ideas," we may say that association can only work when "ideas" have been constituted, *i. e.*, when many mental dispositions have become differentiated and organized in systems. The mistake of the association psychology was to assign to association also the work of making "ideas."

Association makes nothing new; it merely connects together "ideas" or dispositions previously formed, previously differentiated by discrimination and logically ordered by apperception. It sets up a rich network of cross-connections between the multitude of dispositions; a network of connecting threads, the woof formed by the shuttle of time, which, shooting to and fro across the warp of mental structure formed by the proliferating systems of dispositions, weaves them into a connected mass.

This connecting thread may be started into activity by some sense-impression or perception, at any point corresponding to some moment of past time; then in its simplest cases, namely, in simple redintegration, it operates like a fuse which, ignited at any point, conducts the exciting spark in one direction only, namely, in the direction from the past toward the present, igniting one disposition after another, and so bringing to mind the corresponding objects in the order of their perception, the order in which the shuttle reached them.

But this process of redintegration never continues long without interruption, for two reasons. First, in weaving the pattern of associations, the shuttle of experience returns again and again to the same dispositions, crossing and recrossing its old paths; that is to say, sense-impressions lead us to think of the same object in different temporal and spatial connections upon successive occasions; and so the woof of connecting threads, or associations, becomes immensely tangled; each disposition becomes associated with many others, so that the spreading spark, on reaching any one disposition, may have many alternative routes open to it. If, then, it follows any route other than the original path of the shuttle, we have divergent reproduction. If, for example, the same person, *X*, has figured twice in my experience in two different connections, *A* and *B;* then, when the redintegrating spark reaches the disposition, *X*, it may follow either the route representing the original order of my thinking or perception, on the occasion *a;* or it may diverge along the route of my thought on the occasion *b*. The more varied the experience of the subject, the more numerous will be these alternative lines of association, diverging from each disposition.

The facts of mental structure thus require for their diagrammatic representation a three-dimensional diagram. As such a diagram we may take a bush woven over by a multitude of spider's threads, stretching from leaf to leaf; each leaf being directly connected with many others by these threads. Such is the crude picture we may form of the structure of the mind and of the way the branches, twigs, and leaves of the tree of logical knowledge are woven together by the threads of historical association.

Secondly, in working of system, the quasi-mechanical tendency of the associative threads is not left without control. In simple reminiscence, no doubt, there is approximation to such free play of association. But, in proportion as our thinking is purposive, is a striving to a goal, the solution of a problem, conation interferes with and largely overrules association, accentuating, as a selective factor, the chances of revival of whatever is relevant to the governing purpose. Thus, in reciting a train of incidents, if our purpose is to tell the truth, the whole truth, and nothing but the truth, this purpose may reinforce the redintegrative tendency of pure associative reproduction. But in nearly all cases some other motive is at work. We desire to bring out the guilty or the innocent intention of the person whose actions we describe; or we aim at making the story dramatic and interesting to our hearers; or we desire to put in a good light our own share in the events. And, according to the strength of these motives, of which we may be not explicitly aware, we select, emphasize, and omit, in a way that shapes the course of reproduction, to serve our implicit purpose. And, if we are not aware of the operation of such motives and of the nature of our implicit purpose, we may in all good faith recite a story which grotesquely distorts the actual order of the events we profess to describe.

Assimilation

By some psychologists who followed Locke's way of "ideas," yet saw that "ideas" cannot be generated by association alone, that we do not begin our mental life with a multitude of discrete sensations or simple "ideas" and proceed to associate them together to form complex "ideas," *assimilation* was made the fundamental mode of growth. An "idea" or "percept" was said to assimilate new elements, when we perceive an object like some familiar object, but yet different in certain respects. In simple recognition of an object as the same, it would seem that no growth or differentiation of mental structure is involved; there results presumably merely a consolidation of structure already formed, as in all merely repetitive process, in the simple repetition of action and in simple reproduction or redintegration. If, on the other hand, an object is recognized as like a familiar object, but yet different in some respects, the process, in so far as it results in mental growth, would seem to be essentially one of discrimination. I cannot see, therefore, that assimilation can properly be regarded as one of the fundamental modes of development of mental structure.

CHAPTER XVI

REASONING AND THE SYSTEM OF BELIEFS

We have seen that the feeling or emotion of belief (positive or negative) results from judgment. We have now to discuss beliefs, rather than belief as a mode of experience. A belief is an enduring (though not necessarily permanent) feature in the structure of the mind; judgment produces the structural change which persists as a belief, after we cease to think of the topic and the feeling of belief has died away. We have seen that perception normally involves judgment and establishes belief. In primitive perception the judgment is implicit only; as when the dog recognizes his master at sight. And the belief established by primitive perception is merely a confident anticipation; as when the dog, hearing his master's whistle, confidently anticipates his appearance.

Explicit judgment, giving rise to definite belief, follows upon suspension of judgment in the attitude of doubt and inquiry. It takes place only on that level of mental life at which belief is expressed in the form of a proposition. But, although fully explicit judgment and definite belief may be clearly distinguished from implicit judgment and mere confident anticipation, there is no sharp line to be drawn between them. In our own experience we may recognize many intermediate grades. When I hear the voice of a long-absent friend, I may merely leap to my feet and run to the window; as the dog does on hearing his master's voice without. Or I may exclaim, as I do so, "There's *A*." Or I may listen a moment in doubt, before springing up; the familiar quality of the voice merely arresting my attention and throwing me into the attitude, "What's that?" Or I may formulate my doubt in a question, "Is that *A?*" and then, after listening again, decide "Yes, that's *A*."

A large number of beliefs about particular things result immediately from perception. Others are arrived at by associative reproduction or memory of perception; as when you are asked of a past event, "Did he speak loudly?" or "Did he sing out of tune?" If you answer this question with a confident "Yes" or "No," you are either calling to mind a belief established by explicit judgment at the time of hearing the voice; or you recall the voice as heard and now base your explicit judgment upon this recollection, making explicit that which had remained implicit in your perception, namely, the degree of loudness of the voice or trueness of pitch.

We have seen also that judgment and consequent belief may be determined by communication. In the simplest of such instances, the other person's assertion determines my judgment, either on perception or recollection, merely in virtue of his prestige and my docility; that is to say, my attitude toward him is submissive, and, when he expresses a belief, my submissive impulse works as a force to determine my judgment in conformity with his assertion. This is "suggestion" in the technical sense. It works much more effectively on judgments of recollection than on judgments of perception. Thus, if the question is, "Is he singing out of tune?" your judgment will be less easily determined by suggestion than when the question is, "Did he sing out of tune?" But all communication is by sense-perception,[1] and, therefore, although determination of judgment by suggestion is the source of many beliefs, such beliefs, like those established by judgments of recollection, are directly derived from sense-perception, and involve no principles of mental action radically distinct from those of sense-perception.

Almost all the beliefs of a simple-minded person are derived from sense-perception in one or other of these three ways—perceptual judgment, judgments of recollection, and judgments on suggestion. But there is another great process by which beliefs are established, namely, REASONING.

Most of the more general beliefs of a developed mind are the product of a process in which suggestion is mixed with reasoning. Thus my belief that "this orange is round" is the product of perceptual judgment; but my belief that "this earth is round" is due in the main to communication; and, though those commu-

[1] With the possible exception before noted of telepathic communication.

nications worked upon me originally by suggestion, they have been supported or reinforced by reasoning processes, so that my belief, as I now hold it, is, in part at least, rational, or the product of reasoning. When suggestion and reasoning work together, we properly speak of *persuasion.* The rational factor in persuasion may remain implicit; as when I believe the assertion of another man, because I believe him to be a trustworthy witness and narrator and could rationally justify this belief, although I do not stop to do so; or it may be explicit, as when he reasons or argues effectively in support of his assertion.

The peculiarity of reasoning which justly excites anew in every generation wonder and admiration is that, by means of it, we attain to true beliefs, independently of new perceptions and independently of reproductive imagination or specific recollections. So marvellous is this process that in every age philosophers have been inclined to set "Reason" apart from all other mental functions, on a throne by itself. Aristotle set the fashion with his doctrine of the "creative reason," which, it seemed to him, must be regarded as an influx from some superior realm; whereas all other mental processes were essentially functions of the bodily organism. And long discussions of this topic throughout the middle ages culminated in the nineteenth-century disputes in which, though it became generally admitted that animals share in all the other mental powers of men, some thinkers continued to deny that they have "Reason," and to regard reasoning as a process wholly different in kind from all others. And philosophers and psychologists are by no means agreed as to the essential marks of reasoning; they continue to put forward views of reasoning differing as widely as Plato's differed from the theory of the early Greek materialists. On the one hand are those for whom Reason is a quasi-divine and altogether spiritual function; on the other hand, the frank materialists and the modern near materialists, such as Messrs. C. A. Strong, G. Santayana, Bertrand Russell, and other Neo-Realists. For most of these, reasoning is merely a complex process of associative reproduction, and is essentially determined by the play of physico-chemical processes in the brain, proceeding according to purely mechanistic laws of habit.

From the point of view of psychology we may best define reasoning broadly as follows.

The essence of all reasoning is that judgment and a new belief are determined by beliefs already established in the mind. If these old beliefs are true and the reasoning process correct, then the new belief is true and becomes an effective guide to action. In the most striking cases, the new belief is derived by a complex chain of processes from a number of previously established beliefs; as when the astronomer Adams arrived at the belief that a hitherto unseen planet would be seen at a certain position in the heavens, if a sufficiently powerful telescope were directed to that spot.

But some reasonings are very simple. We may distinguish three principal types of reasoning: (1) First, reasoning from two particular beliefs to a third particular belief. (2) Secondly, reasoning from several or many particular beliefs to a general belief. (3) Thirdly, reasoning from a general belief and a particular belief to a particular belief. The first is not commonly admitted to deserve the lofty title of reasoning. The second, known as inductive reasoning, is also regarded by some logicians as hardly worthy of the name. The third, known as deductive reasoning, has been generally held to be reasoning in the full and perfect sense, the process in which the mystery of mind culminates.

Although these three modes of reasoning are perfectly distinct in simple and typical instances, much reasoning partakes of the nature of all three types. But we may confine our attention to the three typical modes. Reasoning of each mode may be used either as a process of discovering new truth, or as a process of establishing, of demonstrating, truth, of justifying belief in the truth of a proposition which we are already inclined to accept. The former is the more important use of reasoning; it may be called scientific reasoning. The latter is a simpler process, and may be called argumentative reasoning; but here again there is no sharp line.

Let us dispose at once of the contention that reasoning is nothing but associative reproduction. This is the traditional associationist view, which hangs together with the view that belief is inseparable association. We have seen that association is not belief—no matter how inseparable; I must now insist again that associative reproduction is not judgment, though it may determine judgment and consequently belief. The formula of association is "this and that"; the formula of belief is "this is that." From the point of view of mental structure, association is the linkage of distinct dispositions; judgment, on the other hand, produces either differentiation of dispositions (discriminative judgment which, when explicit, results in negative belief—"this is not that") or synthesis of dispositions (apperceptive judgments). In terms of the association psychology, the "idea" of black is very strongly associated in my mind with the "idea" of white; but I have no belief that black is white, and no increase of the strength of association between the two "ideas" would generate or constitute that belief. So, also, I have seen innumerable horses, each of which had four legs and a tail, and I have never seen a horse otherwise equipped; yet I do not believe that every horse has four legs and a tail. And if I believe that every full-grown horse has a mouth, that is not due to association, but to reasoning.

Reasoning from Particulars

When we reason from two particular beliefs to a third, our mental process is essentially one of imaginative manipulation or experimentation. For example, I believe that the city *B* is north of the city *A*, and also that *C* is north of *B*. The question may then arise—is *C* north of *A*? By imagining the relative positions of *B* and *A* and of *C* and *B*, on a map or scheme, however vaguely (just as I might draw them on a sheet of paper), I at once arrive at the belief that *C* is north of *A*. This is a simple mode of reasoning applicable to all questions of less and more, of serial order in space, time, or quality. In practice we often make use of it in determining the relative order in time of past events.

Notice that the mere coexistence in my mind of the two parent beliefs does not suffice to generate the third. It is not until the question arises and I desire to know the answer that judgment takes place and the new belief is established. But, when established, it is no less strong than the parent beliefs.

Closely allied to these judgments of serial order are judgments of identity derived from two previous beliefs. For example, my friend the physician, *A*, remarks one day that his first patient was a dipsomaniac. Another day my much-trusted lawyer, *B*, remarks casually that he was *A*'s first patient. I fully believe both assertions (by persuasion). The two beliefs dwell in my mind without interaction; until at a later date some event, or some remark of a third person, raises in me doubt of the trustworthiness of my lawyer. Perhaps immediately, perhaps at a later time, I suddenly realize—*B* was a dipsomaniac. I have derived a new and important belief from the two previously coexisting beliefs. This is what is commonly called "putting two and two together." Processes of this kind play a great part in detective work.

It may be said that this is merely an instance of mediate association. My "idea" of the lawyer and my "idea" of a dipsomaniac are both associated with my "idea" of Doctor *A*'s first patient; and through this common association they are brought to consciousness in immediate succession and so become associated. But this process of reasoning differs from and is more than association in two respects: First, association is not judgment. The lawyer might be most closely associated in my mind with dipsomania (perhaps because his son or wife is a dipsomaniac) without any belief that he suffered from that affliction. Secondly, the process is highly selective; the two latent beliefs are brought forward in conjunction, because there has been roused in me the desire to know the answer to the question—Is he trustworthy? In this respect the mental process of "experimenting" is not essentially different from experimental observation. I might have set about to find an answer to the question by keeping a close watch on the lawyer. In both cases my mental process would be guided by my desire, would be selective in accordance with my purpose. Both would be processes of "trial and error"; but neither would be entirely random; just as the movements of an animal striving to get out of a cage are not entirely random, but selective because purposive. And they would be effective in proportion as this selectivity of purpose was effective in guiding me to relevant facts; in the one case facts already known or believed; or, in the other case, new facts of observation. As Doctor Rignano[1] remarks: "The simple mechanical association of ideas . . . does not suffice to render the least account of that association, guided and canalized, which constitutes reasoning. Something more is necessary in order that for the associative chaos, for the spontaneous and natural incoherence of ideas, there shall be substituted order, connection, and coherence. And this something more is precisely affectivity. James Mill himself . . . found himself compelled, in order to account for the coherence of a process of thought, to have recourse to the predominance and control, during all the process, of the idea of the end . . . which in reality is no other than the affectivity for the end. From this results the very great importance for the maintenance of coherence during a long process of reasoning of the capacity for persistence and resistance of the affective tendency, which pursues its proper goal among all the successive circumstances simply thought of."

[1] "Qu'est-ce que le raisonnement?" *Scientia*, Vol. XIII. Rignano maintains that all reasoning is of this type, namely, imaginative experimentation. He writes: "Le raisonnement tout entier, sous quelque forme qu'il se présente, n'est pas autre chose, en substance, qu'un véritable et propre 'Gedanken—experiment,' c'est-à-dire . . . une combinaison mentale d'expériences imaginées."

What Rignano here calls "the affective tendency" is what throughout these pages has been called the conative tendency, the impulse or desire striving toward a goal. The desire which sustains and guides the reasoning process is the desire to know the answer to the question on which we are in doubt; such desire may spring directly from the instinct of curiosity, or it may be derived from desires for other goals for the attainment of which the particular knowledge sought in the reasoning process is a necessary means. The selectivity of this desire is what James has well named sagacity, that factor which distinguishes the good from the poor reasoner. Two men may have equally rich stores of knowledge or true beliefs; yet in the more sagacious man the governing purpose selects among those stores the items that are relevant; he "puts two and two together"; while the less sagacious man does not reach the conclusion, because the relevant facts are not brought to bear on the problem.

This selectivity or sagacity, which is the all-important factor in reasoning of this kind, is not, then, a new factor. It is the same kind of factor which, on the plane of practical trial and error, makes the process, whether in men or animals, other than a purely random process. It is the factor which at all levels, from Amœba to Man, is the essence of Intelligent adaptation.

Inductive Reasoning

Consider now the second type of reasoning, the inductive. From various observations and communications, I have learned that this and that and the other species of ungulate mammals are herbivorous. Then I come across or capture an ungulate mammal of a kind I have never seen or heard of, such as the Okapi. The question arises, "What does he eat?" I go over in my mind various instances of such mammals known to me. They are all herbivores; and I conclude that this creature also is a herbivore. This instance is instructive, because in reality, like so many of our actual reasonings, (1) it involves both induction and deduction: (2) it yields, not a positive belief, but rather a tentative belief, an hypothesis, which serves as a guide to action; the conclusion of the process is "He is probably herbivorous; try him with grass": (3) the steps of the reasoning process are more or less implicit rather than explicit.

The inductive part of the reasoning is the going over in my mind instances of other ungulates, which process, if all the instances are concordant, leads me to judge, "All ungulates are (probably) herbivorous." The deductive part is "This is an ungulate, therefore he is herbivorous." The inductive process may vary from the perception or recollection of a single instance to a very extensive enumeration. My native huntsman may say "He's rather like a mule; give him some grass." My scientific companion may enumerate all the species of ungulates known to science.

The simplest form of the inductive process, or the germ of it from which it develops in a perfectly gradual manner, is confident anticipation founded upon a single experience; as when the burnt child dreads the fire, or the animal, hurt and frightened by one man, runs away in fear from any other man. The logician who is painfully bitten by a strange animal on taking it into his hand, and who, on meeting a second specimen of the same species, shrinks from it in fear, might justify his behavior by explicating his mental process and displaying it at length as a process of induction followed by deduction. He might reason as follows: "This animal looks very like that other; animals that look very much alike belong to the same species; all animals of the same species are likely to behave in the same way under similar circumstances; that one bit me, therefore this one will bite me; therefore it is wise to get out of his way."

Very many of our reasonings are such attempts to justify our expectations, or our actions, by such explication of the grounds of them.[1] A single experience of an object suffices to determine expectation, if that object has excited a strong conative reaction. If the reaction is less strong, repetition of the experience may be necessary; and the more frequent the repetition, the stronger becomes our expectation. Thus, after every occasion of eating cheese, I suffer discomfort; in the end I make the induction: every eating of cheese is followed by discomfort. And, when I am offered a dish and am told that it contains cheese, I refuse it; that is to say, I deduce from my general rule the conclusion that this dish will be followed by discomfort. My refusal is reasonable and rational. The mental process which leads to the refusal can hardly be denied the name of reasoning; for it involves explicit judgments and the derivation of a new

[1] As Mr. Alfred Sidgwick, one of the most reasonable of the logicians, says: "In ordinary life and in science we normally suspect a truth before we prove it; our reasonings lag behind our guesses, and are an attempt to review the grounds of a belief which has already begun to take shape." —"The Use of Words in Reasoning."

belief from others previously established. Yet the inductive part of the reasoning by which I reach my generalization is a simple enumeration. It is a going over in my mind of past instances; it is imaginative arraying of few or many particular instances. Pure induction is always and essentially of this nature.[1]

Efficiency in induction depends, as in the first form of reasoning, on the effective selectivity of the reproductive imagination in bringing to mind relevant instances; that is to say, on that same factor of sagacity. Inductive reasoning is, then, in its pure form nothing more than the use of language to raise confident expectation (determined by past experiences) to the level of explicitly formulated belief. It involves no principles of mental activity not found at lower levels.

It is both a merit and a weakness of our minds that we are so readily led to expect that any sequence of impressions will repeat itself, when the initial members of the series recur, especially when any strong impulse is aroused by them. This tendency leads us to avoid hurtful things and to pursue gratifying things, after one or few experiences of them. But the same tendency leads to those hasty and imperfect generalizations which are the commonest flaws in our reasonings and lead us often to false conclusions. In both these respects the use of language greatly accentuates our natural tendency. To use any common noun or name is to generalize, is to assert that the thing named has essentially the same nature as other things so named, and that we may and should and do form the same expectations of it as we have of those other things. Thus, in the example used above, as soon as I accept the assertion, "This is cheese," I expect from this dish the consequence I have observed to follow on eating of cheese in other forms. And the use of the noun has played a great part in facilitating my generalization (implicit or explicit) that cheese does not agree with me. Applying common names is thus essentially a process of inductive generalization. It works admirably, when we are dealing with pure chemical substances, and very tolerably in respect to such standard common "elements" as earth, air, fire,

[1] In scientific induction the process is much complicated by metaphysical assumptions about identity or sameness and causation, which in the physical sciences are found to be good working hypotheses. We are apt to assume that the same assumptions may be safely used in the biological sciences; and that is the essence of the mechanistic dogma. As a matter of fact, some of the most generally accepted biological generalizations are founded on simple enumeration; *e. g.*, the generalization that all animals are mortal or must die. This purely inductive generalization seemed well established, until Weismann pointed out that some animals (certain protozoa) do not die or are not mortal. The rule that all bodies fall to the ground when unsupported, or that every particle of matter attracts every other, is and remains, I believe, a purely inductive generalization based on enumeration of many instances.

and water. It works well also in respect of animals and plants; just because Nature has grouped these in species and distinguished all the members of each species by marks that are in general easily recognizable by us. But it is very much less effective, when we deal with classes of things constituted by human convention; then common names are apt to imply generalizations that are very misleading; as when we call a particular man a rational animal, a socialist, a philanthropist, a rogue, or a conservative. To react to a new member of a class of objects as we have learned to react to another member (as when the burnt child dreads the fire, or the puppy flees from Tommy because he was kicked by Billy) is to exercise inductive generalization at the lowest level. To apply a common name to an object (as to say "This is fire" or "This is a boy") is to exercise the same function at a higher level. To think of a number of examples of the class (either perceptually or imaginatively) and note in each the presence of the quality in which we are interested (burning or cruelty) and then to say, "All fire burns" or "All boys are cruel," is to exercise the function at a still higher level. What we do in scientific induction is, not to attempt to examine and enumerate all members of the class, but to find marks which suffice to indicate essential similarity of all members of the class, and then to appeal to the principle of causation—like causes produce like effects—and use this as a major premise of a deductive reasoning.

This tendency to inductive generalization is, then, fundamental and is exhibited at all levels of mental life. At the lower levels, it is merely the tendency to react to similar things, things presenting similar sensory cues, as though they were essentially the same thing over again; and, because the world is so full of a number of things which do fall into natural classes, the members of each of which present similar sensory cues and are essentially similar for our purposes, this tendency in the main serves us well; and, in spite of the errors to which it gives rise, it is the source of our highest scientific generalizations or laws.

Deductive Reasoning

It is, then, in the deductive stage of the reasoning process, if anywhere, that we must expect to find the distinctively human or quasi-divine or supernatural factor which is implied when Reason is set over against all other mental functions, as radically different and incapable of evolution from them.

Suppose we come upon a strange organism, say a sea-cucumber, and we dispute whether it is animal or plant. Suppose, further, we both believe that all organisms that breathe air are animals. We examine the creature, and I point out that it has organs which are unmistakably of the nature of gills for the breathing of air. "Therefore" I say "*This* is an animal." For your mind the reasoning process evoked by my words is simple and pure deduction of a new belief from the two parent beliefs, namely: (1) All air-breathers are animals. (2) This is an air-breather. It matters not how you have come by these beliefs, nor that the former is not strictly true.[1] If they are established in your mind and *if* you desire to know the answer to our question, my demonstration is conclusive; you cannot refuse to assent; and the assenting is judgment which establishes the new belief.[2]

Your parent belief (1), expressed as the major premise of the argument, is the existence in your mind of a mental system (an "idea"), formed by the apperceptive synthesis of two other sys-

[1] None of our general beliefs, outside of mathematics, are strictly true. They are at the best good working hypotheses. In reasoning about abstract number and space, we are able to reach conclusions that are strictly true, because the terms of our reasoning are adequately and exhaustively defined. This is true of no other reasoning involving general assertions. In physical science we are able to make general assertions and hence reasonings which are very nearly strictly true; as when we are concerned with the volume of a gas under various conditions of pressure and temperature; or as when we say that ten quarts of water weigh ten times as much as one quart. Such a statement as the last is only true, if all the water is pure, and if the conditions of temperature, distance from the earth's centre, and so forth, are strictly the same. But as these conditions are never strictly realized, our reasonings are never strictly true.

In biology, psychology, and all the human sciences, and especially in metaphysics, we are in much worse case. In vain philosophers have attempted to formulate certain general assertions which shall be strictly true without being tautological, and which, like the axioms of geometry, may serve as major premises to syllogisms which will lead to new and strictly true assertions. In these spheres our knowledge is incurably empirical, and our general terms or "universals" are wofully lacking in definition. Hence, at the best, our reasonings do but lead to assertions having an indefinable degree of probability; that is to say, to hypotheses which serve as guides to action, working hypotheses which are held to be true in proportion as they work well. Men of science have long recognized that this is the nature of their general truths, laws, or principles. When the late William James pointed out that the general assertions of other disciplines, such as history, ethics, and metaphysics, are of similar nature and that, in fact, the adjective "true" applied to general assertions can only mean that such assertions are good working hypotheses, this simple extension of scientific insight was generally repudiated and denounced as a philosophical heresy under the name of Pragmatism.

[2] If you are dominated by a strong desire for some state of affairs inconsistent with the conclusion, and if this prevents you from desiring to know the truth, the argument has no compelling power over you.

tems ("ideas"), corresponding to "all air-breathers" and to "animals" respectively. Call these *a* and *b* and call the combined system *ab*. Your parent belief (2), expressed as the minor premise of the argument, is similarly the existence in your mind of a system (an "idea") formed by the synthesis of two systems ("ideas"), one, *c*, corresponding to "*this* organism," and the other, *a*, to "air-breather." That is to say, the system *a* ("air-breather") is fused on the one side with the system *b* ("animals") and on the other side with the system *c* ("this organism"); and the result of bringing the three systems into play in immediate succession is that a new apperceptive synthesis takes place between *c* and *b*. From the point of view of mental structure, deductive reasoning is thus a process of mediate apperception. Apperceptive synthesis of *c* with *b* takes place, because both are already fused with *a*.

It may be said that this deductive process is then, after all, merely association. We have three "ideas," *a*, *b*, and *c*: *a* is associated with both *b* and *c*; and when *a* is reproduced first with *b* and then with *c*, *b* and *c* become associated. But, I repeat, association is not belief, and associative reproduction is not judgment. Note that synthesis of two systems does not involve their fusion to the point of loss of all distinction between them. The mere fact that, after apperceptive synthesis, we can still think and speak of the two objects as distinct, although we partially identify them when we say "this is that" ("air-breathers are animals"), this fact shows that the apperceptive process is not a complete, but rather a partial, fusing of systems. However we may conceive of the association and of the synthesis of systems (or "ideas"), we must recognize that they are very different processes, and that they result in very different relations between the systems concerned, relations which are expressed by the formulæ "*c* and *b*" (association) and "*c* is *b*" (apperceptive synthesis) respectively.

Notice now the importance of the word "all" in the argument, and the important part played by its meaning in the play of meanings which is the reasoning process. The word "all" may be omitted from the verbal statement, which then runs

a's are *b*'s
c is an *a*
Therefore *c* is *b*

This verbal formulation leaves it unclear whether all *a*'s, or only some *a*'s, are meant. In the latter case we have an "undistributed middle term," and the argument is inconclusive. It is only by introducing the word "all" in the major premise (by making the assertion universal) that the argument is made compulsive.

In ordinary reasoning we often omit the word "all," though we may mean "all." The explication of the reasoning, by throwing it into the form of a syllogistic argument, serves to bring forward more prominently the meaning "all." The universality expressed by the word "all" is sometimes made much of, as the essential and peculiar feature of reasoning; and man is set apart from the animals, on the ground that he thinks in "universals," while the animal thinks only of particular objects. This involves an error which we have already noticed,[1] namely, the error of supposing that the primitive mind perceives particular individual objects as such, and that development proceeds by the coalescence of particular "ideas" to form general "ideas." As we have noticed, the universal is already implicit in the thinking of the burnt child who dreads the fire, and in that of the animal who flees from all men after maltreatment by one.

It is when the argument is thrown into the hypothetical form that the deductive reasoning process acquires, in the highest degree, that character of detachment from, and superiority to, all content which has served to set it apart as something unlike all other mental functions. We say—if all x's are y's, and if z is an x, then z is a y; no matter what x, y, and z stand for. Here, it may be said, we have a reasoning process which compels assent; and yet the conclusion cannot be said to proceed from beliefs already established; reasoning rises superior to all content, to all belief in matters of fact, and soars into the empyrean of pure thought; it operates, not with beliefs, but with forms of abstract thought. This is indeed evidence of the power of the mind to think in terms of abstract symbols; but still there is involved no essentially new principle or type of function, none not found in the lower forms of reasoning.[2]

[1] P. 380.

[2] These highly abstract reasonings serve to illustrate forcibly the futility of the attempt to exhibit reasoning as merely the play of associative reproduction, as also the futility of the more recent *reductio ad absurdum* of that doctrine, which

Consider now the deductive process as it is used, not for the demonstration, but for the discovery of truth. When I point out to you—This organism is an air-breather, therefore it is an animal, I do more than merely state the argument. Under the impulse to find an answer to the question, "Is this an animal?" I select a *relevant* feature of the organism, either perceptually or imaginatively, namely, its air-breathing. That again is the exercise of the selective function which, following James, we have called sagacity. This, as we have seen, is essentially the same function which at all levels characterizes purposive activity and makes the process of trial and error other than a purely random process. This sagacious selection of the relevant belief is, then, the essential feature of the reasoning of discovery, in all our three main types of reasoning.

And, though this selectivity characterizes mental or purposive activity at all levels, we may best hope to gain some insight into the essential nature of the function as it is displayed most explicitly at this highest level in the reasoning of discovery. Let us go back to our instance of "putting two and two together," the case of the physician, *A*, and the dipsomaniac lawyer, *B*. I carry in the structure of my mind the two parent beliefs, hitherto unrelated to one another. Then I am led to doubt *B*'s trustworthiness; and the desire to know, to find the answer to this question, springs up and works within me, whenever I think of *B*. The impulse, striving for satisfaction, keeps me mentally active; it brings up one memory after another connected with *B*, but not wholly at random; the various forms and evidences of untrustworthiness known to me are the objects of which I think. The dispositions corresponding to all these have been organized in a single system by apperceptive processes, in which language has played a leading part. My impulse, my desire to know, is led into this system and rummages within it, keeping the whole system in subconscious excitement, leading me to think more or less explicitly of the various forms of untrustworthiness in turn. When I think of secret drinking and dipsomania, the impulse strikes across to Doctor *A*'s

asserts that reasoning is the mere play of language mechanisms. Compare the two arguments:

All x's are y's, z is x, therefore z is y
All x's are y's, z is y, therefore z is x

Any normally developed human mind can be brought to see that the former is a conclusive argument and that the latter is not. But no one not already familiar with abstract verbal formulæ of this kind could make this distinction without taking the meaning of the words, especially the meaning of "all" and of "is." Yet for such a person there is nothing in the associations or verbal habits into which these words and letters (as mere sounds and motor mechanisms) have been worked up by previous hearing and speech that can account for the distinction he makes.

first patient, and then, because the whole system of activity is connected with B, the belief "B was A's first patient" is stirred, judgment takes place, and my desire to know attains its goal in the new belief.

All the types of reasoning, then, are processes of mediate apperception; they all make use of a "middle term," an object which, being apperceived as partially identical with two others, serves to bring about apperception of some essential similarity between them. And this use of a "middle term" is the sole essential feature of reasoning, in which it differs from other mental processes. But this mark of the reasoning process does not enable us to draw any sharp line between reasoning and simpler processes of judgment; for the middle term, or mediating belief, may be used with all degrees of explicitness. When Robinson Crusoe saw the footprint on the sand, he started back in a state of highly complex and confused emotion. We naturally say that he inferred, from the footprint, the recent passage of a human visitant. For his emotion, though it might seem to be an instantaneous response to the visual impression, was the consequence of his belief that a man had stepped upon the beach. And that belief could be justified only by a considerable train of reasoning. If a similar print were uncovered to-morrow in a quarry of oolitic rocks, the world would be flooded with thick volumes of argument as to the significance of that print. I think we are bound to admit that in Crusoe's mind a process of reasoning preceded and determined his emotion. It was not merely the strangeness of the visual impression. He may have seen his own footprints on the sand many times every day for months. The reasoning by which he could have justified his emotion must have run somewhat as follows: "All such prints are made by men, therefore this was made by a man. I have not been here before, therefore it was not made by me, but by some other man. And it has been made recently, for last night the tide came over this sand. Therefore some other man is close at hand." Yet no such train of explicit reasoning preceded and determined his emotional response. This is an instance of a not uncommon kind, which seems to justify the statement that reasoning, even reasoning of a complex kind, may go on very rapidly and effectively without the use of language.

The many levels of explicitness of reasoning may be illustrated by another quasi-historical incident. When the dove returned to the ark bearing a leafy twig, we may fairly suppose that his appearance provoked the following reactions: The ox lowed in vague anticipation of green fodder; the elephant lifted up his trunk and sniffed in all directions; the apes chattered excitedly and keenly scanned the horizon. Ham said "Well, I never; wherever did he get that?" Shem said "I guess he's found a tree somewhere." Japhet said "Now we sha'n't be long." Mrs. Noah said "Heaven be thanked! Those are young leaves, only just sprouted. I don't mind admitting now that I'm sick and tired of this dirty old ark." And Noah: "My children, the Lord has completed his work, the wicked are destroyed. Let us praise the Lord, and then make ready to disembark the animals." Who shall say at which point in this scale of increasing explicitness we should recognize reasoning?

Systems of Beliefs

The structure of every developed mind comprises a multitude of beliefs. Many of these concern particular things and events; these are either isolated or hang together merely in temporal sequences or spatial systems. When we speak of a man's beliefs, we usually mean beliefs of a more or less general nature; in every normal human mind, these are in some degree organized in systems. In the highly organized mind that we call a scientific intellect, this organization renders most of the general beliefs coherent and reciprocally supporting,[1] like the stones of a dome of masonry. The true description of the structure and mode of growth of this dome of scientific belief is the task of the logicians; and they are far from agreement. There are those, the empiricists, who assert that the dome stands on its wide base of a myriad facts or beliefs of observation, and tapers to its summit of general principles. Others maintain that the dome stands inverted upon one or a few keystones, which they describe

[1] The intimacy and mutual dependence of such general beliefs are often overstated. The late Professor Münsterberg, for example, was never tired of asserting that a proof of the occurrence of telepathy would shatter the whole system of his scientific beliefs.

as the principle of causation, or an instinctive belief in causation, or the categories of the understanding, or innate ideas of time, space, cause and effect, identity, difference, and so on.

There is no more difficult problem than this of the nature and extent of the intellectual equipment provided by nature or by heredity. Hitherto, in spite of centuries of controversy, we have hardly devised words with which the discussion can be profitably conducted. My own opinion is that both the extreme parties to the controversy are wrong, and that the truth lies somewhere in between. If that is so, the simile of the dome which I used just now is misleading; for the structure rests upon, and grows up from, neither a broad base of particular facts nor from a few keystones of general principle. Rather, the structure grows and expands in all directions like a marine organism, constantly in touch with its environment, growing by what it absorbs from that environment, and shaped partly by the accidents of that environment; yet all the while shaping and organizing its structure, according to the laws of its own nature, which laws are such as to adapt it to deal effectively with its environment. Some such view was implied in what I have written on earlier pages of mental development and of spatial thinking.

Leaving this deep question with only this hint, we may notice that few minds entertain one wholly coherent and consistent system of general beliefs. Returning to the imperfect simile, and likening the perfectly coherent system of a scientific intellect to a classical building surmounted by a single dome, we may liken the intellect of another man to a Gothic cathedral with twin spires, which stand independently without mutual support. Such is the man who builds up systems of religious and of scientific beliefs, in almost complete independence of one another. In terms of the same simile, the beliefs of the ordinary man may be likened to a Gothic building of great irregularity, lacking all unity or consistency of plan and covered with queer gables and towers, each of which may be pulled down or remodelled without seriously affecting the rest.

Such more or less detached systems of belief, more or less logically incompatible with one another, are formed through the working of different conative tendencies organized in great sentiments, such as the religious, the patriotic, and the family sentiments. These we have to discuss in our next chapter. At present it must suffice to remark that the harmonization of beliefs in a single consistent system is only approximately achieved by those persons who are moved, as we say, by a "disinterested love of truth." This phrase is, of course, a contradiction in terms; as we see, if we transpose it into its equivalent—"a disinterested interest in truth." What is implied is a cultivated sentiment for true beliefs, or truth, which shall be strong enough to counteract or correct the strong bias, toward this or that system of beliefs, which springs from every other type of sentiment.

CHAPTER XVII

GROWTH OF MENTAL STRUCTURE (CONTINUED). THE DEVELOPMENT OF SENTIMENTS AND THE ORGANIZATION OF CHARACTER

What is Character?

We have discussed the processes of organization of intellect in artificial detachment from character, while recognizing that the intellect, or cognitive organization, is essentially the instrument of our purposes, that it is brought into play in the service of our desires, the driving forces of the organism.

We have seen that desires are identical with the impulses, the conative tendencies of our instincts, working on the plane of imagination rather than of mere sense-perception. The organized system of these tendencies, directed upon a variety of objects and toward the realization of various goals connected with these objects, constitutes what we call character. Character is the system of directed conative tendencies. It may be relatively simple or complex; it may be harmoniously organized or lacking in harmony; it may be firmly or loosely knit; it may be directed in the main toward lower or toward higher goals. Character of the finest type is that which is complex, strongly and harmoniously organized, and directed toward the realization of higher goals or ideals. Such character may be attained by the individual whose intellect is relatively simple and ordinary. But the better organized and richer the intellect, the more efficiently will character work toward the realization of its goals.

The Nature of Sentiments

The units of character are the *sentiments* or *complexes*. There is at the present time some lack of agreement among psychologists as to the use of these two words. Some writers treat them as synonyms. Both are used to denote acquired trends, or the settings of our conative tendencies that are acquired through individual experience. The best usage, I think, restricts the term "complex" to acquired conative settings which are in some degree morbid, by reason of their lack of harmony with the rest of the character. Adopting this usage, we shall have the word "sentiment" as the most general term to denote all acquired conative trends; and "complex" will be used to denote sentiments that are in some manner and degree morbid or pathological; while "instinct" remains our name for directed conative trends which are given as such in our innate constitution.

The proposed usage of the word "sentiment" involves some specialization of the word, such as is necessary to render any of the psychological terms of common speech, or of the literary tradition, suitable for scientific discourse. In common speech and in much psychological writing, "sentiment" is not clearly distinguished from "emotion." Yet common speech does vaguely recognize a difference between them, a difference which is of the first importance. We speak of an emotion of anger, but of a sentiment of hatred; of a wave of patriotic emotion or an outburst of patriotic activity, but of a sentiment of patriotism or love of country; an emotion of outraged honor or justice, but of a sentiment of honor or of justice; of a gust of tender emotion for a person, but of a sentiment of love or affection or devotion to that person. In all these cases common speech properly recognizes the all-important distinction which I am trying to make clear, and which psychologists are very slow to recognize or observe. The distinction is one on which I have insisted throughout these pages, namely, the distinction between facts of mental structure and facts of mental functioning or activity, between structure or enduring dispositions and systems of dispositions, on the one hand, and experiences or activities determined by structure, on the other. The emotion is a mode of experience, a way of functioning, and a fact of activity; the sentiment is a fact of structure, an organized system of dispositions, which endures, in a more or less quiescent condition, between the occasions upon which it is brought into activity.

It is the same distinction that we have drawn between a train of instinctive activity and an instinct as an enduring structure; between thinking of an object and the enduring cognitive disposition that enables us to think of that object, and which is developed through every successive thinking of the object; between belief as a feeling or "derived emotion" and "a belief," which is the form into which our cognitive dispositions are developed through explicit judgment and reasoning.

A sentiment involves an individual tendency to experience certain emotions and desires in relation to some particular object. It is an enduring conative attitude toward some object induced by experience of that object. We have already seen that the higher animals are capable of acquiring very simple attitudes of this sort. Consider the case of a puppy-dog that is repeatedly teased and maltreated by a particular boy whom it meets on the street. It quickly acquires the tendency to run away in fear, at the mere sight or sound of this boy in the distance. We should do some violence to language, if we spoke of this as a sentiment of fear for the boy. It is merely an emotional habit. But it is a rudimentary sentiment. The dog does not show the behavior and symptoms of fear continuously; but he shows them, whenever he perceives the boy. In a similar way, a child may acquire a habit or a sentiment of fear for another person; as the small boy for the big bully. The main difference between the case of the dog and that of the boy will be that the boy, owing to his greater power of imagination, will be apt to be reminded of the bully, by conversation or otherwise, when the bully is not present; and, just because he has acquired this sentiment of fear for the bully, he will be apt to dwell upon him in imagination; and, as he imagines him, he will experience in some degree the emotion of fear, and the impulse of fear will determine him to work out in imagination plans for avoiding the bully. Such a most simple sentiment is formed through the repeated evocation of some one instinctive response by some one object. It may be regarded as consisting of a single cognitive disposition associated or functionally linked with a single affective-conative disposition—namely, that of the instinct of escape.

The Sentiment of Hatred

If the small boy is not utterly lacking in spirit, not entirely without pugnacity, his sentiment for the bully will inevitably grow more complex. Sometimes he will angrily resent the bully's interference with his actions, perhaps actually by angry blows and words, perhaps only when the bully is remote; on thinking of the bully, the small boy rages within himself, plotting vengeance. In this way, the affective-conative disposition of the combative instinct becomes directed or set toward the bully; that is to say, in stricter language, this disposition also becomes functionally linked or associated with the cognitive disposition concerned in all thinking of the bully. Or, if we use the word "idea" as the more convenient name for a cognitive disposition or system, we may say that the "idea" of the bully has become associated with the affective-conative dispositions of two instincts, namely, those of escape and of combat.

The conative dispositions of the two instincts are not directly connected with one another; they become parts of one system only because each becomes connected with the same cognitive disposition. The whole of this system, built up through repeated experiences of fear and anger, evoked by this one object, constitutes a sentiment of hatred for the bully. The sentiment cannot be identified with any one kind of emotion; because, when once formed, it is the enduring condition of a considerable range of emotions and desires; namely, fear and anger imperfectly blended in various proportions on different occasions, and always painful, because their tendencies or desires are always more or less in conflict; and also the whole range of the derived emotions of these two fundamental desires, confidence, hope, anxiety, despondency, despair, regret, and chagrin. The particular complex blend of emotional qualities, experienced upon perceiving or imagining the object on any one occasion, will depend upon the particular situation of the object (perceived or imagined) in relation to the subject.[1] We touched on all this before, in describing

[1] Common speech seems to recognize an emotion of hate distinct from both fear and anger; it may, for example, describe a man as showing at once anger, fear, and hate. But this is mere loose redundancy. If "hate" can be appropriately used to denote emotional experiences of any one kind, those are experiences in which the qualities of fear and anger are blended. The importance of this simple truth as an aid to clear thinking was abundantly illustrated during the war. We had endless discussions of the question whether we hated, or should hate, the enemy. And the moralists who admitted that we might rightly be angry with the enemy for his wanton destruction in Belgium and France, and who could hardly deny us the right to fear him, when he was murdering our women and children by throwing

the life of the natural man. I dwell tediously upon it here, because experience has shown me that it is very difficult to get students and even many professed psychologists to grasp clearly these simple fundamental facts of the nature and mode of formation of sentiments. The sentiment of hatred or dislike is one of the great types of sentiment.

The Sentiment of Love

Now consider the formation of a sentiment of another principal type—the sentiment of love. Suppose that you are a lonely student, living the life of a recluse, absorbed in your studies, with few human contacts and those more or less cold and formal. One winter day, as you return to your lonely lodging, you notice, crouching against the wall, a miserable-looking dog, dirty, cold, and emaciated. You stop and look at him, perhaps out of mere curiosity, wondering where he has come from. He looks up at you, shrinking timidly; and you are moved by the emotion we call pity.[1] You speak gently, look more closely, and see that he has a crushed foot. "Poor beast," you say; and your voice and gesture express your emotion and tendency. The dog responds with a faint movement of his tail and eyes. You feel you can't leave him like this, huddled in misery and pain. You gently coax him to follow you home. There you make him a warm bed, give him meat and drink, and bind up his wounded foot. The dog accepts all your help in pathetic submission. He licks your hand; his eyes follow you about; he feebly wags his tail when you come near. You find a strange satisfaction in all your kindly actions. You take infinite trouble to make him comfortable, although it interferes with your work, breaks your

bombs and shells upon our open cities, pretended that it was wrong to hate him. The truth of the position here taken is well illustrated by the changing attitude of the German masses. During the earlier stages of the war they were properly said to hate the British, but not the French. For they both feared the power of British arms and angrily resented the British intervention, which, they felt, had prevented the rapid realization of their designs upon France. They did not hate the French, because they felt themselves able to crush them, and therefore neither feared nor were angry with them. But since 1918 they have learned to hate France, because France has had the power and the will to thwart their plans and to inflict punishment upon them.

[1] Cf. p. 335.

night's rest, and altogether upsets your calm routine. And so it goes on. The dog becomes more and more responsive. His timid shrinking gives place to joyous welcoming. He responds to your every action, emotion, and mood. When you sit despondent, he puts his head on your knee, gazing intently into your eyes; and the world seems less dark. When you take up your hat, he dashes to the door. When the neighbor's big dog attacks him, you rush furiously to his defense. When your neighbor complains of the noise he makes, you resent his aspersions and find extravagant excuses. You have become his god; and he is your child. And one day, as he bounds out on the street, careless in his delighted anticipation of a walk with you, the wheel of a motor-lorry goes over his little body. You pick him up and tenderly carry him into the house, and, as he licks your hand for the last time, you are blind with rage and with pain that is greater than his own. When he lies stiff and cold, a mere dead dog, you know the pangs of sorrow. You cannot bring yourself to throw him into the dust-bin. Half-ashamed of your actions, you bury him tenderly in the garden and plant a bush upon his grave; and his photo stands on the shelf over your fireplace, till it is faded and worn out, a reminder that love and loyalty are real and that the world is not wholly evil.

Such is the sentiment of love in its simplest form.[1] In this instance, the tender impulse of the protective or parental instinct is first directed to the object in the form of pitiful ministrations, and is evoked by the same object again and again. The affective-conative disposition from which it springs becomes in consequence firmly linked with the growing cognitive system of knowledge and belief about your little friend; so that every thought of him is tinged with that emotion; and, even when he angers you, your emotion is reproach, rather than crude anger. But the system becomes more complex by the linkage to it of other conative dispositions. Especially, your responsibility for the dog requires you to exert authority over him; and his submission to

[1] I have chosen for description the love of a dog, in part because this may serve as a *reductio ad absurdum* of the Freudian dogma that all love essentially involves the sexual instinct.

your commands gratifies your self-assertive impulse; so that this disposition can hardly fail to enter into the sentiment.[1] Again, the dog's companionship brings into play and gratifies your need of company, that is to say, your gregarious impulse; and his unfailing responsiveness to your emotions and moods sets up between you the relation of active sympathy.[2]

In these ways the sentiment of love, which began merely as pity, rendered habitual by repeated evocation, grows more complex and becomes the source of many and various emotional experiences, in which the primary and secondary emotional qualities are blended with the derived emotions in a multitude of different combinations

Notice that, when any conative disposition has entered into the composition of a sentiment for one object, it is not monopolized by that sentiment; it remains, as before, ready to be brought into play sporadically by any appropriate object; and it is not precluded from becoming habitually directed upon other objects, that is to say, from entering into other sentiments. A man may love his dog, without ceasing to love his wife or children; and his love for each such object is a distinct and separate sentiment, unique in composition and in the relative prominence of the several conative tendencies that are comprised in its system. Though it must be admitted that similar sentiments for distinct objects are to some extent rivals; because they draw upon or derive their energy from the same springs. Hence the man of a single love, or hate, is apt to manifest a more passionate intensity of emotion and to expend a greater quantity of energy in the service of the desires of his one sentiment, than the man of many loves, or hates, puts forth in relation to any one object.

Sentiments of Contempt and Respect

Beside love and hatred, we must notice two other great types of personal sentiment, namely, contempt and respect.

[1] In the attitude of some men toward their dogs this is the principal factor. They have little or no tenderness and a minimum of sympathy. When you see a man flourishing a long dog-whip, while several large and expensive dogs run at his heels, you may safely infer a crude sentiment of this kind.

[2] Cf. pp. 424 and 432.

Contempt, which in its milder forms may be called condescension, is an habitual attitude of self-assertion and self-display over against the object of the sentiment. It may involve no other conative disposition than that of the self-assertive instinct; but it is apt to be associated with, and partly blended with, the form of self-regarding sentiment that is properly called pride, to form a bipolar sentiment of pride in oneself and contempt or condescension toward others.[1]

Respect is the opposite of contempt. Imagine a fellow-student toward whom you have been indifferent or, perhaps, inclined to be faintly contemptuous. He is ill-dressed, has few friends, and no outward signs of distinction. Then you discover that he is a student of unusual brilliance; that he has worked his way through college in face of great difficulties, perhaps helping to support his mother at the same time, and that, before transferring to this college, he has run a mile in four minutes and thirty-two seconds. Your attitude becomes one of enduring respect, or even of admiration. It is a sentiment of which the essential attitude is that of looking up to the object, the impulse is that of the submissive instinct; for he has shown, in certain regards, powers that are greater than your own. You have acquired an habitual deference or docility toward his opinions, admiration for his achievements, and respect for his personality as a whole.

Sentiment of Friendship

If, now, you are thrown together by your studies, you begin to rely upon one another, you exchange courtesies and services, you are mutually helpful; and, especially, you begin to find in him satisfaction of your social or gregarious impulse. When you get good or bad news, or think of a good joke, or see an exciting incident or a good play, you feel the need of telling it to some one; and, if your fellow-student responds to these communications by sharing in some degree your emotional reaction, you derive satisfaction from the fact, an increase of enjoyment or a diminution of pain. In this way you gradually establish a relation of *active sympathy* with him. You no longer merely respect him,

[1] Cf. pp. 426 and 437.

and casually share in some degree his emotional reactions; but you actively seek to share your experiences with him. Further, in his time of trouble, you pity him; and you repeatedly have occasion to feel some gratitude for the services he renders you. In this way the tender impulse may find a subordinate place in your sentiment. That is the sentiment of friendship. It naturally tends to grow stronger and more enduring the greater the mass of memories that you have in common, especially memories of events in which you have co-operated sympathetically. Whether all such memories should be regarded as forming a part of the sentiment, as entering into its constitution, it is not easy to say. But, certainly, in so far as you have exerted judgment and established beliefs about him, such as that he is the best fellow in the world, such beliefs are part of the system of the sentiment.

The Tender Passion

If this fellow-student is of the opposite sex, this sentiment may easily become more complex, chiefly by the association of two other impulses with the object, the inclusion of the affective-conative dispositions of two other instincts within the system of the sentiment. A certain physical weakness and delicacy (probably moral also) about the *normal* young woman or girl constitute in her a resemblance to a child. This resemblance, working in the way that we have called intuition or implicit apperception,[1] throws the man habitually into the protective attitude, evokes the impulse and emotion of the parental instinct. He feels that he wants to protect and shield and help her in every way.

Lastly,[2] the sexual impulse may add its immense energy to the system. Then, though kept in check by the tenderness and respect which are already established, it is apt to dominate the

[1] Cf. p. 391.

[2] It may be lastly, it may be firstly. Those attachments in which the sexual impulse begins to play its part in the relation late rather than early are, no doubt, the safer, the more likely to run a prosperous and enduring course. But it would be foolish to deny that, in some cases, a sentiment of the best type begins with an attraction which is predominantly sexual.

scene, for a time at least, becoming the principal source of the desires from which the whole gamut of the derived emotions repeatedly springs, and determining judgment and belief in the familiar way expressed in the dictum that love is blind.

The Sentiment of Self-Regard

We cannot fully describe the sentiment of love, in all the complexity of the most developed types, until we have considered the sentiment of self-regard. This is the most important of all the sentiments, by reason both of its strength and the frequency and far-reaching nature of its operations.

A few words must be said about "self-consciousness" in general. Some psychologists make a great mystery of "consciousness of self." But whatever mystery is involved in thinking of oneself is the mystery of thinking in general, of consciousness or awareness of anything. The mystery of self-consciousness is not a new and additional mystery. We have seen that our belief in things of all kinds, in continuously existing self-identical realities, is founded upon our experiences of striving, of effort, of putting forth power or energy in the pursuit of our goals. One thinks of oneself as that which knows and strives, enjoys and suffers, remembers and expects.

No doubt, this object is thought of very vaguely by the young child; but language quickly comes to his aid; and his own proper name becomes a handle by aid of which he gets hold of himself, acquires facility in thinking and speaking of himself as an agent, a striver, a desirer, a refuser. He learns to think of his limbs and other organs, as he learns to think of his toys and tools; but they are his in a peculiarly intimate sense. He controls them more easily than other things; and they are always with him; and his hurts and pains seem to be in them. But they remain his, not him; mine, not me; baby's finger or foot, not baby himself. Above all, other persons interest him; because they satisfy his wants, relieve his distress or fear, yield to or refuse his demands, or compel him against his best efforts. Hence they are very real to him; and his thinking of himself becomes richer in meaning, as he learns to think of them more adequately, to expect and remember, to yield, or to assert himself against them more effectively.

Presently, these other persons begin to bring him rewards and punishments, praise and blame, approval and disapproval, admiration and contempt, reproach and ridicule. To these influences he responds appropriately, asserting himself where he can, yielding submissively where he must, because he has within him the instincts of self-assertion and of submission. And, as he learns the meaning of his own emotional excitements in terms of the tendencies to action that go with them, so he learns to interpret the emotional expressions of others and to give, both to them and to his own stirrings, more or less appropriate names. Gradually he learns his own capacities and limitations, in relation to things, to animals and to persons, learns his enduring likes and dislikes, his main tendencies, his strength and his weakness.

Gradually he becomes extremely sensitive to the expressions of other persons toward himself; both because these expressions are significant of satisfactions and of pains to come, and because they bring immediate satisfactions and pains; the elation of praise and admiration, augmenting all his satisfactions of success; the pain of thwarted self-assertion and self-display, increasing the pains of failure. And, as he grows older, he realizes that moral approval and moral censure represent, not only the attitudes of the person who administers them by word or glance, but also the attitudes of the world at large, of organized society, with its fixed traditional code of right and wrong and its system of rewards and punishments; an immense vague power, which, when it confronts him with its "thou shalt not," its vague threats, and its vague promises of great rewards, can hardly fail to evoke the submissive impulse.

At last he learns, under the guidance, the suggestions, and the persuasions of those toward whom he is docile, to pass judgment upon himself as upon others, and so to build up a system of beliefs about himself and about conduct and character in general. In these ways the word "I" or "me" grows richer in meaning, as he builds up a system of beliefs about his own nature, a system of beliefs which is rooted in, because in the main sprung from, the two great conative dispositions of self-assertion and submission.[1]

This object "me" thus becomes represented in the structure of the mind by a system of dispositions of extraordinary extent and complexity, a system also which is associated with a multitude of past events and objects, located more or less definitely in time and place. And the conative dispositions of the system, being brought into play so frequently, by every social contact, whether actual or only imagined, become delicately responsive in an extraordinary degree, as well as very strong through much exercise. Such is the sentiment of self-regard. In the normal man, the two main tendencies of the sentiment, the impulses of self-assertion and submission, are duly balanced, and the sentiment is properly called "self-respect." When the self-assertive tendency is unduly preponderant and takes the relatively passive form of finding satisfaction in merely contemplating the superiorities of the self, of enjoying the elation brought by the deference and homage of others (whether actual or fancied only), we call the sentiment "pride"; and when the superiorities (fancied or real) in which satisfaction is chiefly found are trivial or of the body merely, we call it "vanity." When this impulse assumes a more active role and seeks progressively and insatiably to compel the admiration, deference, homage, and submission of an ever larger number of men, we call the sentiment "ambition" or the "will-to-power," or, in extreme cases, "megalomania."

The Extension of Self-Regard

Now notice how the impulses and desires of self-regard become extended beyond the actual bodily and mental self. One's clothes, which so largely determine one's appearance in the eyes of others, and which commonly do express in some degree one's

[1] It is natural that this thinking of self, so rich in meaning and rooted in so extensive a system of dispositions, one built up by a multitude of experiences, this "idea" of self, should present a special difficulty to those psychologists for whom "an idea" is merely a cluster of sensations and images. This banal doctrine seems threadbare to the point of absurdity, when we are told that the "meaning" of the words "my mother" or "my wife" is merely a cluster of images; and it collapses spontaneously when applied to that most complex of all "meanings," the meaning of the word "myself."

personality, are subject to the regards of others, their praise, admiration, approval, their ridicule, censure, or disapproval. Most of us are very sensitive to such regards; we react to them as we react to similar regards paid to our actual selves—with pleased elation in response to admiration and approval; in response to contempt or disapproval, with the pain of thwarted desire, or with that inharmonious and therefore unpleasant blend of self-assertion and submission which we call embarrassment. And, in this sphere also, the individual is felt to voice the opinion of the mass; so that, for many of us, conformity to the prevailing fashion in clothes becomes a prime essential for peace of mind.

Again, the works of our hands and brains, whether it be a house, a picture, a book, or a furnished room, are subject to judgments which affect us hardly less than those passed upon our persons. And all our possessions, in so far as we have chosen or made them, or in any way expressed ourselves in them, are judged as such expressions. Hence our sentiment of self-regard is sensitive to all such judgments and attitudes expressed by others. This is the fact sometimes expressed by saying that all such things become part of the larger self, or are identified with oneself.

The most important objects to which a man's self-regard normally becomes extended are his family (especially his children) and other social groups of which he is a member, his school, his college, his city, his profession, his nation. For each such object, individual or collective, he may form some special sentiment; but, in each case, the person or group is a part also of his larger self, is more or less identified with himself and he with it, both in his own mind and by the world at large, and therefore is an object also of his self-regarding sentiment. For each such object he may be said, then, to acquire a compound sentiment.[1] This is most obviously and generally true of a man's children. The sentiment of love, which in its purest form is

[1] An ego-altruistic sentiment, which is both a form of self-regard and a love of the object. Such extensions of self-regard are facts of prime importance for all social life and for social psychology, as shown in my "Group Mind," New York, 1920.

wholly "disinterested," that is to say altruistic, its main impulse being to protect and cherish its object, is complicated by the extension of self-regard to its object; for the child is rightly held by the world to express the parent, who therefore can hardly fail to be elated by the acknowledgment of its excellencies and pained and shamed on the display of its defects. In the loves of parents for their children these altruistic and egoistic constituents are present in very various degrees.

We see, then, how very complex the sentiment of love normally becomes: for even the already complex sentiment of the lover is apt to undergo this complication; especially when the loved person becomes his wife, the chosen embodiment of his ideals and, as the old phrase has it, the guardian of his honor. In those countries in which it is not unusual for a man to give his love to a mistress but to extend his self-respect to his wife, a man who follows this fashion runs the risk of disturbing inner conflicts which may easily prove disastrous.

In common speech the word "love" is used with amazing laxity. Two ambiguities are chiefly noteworthy. First, common speech does not distinguish clearly between the sentiment of love and the various emotional excitements which it calls "love." It is clear, I think, that it is apt to give the name "love" to every emotional excitement in which the quality of "tender emotion" is prominent.[1]

Secondly, common speech and thought, with that deep-lying tendency to accept as essentially alike whatever things are given the same name, fail to recognize the great variety of sentiments all of which may properly be called "love." We speak of "the

[1] This ambiguity and the fact here indicated are well illustrated by that beautiful old sentence, "As a father pitieth his children, so the Lord pitieth them that fear Him." This element of tender emotion, with its impulse to cherish, succor, and protect, which enters into pity, gratitude, reverence, sorrow, and what is popularly called "sympathy," and is the active root of all such qualities as charity, kindness, benevolence, mercy, and philanthropy, is what Schopenhauer called "loving-kindness" and rightly designated as the essential basis of all altruism, and hence of all true morality. For it is the one and only strictly altruistic element in human nature. Without it, a man might possibly learn to obey "the categorical imperative," and even become a slave to duty; he might be just and upright and loyal to the group with which he was identified; but his justice would be untempered by mercy, his uprightness would be the honesty of the best policy, and his loyalty

love of the mother for her child," as though this phrase implied a sentiment of a perfectly definite type, the same in all instances; and the phrase has some justification, for it implies that type of love in which the tender protective impulse vastly predominates over all other factors. But we must recognize that each sentiment for each object is unique. Even the mother of many children loves each child in a different way; her sentiment for each child is a distinct formation, having its own unique balance of tendencies. We see this clearly, if we contrast her love for her brilliant, masterful, successful son with her more purely tender and altruistic love for her little, crippled and, perhaps, mentally defective daughter.[1]

In respect not only of the self proper, but also of all the many objects that become "included in the larger self" or, more exactly, all the objects to which the sentiment of self-regard is extended, we are apt to be very sensitive to the collective voice of society, of the group, of public opinion, however expressed. This is true, no matter what particular form the sentiment may take, whether pride, vanity, ambition, undue humility, or a well-balanced self-respect. To have the sentiment in any form is *ipso facto* to be sensitive to public opinion; for the two fundamental impulses of the sentiment are evoked not merely by the contemplation of the self, but by the attitudes of other men toward oneself; they are primitively, in their simplest and crudest operation, reactions towards other men; they are fundamentally social. It is, then, a serious error to pretend, as some writers do, to distinguish between our self-regarding tendencies and our regard for public opinion or the judg-

would never prompt him to postpone his own good to that of his fellow-men. It is remarkable that Schopenhauer, after brilliantly vindicating the reality of this altruistic element in man against all the cynics and the pedants, ruined his psychologically true account by seeking an extravagant metaphysical explanation of the facts. Instead of identifying this altruistic element of human nature with that parental impulse which is so powerful in the higher animals, and which I have called Nature's brightest invention, because it, and it alone, rendered possible all the higher development of mankind (cf. p. 130), Schopenhauer revoked his defense of the reality of altruism by explaining it away metaphysically, saying that, when we are moved to act on behalf of a fellow-creature, it is because we know unconsciously that all living creatures are one being. (Cf. "The Basis of Morals.")

[1] I do not delay to criticise in detail the popular Freudian dogma that all love is sexual. I reject it, not because it offends my "moral sense," but because it is so obviously untrue and is based upon implicit reasoning which is so obviously fallacious. The main fallacy is the common one that whatever things have the same name are essentially similar. Another is that, because children are produced through the agency of the sexual instinct, therefore all interest in them is sexual. These are supported by a number of false assertions, such as that the love between the parent and child of the opposite sex is always or usually stronger than between

ments of society upon us. Professor A. G. Tansley[1] has elaborated this common error most explicity. Using the word "complex" where I should use the word "sentiment," he states that we must recognize in all normal men three great universal complexes, besides various minor complexes more or less peculiar to individuals. These three are said to be the "ego complex," the "herd complex,' and the "sex complex"; and the two former are discussed as though they were entirely separate formations, with distinct spheres of operation and influence. Mr. Tansley seems to have fallen into this error through the persuasive influence of Mr. W. Trotter's brilliant but "popular" little book, "The Instincts of the Herd," in which all social phenomena, and especially all influences of society on the individual, are explained by uttering the blessed word, "herd-instinct." I have recognized (Chapter V) that the human species has the gregarious instinct, and that the self-assertive and submissive impulses were presumably evolved or acquired by the race secondarily to the gregarious tendency. And I recognize that the gregarious instinct does play a part in giving society its great hold upon us, namely, as follows: Its impulse becomes on the human plane the desire, not only for the physical proximity of other human beings and for intercourse with them, but also for the sharing of our emotions with other men; for it is only then that the gregarious impulse attains its fullest satisfaction. On the primitive human plane, this satisfaction is attained by physical immersion in the crowd; for then the primitive sympathetic tendencies[2] secure uniformity of emotion in all members. On a higher and imaginative plane this desire for community of emotion becomes what I have called "the principle of active sympathy"; that is to say, it prompts us to desire to be in emotional harmony with those about us, and it renders us uneasy and dissatisfied, so long as we feel that in any matter our emotional attitude is widely different from that of our group

parent and child of the same sex. Again, all human relations are either relations between persons of opposite sex or between persons of the same sex; that is to say, all human relations are either heterosexual or homosexual; therefore all human relations are sexual and it is mere prudery (due to a repressed incestuous desire) to deny that your affection for your father or grandmother or your little daughter or grandson is sexual. The way in which such "reasonings" are accepted and repeated (for the most part implicitly) is melancholy evidence of the weakness of the human intellect. The sensational psychology, based on such rotten foundations as these, serves to sell the books which contain it by the hundred thousand; but I am not sure that the popular interest in psychology of this kind gives ground for rejoicing. It is useless to attempt to argue with a Freudian; he is a devotee of a sect, not a man of science, and, like all sectarian enthusiasts, he is impervious to the shafts of reason. If he is an unusually open-minded specimen, you may succeed in pinning him down to the admission of the fallacies by which the sexual dogma is defended; but he will always elude you in the end, by retorting that Freud does not use the word sexual in the ordinary sense. And neither he nor Professor Freud himself will ever tell you in what sense he does use the word. The Freudian reasoning is in the main a peculiar process which can only be characterized as "persuasion by innuendo." I say this, while freely admitting that Professor Freud has rendered great services to psychology. What those services are I shall try to show in Part II.

[1] In his otherwise excellent book, "The New Psychology." [2] Cf. p. 155.

or social circle. In matters in which society at large, including all the minor groups or circles of which we are members, expresses unmistakably a common emotional attitude, as in the fundamentals of common morality, this desire to be at one with our fellows works in fullest strength; and, if we find ourselves out of harmony with such general emotional attitudes, we cannot avoid some enduring uneasiness.[1] In this accessory fashion, the impulse of the gregarious instinct works within the system of self-regard; the conative disposition of that instinct becoming incorporated in the sentiment. The self-regarding sentiment has, then, always as its object the self-in-its-social-setting, rather than a self thought of in isolation. This is true even of those persons who fail to develop any group loyalty, any sentiment of attachment to any group. But in the normal child, brought up in a reasonably harmonious family, some such sentiment of devotion to the family group can hardly fail to grow up, and to prepare the way for the development of similar sentiments for the larger groups of which the adult naturally becomes a member. And, when a man is a citizen of a nation that has a proud history and a great place in the world, he can hardly fail to develop some sentiment of devotion to that comprehensive group, some patriotic sentiment. In the patriotic sentiment, the protective impulse and tender emotion may play so subordinate a part that it hardly can be called love. Yet, even then, patriotism is a potent factor; because it is a form of extended self-regard, and because it is in some sense a synthesis of all a man's loyalties to lesser groups—the crown of a system of group sentiments, all of which contribute something of their strength to this sentiment for the major object, the nation, which is seen and felt, more or less obscurely, to comprise and to be the guardian and preserver of all those lesser objects.[2]

These group-sentiments, then, essentially involving extension of self-regard to the group, carry yet further that intimate connection in the mind which makes it impossible to think of the self apart from its social setting; a fact of fundamental importance which is ignored and implicitly denied by those who, like Messrs. Tansley and Trotter, describe the "ego complex" as one thing and the "herd complex" as another.

This rapid sketch of the sentiment of self-regard and its many ramifications will serve to indicate how in the normal adult the fundamental impulses of the sentiment, those of self-assertion and submission, which on the plane of merely instinctive life are of relatively feeble and infrequent operation, become extremely sensitive and powerful and all-pervasive; for they are brought into play through so many channels, and so are strengthened by almost perpetual exercise. We see, then, why these impulses

[1] Perhaps the best illustrations of this are afforded by certain instances of high-minded persons who have decided that they were justified in defying the custom and moral code of their society in respect to marriage.

[2] I have discussed the role of the group sentiments in more detail in my "Group Mind."

become dominating factors of our personality; the sources of our most acute pains and of our most intense and enduring satisfactions; why disgrace and social ostracism are the severest penalties, and social esteem the most prized reward and the dearest and most enduring goal of our desire. It is said that some savages have lain down and simply died under disgrace; and we know that many a man of higher culture has preferred death to dishonor, and that many another has sacrificed every other good in order to retrieve his position in the eyes of his fellows.[1] We see also why the desire for revenge is a so powerful and persistent motive of human action, at all levels of culture; for this desire, with its painful emotional excitement, which is sometimes called "the emotion of revenge" (not mere anger, but anger rendered painful by an admixture of thwarted self-feeling, and perhaps also of fear) is essentially the desire "to get even with" the adversary. It springs from the sentiment of self-regard, and is evoked, not by mere injury or aggression or obstruction, but by the injury that is combined with insult, that is to say, the injury which lowers us in our own eyes and in the eyes of the world.

[1] We may see also why the literary man and the artist so generally are extremely "touchy" or sensitive to all indications of approval and disapproval, so profoundly disturbed by disapproval, so absurdly elated by praise or appreciation. For men of these callings devote their best energies to work which is wholly designed to win the approval of their fellows and whose value can only be determined by the appraisal of the public. The carpenter, the engineer, or the chemist may find satisfaction in knowing that the creation of his hands and brain is being used by his fellow-men and contributing to their welfare, though they know nothing of his share in its production. But, if the public remains indifferent to the works of the writer or the artist, he can only console himself with the desperate hope that posterity will appreciate them. What writer of books has not lain awake long hours, in consequence of some depreciatory remark of an unknown critic; or has not felt half-ashamed of his own elation on finding some word of appreciation? We see also why ambition is "the last infirmity of noble minds." The enormous power and imaginative range of this motive, the self-assertive impulse, are illustrated, in the most striking way of all, by the immense labors that are sustained by the desire of posthumous fame. If any reader is inclined to think that I overestimate the role of this impulse in human life, he should read Mr. Lytton Strachey's "Eminent Victorians." There he may learn how, in the most pious and philanthropic personalities, this protean impulse plays its subtle part in energizing action, sustaining immense undertakings, and complicating the most admirable and altruistic motives. He should also reflect upon the dictum, "hell has no fury like a woman scorned."

The Moral Sentiments

Moralists have written many chapters about the moral sentiments; but, with their confused popular terminology and their lack of psychology, they have not succeeded in throwing much light upon them. Yet the moral sentiments are real and important constituents of character; not of all character, but of moral character. We speak of love of justice or of truth, hatred of cruelty or dishonesty, dislike of untidiness, and so on. These are not empty forms of speech. They denote real concrete sentiments for abstract objects. It is possible to acquire a sentiment for any object of which one can think, be it particular and concrete, or general or abstract. And any object, of any of these classes, of which we have occasion to think again and again with similar emotional stirrings, inevitably becomes the object of a sentiment of some sort, however rudimentary. Even our sentiments may become objects of sentiments; that is the peculiarity of the "sentimentalist," the "man of sentiment," who cultivates and cherishes his sentiments, his patriotism, his religion, his "honor," his love of this or his hatred of that, for its own sake, because he has reason to think it a fine thing, a mark of distinction on which he prides himself.

How, then, do we acquire these sentiments of like and dislike for moral qualities, qualities of character and conduct. In order to understand the process, we must realize that a large number of such moral sentiments are traditional in every nation; and that each social group within the nation that continues to exist from generation to generation has its own peculiar moral tradition, consisting of the moral sentiments common to the whole nation, but modified by special emphasis on this or that sentiment and by comparative indifference to other qualities. Thus, as is well known, every great profession has its own peculiarly modified form of the common moral tradition; and the same is true in less degree of every enduring community, such as a religious sect or a great school or college.

The isolated individual could never acquire more than the most rudimentary moral sentiments. In the first place, he needs the aid of language to enable him to think of the various moral qualities as such. And as, with the aid of language, he learns to think of these abstract objects, he almost inevitably begins to build up sentiments about them: for the traditional emotional attitudes toward these objects are generally expressed by his fellows in words, in tone of voice, in gesture, or in other more energetic ways, whenever the objects are mentioned. Further, the child, when he comes into practical relations with persons by whom the various moral qualities are prominently displayed, experiences in his own person pleasant and unpleasant effects. Such experiences give richer meaning and emotional reality to the words by which the moral qualities are denoted.

But, in the main, it is by sympathetic contagion and by suggestion from admired personalities that the child's moral sentiments are shaped. Admiration for a person is itself a sentiment, one which is apt to develop into love or reverence, though it does not necessarily do so.[1] It is an habitual attitude of submission and of wonder in face of the admired person; and the child who has acquired this sentiment for an older person can hardly fail to share contagiously his emotional reactions to acts and qualities of character, and to accept his judgments upon them; and also he will in all probability desire to be, or to become, like the admired person, and therefore to cultivate, more or less deliberately, the moral as well as the physical attitudes of that person. As the child becomes acquainted with literature and art, his range and choice of models for admiration are vastly increased; and he may find his moral hero in some legendary or historical personality, in Socrates or Jesus, St. Francis of Assisi or Robert the Bruce, Washington or Lincoln or Florence Nightingale, Buffalo Bill or Jack Kelly. The influence of such personalities may, for a time, far outweigh that of all the persons with whom he comes into actual contact. But, in the end, the moral sentiments of the group in which his life is mainly passed tend to mould his into conformity with themselves; for his group enforces its traditional code with rewards or punishments, praise or blame, admiration or scorn and ridicule, according as he conforms in word and deed, or rebels and stands apart. And, if a man belongs to several groups, each having a distinct

[1] Cf. pp. 333 and 424.

code, he will, as it is picturesquely said, be liable to develop as many distinct selves; or, more accurately, he will, in each of these moral atmospheres, be liable to conform to it by emphasizing this or that member of his system of moral sentiments.

It is a peculiarity of our moral sentiments that each one is apt to be bipolar. For each moral quality that we name and recognize has its opposite; and, in learning to love the one, we can hardly fail to learn to hate in some degree its opposite. Justice and injustice, kindness and cruelty, honesty and dishonesty, truth and falsity, loyalty and disloyalty, are such pairs of opposites. According to a man's native disposition and the course of his experience, his moral sentiments will tend to be more of the positive nature of love, or of the negative nature of hate; but he can hardly love justice without in some degree hating injustice; though perhaps the converse proposition is not generally true. And our bipolar moral sentiments are apt to manifest themselves more energetically at the negative pole, as impulses of anger, disgust, and contempt, than as positive efforts on behalf of the esteemed qualities.

Consider a single instance, the formation of a bipolar sentiment of hatred of cruelty and love of kindliness. The child encounters cruelty, at an age when he is already familiar with kindliness under many forms; it may be cruelty directed toward himself or toward some animal, perhaps his cherished kitten. In either case, he angrily resents it; in the former case, because it thwarts him in some way (and in this case probably fear mingles with his anger); in the second case, because it thwarts his tender protective impulse. Repetitions of such experiences confirm and render habitual these emotional attitudes toward the person or persons whose cruelties he encounters. He soon learns to apply the adjective "cruel"; and, from this, it is a small step, under the guidance of language and precept and example, to think of cruelty in the abstract as something hateful, something the mere thinking of which suffices to stir his emotional resentment; thus he becomes able to say truly "I can't bear cruel people," or "I hate cruelty." In similar ways, he soon learns to say "That is a kind man; I like people who are kind." And then, as he realizes that cruelty and kindliness are opposite and incompatible qualities, the two incipient sentiments co-operate, and, in co-operating, become fused to one.

The moral sentiments give to conduct a greater consistency than it could have in their absence. The child with a tender heart will generally be kindly; yet he may be found by an elder curiously tearing to pieces a living fly, or making dreadful experiments on a frog or a worm, or even on his own pet kitten. Then, when he is told, "That's cruel," or "That's cruelty," he will, if he has learned the meaning of the words and acquired in some degree a hatred of cruelty, realize the truth of their application to his own action and will not so readily, so "thoughtlessly," as we say, repeat such actions.

This stabilizing influence of the moral sentiments has been made the subject of experiments which reveal instructively how importantly they contribute to consistency of right conduct and how insufficient is the "habit theory," which so many practical moralists unduly stress, and which so many psychologists would falsely make the key to all problems of human conduct and animal behavior. A mere habit of action is specific, peculiar to the particular circumstances under which it has been induced. A sentiment for a particular quality of conduct or character is perfectly general in its application and influence; for language and the powers of abstraction and induction here perform for the moral nature a service similar to that rendered by them to the intellect.

The experiment I refer to consisted in developing assiduously, in a class of school-children, a habit of neatness and tidiness in respect of one particular task. The habit was readily acquired in various degrees by all the children; but it was observed that, as might be expected, it had no "spread"; the quality of tidiness did not transfer itself to other tasks and daily actions. In respect of these, the children remained as untidy as before. Then a sentiment for tidiness as a general quality was cultivated in them; and soon its effect was manifest throughout a wide range of behavior: for the average child can readily apply for himself such an abstract term to kinds of behavior and to situations to which he has not heard it applied, and so can bring his growing sentiment into play.[1]

[1] Cf. W. C. Ruediger, "Educational Review," Vol. XXXIV.

Every man, then, inevitably acquires a number of moral sentiments; and moral culture largely consists in the refinement and harmonization of these sentiments by reflection and reasoning upon the various qualities of character and conduct; for, by such reflection and reasoning, we become able to think of these qualities with greater precision and to form well-grounded beliefs as to their relative values or importance.

Moral Character

In comparison with the great sentiments of self-regard and of love and hate for persons and with the stronger of the crude instinctive promptings, the impulses of anger, fear, hunger, and lust, in comparison with any of these, the moral sentiments are but feeble springs of action. We have, then, still to inquire, "How is the conduct of a good man constantly regulated in accordance with his moral sentiments? By what magic do these relatively weak tendencies of the moral sentiments control those immensely powerful impulses? How are we to explain the fact that in some cases men have been able, when perishing of thirst or hunger, to pass the cup or the crust to another, saying "His need is greater than mine"; or to forgive a gross and wanton injury; or to stand fast when shaken by horrible fear; or to resist a fierce sexual temptation?

This is the crux of the problem of moral conduct.[1] Shall we be content to say, with Plato and some modern moralists,[2] that Divine Reason sits in the head, controlling fierce passions that reside in the belly, as a charioteer controls with whip and rein a team of savage steeds? Hardly! Reasoning plays an important part, as we have recognized, in refining and harmonizing the moral sentiments. And reasoning may help us to acquire a moral creed, a belief that some one formula may express the ultimate goal of moral effort; such as "the greatest happiness of the

[1] It was well defined by William James as follows: Ideal impulse $<$ Instinctive propensity; Ideal impulse $+ X >$ Instinctive propensity. The problem then is—What is this X which turns the scale of the moral conflict in favor of the ideal impulse, the prompting of a moral sentiment, and enables it to triumph over the far stronger instinctive propensity?

[2] Cf. Dean Hastings Rashdall's "Is Conscience an Emotion?" and my reply in *The Hibbert Journal*, 1920.

greatest number"; or "self-development"; or "the promotion of the good"; or "the realization of the good life"; or "the promotion of the higher culture"; or "the realization of the perfect State." And reasoning also helps us to determine what forms of conduct and what qualities of character are most conducive to the realization of the highest good, however we may have defined it. But "Reason" is not a conative energy that may be thrown on this side or that, in our moral conflicts.[1] Reason is not that X of which we are in search; though it plays an important part in bringing that X to bear.

Shall we say, with the utilitarian divines of the eighteenth century, that fear of punishment or desire of reward in the life after death is this moral X? The doctrine is sufficiently exploded; though it has some truth as applied to particular cases.

Shall we say, with Shaftesbury, that this X is "good taste"? Or, with Bishop Butler, that it is "conscience"? Or, with Adam Smith, that it is "the impartial spectator within the breast"? Or, with James and many others, that it is "the fiat of the Will"? No one of these statements can be said to be wholly false. But, recognizing that each of them is vaguely true, we still have to ask, "What is 'good taste'? What is 'Conscience'? What is this 'man within the breast'? What is the 'will' and what is its 'fiat'? And how do these agents effect these marvels of the moral life?"

The approximately true answer to these questions has been given, I believe, in my "Social Psychology." I will restate it here very briefly. The X, the unknown quantity of which we are in search, is always an impulse awakened within the sentiment of self-regard. It is the desire that I, the precious self, that being which I conceive proudly or humbly, more or less adequately, more or less truly, and more or less clearly, accord-

[1] As well say that the Reason of Marshal Foch was the force which, in the last stage of the Great War, gave victory to the Allies. The forces concerned were the vital energies of the armies and the physical energies of the mechanisms of war. The Reason or intellect of Foch, by directing those energies, assembled and applied them in the most effective manner, without being itself an energy that could by mere addition make an appreciable difference. It is the paradox of Intelligence that it directs forces or energies without being itself a force or energy. This point will be developed in the chapter on "Body and Mind" in Part II.

ing to the degree of development of my powers, the desire that this self shall realize in action the ideal of conduct which it has formulated and accepted.

The way in which moral sentiments are built up has been sufficiently indicated. The ideal of character is the synthesis or harmonized system of moral sentiments. We have seen, also, why it is that a man is swayed so powerfully by the regards of his fellow-men, and strives to conform, or to appear to conform, to the standards demanded by his social group. The only serious problem that remains is: How is it possible that, in the highest flights of moral effort, a man may stand apart from his group and from the whole of organized society, defying the general opinion and the forcibly expressed common sentiments, and saying "You are mistaken; this is right and I will do it, though I go to prison and disgrace, or to hell"?[1]

It is, I think, true to say that, even in the most extreme of such cases, the explanation is not in principle other than that we have found for the more ordinary type of moral struggle, in which a man's self-regard is thrown on the side of some generally approved moral sentiment and carries it to victory over some stronger cruder tendency. The difference is in the nature of the social group, the body of spectators, the tribunal, before which the subject imaginatively displays himself, in whose eyes he desires to stand well. The man who stands up against the prevailing public opinion and sentiment is the man who has found some higher court of appeal, the verdict of which he esteems more highly, whose disapproval he shrinks from more sensitively, and whose approval he desires more strongly, than that of the mass of mankind.

This court, this tribunal, may be his particular moral hero or select group of heroes; it may be his dead mother, or his best friend; it may be what he believes to be the group consisting of the best men of all ages; it may be the Christian saints; or it may be God. And, when he resists the temptation to follow the

[1] However strongly we may disagree with the ultra-pacifists, we must, I think, recognize that some of the "conscientious objectors" of the Great War nearly achieved this sublime superiority to the opinion of the mass of their fellow-men. Of course, each of them knew that he was not entirely alone, that there were others like himself who approved his line of conduct.

easier way, he believes that, though his chosen line of conduct may never become known to this tribunal, yet, if it were known, it would be approved; and he believes that its opposite would be condemned or regretted. In short, he has learned to judge his conduct as it would appear to a purely ideal spectator, and to be moved to assert himself as that which this spectator would approve. In this way, by the construction of an ideal in which his moral sentiments are synthesized and harmonized, a man may become, as it is said, a "law unto himself." This is not the place to discuss the ethical status of such conduct, its advantages and its very real dangers. We are here only concerned with the psychological principles involved in such moral autonomy.

Volition

Conduct of the type we have last discussed is generally admitted to involve volition in the fullest sense. It is decision and action in the line of most resistance, after moral conflict and deliberation. The student may ask "What, then, is the Will? And what is Conscience?" The answer is that neither "the Will" nor "Conscience" is a faculty, an entity of any kind, distinct from the rest of the personality. "The Will" is character in action; and "Conscience" is moral character—character developed under moral guidance, character in which the moral sentiments are duly incorporated in the system of the sentiments and, through the medium of the sentiment of self-regard, are given due weight in all moral issues; character consolidated by habitual and consistent decision and action, in accordance with the promptings of the moral sentiments and of an unyielding self-respect.

It is worth while to support this brief account of moral character and volition, by considering certain defects of character and some peculiar and lower forms of volition. Notice first that character goes to pieces and volition is undermined, if self-respect is destroyed. This is what so often happens to the man who becomes the victim of alcohol or of other such drugs. In the good old days, when every gentleman was carried to bed in his boots five nights a week, a man could drink heavily with little loss of self-respect; and he was under no temptation to take to secret drinking; and might remain a reasonably efficient member of society, so long as his liver and his brain-cells withstood the chronic poison. In the modern world there are but few social circles which will continue to approve or to tolerate the habitual drunkard; his self-respect is therefore in more danger than his liver. The loss of will-power that necessarily follows a severe blow to a man's self-respect was one of the striking features of the so-called "shell-shock" cases so frequent in the War. In all such cases, the only means of retrieving character and will-power is to restore self-respect; everything that contributes to that is good; everything that makes in the other direction confirms the condition. The beachcomber of the magic isles of the Pacific is the extreme type of the man who has lost self-respect and therefore has no "Will." To lose the respect of others is only the first step on this path of disintegration of character. So long as a man still believes in himself and is capable of shame and of resenting an insult, his case is not hopeless. But, as soon as he can say "I'm a rotter," and doesn't care who knows it, he is beyond the power of human aid.

At the other end of the scale of sheer will-power, is the man who has made a cult of self-control, the man who habitually and ostentatiously denies himself every indulgence, who in winter daily breaks the ice of the public pond to take his morning bath, who can always be relied upon to tackle the disagreeable task shunned by others, who finds his chief satisfaction in proving to himself and to the world that he can do the hard thing. Such moral athletes are the victims of an ideal of character which, admirable as it is, tends to make a narrow, hard, and unintelligent personality. Some such ideal seems to have been traditional in those tribes of North American Indians whose young men subjected themselves publicly to bodily tortures. The same geographical area seems now to be producing a somewhat similar ideal, the ideal of "aggressiveness," the ideal of the "hustler," who, without knowing what he wants, is determined to get it at all costs.

Another type of strong will-power is that of the naturally self-assertive man who is but little given to reflection upon himself and who has no clearly formulated ideal. He may be slow to undertake any task; but, once set upon it, he pursues his goal with the utmost tenacity, not merely because he is by nature of steadfast temper,[1] of that constitution in which all conations are persistent, but also because his self-assertive tendency is evoked by every difficulty. To such a man, every check, whether from human or other source, is an immediate challenge and stimulus to increased effort. Recently, after a rainy day, I set out for an evening stroll, in company with a square-jawed extrovert. Our purpose was merely to get a little exercise and fresh air. Sighting a deserted farm-house, on a hill a little way from the road, we turned toward it, moved merely by a very mild curiosity. Very soon we had lost our direction among the trees. The mosquitoes swarmed, it was unpleasantly damp underfoot, and the undergrowth was dense. But in vain I suggested a return to the road. My companion kept trying one direction after another. At last I put it to him, "Why are you so set on finding that house?" At once the reply came, "Oh! I hate to be beaten." And, *pace* our Freudian friends, I believe his reply expressed the whole truth. Of this type is the inveterate rock-climber, who, caring nothing for scenery and bored by a walk over the hilltops, spends every holiday in scrambling up "chimneys" and precipices and in devising new and more difficult ways of getting to the top of a mountain.

Somewhat similar is the motive of the financier or business man who sets out to make a fortune and who, having made it, cannot rest or take up any rational mode of life, but persists in seeking new worlds to conquer. The repeated satisfactions of his self-assertive impulse, attained along the one line of activity, have confirmed him in that line; and he can anticipate no success along any other.

Yet another type of specialized and unbalanced character is that formed under the influence of a master sentiment for some one object. The object may be a person, or an animal, or a house; it may be "the single-tax" or "prohibition"; it may be old china, or pewter, or first editions, or beetles. In respect of all other goals, the man may be vacillating and weak; but in respect

[1] Cf. p. 352.

of his one hobby, he shows the utmost persistence. Such activity in its simpler forms can hardly be called volitional; yet the master-sentiment serves to give consistency to conduct and a certain firmness to character.

The contrast between the man of the last type and the moral athlete illustrates an important fact, namely, that the self-assertive impulse is unique in that it is a motive of universal applicability; whereas every other motive is more or less restricted in the range of objects and situations by which it may be brought into play. Even a universal love for mankind, or for all living things, may leave a man irresolute and weak in many situations. But the self-assertive impulse, made strong and delicately responsive by much and varied exercise, may come to the reinforcement of any other motive and may support us to the bitter end in any task, trivial or serious, to which we have once set our hands.

Resolve

Some authors have asserted that volition always involves explicit judgment, the judgment "I will do this." This seems to me to restrict the term "volition" unduly. There are many actions, even among those that succeed to deliberation, which, as it seems to me, may properly be called volitional (because the issue of a balance or conflict of desires is determined by the accession of an impulse from the sentiment of self-regard) and which nevertheless are preceded by no explicit judgment. Nevertheless, in the most developed or complete volitions, explicit judgment does precede action. This is most clear in respect of deliberate decision or choice of alternative goals, with resolve to act in a certain manner when and if the occasion shall arise. In such cases of decision preceded by reasoned deliberation, we have the most intimate and subtle interplay of the cognitive and the conative processes.

Without conflicting motives, we do not deliberate on our choice of goal; though we may deliberate on choice of means to a goal already adopted. In such cases the choice of means is a process as nearly purely intellectual as any can be; our desire is simply to know what are the best means for the purpose in hand.

The choice of a goal, on the other hand, is always a process in which desire largely determines judgment; and in this case every anticipated circumstance or result of action influences us, according as it promises to promote or thwart our conation, strengthening or checking our inclination toward this or that goal. Yet, when the decision is reached, the process of deliberation terminates in an explicit judgment, expressed in some such assertion as "That is my line," "That's what I will aim at." By such judgment a belief is established, a belief which, like all beliefs, tends to endure in its own right. But, if the moment for action is long postponed, the volitional process may renew itself to sustain and confirm this belief. The appeal is again to the sentiment of self-regard; and we say "No, I must not change my mind; that would be weak. I must be resolute and hold to my choice, or I shall seem like a poor volatile creature." In some persons this form of volition gives rise to an unintelligent obstinacy.

The role of judgment and belief in volition may also be illustrated negatively. If, in the process of deliberation as to the choice of goals, I become persuaded in any way that one of the alternative goals is impossible of attainment, then I am thereby prevented from judging that I shall attain it; then also I am prevented from willing that goal, no matter how strongly the motives urging me toward it may predominate over all others. If, on the other hand, I am led to believe, whether by pure suggestion (as in the hypnotic subject) or by reasoning or persuasion, that I shall strive for a certain goal or shall perform a certain action at a given moment in the future, this belief will greatly facilitate such action when the time comes, rendering effective a motive which otherwise might be too weak to determine action.

Freedom of the Will

I have made it clear, I hope, that in my view the resolutions of the will are not "bolts from the blue," of a nature unconnected with the lower or more primitive functions of the organism. Will, as I have said, is character in action; and in our most complete volitions, following upon deliberation, the intellect co-operates fully with character. Volition then becomes the expression of the whole personality. But it is still the working of the conative impulses that spring from the instinctive dispositions, impulses working, not sporadically and in detachment from one another, but within a delicately balanced and more or less harmonious and unitary system. Does it then follow that we must accept the determinist position, must deny completely all freedom of the will, all power of voluntary decision to influence a course of events which has been predetermined from the beginning of the world? Or may we believe that the course of things is not strictly determined and predictable, and that human decisions are what they seem to be, real determinants, new beginnings from which new lines of determination run on into the future? To me it seems that all we know of Nature and of the human mind justifies the latter alternative. The only ground for doubting it, offered by the strict determinists, is their belief in the universality of "the law of causation." But this belief, however stated, is not susceptible of being proved.

The determinist argument explicitly stated runs in some such way as follows: Similar (or the same) causes produce similar (or the same) effects. This human decision is a similar effect, therefore it has a similar cause. This syllogism is obviously foolish. Both its premises are gratuitous assumptions; and in no way can we establish premises from which the determinist conclusion follows. If it be said that some such major premise as "all events are strictly determined or caused" is a necessity of thought, we may point to the various scientists and philosophers who tell us that any such assumption is ridiculous, that the notion of cause and effect always has been obscure and muddled, incapable of being clearly thought or expressed, and that, however useful it may have been and still may be in a limited way, it has had its day and now is merely a clog on speculation.

That the human mind, in its highest flights, creates new things, thinks in ways that have never been thought before, seems undeniable in face of any of the great works of genius. Those who tell us that the mere shuffling of the letters of the alphabet in a dice-box will produce a great work of literary art, or even a single perfect verse, may be speaking literal truth, if we grant them the continuation of the process through unlimited time. But the striking peculiarity of the human race is that, in the last few thousand years, it has produced such things, created such novelties, over and over again.

If, then, the human mind is greatly creative in its highest forms and flights, how can we deny that it may be creative, in a small way, in the moral struggles of the common man. By a long series of such creative acts on the part of men both great and small, the moral tradition, the highest product of organic evolution, has been painfully and slowly evolved. Why should we doubt that organic evolution is a creative process and that Mind is the creative agency? We have no theory of organic evolution remotely adequate to the problem. But it seems clear that any theory which ignores Mind condemns itself to triviality.

The belief in a certain creative power of original determination is a necessity of our moral nature. Without it, we are paralyzed; unless we suffer a degree of dissociation which permits us to hold, like the insane patient, incompatible beliefs. The belief in "strict determinism" on the part of a man who actively pursues his goals and puts forth strenuous efforts is, then, merely a symptom of mental disorder of so mild a nature that there may be good hope of his recovery.

The Main Stages of Evolution

I have tried to show my reader that the modes of purposive striving form a continuously graded series, from the pursuit of its prey by the Amœba to the moral struggles of Man. Nevertheless, it is useful to distinguish a number of stages in this evolutionary scale, as follows: (1) The vague, almost undifferentiated striving of the animalcule in pursuit of his prey. (2) The strivings of animals in which the instincts are sharply differentiated and directed toward specific goals that are vaguely anticipated by the creature. (3) The instinctive strivings of primitive man toward goals more fully imagined and anticipated; the strivings of instinctive desire. (4) The strivings of men prompted by desire for instinctive goals, but directed also to goals which are conceived and desired only as means to the instinctive goal. (5) Conduct of the lower level; that is, instinctive desire regulated and controlled, in the choice of means, by anticipation of rewards and punishments. (6) Conduct of the middle level; that is, the same instinctive impulses regulated in the choice of goals and of means by anticipation of social approval and disapproval. (7) Conduct of the higher level; that is, striving regulated in the choice of goals and means by the desire to realize an ideal of character and conduct, a desire which itself springs from an instinctive disposition whose impulse is turned to higher uses by the subtle influences of organized society embodying a moral tradition.

Such are the seven ages of life through which we all must pass, as our ancestors have passed before us. Does the future hold further and higher stages of evolution? Who shall say?

Some Problems of the Future

In the foregoing pages I may seem to the reader to have written dogmatically and arrogantly; as though I believed that my account of mental process and mental structure is true, or truer than any other. But I believe only that it is the best I have been able to achieve by thirty years of strenuous study. I know that my conclusions are only working hypotheses, which may be far more wrong than right, and which at the best are only the crude foundations for psychology. It may help the student, if I try to define here some urgent problems in respect of which, as it seems to me, we are still almost wholly in the dark. For I am anxious above all to avoid giving the impression that psychology has hitherto done more than make a fair beginning. And in this science, more than in most others, the adequate statement of problems is difficult and important.

1. What are the nature and extent of the innate basis of the mind? This problem has two main divisions: (*a*) What are the nature and extent of the conative basis? If the account I have given of the instinctive basis is in the main on the right lines, are the instinctive dispositions inherited as simple unit factors? Or are they in some degree organized, or predisposed by heredity

to become organized, in the great sentiments common in some degree to all men? And, especially, is there any innate predisposition to the growth of moral sentiments? (*b*) Is there any innate basis of intellectual development other than the instincts, the plasticity of the nervous system, and that general power of adaptation to novel conditions which in these pages has been called "Intelligence" or, in its higher manifestations, "sagacity"? Is there some inborn impulse, distinct from the impulses of the instincts, which functions in some general way to promote intellectual growth? Is there anything in our innate endowment that in any manner or degree justifies the old doctrine of "innate ideas"? Are there any innate cognitive dispositions, beyond those involved in the structure of the instincts? The same problems may be stated in a more concrete fashion, as follows: What is the innate basis of the special intellectual aptitudes which distinguish one man from another and often seem to run in families and to crop out in various members of successive generations? It does not seem probable that these differences and likenesses can be explained in terms either of environmental influences or of accidents of the spontaneous developmental processes.

The doctrine of association of "ideas," from Locke and Hume onward, has masked and confused these fundamental questions. These and many other problems are bound up with that major problem which, throughout this book, I have consistently avoided, namely, the problem of the relation of mind to matter, of soul to body. I have aimed only at inducing in the student an open mind toward this master problem, so central for both psychology and philosophy, insisting only that, so far as we can at all see at present, purposive action cannot profitably or plausibly be regarded as a special case of mechanical process. The disorders of mental life, the abnormal and quasi-abnormal modes of mental functioning, have very intimate bearing upon this great problem: therefore I have postponed all discussion of it to the final chapters of the book on abnormal mental processes which, I hope, may follow and supplement this volume.

INDEX